PETER J

TRAVELLER'S GUIDE TO
SOUTH AFRICA

STRUIK

Struik Publishers (Pty) Ltd
(a member of the Struik Publishing Group (Pty) Ltd)
Cornelis Struik House, 80 McKenzie Street, Cape Town 8001.

Reg. No.: 54/00965/07

First published 1991
Second edition 1992
Third edition 1996

Copyright © in text: Peter Joyce 1996
Copyright © in photography: as credited on page 4
Copyright © in maps: Globetrotter Travel Maps 1996
Copyright © in published edition: Struik Publishers (Pty) Ltd 1996

All rights reserved. No part of this publication may be reproduced, stored in a retrieval system
or transmitted in any form or by any means, electronic, mechanical, photocopying, recording
or otherwise, without the prior written permission of the copyright owner(s).

ISBN 1 86825 777 0

MANAGING EDITOR: Annlerie van Rooyen
EDITORS: Joy Clack, Lesley Hay-Whitton and Laura Twiggs
DESIGN MANAGER: Odette Marais
DESIGNER: Chris Abrahams
DTP MAPS: Karen Bailey
INDEXER AND PROOFREADER: Sandie Vahl

Reproduction by cmyk Prepress
Printing and binding by Tien Wah Press (Pte.) Ltd, Singapore

The travel, accommodation and other facilities described in this book represent a major
portion of those available at the time of going to press in mid-1996. The tourist world, though,
is in its nature subject to rapid change, and while every effort has been made to ensure accuracy,
some of the information will inevitably become outdated during this edition's life-span.
Travellers are therefore advised to consult local publicity associations and other sources before
embarking on visits to specific venues. The contact addresses and telephone numbers of these
associations and sources appear in the relevant Advisories at the end of each regional chapter.

For their part, the publishers would appreciate advice – from readers and from organisations
that provide tourist amenities – relating to new or upgraded (or indeed defunct) facilities for
incorporation into subsequent editions. *Please write to:* The Editor, *Traveller's Guide to South
Africa*, Struik Publishers (Pty) Ltd, PO Box 1144, Cape Town 8000.

PHOTOGRAPHIC CREDITS

Copyright for the photographs rests with the photographers and/or their agents as listed below.

SIL = Struik Image Library ABPL = Anthony Bannister Photo Library INPRA = International Press Agency

Adey, Shaen: pp. 41 (SIL); 113 top (SIL); 149 (SIL); 163 bottom (SIL); 232 (SIL); 256 (SIL) **Benjamin, Shawn:** pp. 39 bottom; 203 **Best, P.B.:** p. 194 left **Bressler, Ray:** p. 115 **Colour Library:** p. 211 (SIL) **Copyright Unknown:** p. 127 **Cubitt, Gerald:** pp. 62; 124; 151; 209 **De La Harpe, Pat:** pp. 120; 133 **De La Harpe, Roger:** spine (SIL); cover: middle left; pp. 3 (SIL); 13 (SIL); 71; 113 bottom (SIL); 125 (SIL); 134; 135 top; 135 bottom (Natal Parks Board); 136 top (Natal Parks Board); 136 bottom (SIL); 140 (Natal Parks Board); 144; 152 (Natal Parks Board); 154 top (Natal Parks Board); 188 (SIL); 224 (SIL); back cover (SIL) **Dennis, Nigel:** cover: top right; pp. 8 (SIL); 12 (SIL); 72 (SIL); 74 (SIL); 78; 79 left (SIL); 80 left (SIL); 114; 138 (SIL); 155 (SIL); 208 (SIL); 210 **Dreyer, Gerhard:** pp. 18 (SIL); 185 (SIL); 186 top left (SIL); 186 top right (SIL); 186 bottom left (SIL); 186 bottom right; 192 top left (SIL); 192 top right (SIL); 192 bottom (SIL); 193 (SIL); 265 bottom (SIL); 266 left (SIL); 266 right (SIL); 268 bottom (SIL) **Frankenfeld, Henner:** p. 23 (SouthLight) **Haagner, Clem:** p. 101 (ABPL) **Heymans, Piet:** p. 79 right **Hoffman, Leonard:** p. 262 (SIL) **INPRA:** p. 24 **Johnson, Anthony:** p. 227 bottom left (SIL); 227 bottom right (SIL) **Knirr, Walter:** cover: bottom right; pp. 15 (SIL); 19 top (SIL); 21; 27 (SIL); 29; 32 (SIL); 34; 39 top right (SIL); 41 left; 42 bottom; 43; 47; 50; 51; 65; 67; 68; 70; 84 (SIL); 85; 87; 91; 92; 96; 102; 103 top (SIL); 103 middle left (SIL); 103 middle right (SIL); 103 bottom; 106 (SIL); 109 (SIL); 110 bottom; 111 bottom; 118 (SIL); 119; 130 (SIL); 148 (SIL); 153 (SIL); 157 (SIL);191 (SIL); 200 (SIL); 214 (SIL); 218; 220; 246; 249 bottom (SIL); 271 (SIL); 272 (SIL); 273 top (SIL); 274 (SIL) **Laing, Anne:** pp. 14 (Action Shots); 30 bottom (Action Shots) **Mackinnon, Jeannie:** pp. 39 top left; 49 bottom; 121; 227 top; 233 top; 251 top **Morris, Jean:** pp. 37; 122 top; 126 **Murray, Jackie:** pp. 42 top (SIL); 45 left (SIL); 45 right (SIL); 54 (SIL) **Pickford, Peter:** pp. 9 (SIL); 55 (SIL); 56 (SIL); 137 (SIL); 154 bottom (SIL) **Pillay, Gonsul:** p. 16 (Durban Publicity Association) **Potgieter, Herman:** pp. 44; 46 **Proust, Alain:** p. 104 **Skinner, Mark:** cover: top left; pp. 17 (SIL); 19 bottom; 184; 217 top; 221 **Soule, Lionel:** pp. 25; 28 **Stanton, Lorna:** pp. 40; 73; 80 right; 267 **Sun International:** cover: bottom left **Sycholt, August:** cover: middle right; pp. 49 top; 53; 132; 182; 190 **Szymanowski, Janek:** pp. 122 bottom; 128; 147; 178 **Thiel, Erhardt:** pp. 11 (SIL); 31 (SIL); 197 (SIL); 219 top (SIL); 219 bottom (SIL); 225 top right (SIL); 225 bottom (SIL); 226 (SIL); 230 bottom (SIL); 236 top (SIL); 239 top (SIL); 241 (SIL); 249 top left (SIL); 249 top right (SIL) **Turner, Ken:** p. 223 **Van Aardt, Mark:** pp. 230 top; 233 bottom; 238; 251 bottom **Von Hörsten, Hein:** pp. 33 (SIL); 38; 97 (SIL); 160 (SIL); 164 (SIL); 165 (SIL); 166 (SIL); 167 top (SIL); 167 bottom (SIL); 171 top (SIL); 171 bottom (SIL); 172 top (SIL); 172 bottom (SIL); 173 left (SIL); 173 right (SIL); 174 (SIL); 175 (SIL); 176 (SIL); 195 (SIL); 217 bottom (SIL); 235 (SIL); 239 bottom (SIL); 253 (SIL); 255 (SIL); 257 (SIL); 259 (SIL); 265 top (SIL); 268 top (SIL); 269 bottom (SIL); 270 (SIL); 276 (SIL) **Von Hörsten, Lanz:** title page (SIL); pp. 10 (SIL); 66 (SIL); 69 (SIL); 81 (SIL); 89; 169 (SIL); 170 (SIL); 194 right (SIL); 217 middle (SIL); 225 top left (SIL); 228 (SIL); 231 (SIL); 236 bottom; 237 (SIL); 240 (SIL); 250 (SIL); 252 (SIL); 269 top (SIL) **Whelan, Colin:** p. 30 top (Action Shots) **Young, Keith:** pp. 77 (SIL); 110 top (SIL); 111 top (SIL); 163 top (SIL); 204 (SIL); 205 (SIL); 206 (SIL); 229 (SIL); 277 (SIL)

FRONT COVER: *Top left:* Cape Town's Victoria and Alfred Waterfront; *Top right:* A magnificent male lion of the Kruger National Park; *Middle left:* Zulu girls at Shakaland; *Middle right:* The Drakensberg's Amphitheatre; *Bottom left:* The Lost City at Sun City; *Bottom right:* Clifton with the Twelve Apostles as a backdrop. SPINE: Young Zulu maiden. BACK COVER: A giraffe at Hluhluwe-Umfolozi Park. TITLE PAGE: Windmill at sunset in the Kalahari Gemsbok National Park. PREVIOUS PAGE: Tranquil forest scene at Injasuti, part of the Giant's Castle Game Reserve.

CONTENTS

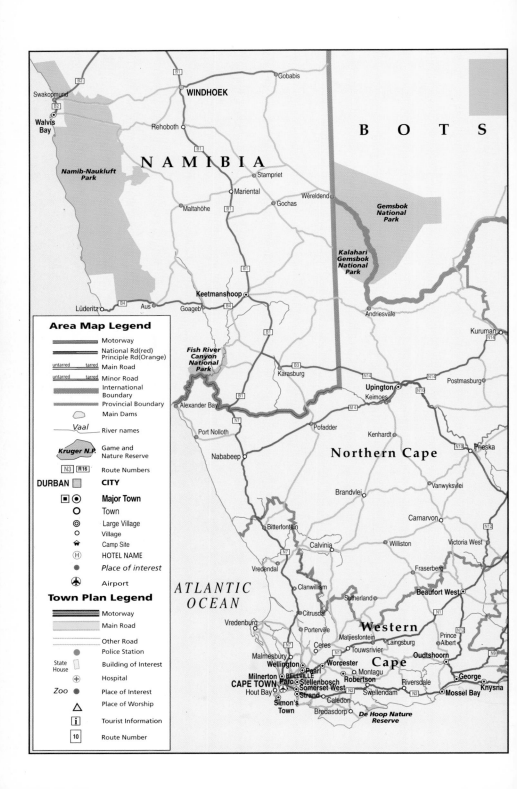

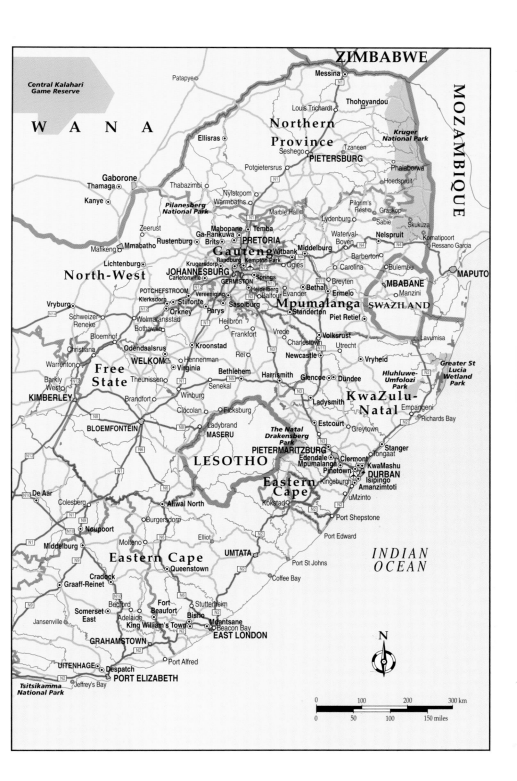

PART ONE

AN INTRODUCTION TO SOUTH AFRICA

South Africa is five times the size of Britain, about as large as Holland, Belgium, Italy, France and former West Germany combined. It stretches from the Limpopo River in the north to blustery Cape Agulhas, nearly 2,000 km (1,240 miles) to the south, from Namaqualand along the barren western seaboard 1,500 km (932 miles) to subtropical KwaZulu-Natal and the humid Indian Ocean coast: a total land area of 1.3 million km² (500,000 square miles).

It is a land of remarkable diversity: variety and contrast are vividly evident in the bewildering mix of race and language, creed, colour and culture. The diversity is there, too, in the nature of the land; in its geological formations and regional climates; its mountains, plains and coasts; its rich farmlands; its bushveld scrub and arid deserts – each of the many different parts supporting its own distinctive plant and animal life. Truly, a world in one country.

LEFT: *Skeletal trees are etched against the darkening sky at one of the world-renowned Kruger National Park's many waterholes.*
ABOVE: *A pair of sociable elephants take their fill of the life-giving waters.*

9

THE·LAND

MOUNTAINS AND RIVERS

If you were to look down on South Africa from an orbiting satellite you would see a clear, quite simple topographical pattern. The land falls into two distinctive physical regions: the great interior plateau, semicircular and occupying most of the subcontinent; and the 'marginal zone', which is the relatively narrow coastal and hinterland strip fringing the plateau on three sides. A third, strikingly obvious geographical feature is the division between the two regions: the highly (in the most literal sense) conspicuous and continuous necklace of mountains and hills known as the Great Escarpment.

The plateau is actually the southern tip of the Great African Plateau that rises in the Sahara Desert, some 5,000 km (3,000 miles) to the north. In southern Africa its altitude varies from the comparatively low 600 m (2,000 ft) of the Kalahari basin to an impressive 3,400 m (11,155 ft) in the towering Maluti mountains of Lesotho and the Drakensberg of KwaZulu-Natal.

Three hundred million years ago, when the single great land mass called Pangaea first began to succumb to continental drift, slowly, over hundreds of millennia, breaking up to create the global land patterns we know today, the stretch and pull of the earth's crust fashioned the most striking portion of South Africa's marginal zone – the Cape Fold Mountains, a series of high ranges running parallel to each other and rising magnificently over the valleys of the southern seaboard.

Only part of South Africa is blessed by good and regular rains. Just a quarter of the country is nurtured by perennial rivers. There are no real lakes – the largest expanse of water, Fundudzi in the Northern Province, was born of a massive landslide; the tourist-frequented 'lakes' of Zululand and the Knysna district of the southern coastline are in fact lagoons. Even the flow of the perennial streams and rivers depends on seasonal and, latterly, erratic rains. As for the great spaces of the western interior, their riverbeds fill and flow only after rare summer storms.

Biggest of the river systems is that of the Orange, running westwards from its headwaters in the Drakensberg for 2,250 km (1,400 miles)

to the Atlantic. Its tributaries include the Caledon and the Vaal (actually longer than the Orange but less voluminous). The Orange drains almost the entire plateau – 47% of the country.

The eastern slopes of the plateau, in contrast to the western regions, are comparatively well watered by their small rivers (one of the more substantial is the Letaba, well known to game viewers in the Kruger National Park). They drain just 12% of the country's surface area but contribute 40% of the total run-off. Of the plateau's other rivers, Kipling's great grey-green Limpopo is the most renowned, demarcating South Africa's northern frontiers with Botswana and Zimbabwe, gathering volume and momentum as it makes its way to the Indian Ocean north of the Mozambican capital Maputo. Despite its legend in literature, though, it is not a major river by African continental standards.

Significant rivers of the coastal belt include the Sundays and Great Fish, both of which were crucial lines in the often violent territorial disputes between white settler and black tribesman in the 19th century; the beautiful Berg River of the Western Cape; and KwaZulu-Natal's Tugela, where some of the most savage and, for the British, unrewarding battles of the Anglo-Boer War were fought.

All told, though, South Africa's rivers do not amount to much in world terms: their total run-off is equivalent to that of the Rhine at Rotterdam, and to just half that of the mighty Zambezi 1,000 km (620 miles) to the north.

BELOW: *The Orange River, by far South Africa's largest watercourse, flows through the desolate Richtersveld before discharging into the Atlantic.* OPPOSITE: *A brace of splendid West Coast crayfish.*

SEAS AND SHORES

Lapped by two oceans, South Africa's coastline runs 3,000 km (1,860 miles) from the Atlantic wilderness of the Orange River mouth in the north-west, round the often stormy Cape to KwaZulu-Natal and the Mozambican border in the east. Large stretches reward the traveller with spectacular scenery; some are a paradise for the angler, surfer, camper and sun-worshipper.

Broadly speaking, the oceans fall into two type-categories – warm and cooler – the nature of each determined largely by the dominant currents of the subcontinental seas. The warm waters along the east coast emanate from the tropics and flow rapidly south and south-east as the Agulhas Current, which more or less hugs the coast until, close to Cape Agulhas, it turns south and east. Along the west coast, the principal waterbody comes from the South Atlantic in the form of the north-flowing Benguela Current, and is much cooler.

THE WEST COAST is a barren region of rocky, sand-blown shorelines backed by the legendary raised beaches and, stretching inland for anything between 30 and 50 km (20 and 30 miles), terraces of deep, soft, often-shifting sand. Dunes are covered by sparse greenery (technically, dwarf bush vegetation), and the land is classed as sandveld. In the far north, around the mouth of the Orange, the terrain is rich in diamonds, swept down by the river over the ages and then distributed by currents.

The country's once-dynamic, now ailing but still enormously productive fishing industry has its home along the west coast. Here, during the upwellings of the Atlantic – usually during spring and summer – rich plant nutrients are carried to the inshore zone, so favouring the proliferation of plankton, basic to the area's stocks of mussels. These shellfish are primary feeders, and in turn support massive populations of rock lobsters (crayfish, also known as 'kreef'), snoek and stockfish (Cape hake). In the south the sea at times abounds with tunny, marlin and yellowtail.

THE SOUTH AND EAST COASTS are much more heavily populated and, in tourist terms, more popular. In the south, one stretch of shoreline and its hinterland is especially beautiful: the 220 km (137 miles) Garden Route that extends roughly from Mossel Bay in the west to the Tsitsikamma Forest and Storms River in the east. This is a green and flowered

region of charming bays, cliffs and pounding surf overlooked by the not-too-distant and splendid Outeniqua Mountains.

Equally enticing to holiday-makers are the coasts to either side of the city of Durban in the east: wide, dune-backed sandy strips fringing a remarkably straight shoreline (Durban itself, with its 16-km-long/10 miles Bluff and vast bay, is something of an exception). In fact, there are precious few good natural harbours along the entire length of the Republic's coastline. (Saldanha Bay is the best, but it was passed over by early seafarers in favour of the more exposed but better watered Table Bay.) It is an even coastline, without many pronounced embayments, and most of the otherwise-suitable estuaries are blocked by sandbars, the product of currents and of the heavy sediment brought by rivers with steep gradients and sporadic flow.

East London, in the Eastern Cape, is South Africa's only river port and its harbour, on the Buffalo, is constantly dredged. Durban's bar is notorious. The city's port is one of the southern hemisphere's biggest and busiest, but only in 1892, after many experiments with breakwaters and sand-pumps, did the 2,820 ton *Dunrobin Castle* manage to sail into the harbour – the first ocean-going liner to do so.

SOUTH AFRICA'S FLORAL WEALTH

South Africa is divided into a number of widely differing vegetation zones. Much of the centre and west – the great, dry Karoo and the Atlantic coastal belt – sustain hardy succulents, many of which bloom in springtime. Dense thornbush savanna covers the lower areas of the north and north-east; the Highveld and other parts of the west-central interior comprise grasslands largely bare of trees.

Remnant and magical swathes of natural forest – of yellowwood, ironwood and other hardwoods – are found along the southern seaboard and on the Mpumalanga (Eastern Transvaal) uplands. Along KwaZulu-Natal's balmy Indian Ocean shoreline there are patches of evergreen subtropical trees, among them raffia and ilala palms and here and there, in the swampier parts, mangroves.

South Africa's botanical pride, however, is the Western Cape's *fynbos* (literally 'fine bush'), a plant type rich enough in its variety to merit the tiny region's ranking as one of the world's six Floral Kingdoms.

The lovely ray-flowered protea, one of the Cape Floral Kingdom's nearly 370 species of the family Proteaceae.

CLIMATE

Weather patterns, influenced by different ocean currents, by altitude and prevailing winds and by the ever-changing nature of the land, are subject to sharp regional variation. Climatically, South Africa could be half a dozen entirely separate countries.

When it comes to rainfall, however, there are three broad but very distinct regions. The south-western tip of the subcontinent which centres on the lovely city of Cape Town, experiences winter precipitation; the southern and eastern coastal belts enjoy (in good years) perennial showers which are heavy, almost tropical, in KwaZulu-Natal. Rains over the remainder of the country – on the great central plateau and towards the east – come in the form of sudden downpours during often violent summer thunderstorms.

This is not to say that the country, as a whole, is well watered. On the contrary, South Africa is one of the world's drier countries with an annual rainfall of a little over 460 mm (18 in) compared with the global average of 857 mm (34 in). The rains, too, tend to be sporadic and unpredictable; drought has been the norm

rather than the exception in recent times. And the farther westwards one travels the less generous the heavens are.

Average annual temperatures are more constant. The northern areas are not, as one might expect, very much hotter than the southern because the land rises to the high central plateau, which is generally cooler than other parts of the world lying within the same lines of latitude. Cape Town can be suffocating and its annual average temperature is 17 °C (63 °F); Pretoria, a full 1,500 km (930 miles) nearer the tropics, can freeze and its mean temperature is only a half degree centigrade more.

But temperature inversions vary, quite dramatically, from place to place. They are least at the coast and greatest in the interior, where clear-skied winter nights are bitterly cold while the days remain sunny and mild.

South Africa, in fact, is blessed with a great deal of sunshine, the average number of cloud-free hours a day varying (depending on the region) from 7.5 to 9.4, compared with New York's 6.9, Rome's 6.4 and London's 3.8. Indeed, some parts of the country, the dust-dry western districts for instance, register a bare 10 or so overcast days a year.

WILD KINGDOM

South Africa's wildlife heritage is remarkable in its richness: the country covers less than one hundredth of the earth's land surface, yet it accommodates nearly 5% of its mammal and 8% of its bird species. Much of this splendid diversity can be seen and enjoyed in the 600 or so protected areas that have been set aside for conservational purposes.

Best known of these is the Kruger National Park, a vast expanse of sun-drenched bushveld that occupies 20,000 km² (7,700 square miles) of the north-eastern lowveld region and which contains more types of wildlife than any other sanctuary in Africa. Among its myriad drawcards are lion and leopard, the endangered rhino, buffalo and elephant – the famed 'big five' so sought after by the visiting game viewer.

The Kruger National Park, though, is just one of many superb wilderness destinations. Along the eastern seaboard are the reserves of Zululand, a region blessed with a unique mix of ecosystems and a stunning profusion of life forms. The Eastern Cape has its Addo Elephant National Park. To the north-west of Johannesburg are the broad grasslands of the Pilanesberg, location of one of Africa's most impressive game-stocking enterprises. Drive westwards and you'll eventually reach the great sandy plains and red dunes of the Kalahari Gemsbok National Park, whose sparse grasses, improbably, nurture enormous herds of antelope. South Africa's conservancies, in fact, rival those of Kenya in their sheer variety, and in what they can offer the visitor in the way of amenities.

Not that all is well with the country's wild regions. They are well protected, well managed but, as in so many other parts of Africa, they remain under constant threat – from poachers; from mining and industry; from domestic cattle and the spreading farmlands; and from the voracious appetite of the rural communities for water, grazing, firewood, medicinal plants, thatching materials and living space. To people long deprived of their rights to good land, the existence of large tracts of fertile, protected and apparently unused countryside makes very little sense, and the temptation to encroach is often irresistible.

These are the intractable problems of Africa, and indeed of the entire Third World and much of the First, and they are likely to remain with us for a long time to come.

There is, though, room for optimism. The priorities in South Africa, as elsewhere, have undergone a dramatic change, and the voice of the conservationist is heard and understood a lot more clearly than it was even a decade ago. Humankind's assault on the environment simply must be brought to a halt if the earth as we know it is to survive.

Moreover, those who make the decisions understand that the wilderness is worth preserving, not only as an investment for future generations but for the *immediate* rewards that it brings – in short, that ecotourism is capable of generating both jobs and money, much of the latter by way of valuable foreign exchange.

In this context, one trend is especially hopeful. There is now a general conviction that the wellbeing of the wildlife and the interests of tourism need not be in conflict with the needs of the rural people, and recent years have seen the emergence of what is variously called the 'multi-use', the 'resource' and the 'game management' area – integrated reserves in which the people on the ground, instead of being excluded, remain on the land, help conserve the environment and, in return, share in its valuable resources and benefit from tourism development. It is a win-win scenario, and it holds great promise for the future.

A lone leopard rests up during the heat of the day. These handsome cats, who are one of the 'big five', hunt at night, preying mainly on small buck.

THE PEOPLE

South Africa has an estimated population of around 42 million. One cannot be more exact because, although censuses are periodically taken, they are soon outdated, and the very nature of society and the mobility – and until recently the hostility – of some of its elements have made it difficult, if not impossible, to paint a precise statistical picture.

Of the four major racial groups, black people number 32 million; whites nearly five million; those of Asian origin just under a million; and the coloured community three to four million.

Growth rates vary sharply among groups – predictably, since South Africa is anything but homogeneous. Most blacks have their roots in the countryside. Cultural taboos and perceived economic necessity inhibit family planning; the extended family is an accepted and effective form of social security. Southern Africa is no different from the rest of the world: poorer, less educated people tend to have large families. With greater urbanization and higher standards of living a decline in the birth rate can be expected. At present, the black population is increasing by 2.7% a year, which projects a total of close to 40 million by the end of the century. By contrast, the annual white growth rate is 1.5%, which indicates (if one discounts the migration factor) about 5.5 million in the year 2000.

A crucial feature of the past few decades has been urban drift, the migration of people – especially black people – from the countryside to the cities. Industrial expansion since the Second World War has meant jobs, or at least the prospect of jobs, in and around the major centres: an irresistible lure to the hundreds of thousands who would otherwise have to scratch a meagre living from the soil in areas not favoured by many modern amenities, and where, because of drought and overstocking and erosion, the land is poor and becoming ever poorer.

With the dismantling of apartheid and the coincident pressures of drought and deep recession (both were features of the early 1990s), the rate of urbanization increased dramatically. In 1994 it was estimated that 700 000 people were abandoning the rural lifestyle each year.

BELOW: *Flag-waving rugby fans pack the stands at Newlands in Cape Town.*
OPPOSITE: *Brightly patterned murals adorn this traditional Ndebele home north of Pretoria.*

TRADITIONAL AFRICA

Although there are close historical and cultural affinities, the black communities of southern Africa have their ethnic divisions: they are clearly distinguished by custom, social system and language into a number of groupings. The divisions are not clearly evident in the party-political arena nor in the context of increasingly detribalized urban life, but in other respects the principal black groups can be regarded as distinctive societies.

These societies comprise the Zulu, the Xhosa, the Swazi (all three of these groups are related, belonging to the Nguni group of peoples); the Northern Sotho, the Southern Sotho and the Tswana (again, of the same major Sotho group: the Tswana are the western branch); the South Ndebele and the North Ndebele; the Venda and Lemba; and the Shangaan-Tsonga.

These ethnic groupings might suggest that South Africa's black communities have clung tenaciously to traditional African ways and remain outside the mainstream of Western influence, which of course is patently not so.

But custom, tradition and ancient loyalties do persist, most obviously in the rural areas. They are enshrined, for instance, in the rules of courtship and marriage; in matters of inheritance and guardianship and seniority within the clan; in kinship bonds, the social order and the spiritual force of ancestry; and in the assumptions underlying land tenure and in concepts of wealth.

Digress from the KwaZulu-Natal highways and you'll see elegantly crafted 'beehive' huts and the plumed and furred ceremonial regalia of an earlier and more romantic age. Ndebele women still decorate their homesteads with colourful geometric patterns and wear tight, multi-ringed metal necklaces and anklets that can never be removed. Venda girls enter womanhood by performing the sinuous *domba* snake-dance. During the year's first new-moon phase the Swazi of Mpumalanga's KaNgwane district honour their ancestral chiefs and their nationhood, and celebrate the first fruits of the soil, in the Great Incwala, a week-long festival of ritual, song, dance, feast, game and endurance tests.

Farther south, in the land of the Xhosa, rural folk of both sexes smoke long, carved pipes in the manner of their forebears, and teenage boys undergo the complex and painful rites of circumcision and initiation. Different styles of dress identify status within family and clan; intricate beadwork patterns – here and farther east, in Zululand – convey subtle messages.

But that is the old Africa. The new co-exists (often uncomfortably) and will in due course supersede. A large number of the 10 million urban blacks are second and third generation townsmen; hundreds of thousands are migrant workers; all have been exposed to the blessings and curses of the acquisitive society. The tribal order, in the towns, has been largely eroded, to be replaced by a transitional but distinct sub-culture that encompasses (engulfs, in many tragic instances) everything from social structure and family life to music and language.

15

A SMALL CORNER OF INDIA

A need for labour to harvest the crops of the then Natal's new and vast sugar plantations in the mid-19th century prompted the importation of thousands of workers from India. They were indentured (contracted) for a period of between three and five years, after which they had the choice of repatriation, of renewing their contracts, or of accepting Crown land and remaining as settlers. Most took up the land option, and settled.

The first shipload disembarked in 1860. In due course they were joined by non-indentured 'passenger' immigrants from the Indian subcontinent – British subjects able to travel freely within the Empire, and choosing the sun-bathed spaces of Natal as their future home. Today, South Africa's Asian community numbers some 900,000, most of whom – around 85% – live in and around the Verulam-Durban-Pinetown complex.

Nearly all the remainder, about 100,000 people of Asian origin, are settled in Gauteng province, on the Witwatersrand and in Pretoria. Among them are 10,000 or so citizens of Chinese extraction who have managed to retain their own cultural identity.

The Indian society, generally a prosperous one, has its own distinct traditions which are underpinned by religion and by kutum – the disciplined, patriarchal, extended family which regulates relationships and social interaction. The community as a whole is remarkably unified but also strictly organized according to faith – Hindu and Muslim.

The Hindu element is in turn divided into four language groups – Tamil, Telugu, Hindustani and Gujarati – and subscribes to its own strict rules governing modes, manners, ritual, food and drink.

The Muslims speak Gujarati – the language of western India – and Urdu, and they also observe precisely defined codes of both belief and behaviour.

Again, though, traditions are being eroded on an ongoing basis, especially among the younger generation. The izar and qami, the dawni and sari are giving way, if not always to T-shirts and jeans and trainers, certainly to the more conservative Western styles of dress; there is movement away from the multiple towards the smaller and more independent family; traditional male authority no longer goes unquestioned; young Indian women lead far freer and more diversified lives than their mothers and grandmothers; and English is the main means of communication.

BELOW: *An Indian duet goes through its delicate paces outside Durban's Victoria Street Market.*
OPPOSITE: *Part of the huge gathering of 'Coon Carnival' minstrels that enliven Cape Town's streets at New Year.*

THE COLOURED COMMUNITY

The country's three million-strong coloured community, the majority of whom live in the Western Cape, has diverse origins. The early Dutch settlers imported slaves from Holland's eastern possessions, from elsewhere in Africa and from some of the islands of the Atlantic and Indian oceans, and admixtures steadily and inevitably followed, Hottentot, Xhosa and white settlers adding their own progeny over the following decades.

Significant and distinct subgroups include the Griquas of the north-eastern and north-western region, the product of European-Hottentot miscegenation; the coloured people of KwaZulu-Natal, many of whom trace their ancestry far back to immigrants from Mauritius and St Helena; and the 200,000 Cape Malays of the Peninsula, a close-knit, homogeneous society that has maintained its strict Islamic ways over the centuries.

In general terms, though, the coloured people of South Africa are culturally very much part of the Western world. Some 87% are of the Christian faith; the majority speak Afrikaans; and they are barely separable in lifestyle and social organization from people of exclusively European origin. There seems no good reason why they should have been subjected to any special classification (not that formally imposed racial categories of any kind can ever be justified), and for centuries in fact were more or less an integrated part of the Cape community as a whole, enjoying, among other things, the constitutionally entrenched common-roll franchise until it was cynically removed in the 1950s.

Under the apartheid regime coloured residential areas were delineated; the famed District Six, close to the heart of Cape Town, was demolished and most of its inhabitants moved to the huge, new and somewhat characterless townships such as Mitchell's Plain on the Cape Flats. The callous forced removal created lasting bitterness and for decades the site of District Six remained undeveloped, a scar on Cape Town's landscape and on the minds of its citizens.

Whatever the indignities suffered, though, the Cape coloureds have remained an exuberantly resilient community with, among other things, a lively musical tradition of its own. The origin of many of the songs are obscure, but the melodies and the cheerful, often racy words are still heard at such gatherings as the annual New Year's 'Coon Carnival', a joy-filled festival in which hundreds of brightly dressed minstrel troupes parade through the streets. The occasion owes something to traditions borrowed from the American Deep South, but its flavour – and the characterful *ghommaliedjies* that you hear – are distinctively Cape.

17

THE WHITE TRIBES

For much of the 20th century South Africa had two official languages (today there are 11, though English is fast gaining favour as the principal means of communication), reflecting the dual origins of what were, until the recent transition to full democracy, the country's politically dominant groups.

THE AFRIKANERS, descendants of the early Cape-Dutch settlers and of the people of many other nationalities they absorbed – notably German and French – number over 2.5 million. High Dutch was the stem from which the Afrikaans language branched, taking on new words and a different shape over three centuries of isolation from the original homeland and, later, from the principal Cape settlement.

The other nationalities are significant: the Afrikaners, in fact, have a rich mix of cultures in their blood, one official estimate pegging the ancestral ingredients at only 40% Dutch, a surprising 40% German, 7.5% British (mainly Scottish), 7.5% French and 5% other. The French connection, through the hardy Protestant Huguenots who fled persecution in Europe in the 1680s, can be discerned in names such as Du Plessis, Du Toit and Marais; the Dutch in the 'van' prefixes. Curiously, by comparison, there seems to be little that is clearly German in language, custom or nomenclature – assimilation seems to have been total.

The Afrikaner community expanded from very small beginnings, more as a consequence of natural increase than from immigration (hence the proliferation of certain names – Botha and Malan, for instance). Families have always tended to be large, patriarchal, Calvinistic and close-knit, and groups of families clannish – the universal characteristics of frontierspeople.

Until fairly recently the Afrikaners were a predominantly rural people, but the ravages of the South African War (1899–1902), drought, cattle disease and rapid industrialization led, from the early years of this century, to a large-scale and continuing drift to the cities. This forced migration caused a great deal of hardship: thousands of families with their roots in the countryside found it impossible to adjust to urban life, and few had the skills to compete on the job market. In 1931, at the height of the Great Depression, a Carnegie-funded commission reported that, of a total white population of 1.8 million, over 300,000, most of them Afrikaans city-dwellers, could be classed as 'very poor'. Today, however, much of commerce, industry, banking and insurance is in the hands of Afrikaans-speaking businessmen.

THE ENGLISH South Africa is home to just under two million English-speaking whites, and their legacy is entirely different from that of the Afrikaners. The background is colonial rather than pioneer; urban-industrial rather than rural.

The origins of this segment of South African society can be traced, for the most part, to the British occupation of the Cape in the early 1800s, and to the colonial government's 'anglicization' policy, one major consequence of which was the landing, in 1820, of 4,000 British settlers at Algoa Bay, now Port Elizabeth, in the Eastern Cape (*see* page 161). Farther east, the colonization of Natal – a more independently motivated exercise – gathered momentum from the 1840s with a series of private immigration schemes. Thereafter, the discovery first of diamonds in the northern Cape and then of gold on the Witwatersrand attracted an avalanche of *uitlanders* (foreigners), most of them English-speaking, to the northern areas.

More recently, post-war immigration, and immigrants from Britain's former colonies in East and Central Africa, and especially from rebel Rhodesia (now Zimbabwe), added substantially to the numbers. The strongholds of the present English-speaking people were thus historically determined. It is no accident that South Africa's 'English' universities are at Cape

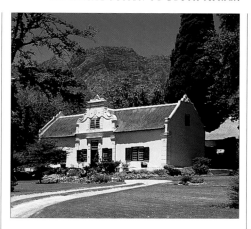

Town (University of Cape Town), Grahamstown (Rhodes University), in KwaZulu-Natal (Durban and Pietermaritzburg) and in Johannesburg (Wits). Excluding significant English-speaking farming enclaves in the Eastern Cape and in the sugar and fruit-growing areas of KwaZulu-Natal, it is largely an urban community.

WHITE MINORITIES A number of smaller ethnic and linguistic groups make up the remainder of the white community. Most substantial – estimates vary widely but there are probably about 75,000 – are South Africans of Portuguese extraction, most of them former residents of Lisbon's African territories of Mozambique and Angola, both now independent, though a fair number hail from the Atlantic island of Madeira. In descending numerical order the additional groups are the German (40,000); Greek (17,000); Italian (17,000); and French (7,000).

A significant subgroup of English-speaking South Africans are the Jewish people, comprising about 2.5% of the white population. Though relatively small in number, Jewish South Africans have contributed disproportionately to the business and industrial development of the country, and to the performing, literary and visual arts.

OPPOSITE: *A replica of Bartolemeu Dias's ship, whose arrival in 1487 heralded the colonial era, is on view at the Mossel Bay museum.*
LEFT: *An imperious Queen Victoria still stands in front of Port Elizabeth's public library.*
ABOVE: *'La Dauphine', an elegant farmstead in the lovely winelands and part of the country's gracious Cape Dutch heritage.*

THE PAST

Both the black and the white man is a relative newcomer to the southern subcontinent. Millennia ago, long before their arrival, bands of nomadic Bushmen (or, more correctly, San) hunter-gatherers, a gentle people wholly in harmony with their environment, roamed the great sunlit spaces in search of sustenance and solitude. Then, about 2,000 years ago, some of these groups acquired sheep from the Sudanic peoples of the north, and in doing so set in train a 'pastoral revolution' that, for the first time, introduced the concept of property ownership, and of territory, into the relationships between the clans.

The new, wealthier and more powerful San, known as the Khoikhoi ('men of men') and also for a time as Hottentots – a name invented by the Dutch – concentrated in loose federations: the Korana in the north-central regions, the Einiqua in the far west and the Namaqua in the south-west. The Namaqua later divided, some migrating down the coast to the Cape Peninsula. These were the first southern Africans to come into contact with the European seafarers of the 16th century, and with the settlers who came after them.

Meanwhile, other peoples of quite different cultures – Bantu-speakers who used iron and kept cattle – had appeared in parts of what is now Zimbabwe, to be followed, around AD 1100, by a second and stronger migratory wave that washed south through the great interior and down the east coast. By the seventeenth century its vanguard, the Xhosa, were in occupation of the southern seaboard

The colonial era

Although the Portuguese navigators (notably Dias and Da Gama) pioneered the sea lanes to India, it was the Dutch who first established a presence on the southern coast of Africa, a halfway house along the route.

In April 1652 Jan van Riebeeck and his small party made their landfall on the shores of the bay beneath Table Mountain. Their aim was to create a victualling station for the Dutch East India Company's passing fleets, but before long Van Riebeeck was finding it hard to feed his own people, let alone serve the crews of visiting ships. In some desperation he turned to private

enterprise, releasing Company employees from their contracts to set themselves up as farmers and tradesmen. He also solved the labour shortage by importing slaves from other parts of Africa and from the Far East.

Both moves were to prove significant. The Cape outpost was now no longer simply a garrison with limited objectives, but a colony capable of growth, and over the following decades it expanded steadily as 'Free Burghers' took over the countryside, pushing the Cape's boundaries ever outward. In the east they came up against the Xhosa and, inevitably, mutual distrust and competition for the best grazing land led to dispute and confrontation. In 1779 the first of nine 'frontier wars' erupted.

White expansion

By the end of the 18th century the power of the Netherlands was in terminal decline, and in 1795 the British took over control of the Cape. They withdrew for a brief period eight years later, and then returned in 1806 to rule the colony for the rest of the 19th century, a period during which the extent of white settlement expanded to cover the entire South African region. The story unfolded in three principal areas of conflict:

THE EASTERN CAPE: Constant skirmishing along the ill-defined eastern frontier, and especially a Xhosa onslaught on the garrison of Grahamstown in 1819, persuaded the colonial government in Cape Town that only large-scale immigration could bring some stability to the region. In 1820 some 4,000 British farmer-colonists were brought in to form a 'buffer zone' between the warring groups. For a time it seemed that proper borders could be agreed, and that the Xhosa would be left in peace, but eventually the eastward push was resumed and the black clans subdued.

KWAZULU-NATAL: British settlers began to arrive on the far eastern coast during the 1820s, at a time when the *Mfecane*, a catastrophic series of forced migrations, was in full flood. The *Mfecane* had been triggered by the meteoric rise to power of Shaka, whose newly fashioned Zulu armies set out on a bloody war of conquest, igniting a chain reaction of violence that engulfed the whole of the eastern seaboard and much of the interior.

Other whites rolled in from the west in the 1830s, Boer (Afrikaner) trekkers who, in their quest for a homeland, came into sharp contact with Shaka's successor, Dingane, whom they finally defeated at Blood River in December 1838. But it was the British who eventually prevailed – over both trekker and Zulu. The former were eased out of the fledgling colony of Natal in 1842; the latter, after a stunning victory at Isandlwana, were crushed at Ulundi in 1879.

THE NORTHERN REGIONS: By the 1830s many Dutch-speaking Cape settlers had become disenchanted with what they regarded as an arrogant and too-liberal British authority in Cape Town, and, after slavery was formally abolished in 1833 (this deprived the farmers of cheap labour), began to in-span their oxen and head into the interior in a mass migration that became known as the Great Trek.

The exodus, which started in a fairly small way, gathered momentum over the next few turbulent years, and, when the wanderers eventually became farmers again, white people were in occupation of much of the territory north of the Orange River. In the early 1850s their settlements were entrenched and strong enough to warrant the creation of two independent republics: the Orange Free State and the Transvaal.

War and Union

The battle lines now changed. Some of the black peoples had been defeated in war, the rest neutralized through treaty, and the white tribes turned against each other.

The Voortrekkers had sought seclusion and the right to govern themselves without interference from the Cape, but the discovery of the fabulous Kimberley diamond fields at the end of the 1860s and of the Witwatersrand's golden reef about a quarter of a century later destroyed any chance of a lasting peace. They turned South Africa from a colonial backwater into a major pawn on the international political chessboard, and the northern region into a prize well worth competing for.

Britain and the Transvaal fought it out on the slopes of Majuba Hill in 1881 (the Boers won) in a battle that left the former humiliated and the latter, in the person of President Paul Kruger, deeply suspicious of British imperial intentions. In the event, Kruger's suspicions were to be vindicated – most notably by the abortive Jameson Raid of 1895/6 – and in the closing months of the century the two countries found themselves at war again. The Anglo-Boer conflict lasted nearly three years, reduced much of the northern countryside to a barren wilderness, and left a legacy of fierce bitterness: Afrikaners would be slow to forget, and some of them could never forgive, Kitchener's devastating scorched earth policy and the horrors of the concentration camps.

The British, however, were determined on reconciliation. Their peace terms, set out in the Treaty of Vereeniging (1902), were generous to the vanquished; Lord Milner, chief architect of the war, praised the Boers' 'dignity in victory and stoicism in defeat', and his team of talented young administrators, known as the 'Kindergarten', contributed brilliantly to the process of post-war reconstruction.

In 1908 and 1909 an all-white National Convention debated unification, and on 31 May of the following year the two former Boer republics (the Transvaal and Orange Free State) and the two British colonies (the Cape and Natal) became provinces of the new Union of South Africa. The country's first premier was Louis Botha, his deputy Jan Smuts; both were Afrikaners of the 'enlightened' (pro-British) kind, though each had led commandos against the Imperial forces, with stunning success, during the war.

The black people – the vast majority – had not been consulted in the creation of the unified state, and had practically no democratic rights under the new arrangement.

A Boer soldier, part of the Paul Kruger monument in Pretoria's Church Square.

THE APARTHEID YEARS

The nationalists of the 1950s and 1960s did not invent apartheid: numerous race laws had been enacted during the four decades following Union in 1910. What they did do was tie together the existing threads of racial prejudice to create one of the most all-embracing bodies of restrictive law ever devised.

Lynchpin of the system was the Group Areas Act (1950) which further segregated cities and towns. Other statutes involved freedom of movement; racially based identity documents; classification according to colour; regulation of the workplace; the prohibition of mixed marriages; an amended Immorality Act (criminalizing sex across the colour line); the Reservation of Separate Amenities Act (this erected 'whites-only' signs over places such as libraries, public gardens, beaches, benches and entertainment venues), and a huge arsenal of security regulations.

One of the chief architects of apartheid was Hendrik Verwoerd who, as Minister of Native Affairs and Prime Minister, contrived the massively destructive Bantu Education Act and laid the foundations of the homelands system – the 'Grand Apartheid' design that carried segregation to its ultimate, insane conclusion. Verwoerd died in 1966, victim of a deranged assassin's knife. Major events during his ruthless premiership were the Sharpeville shootings (1960); the subsequent banning of the African National Congress (ANC) and other opposition groups; South Africa's expulsion from the Commonwealth and its transition from dominion to republic (1961).

The liberation movement

Black opposition had its roots in post-Anglo-Boer War disillusionment, a sense of betrayal reinforced by the exclusion of the black majority from the process leading to Union in 1910. Nevertheless the ANC, formed as the South African Native National Congress in 1912 (it changed its name in 1925), remained committed to peaceful solutions for the next half century, during which time black rights were relentlessly eroded. It retained its non-racial, liberal stance even during the bitterly waged 'defiance campaign' of the early 1950s. This moderation, which had failed to advance the cause, prompted a breakaway by radical elements who, in 1959, formed the Pan-Africanist Congress (PAC). A year later, after the massacre at Sharpeville, both bodies were banned and went underground.

Soon afterwards the ANC launched its armed wing, Umkhonto we Sizwe ('Spear of the Nation') and embarked on a programme of sabotage that led, in 1963, to the arrest of Nelson Mandela and other prominent figures.

Protest and reform

Sharpeville, where 69 black demonstrators were gunned down by police, was a turning point in the country's affairs. Before the shootings South Africa was an accepted member of the community of nations; after March 1960 it faced isolation abroad and growing racial conflict at home.

Verwoerd's successors, BJ Vorster (1966–1978) and PW Botha (1978–1989) tried to stem the tide – the former through a policy of *détente* with independent black states, the latter through domestic reform. Botha's new constitution (1984) gave the Indian and coloured communities a political voice, albeit a limited one, but blacks were excluded from the process – they were deemed to be citizens of one or other of the 'homelands' – and the initiative was doomed from the start.

The seeds of failure had in fact been sown earlier – in June 1976 when 10,000 students staged a protest march through the dusty streets of Soweto and battled it out with the security forces. Lives were lost, buildings and vehicles destroyed, and violence spread to other parts of the country, continuing for eight months. These and subsequent riots established a pattern – of unrest designed to 'make the country ungovernable', of tough police reaction, of a regime increasingly under siege. By the late 1980s the townships were in a state of anarchy, and even conservative whites became convinced that they could no longer hold onto power.

The new era

In 1989 PW Botha suffered a mild stroke and, in due course, resigned the presidency in favour of FW de Klerk, a politician not noted for his liberal views but a pragmatist nevertheless.

The changes that followed were rapid, fundamental and dramatic. On 2 February 1990, at the opening of parliament, De Klerk announced the unbanning of the ANC, the South African Communist Party and about 30 other organizations. Nine days later Nelson Mandela, behind bars for 27 years, walked to freedom.

The decades of white political supremacy were at their end; the new South Africa, its shape as yet undefined, had been born.

CALENDAR OF MAJOR EVENTS

Southern Africa was occupied by the Khoikhoi (Hottentot), the San (Bushman) and, later, by Bantu-speaking (black) peoples long before the arrival of the white settlers. Their history is largely undocumented. Significant dates of the colonial era include:

1488–1497 Portuguese navigators Dias and Da Gama round the Cape.

1652 Dutch settlers under Van Riebeeck land at Table Bay, erect fortress and plant crops.

1659 Khoikhoi protest against white encroachment; first serious armed conflict.

1660s Explorers make their way inland, and along west and south coasts.

1779 First 'frontier war' between Xhosa and settler in Eastern Cape. Eight more were to erupt during the next 100 years.

1780–1783 War between Holland and Britain hastens demise of Dutch East India Company.

1795 British occupy the Cape.

1816–1818 Rise of Zulu empire under Shaka.

1834 Slavery abolished.

1835–1845 Great Trek of Boers into interior and to eastern regions.

1852–1854 Independence of Boer republics of Transvaal and Orange Free State recognized.

1860 First Indians arrive in Natal.

1869 Kimberley diamond fields discovered.

1879 Anglo-Zulu war. Zululand carved up into separate chiefdoms.

1886 Witwatersrand goldfields discovered; Johannesburg born.

1899–1902 Anglo-Boer war devastates country. Vereeniging Treaty generous to Boers.

1908–1910 National Convention of white leaders leads to unification of SA; blacks excluded from process. Louis Botha becomes first premier.

1912 SA Native National Congress (later renamed African National Congress) formed.

1913 Natives Land Act creates 'traditional' black territories (homelands).

1914–1918 SA declares war on Germany; Union troops conquer South West Africa (SWA).

1923 Natives (Urban Areas) Act imposes segregation in towns.

1934 National and South African parties form 'fusion government' reconciling white political interests. DF Malan breaks away to launch white right-wing 'Purified National Party'.

1939–1945 SA joins Allied cause in war against Hitler's Germany and (later) Italy.

1948 Malan's National Party wins election, launching apartheid era.

1950 Population Registration, Immorality and Group Areas acts passed.

1956 Coloured voters removed from common roll after regime manipulates the constitution.

1958 HF Verwoerd becomes prime minister.

1959 Robert Sobukwe forms Pan-Africanist Congress (PAC).

1960 Police open fire on demonstrators at Sharpeville; 69 blacks killed. ANC, PAC and other bodies banned. British premier Macmillan delivers 'wind of change' address to SA parliament. White electorate votes for republican form of government.

1961 Verwoerd withdraws SA from Commonwealth; SA becomes republic. Nelson Mandela leads armed struggle; ANC sabotage campaign begins. ANC's Albert Luthuli awarded Nobel Peace Prize.

1962 Mandela arrested.

1963 'Rivonia' sabotage trial begins; Mandela and others sentenced to life imprisonment.

1976 Soweto riots erupt in June; countrywide unrest follows.

1977 Black Consciousness leader Steve Biko dies in police custody.

1980–1984 President PW Botha launches reform initiative; new three-chamber constitution gives vote to Indians and coloureds, excludes blacks. Unrest escalates.

1989 FW de Klerk succeeds Botha.

1990 Liberation movement (including SA Communist Party) unbanned; Mandela released.

1994 First one-person, one-vote election held; ANC becomes majority party in parliament; government of national unity formed; Nelson Mandela sworn in as president.

Lining up to vote in April 1994.

COMING TOGETHER

The journey towards political settlement and the establishment of a fully democratic order proved long, hard, and fraught with hazard.

Tentative talks between the Nationalist government, the ANC and other organizations began in 1990, and continued more formally during the following year, when the leaders of 19 widely divergent political bodies came together to inaugurate the Convention for a Democratic South Africa (Codesa). Notable absentees from the forum, at least initially, were the Pan-Africanist Congress (which held to its revolutionary principles) and Zulu Chief Mangosuthu Buthelezi's Inkatha Freedom Party.

The issues were complex, some seemingly intractable. De Klerk had, from the first, rejected simple majority rule in favour of a power-sharing formula that contained checks against the 'domination of one group by another' – a euphemism for entrenching white minority rights. He also advocated federalism: the devolution of power from the centre to the regions. Conversely, the ANC and its partners wanted, among other things, a unitary state and a winner-takes-all electoral arrangement.

But hopes of a political breakthrough were raised by the positive results of a whites-only referendum held in March 1992, and were maintained despite the setbacks that occurred in the following months (including widespread violence and the murder of popular radical Chris Hani). In September 1993 Nelson Mandela called for the lifting of all remaining international sanctions. Two months later he and De Klerk shared the 1993 Nobel Peace Prize.

In December, parliament was effectively superseded by a multi-party Transitional Executive Council, and the last of the obstacles quickly (and, it seemed, miraculously) evaporated in April 1994 – just days before the general election – when Zulu leader Mangosuthu Buthelezi agreed to take part in the new order.

After a protracted election process, which proved lively, often chaotic but always – astonishingly in view of past antagonisms – good-humoured, the ANC gained a near-two thirds majority in the proposed National Assembly. It also captured healthy majorities in six of the nine provincial parliaments.

Early in May 1994 Nelson Mandela was sworn in as the first president of a finally liberated, fully democratic South Africa.

MAN OF DESTINY

State President Nelson Mandela.

Nelson Rolihlahla Mandela, member of the royal Tembu (Xhosa) house and first president of the new South Africa, was born in the Eastern Cape's Transkei region in 1918. He gained degrees from the universities of Fort Hare and the Witwatersrand, qualified as a lawyer in 1942, joined the African National Congress two years later, vigorously protested against the hated apartheid system after 1948 and was 'banned' in terms of the Suppression of Communism Act.

Although legally barred from holding party office during the 1950s, he helped reorganize the ANC on a cell basis and formed (and led) its military wing, Umkhonto we Sizwe ('Spear of the Nation'), spent some months abroad, was arrested twice (for high treason and incitement) and eventually, in 1963, convicted on nearly 200 counts of sabotage. He spent the next 27 years in prison, many of them on infamous Robben Island, near Cape Town.

Mandela, a creditable amateur boxer in his youth, is renowned for his phenomenal capacity for hard work and his asceticism (he eats sparingly and neither drinks nor smokes). Vision, statesmanship and genuine humility – a grace rare in politicians – are among the many qualities that have characterized his presidency, and which earned him a share of the 1993 Nobel Peace Prize.

SOUTH AFRICA TODAY

South Africa has seen rapid and fundamental change. In four years – from 1990 to 1994 – the country negotiated a painful transition from autocratic white minority rule to full democracy. Its political and economic institutions have been restructured, its society transformed.

THE CONSTITUTION

South Africa is a republican democracy administered since 1994 by a 'government of national unity'. An Interim Constitution was introduced in that year: Parliament has been busy constructing a final formula. However, the constitutional foundations have been laid, embodied in some 30 entrenched principles. The chief ingredients of the Interim Constitution are:
• A 400-member National Assembly elected on a system of proportional representation.
• A 90-member Senate which acts as a watchdog. It may also introduce legislation.
• An executive comprising the State President, at least two Deputy Presidents and a Cabinet of up to 27 ministers. Parties with 20 or more members in the National Assembly are entitled to a proportionate number of Cabinet portfolios. Decision-making tends to be by consensus 'in accordance with the spirit of national unity'.
• Nine regional administrations, each with its own legislature, premier and cabinet.

South Africa's flag, emblem of the 'rainbow nation'.

• A Charter of Fundamental Rights, or Bill of Rights, which safeguards the ordinary citizen from unjust action by the State and, in certain instances, by other individuals.
• An independent Constitutional Court. The Constitution is the supreme law; statutes enacted by Parliament must be in accordance with its clauses, some of which restrict parliamentary discretion. The Court is the final authority on all constitutional matters.

FOREIGN POLICY

South Africa is a minor player on the world stage, but it ranks as a regional superpower and, in Africa, has a crucial role to fulfil.

The country occupies just 3% of the African continent and is home to a bare 5% of its population, yet it accounts for:
• 40% of Africa's industrial output;
• 25% of gross continental product;
• 64% of electricity generated;
• 45% of mineral production;
• 66% of steel production;
• 46% of its vehicles and 36% of its telephones.
The smaller southern African states rely heavily on and co-operate closely with South Africa. Indeed, the regions of Africa south of the Sahara have many shared interests and they are drawing ever closer together – under southern leadership.

In Europe and America, South Africa is seen as the best hope for a continent ravaged by poverty, disease, famine and, all too often, civil strife. The industrial world has poured billions of dollars into various forms of disaster relief – unrecoverable funds that could have been used to far better effect on economic development, long-term health care and badly needed infrastructure.

United States policy towards Africa, unstructured and even opportunistic in the past, now seems to be taking on a definite shape, best described perhaps by the phrase 'preventive diplomacy'. A great deal more could have been done, so the thinking goes, to pre-empt the horrors of Rwanda, civil war in Angola, disintegration in Somalia, famine in Ethiopia, had more studious forethought been devoted to the ominous trends, and the crises nipped in the bud.

Preventive diplomacy means more than stockpiling food and medicines for the evil day. It calls for a partnership between the United States, and the other G7 nations, with an enlightened, comparatively powerful regional leadership. South Africa is well placed to assume the part.

WEALTH OF A NATION

The South African economy is an uncomfortable mix of First World sophistication and Third World underdevelopment.

On the one hand it has immense natural resources, employs advanced technologies and supports complex industrial and commercial structures. On the other hand, educational standards among many of the people are low; there are too few jobs for the rapidly expanding population; and the 'poverty cycle', if not as horrific as it is in some other African countries, does exist, threatening stability and profoundly affecting the process of economic decision-making.

ECONOMIC POINTERS The biggest non-government contributions to the Gross Domestic Product are made by the manufacturing industry (about 22%), mining (13%), commerce (11%), the informal sector (9.5%), transport and communications (9.1%). Agriculture accounts for a surprisingly modest 5%.

These figures reveal the dramatic transformation from an agrarian-based economy a century ago, before the discovery of diamonds and gold, to today's advanced industrialization. For much of the 20th century mining provided the impetus; after the Second World War there was an impressive growth of manufacturing activity. That sector is now the priority: it is capable of much further expansion (South Africa exports too many raw materials that could be locally fabricated, turned into semi-manufactured or end products) and of absorbing more job-seekers than all the other economic areas put together. This is the vital consideration.

MINING South Africa has the largest-known reserves of gold, platinum, high-grade chromium, manganese, vanadium, fluorspar and andalusite in the world, and massive deposits of diamonds, iron ore, coal, uranium, asbestos, nickel and phosphates – a powerful litany of endowment that underpins the country's vast economic potential.

INDUSTRY A large pool of labour, a wealth of natural resources, technological expertise and, not least, economic and perhaps political necessity have led South Africa towards self-reliance in industrial products.

In the early 1990s, the manufacturing industry employed 1.6 million people and, as we have noted, contributed about a quarter of the Gross Domestic Product. However, industry has enjoyed a high level of government protection,

part of a policy to promote self-sufficiency through subsidies, tariff barriers, import quotas and so forth. These controls are being phased out in terms of the GATT agreements, and manufacturers are having to re-gear themselves to compete on world markets (South Africa's economic recovery will have to be export-led) – and in the domestic market against a growing volume of foreign products. Many industries are finding the process painful. So, too, is organized labour, which must accept that wages are dependent on productivity.

The larger manufacturing sectors include metal products (iron and steel, heavy machinery and equipment); non-metallic products (mostly for the construction industry); transport and equipment (notably vehicle manufacture and assembly); chemicals and pharmaceuticals (the entire range); processed foods (60% of which are exported); and textiles and clothing.

AGRICULTURE South Africa is one of the few food-exporting countries in the world – a testament in a sense to the expertise of its farming community and water engineers, because its natural land resources are poor. Rainfall is mainly seasonal and invariably – certainly in recent years – unpredictable. The soil is not especially fertile; erosion over the millennia and the leaching of Africa's earth during the wetter periods of the continent's history have impoverished the nutrient content over large areas (only 12% of the country's surface area is arable).

Despite these built-in drawbacks South Africa has doubled its agricultural output since 1960 and now exports, in an average year, about R15 billion worth of meat, produce, processed foods and forestry and game products and a further R1 billion worth of wool and textiles.

Land is central to the post-apartheid redistribution issue. For decades, the law reserved more than eight-tenths of the country for 'white' occupation, and the pressures to reallocate this precious resource are intensifying. Direct expropriation without adequate compensation has been ruled out, but the white farmer will no longer be coddled by the State. The ANC government's agricultural policy is aimed at 'improving support for the neglected small-scale farming sector, promoting household food security rather than national food self-sufficiency, boosting rural employment and ending inequality ...'. A great deal of State land will be made available, and thousands of rural people will have access to the more bountiful areas.

SOCIAL SERVICES In the early 1990s nearly half the population of South Africa existed 'below the minimum levels'; 2.3 million people were 'in urgent need of nutritional support' (more than 70 children were dying of malnutrition and related causes each day); the housing shortfall was estimated at nearly 2 million (and growing by the month as thousands migrated from the countryside). The social services were in crisis.

Soon after taking office, the ANC-led government launched its ambitious Reconstruction and Development Programme (RDP), which called for massive investment in education (10 years free and compulsory schooling for every child; subsidized tertiary and adult training; heavy expenditure on schools and equipment); in housing (more than a million low-cost units within five years); the provision of running water and sanitation (to a million more) and of electricity (half a million connections a year); and in health (free care for pregnant mothers and children under six), job creation and social welfare.

Sun-drying fruit in the Western Cape.

POWER LINES

Despite its limited oil resources, the republic is a net exporter of energy. Coal is the principal source: approximately 60% of coal-mining output is applied to the generation of electricity; 17% to the production of synthetic fuels; 6% to the conversion of coke and tar. Three great oil-from-coal plants have been built: Sasol 1 in the Free State, and Sasols 2 and 3 at Secunda in Mpumalanga.

South Africa's largest electricity supply utility, Eskom, which operates 19 coal-fired, two hydro-electric, two pump-storage, one nuclear and three gas-turbine power stations, provides 97% of the electricity consumed (some 140 billion kilowatts annually). Six new coal-fired stations came on stream in the mid-1980s, including the largest dry-cooled plant in the world, at Ellisras in the Northern Province. Offshore oil and gas fields are being worked south of Mossel Bay on the southern seaboard, though their long-term viability is in doubt.

THE ARTS

South Africa's cultural scene is lively – much of it of international standard. Literature, the visual arts, theatre, ballet, opera and classical music thrive in the country's major centres.

The emphases, though, appear to be changing – moving away from the legacy of Europe and closer to the cultural heart of Africa. The country is now free to explore its heritage.

Excellent symphony orchestras are based and give regular performances in Durban, Pretoria, Johannesburg and Cape Town. Music of a different kind – a unique kind – is evolving in the black urban community (*see* further on), a vibrant synthesis of African and western idioms that is beginning to make its mark beyond the borders of the townships.

South Africa has produced more than its share of gifted instrumentalists, opera singers and ballet dancers. The country, though, finds it difficult to retain its own: universities and other learning centres turn out an unusual wealth of young talent which is often lost to the more sophisticated stages and concert halls of Europe and America.

South Africa can claim few literary giants of the kind that one might expect to have emerged in a country of such beauty, complexity, conflict and tragedy. There has been no Steinbeck to give voice to the wrath of the economically underprivileged; no James Baldwin to bring fiery articulation to ethnic consciousness; no Orwell, no Solzhenitsyn. It could, though, be that very complexity that inhibits the pen. Says Nadine Gordimer, a leading contemporary novelist: 'Living in a society that has been as deeply and calculatedly compartmentalized as South Africa's has been under the colour bar, the writer's potential has unscalable limitations.'

Nevertheless, there have been, and are, South African writers of real stature: the much underestimated Olive Schreiner; the eccentric Roy Campbell; the mystic Eugène Marais and, of recent vintage, Alan Paton and Laurens van der Post who, each in his own way, has bared the soul of his beloved country; the acclaimed Nadine Gordimer and JM Coetzee; André Brink and Etienne Leroux; the brilliant Athol Fugard and fellow playwright Gibson Kente.

Among the black people of South Africa there is, too, a powerful tradition of oral literature: the key to their past and, perhaps, the door to the country's literary future.

AFRICAN MUSIC AND DRAMA

The indigenous African people have ancient musical traditions, and a superb gift for rhythm, harmony and spontaneous song.

Folk music in the rural areas is a prominent element in ceremony and ritual. Traditional instruments tend to be few and simple; the Zulu make do with cowhide drums and rattles shaken by hand or worn on the ankle, to which they add the powerful, deep-throated roar of men's voices, the keening descant of the women, the clapping of hands and the stamping of feet to produce a beat derived from a largely militaristic heritage. Other tribal groups use marimbas, xylophones and a variety of stringed instruments developed from the shooting bow.

THE CITY SCENE In keeping with urbanization, a new and distinctive sound has emerged from the townships. It stems in part from the original music of Africa, in which *mbube* or the

ABOVE: *Music, dance and drama flourish in the cities of South Africa. Most of the performances draw their inspiration from Europe's cultural heritage, but the emphases are changing, moving closer to the heart of Africa.*
OPPOSITE: *Zulu dancers go through their paces at the Aloe Ridge complex near Johannesburg.*

'choral band' of the countryside is a prominent feature, but it has so many other ingredients that it defies any simple definition.

Its earliest form was *marabi*, a bouncy, anything-goes sound that borrowed increasingly from American jazz and the big-band music of Louis Armstrong, Count Basie and Duke Ellington. Among later influences was the pennywhistle and homemade guitar – *kwela* street music, which had its origins in Johannesburg's Sophiatown and Alexandra in the 1940s, gaining enormously in popularity during the following two decades. And then there was the soul music (often accompanied by acrobatic soul-dances such as the Monkey Jive) of the 1970s and the Afro-rock of the 1980s.

All of these influences have come together under the loose heading of *mbaqanga*, which is the name for African maize bread and which, like the food to which it refers, fills a void, a deep need. There are as many *mbaqanga* sounds as there are individual bands, but all have something in common: they are fresh, innovative – and exciting.

THE PEOPLE'S STAGE A new art form (or perhaps a very old one) is so-called 'black theatre', in which stage presentations – often an exuberant mix of words, music, song and dance – are conceived, written and performed by black South Africans largely for black audiences.

A strikingly imaginative element of the shows is their sparkling spontaneity, which is in part rooted in African culture: performers tend to share in the creation of the work rather than follow a set script. Despite this looseness, however, some of the productions have reached the conventional stages of South Africa's cities, and a few have enjoyed international acclaim.

Until recently much black theatre reflected the grimness of life under apartheid, but it has now moved away from racial introspection towards more universal themes.

THE SPORTING SCENE

The country's wonderfully sunny climate favours outdoor activity, and South Africans are enthusiastic and, in competitive terms, increasingly successful sportspeople.

The long years of isolation inevitably affected performance standards, but the removal of race barriers, readmittance to the international arena and the launching of development programmes are now, at last, allowing the country's youth to realize its full potential.

The major spectator sports are soccer, cricket, rugby, athletics and boxing.

Within the black community, soccer is supreme: there are more than 12,000 soccer clubs and nearly a million regular players in South Africa. The national team were the victors during the 1996 Africa Cup of Nations, which was hosted by South Africa.

Rugby is especially popular among Afrikaners. The premier provincial rugby competition is the Bankfin Currie Cup (the prefix relates to the current sponsor, and periodically changes); the top sides take part in the annual southern hemisphere series against their counterparts from New Zealand, Australia and the Pacific islands, and to date have done remarkably well. The national team, known for decades as the Springboks, emerged as victors in the third (four-yearly) Rugby World Cup, hosted by South Africa during 1995.

The leading domestic cricket competitions are the Castle Cup and the Standard Bank Cup. South Africa made a welcome re-entry into world competition with a short series against India in 1991, the start of a crowded programme

ABOVE: *President Mandela, wearing the national green-and-gold jersey, congratulates captain François Pienaar after the triumphant final of the Rugby World Cup in 1995.*
BOTTOM: *South African batsman Jonty Rhodes faces up to the England bowling attack.*
OPPOSITE: *Harvesting waterblommetjies ('little water flowers') in the Western Cape's Boland area.*

in which it held its own. Its five-run victory over the Australians and triumph at Lords, both in 1994, were memorable.

Golf clubs, of which there are over 400, welcome visitors; most courses are beautifully maintained. Local golfers compete with honour on the international scene; greats have included Bobby Locke and Gary Player; Ernie Els is currently the most successful competitor.

Watersports attract especially large numbers of participants, not only along the coasts but also on the inland dams and rivers. Most good hotels have their own swimming pools; their managements help visitors organize angling, sailing and other recreational expeditions. Parts of the KwaZulu-Natal, Eastern and Western Cape shorelines provide quite magnificent opportunities for surfing and scuba-diving.

Jogging and cycling are also sociably popular recreations; competitive road-running a prominent sport. South Africa has produced some of the world's best long-distance athletes. The premier annual event is the Comrades Marathon, held at the end of May over the 89 km (55 miles) between Durban and Pietermaritzburg. Almost as popular is Cape Town's Two Oceans marathon, which takes place over Easter.

FOOD AND DRINK

South African meat (including venison), fruit, freshwater and sea fish and shellfish – most notably crayfish (rock lobster) and perlemoen (abelone) caught off the Cape coasts – are of the highest quality. The country's restaurants offer the full range of culinary delights, from Continental classics through country fare to the dishes of a score and more exotic peoples.

There is no such thing as 'South African cuisine' in the sense of a single, coherent philosophy of food – the region is ethnically diverse, as are the eating patterns.

However, the traditions of colonial and immigrant groups – Greek, German, Portuguese among others – have been influential. Fiery curries, tandoori meats and memorable breyanis can be savoured in Durban, which has a large Indian population. In the Cape, some restaurants serve 'Malay' cuisine, an Indonesian style that took on elements of Indian and Dutch cooking and is famed for its fragrant bredies – chiefly made from mutton, onions, tomatoes, chillies, cabbage and pumpkin; there's also a piquant concoction based on waterblommetjies, or 'little water flowers'.

Other equally relished dishes include curry-flavoured bobotles, rotis, spicy meatballs, gooey desserts, puddings, tarts and biscuits adapted from the recipes of the early Dutch settlers; sweet preserves from those of the French Huguenots. Cape Malay curries differ from – sweeter and more gentle on the palate than – those of Bombay and Madras. You'll also find fine 'old Cape' (Dutch/Afrikaner) dishes, prominent ingredients among which are Karoo lamb, venison (springbok pie is delicious), sweet potato and pumpkin.

Afrikaner hospitality, especially in country areas, is legendary. The home-cooked meal you would eat would be substantial and probably rather stodgy: typical fare would include splendid portions of red meat (usually mutton or lamb), sweet potatoes, pumpkin or sweetcorn fritters, mashed vegetables flavoured with cinnamon and sage, milk (or custard) tart, cheesecake, various sweet preserves known as *konfyt* and plenty of good, rich coffee to follow. One of the best-loved of South African social traditions is the *braai* (short for *braaivleis*), a standard barbecue featuring well-marinated meats (lamb, beef, chicken, and the highly-spiced, much favoured *boerewors*, or 'farmer's sausage'), potatoes baked in foil and salads.

Traditional African cuisine is not found on many restaurant menus, though as a gimmick tourist parties will occasionally be introduced to a special delicacy – a dish of fried termites, for example. The indigenous people have not elevated food to cult status: eating remains a practical necessity (and a formidably challenging one in many parts of Africa); the range is limited, the dishes basic – the ordinary meal in the townships comprises maize-meal (samp), boiled vegetables and a little stewed meat.

South African wines are generally very good, some are excellent, a few superb. They were long underrated (and boycotted) by the world but are now gaining an international reputation. And, although prices are rising, they are still relatively cheap.

EXPLORING SOUTH AFRICA

South Africa is a vast country, and it has many faces, many moods, the kaleidoscopic canvas embracing high mountain ranges, broad grasslands stretching to the far horizons, great semi-desert spaces in the interior, lushly covered hills and valleys along the coastal terraces, bustling modern cities, country towns and remote villages that sleep soundly in the sun.

This, the most extensive part of the volume, covers the more significant features and attractions of the various regions. The twelve subsections do not correspond precisely with the boundaries of the provinces: the book has been divided, rather, into coherent tourist areas. Starting with the Johannesburg-Pretoria area, the sequence takes the reader eastwards into the Mpumalanga escarpment and down into the game-rich Lowveld, then north to the Limpopo and west to the Pilanesberg and Sun City. Thereafter, the route leads you through the Free State to KwaZulu-Natal and around the country's 3,000 km (1,900 miles) coastline, with a digression into the great interior.

LEFT: *Cape Town's elegant Clifton suburb.*
ABOVE: *Namaqualand in springtime.*

JOHANNESBURG AND PRETORIA

Just 56 km (35 miles) of somewhat featureless, largely built-up highveld terrain separates Pretoria, administrative capital of South Africa, and Johannesburg, capital of Gauteng province, the country's largest metropolis and financial heart of the southern African subcontinent. Between the two is Midrand, until recently an unremarkable scatter of villages but now a prime growth point destined to become a city in its own right.

Pretoria lies nestling in the warm and fertile valley of the Apies ('little ape') River at an altitude of 1,370 m (4,500 ft) above sea level, the eastern suburbs hugging the foothills of the pleasant Magaliesberg range of hills, the central district overlooked by Meintjes Kop and the imposing neo-classical, semicircular façade of the Union Buildings, designed by Sir Herbert Baker. It's a large city – in terms of both population (546,000) and area (592 km² or 231 square miles) – and a handsome one, too, graced by stately buildings and famed for its many parks, its jacaranda trees, its roses and its splendid wealth of indigenous flora.

By contrast the vast sprawl of Johannesburg – also known as Jo'burg, Joey's, the Golden City and, by the miners who work the seams deep beneath the surface, as Egoli – has few claims to beauty, though it does have its 'green lung' and some of the suburbs, the northern ones, delight the eye with their embowered avenues and luxuriant gardens. Its appeal lies elsewhere – in its equable climate (*see* Advisory, page 57), in its vibrancy, its zest for life, its fine hotels, restaurants and shopping malls.

That is the tourist's Johannesburg, a city that, in common with every major metropolis in the world, has its darker side. There is substantial wealth here, but also extreme poverty in the surrounding 'black' townships; entire communities that have suffered generations of deprivation and discrimination have challenged the old order; the political and social patterns are undergoing dramatic changes; the transition process has provoked uncertainty, instability and, sometimes, violent confrontation.

OPPOSITE: *Nightfall over the Golden City of Johannesburg, the fast-beating heart of South Africa's economy and epicentre of the Witwatersrand complex of cities and towns.*

Johannesburg and its mining, industrial and dormitory satellites are collectively known as the Witwatersrand or, more simply, as 'the Rand' (and also, confusingly, as 'the Reef').

South of Johannesburg, around the Vaal River, is another industrialized area. There isn't much open country between the two, but the densest of the southern urban concentrations are within the Vaal Triangle, which embraces the centres of Vereeniging and Vanderbijlpark.

JOHANNESBURG

In July 1886 an itinerant Australian prospector named George Harrison, together with his friend George Walker, stumbled onto the Witwatersrand's reef, the world's richest natural treasure-house; word of the find spread like the proverbial bushfire, and within weeks the first fortune-seekers were camping out on the dry veld. They arrived in their hundreds at first, then in their thousands and finally, when it became clear that this wasn't just another golden bubble, that a new El Dorado was in the making, in their tens of thousands.

Within three years of its birth, Johannesburg was the country's largest town. In 1928 it became a city, and is now the second biggest on the African continent (after Cairo). It stands 1,763 m (5,784 ft) above sea level and enjoys an average of nearly nine hours of sunshine a day throughout the year. In normal times thunderstorms bring almost daily downpours between November and February, often torrential ones sometimes preceded by showers of king-size hailstones; winter days are sunny and crisp, the nights frosty.

Johannesburg has all the amenities of a major modern city: excellent shopping outlets both in the central area and, especially, in the large and glitzy suburban malls; a range of restaurants to suit most tastes; generally good and sometimes innovative theatre; orchestral music, ballet and opera of a fair standard; an explosively adventurous jazz/rock/new-wave/indigenous music scene, and an art world searching for an identity.

The scene is at its liveliest, perhaps, in Hillbrow, a cosmopolitan inner suburb of packed apartment blocks, eateries, discos, clubs, speciality shops and streets that seldom sleep. Visitors, though, should venture into the area with caution: the level of street crime here – as in many other parts of the metropolis – is high.

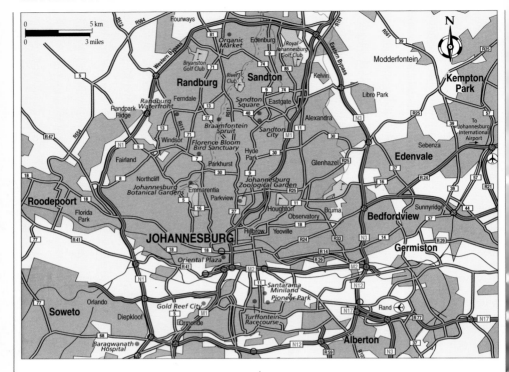

Museums, monuments and landmarks

Johannesburg, a young and reputedly brash city, offers the visitor a surprisingly varied selection of cultural venues. Among the more prominent of these are:

MUSEUMAFRICA (next to the Market Theatre in Newtown). Eye-catching displays that tell the story of southern Africa from the dawn of humankind to the computer age are features of what the curator describes as 'a lively, flexible museum in which everyone can feel at home'.

MuseumAfrica, which opened in 1994, reflects the spirit of the new South Africa as well as its heritage. On view are re-creations of township life (squatter shacks, migrant workers' hostel rooms, shebeens and so forth), and an Apartheid and Resistance section that illuminates key events in the 350-year struggle against white domination (pride of place is given to the often tragically violent years immediately preceding the first free and democratic elections and Nelson Mandela's presidential inauguration). Cultural exhibits include traditional beadwork, musical instruments, hunting and military items, religion

and customs (the tribal love-letters are truly fascinating), replicas of decorated huts and much more. One permanent gallery is devoted to San (Bushman) rock art, another to the Bensusan Museum of Photography. Highlights of the latter include the earliest (1839) pictures and equipment and, for the children, optical toys. Open Tuesdays to Sundays; guided tours.

BERNBERG MUSEUM OF COSTUME (corner Jan Smuts Avenue and Duncombe Road, Forest Town). Period costumes and accessories (fans, feathers, parasols, shoes and jewellery) from 1760 to 1929, attractively displayed in the former home of the Bernberg sisters. Open Tuesdays to Sundays.

JOHANNESBURG ART GALLERY (Joubert Park). Collections include South African, English, French, Dutch traditional, historical and contemporary works; notable is the print cabinet (just under 3,000 items ranging from Dürer to Rembrandt); also sculpture, ceramics, posters, Japanese woodcuts, textiles, fans, furniture. Regular and special tours; lectures, film shows, concerts, poetry readings, dramatic presentations, seminars, workshops; consult the press for details. Open Tuesdays to Sundays.

PLACES OF WORSHIP Among several worth visiting are the impressive Anglican Cathedral of St Mary's (corner De Villiers and Wanderers streets), and the Islamic Mosque (corner Nugget and Market streets).

RAILWAY MUSEUMS The Transnet Museum (formerly the SA Transport Services Museum) is currently sited on the old concourse of the main railway station but at the time of writing was scheduled for relocation. Displays cover the whole public-transport range: railways (including the Transvaal's first locomotive; and a fascinating collection of model trains), road motor services, harbours, airways, lifeboats, tugboat, a photograph room and an excellent art gallery. Open Mondays to Fridays.

Other railway displays – excellent ones – are on view at the Railway Preservation Society's centre near Krugersdorp to the west (historic locomotives and veteran road vehicles), and at the Transport Museum in Heidelberg's old station on the East Rand.

NATIONAL MUSEUM OF MILITARY HISTORY (Saxonwold, next to Zoo). A splendid expo of militaria, with special emphasis on the two world wars: weapons, vehicles, aircraft (including the pioneer Messerschmitt Me-262 jet night-fighter, only one of two in the world to have survived intact). Also Anglo-Boer War memorabilia. Audio-visual presentations on Saturdays and Sundays; open daily.

JOHANNESBURG STOCK EXCHANGE This stock exchange was by no means the country's first – shares were traded at the Cape as early as 1820 – but it's now the country's only physical stock and share market and one of the world's bigger and busier financial venues. Popularly known as 'Diagonal Street', it is a vast, sophisticated and fascinating complex where, although electronic trading is slowly being introduced, 'open outcry' is still the order of the dealer's day and there's plenty of action to be seen. Conducted tours are laid on at 11h00 and 14h00 each day from Monday to Friday.

UNIVERSITY OF THE WITWATERSRAND South Africa's largest English-medium university (18,000 enrolment); the campus is in Braamfontein, near the city centre; tours can be arranged for groups. Of special note is the Standard Bank collection of African tribal art, housed in the Gertrude Posel Gallery, Senate House: ritual material, a collection of traditional beadwork and much else that is rapidly disappearing from the cultures. Other features of

interest include a re-creation of the study used by Jan Smuts, and the original cross (or *padrão*) erected by Bartolomeu Dias near Port Elizabeth.

Also on the Wits campus is the Planetarium (Yale Road): embark on a journey through space and time, enjoyed in comfort. Programmes change frequently to accommodate a variety of topical shows from multi-visual extravaganzas to live lectures. Informative and entertaining; book at Planetarium.

The gold mines

Most of the early workings, those established in and immediately around Johannesburg, have long since closed down, leaving only their silent headgear and their dumps, many of them now decently clothed in greenery, to remind one of those heady days – not too long ago – when the place was more of a diggers' camp than a city. The industry has moved to fresh fields, and now exploits the immense underground wealth of the Rand to the east and west. Visitors who are interested in the world of gold, both past and present, have a number of sightseeing options to choose from. An excellent place to start is the:

CARLTON CENTRE (Commissioner Street). The building is the tallest in Africa, and you'll get a very clear idea of just how extensive the mining network is, how pre-eminently it features in the economic life of the region, from the observation platform (the 'Top of Africa') on the 50th floor. And of course you will see a great deal more than the mines: the entire Witwatersrand

Visitors to one of Johannesburg's working mines can view the gold-pouring process.

GOLD REEF CITY: A JOURNEY BACK IN TIME

To visit Gold Reef City, the vibrant living museum and theme park to the south of the central area, is to rediscover Johannesburg in its exuberant infancy. The re-created pioneer settlement occupies the site of the old Crown, a mine that is honoured in the annals and yielded a huge 1.4 million kg (1,290 tons) of gold during its lifetime – a bounty that would now be worth some R20 billion. The mine also held the world shaft-sinking record for a time.

Visitors can explore the fifth-level underground workings, watch gold being poured, and enjoy traditional (tribal and gumboot) dancing. Some of the many other attractions include train and horse-drawn omnibus trips around the area; a Victorian funfair and tea parlour; dressing up in period costumes and having sepia photographs taken; a replica of the Theatre Royale; a recreation of an early brewery, pub, Chinese laundry, tailor's shop, cooperage, apothecary, newspaper office and stock exchange. A permanent exhibition features minting displays and coins. There are also speciality shops (glassware, pottery, lace, brassware, copperware, leatherware, diamonds, coins, stamps, curios); house museums furnished in period style; restaurants (The Crown is excellent); fast-food outlets; taverns; a beer garden; and a night-club (Rosie O'Grady's). The luxurious, period-style Gold Reef City Hotel caters for overnight guests (*see* Advisory, page 58).

Open daily; special group tours are available to foreign-language visitors.

Traditional dancers at Gold Reef City.

conurbation lies before you, which, if you are a first-time visitor, will help you to orientate yourself and to establish your bearings. Additional attractions at the 'Top of Africa' are a number of fascinating displays, including a Hall of Fame; exhibits relating to the apartheid era and other interesting elements of MuseumAfrica (*see* page 36) as well as various temporary expositions and interesting promotions.

AN UNDERGROUND VISIT to a working mine provides an unforgettable experience and may be arranged through the Chamber of Mines in Hollard Street.

GOLD REEF CITY, a splendidly imaginative reconstruction of pioneer Johannesburg (*see* panel, opposite), built on the Crown Mines site 6 km (4 miles) from the city centre (it's just off the M1 South highway to the Free State; look for the Xavier Street exit).

Gardens, parks and reserves

Central Johannesburg is not well known for its greenery: there are few tree-shaded city squares; space is at a premium, and nearly all of it is filled by high-rise development. But first impressions are deceptive: the city council administers over 600 parks and open spaces, most of which grace the suburbs, covering a combined area of some 4,600 ha (11,366 acres). In fact, Johannesburg, with its 4 million trees, is said to be the world's most treed city. Not very far outside the central area is:

BRAAMFONTEIN SPRUIT, a stream that slices through the suburbs and northern municipalities; it is possible to follow its park-like course from Westdene Dam to the Klein Jukskei River – a distance of about 25 km (15 miles) – almost without touching concrete. This is South Africa's oldest and longest urban trail (though there are shorter alternative routes: one can join it at any point), and Johannesburgers count it among their more prized community assets.

PIONEER PARK (Rosettenville), a leisure area developed around an attractive stretch of water known as Wemmer Pan, is a pleasant place for strolling, and for viewing Johannesburg's skyline. There's a swimming pool, restaurant, picnic spot, and a series of illuminated musical fountains that present evening light-and-sound shows from September through to June.

The main drawcard for the first-time visitor, though, is the James Hall Museum of Transport. This museum features the full range of land

TOP LEFT: *The emerald reaches of the Braamfontein Spruit, the country's longest and oldest urban trail.*
ABOVE: *The full-scale replica of the Drommedaris can be seen at Santarama Miniland.*
LEFT: *Sunday morning strollers at Zoo Lake.*

conveyances except railways (*see* Railway Museums, page 37) including animal-drawn and steam-powered vehicles, trams, buses as well as fire-engines. Open daily.

Nearby is Santarama Miniland: scale replicas of prominent South African buildings and landmarks (Cape Town's Castle, Kimberley's Big Hole and so forth) and a full-size reproduction of the *Drommedaris*, the little sailing ship that brought the first white settlers to South Africa.

JOHANNESBURG ZOO, situated within the Herman Eckstein Park, is located on either side of Jan Smuts Avenue. More than 3,000 animals, birds and reptiles are in residence, 30 of them on the endangered list; the ape house contains gorillas, orang-utans and chimpanzees. Zoo Lake, on the other side of the road, is popular among boaters, picnickers, strollers and lazers. The Museum of Rock Art is within the area. There is also an excellent lakeside restaurant; illuminated fountain; open-air art exhibitions and occasional (Sunday afternoon) country-music get-togethers.

JOHANNESBURG BOTANIC GARDEN, Thomas Bowler Avenue (Emmarentia), boasts a lovely rose garden (4,000 plants, fountains, pools), rose-trial grounds, herb garden, ground-cover demonstration area, hedge display section, many exotic trees, and the Sima Eliovson Florium, venue for floral exhibitions. Open daily; guided tours at 09h00 on the first Tuesday of each summer month. The grounds are on the western shore of:

EMMARENTIA DAM, where yachtsmen, board-sailors, wind-surfers, scuba-divers and model-boat enthusiasts enjoy themselves.

FLORENCE BLOOM BIRD SANCTUARY, situated between Blairgowrie and Victory Park, is part of the Delta Park conservation centre, headquarters of the Wildlife Society. The sanctuary is haven to about 200 bird species, many of which congregate around the two dams where hides have been established. The bird sanctuary is open at all times.

The Nature Conservation Centre maintains an auditorium and exhibition halls (featuring superb environmental displays) within the sanctuary comprising a Natural History Museum, an educational resource complex and a meditation room. Future plans include an astronomical observatory. The area is along the Braamfontein Spruit trail (*see* page 39). Closed on Sundays.

LION PARK, on the northern city fringes (accessible via William Nichol Drive). Here, a 10 km (6 mile) driving trail enables you to observe lion, zebra, ostrich, wildebeest, spring-bok and other game species at close quarters (keep your windows closed, and keep moving). Some visitors enjoy being photographed holding a tame lion cub; other popular features are the Ndebele village, pets' corner, picnic/barbe-cue area, swimming pool and curio shop. Light refreshments available.

Shopping

Major concentrations of general and speciality outlets – 'worlds in one' that encompass restaurants and cinemas, banks, travel agents and other services as well as shops – are the Carlton Centre in Commissioner Street; Rosebank Mall and The Firs on Cradock Avenue, Rosebank; the giant Eastgate Centre on Broadway Extension, Bedford-view; Hyde Park Corner on Jan Smuts Avenue;

LEFT: *Shoelaces and other colourful accessories on sale at one of the city's myriad fleamarkets.*
OPPOSITE: *The Johannesburg Stock Exchange and its Diagonal Street neighbour, the futuristic First National Bank building.*

the Killarney Mall on Riviera Road, Killarney; the Sanlam Centre on Hill Street, Randburg. There are also a great many outlets in and around Johannesburg that cater specially for the visitor, offering an array of African craftwork, curios, hides and skins, locally made pottery and so forth.

Among shopping areas with something different to offer are:

THE MARKET THEATRE MALL, within the multi-purpose theatre complex (*see* page 43). The pretty shopping arcade includes an antiques and collectibles corner and a flower market.

SMAL STREET, the modern pedestrian mall near the Carlton Centre: sophisticated boutiques, speciality shops and outdoor cafés.

DIAGONAL STREET, near the Stock Exchange: small shops selling wares ranging from fruit and vegetables to spices, African blankets and traditional medicines.

ORIENTAL PLAZA, featuring the Indian market in Main Road, Fordsburg (there is also access from Bree Street and Lilian Road) is a colourful cluster of some 270 stores, stalls, eateries and a flower, fruit and vegetable market that beckon the bargain hunter. The emphasis is generally, though not exclusively, on eastern

WARES FOR AFRICA

Among Diagonal Street's special and more unusual drawcards is the unforgettable Herbalist Shop (No. 14), a place that stocks a multitude of veld products used by traditional African healers, often mistakenly referred to as 'witchdoctors'. Many of the herbs and other plants are known by modern science to have valuable curative powers. You'll see bones, animal skins and other tools of the traditional doctor's trade. The shop is open during normal business hours, and guided tours are offered.

Next to the produce market (*see* page 43) is the Multiflora Market, the country's largest flower auction. Also on sale are pot plants and garden requisites. Other open-air venues are:

• **The Johannesburg Fleamarket,** held opposite the Market Theatre complex in Bree Street: more than 400 stalls, selling everything from handicrafts to cockatoos; buskers entertain you. Saturdays from 09h00 to 16h00.

• **The Organic Market,** held on the corner of Culross and Main roads, Bryanston: cottage industries; handicrafts; natural-fibre clothing; African carpets; organically grown vegetables; fruits and spices. The market is held on Tuesday and from Thursdays to Saturdays.

• **Artists' Market,** Zoo Lake. An art and craft expo held the first weekend of each month.

• **Collectors Forum & Fayre,** at Parktown Convent, 40 Oxford Road, Forest Town. The market takes place on the last Sunday of each month from 10h00 to 16h00.

• For information on craft and fleamarkets in and around the city, contact the Johannesburg Publicity Association (*see* Advisory, page 61).

Plants of the veld on display in one of central Johannesburg's herbalist shops.

merchandise; some of the fabrics are exquisite; a minaret clock-tower and peacock fountain add atmosphere. Highly recommended.

FISHERMAN'S VILLAGE, a new development, created on the shore of Bruma Lake in Bedfordview and billed as a 'Mediterranean oasis'. The concept is certainly imaginative, the content appealing, most of it taken up by boutiques and speciality stores, coffee shops and restaurants (about 15 of them in all, including Greek, Italian, Portuguese and Israeli establishments) fronting on cobbled, flower-bedecked streets and alleyways. There's also a boardwalk, and boating and wind-surfing on the lake.

SANDTON CITY, the commercial centre, is one of the largest and most sophisticated shopping and business complexes in South Africa and indeed in the southern hemisphere.

SANDTON SQUARE COMPLEX, a brand new shopping, business and arts centre that takes its inspiration from Venice's St Mark's and other great European squares (marble is much in evidence). It was still under development at the time of writing.

RANDBURG WATERFRONT, an extensive and lively suburban leisure complex of restaurants (55 of them), speciality shops, colourful market

stalls, pubs, cinemas, live music and many other entertainment venues. All of this activity takes place around a pleasant little lake that hosts both the leisurely pedal-boater and the

ABOVE: *A group of street musicians enlivens the scene at the Fisherman's Village fleamarket.*
BELOW: *Part of the Randburg Waterfront, a stone's throw from central Johannesburg.*
OPPOSITE: *Outside the Market Theatre complex in the city centre.*

more energetic watersports enthusiast. The musical fountain in the 'harbour' is said to be the biggest and best in the world.

MARKETS South Africa's largest produce market is the complex of six halls and 39 cold storage chambers that does business (from Monday to Saturday; starting at six in the morning) at City Deep. Hall 2 is reserved for the fish traders (this is the country's first and to date only inland fish market) and general dealers; meat, eggs and groceries are also on sale. There are banks (five of them), cafeterias and a petrol filling station; parking is plentiful; most of the business conducted is on wholesale (bulk) basis but the complex welcomes individual buyers. The staff are expert and helpful and the merchandise (seafood exotics such as smoked marlin, live crayfish and queen prawns) is top quality.

Theatre

The performing arts are alive and very well in Johannesburg; the morning newspaper *The Star* gives details of what's on in its 'Tonight' section; the monthly magazine *Hello Johannesburg and Pretoria* is available from the Publicity Association and from hotels and shops.

Many of the grander shows – drama, opera, ballet, orchestral – are staged by the Performing Arts Council of the Transvaal (Pact) on a regular basis at the Civic and Alexander theatres.

There are a number of other, smaller but lively and talented companies, some of them of the highly enterprising, informally experimental workshop type.

Among the latter are productions conceived, written and performed by black artists largely for black audiences, a distinct art form termed 'black theatre' and noted for its sparkling spontaneity, an element rooted in African tradition: performers tend to share in the creation of a work rather than follow a predetermined script. Despite this looseness, though, some of the shows have enjoyed international as well as wide local acclaim.

Until recently much of black theatre reflected, and protested against, the harshness of life under the apartheid system, but it is now tending to move away from racial introspection and towards more universal themes.

Johannesburg's principal venues are the:
MARKET THEATRE COMPLEX, which houses three auditoriums, restaurant, bar, coffee bar, art and photographic gallery, an exclusive bookshop and a precinct (next door, but part of

the whole) noted for its shopping arcade, bistro and for its unusual 'Kippies' jazz bar. The 80-year-old building formerly did duty as the Indian Fruit and Citrus Market, and is full of character. The theatres cater for all tastes: there's a lot of local, sometimes experimental drama on offer, but the line-up can also include drawing-room comedy (*see* also box, Newtown, page 44). Bookings through Computicket.

CIVIC THEATRE, (Braamfontein) Johannesburg's biggest (1,120-seat; its orchestra pit accommodates 100 musicians) and most prestigious auditorium; venue for opera, ballet, operetta, musical comedy productions, solo recitals and orchestral concerts (and for marionette shows, which are something of a speciality). Its Chamber Theatre, in an adjoining hall, provides playwrights, directors and actors with a well-equipped workshop. It's also a venue for exhibitions (in the large foyer), conferences and seminars; there's a good restaurant (the Symposium) on the premises. Behind-the-scenes tours on Tuesdays and Fridays. The municipal car park is across the road; book at Computicket.

THE ALHAMBRA in Beit Street, Doornfontein, is Johannesburg's oldest theatre. A 370-seat auditorium, it is now part of a group run by Pieter Toerien Productions. The others in the group are the Rex Garner (upstairs at the Alhambra); and the Richard Haines Theatre. Generally, these three venues present straight drama, though there's the occasional musical show. Bookings through Computicket.

Feeding the ducks in one of the city's 600 parks.

ARENA THEATRE, Cradock Avenue, Rosebank. A quite small and intimate venue, the Arena is used by the Performing Arts Council of the Transvaal (Pact) for staging a number of highly innovative productions.

WITS THEATRE, University of the Witwatersrand. This is a very modern theatre and is used as a venue for university drama productions. Bookings through Computicket.

NEWTOWN

Johannesburg's city centre is being transformed by an ambitious urban renewal programme focused on the Market Theatre complex. Some exciting features of the Newtown development include MuseumAfrica (*see* page 36); the Afrika Cultural Centre; the railways museum, lively performing arts venues that include Mega Music and Dance Factory; various theatres, restaurants, jazz and other clubs, pubs, speciality shops, arts and cultural exhibition halls – the whole pleasantly embowered with palm trees. More than 20 cultural organizations have located their headquarters within the precinct.

Music and entertainment

The SABC's National Symphony Orchestra presents seasons each year (two concerts a week), giving something over 60 symphony concerts – in the Linder Auditorium at the Johannesburg College of Education – and many gala, campus, special-event, choral and symphonic-pop performances. Seasonal programme available from the Johannesburg Publicity Association; bookings through Computicket.

Opera, ballet, oratorio and orchestral performances are staged by the Performing Arts Council of the Transvaal. Details of these, and of the other chamber music, celebrity recital and other musical presentations, are available in the daily press, notably *The Star*; also consult the Johannesburg Publicity Association (*see* Advisory, page 61) for more information.

Jazz standards are high, the scene lively and innovative, and it is informatively covered in the *Saturday Star's* jazz column.

Johannesburg, like any big city, offers a wide variety of nightspots – intimate nightclubs, noisier discos, quiet dinner-dancing venues (at some of the hotels and bigger restaurants). For details, consult the local newspapers.

Dining out: the city is exceptionally well endowed with restaurants. (A select list appears in the Advisory, pages 60–61.)

SOWETO

South Africa's largest and best-known 'black' city (though the demise of the Group Areas Act has rendered the term obsolete), Soweto sprawls across 95 km² (37 square miles) of dusty terrain to the south-west of Johannesburg – its name is in fact a contraction of South Western Townships – and it is home to over a million people, perhaps as many as three million.

Much of Soweto is now electrified; some roads have been properly surfaced; and schools, clinics and hospitals have been built (the 2,000-bed Baragwanath Hospital at Diepkloof is one of the southern hemisphere's largest).

In 1987 the Soweto campus of Vista University was inaugurated. The more affluent Sowetans – the ever-increasing number of entrepreneurs, professional people and highly qualified executives – have substantial and attractive homes. But development has, unfortunately, been both haphazard and slow, and most people still live in grossly overcrowded conditions.

Soweto has functioned primarily as a dormitory city, neglected (for reasons of law rather than of choice) by big business; commercial activity resides in the more than 3,000 'spaza' shops (tiny home-based stores), and in the myriad small enterprises within the so-called 'informal economy'. Social life tend to revolve around the football stadiums and grounds, the huge number of shebeens (social drinking and conversation venues), in the much more exclusive and up-market clubs (music, dancing), and in the community halls and recreation centres of various kinds, from which is emerging, among other things, a distinctive and vibrant musical culture.

With the advent of the new political order and given political stability, it is likely that industries will be attracted to the area by the huge and increasingly skilled labour pool, and commerce by the massive buying power of the community. So one can expect dramatic improvements in the range of amenities available to Sowetans and, hopefully, in the quality of their lives.

Tours of the city take in the housing developments, schools, workshops, the Sangoma Centre, 'cultural kraal', workshop for the handicapped, as well as shebeens and private homes. For more information contact the Johannesburg Publicity Association (*see* Advisory, page 61).

BELOW: *Patriotic graffiti in Soweto.*
RIGHT: *Sign of the new South Africa.*

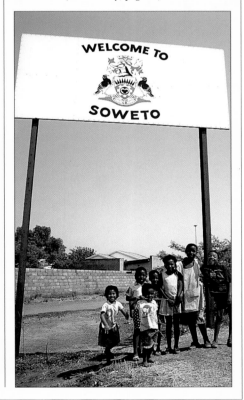

Sport and recreation

There are excellent facilities for bowls, tennis, squash, swimming, sailing (among the pleasant stretches of water are Wemmer Pan and Emmarentia Dam) and other watersports; jogging, cycling (visitors are welcome on group outings; contact the Transvaal Pedal Power Association), and freshwater fishing. For this last, you'll need a licence (available at any sports shop). There is no closed season for trout.

Excursions and tours

Johannesburg is well situated to serve as a base from which to explore other and perhaps more enticing parts of the country. Within comfortable driving distance from the city are the pleasure palace of Sun City (*see* page 102), the hills of the Magaliesberg (*see* page 98) and the lovely Escarpment region of Mpumalanga as well as its celebrated big-game areas (notably the Kruger National Park, *see* pages 71–81).

Tour operators in and around Johannesburg offer a huge number and variety of packages – among them conventional coach and air (including helicopter) trips; photographic and hunting excursions; guided walking and cycling trails. They also have adventurous river-boating (or 'wild water') safaris; hot-air ballooning over the bushveld of the Pilanesberg (*see* page 101) and a number of evocative steam-train trips ranging from a day's outing among the Magaliesberg hills to Rovos Rail's four-day, Edwardian-style luxury journey eastwards to the mountains and the game-rich Mpumalanga Lowveld region. More detailed information on these and other options is available from the Johannesburg Publicity Association.

Recommended local excursions (self-drive or conducted) include those to a gold mine (*see* page 37), Gold Reef City (*see* pages 38 and 39) and Soweto (*see* panel, page 45). Also worth a morning of your time is the:

STUDIO ROUTE About 20 suburban artists and craftspeople open their studios and workshops (some of which also function as galleries and shops) to the public on the last Sunday of each month, and at other times by appointment. The range of creative endeavour is wide, taking in painting, sculpture, graphic arts, pottery, stoneware, silkscreening, calligraphy, jewellery, stained glass, African art and crafts, spinning, weaving, clothing design, fibre art, quiltwork and needlecraft. The Johannesburg Publicity Association will provide details.

HEIA SAFARI RANCH, about 40 km (25 miles) to the west. Sunday visitors are treated to some spectacular Zulu dancing (by the 16-strong Mzumba Dance Group) and to a typical South African *braai* (barbecue). African *rondavels* (round thatched huts) and wildlife (zebra, antelope, the occasional giraffe) are features of the grounds. The nearby Hotel Aloe Ridge, under the same ownership, boasts a 'living museum' Zulu village called Phumangena uMuzi (dancing, ethnic crafts; visitors can overnight in the traditional 'beehive' huts and sample Zulu food and drink) and a 2,000 ha (5,000 acres) game reserve.

THE VAAL DAM AND RIVER, located on Gauteng's southern border, is a prime recreation area and weekend retreat. The dam is large and deep; the river's banks pleasantly willow-shaded; both are well endowed with resorts and with facilities for angling, sailing, power-boating, water-skiing and golf (two courses). The approaches are heavily industrialized; the main smokestack centres are Vereeniging (which has an excellent museum) and Vanderbijlpark, a surprisingly attractive place with a pleasant 8 km (5 miles) river frontage.

KRUGERSDORP GAME RESERVE, near the mining centre of Krugersdorp to the west, is a 1,400 ha (3,500 acres) expanse of open grassland that sustains white rhino, buffalo, kudu, sable, the rare roan and several other types of antelope; more than 160 bird species, and the carefully preserved plant life that covered the

OPPOSITE: *The Vaal Dam, popular among yachtsmen and other watersports enthusiasts.*
ABOVE: *Sewing beads at Heia Safari Ranch.*

area before man came with his mining madness to devastate the land. The reserve embraces a 200 ha (500 acre) lion camp. Accommodation comprises self-contained chalets and a caravan/camping ground; for the day-visitor: a tearoom, swimming pool, and a pleasant 1 km (½ mile) 'educational trail'. Just under 10 km (6 miles) to the north-west of Krugersdorp are the:

STERKFONTEIN CAVES The complex was once described by the great Dr Robert Broom as the 'anthropological treasure-house of the world', a mantle later assumed by Leakey's fossil-rich Olduvai Gorge in Tanzania. Broom began excavating in 1936, but it was only in April 1947 that he unearthed his most important find – the million-year-old fossilized cranium of a female man-ape. This, together with Raymond Dart's identification of the discoveries at Taung (in the North-West), revolutionized scientific theory on the origins of man.

In mid-1995 'Little Foot' was discovered among bones dug up in the 1920s – a hominid foot dating back 3.5 million years, at least half a million years older than previous South African hominid fossils.

There are conducted tours of the caves (every half-hour); next door is the Robert Broom site museum, housing exhibits of immensely ancient animal and bird life.

The site, though, offers more than scientific interest: part of the complex consists of six cathedral chambers, largest of which is the dripstone-decorated Hall of Elephants, 23 m (75 ft) high and 91 m (300 ft) long, and an underground lake with an air of enchantment about it (it features prominently in local African lore).

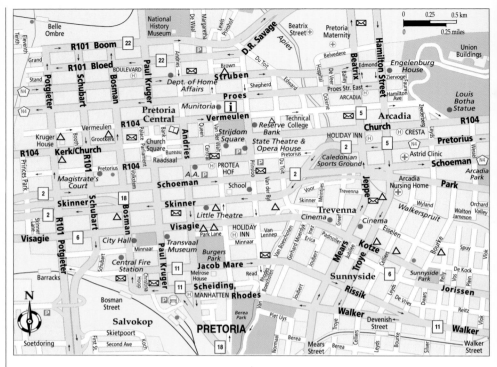

PRETORIA

Pretoria became the officially designated capital of the independent Voortrekker republic of the Transvaal (the South African Republic) in 1860, although the settlement's origins went back a further two decades. The first homestead belonged to a farmer called Bronkhorst, who settled in the Fountains Valley area in 1840.

More families put roots down in and around the nearby village of Elandspoort which, in 1854, was proclaimed the *kerkplaas* for the central Transvaal – the focal point for *nagmaal* (communion), baptisms and weddings. The next year it was renamed Pretoria Philadelphia ('Pretoria Brotherhood') in honour of Andries Pretorius, the victor of the Battle of Blood River (*see* box, The Battlefields Route, page 150).

With capital status came a degree of elegance: some fine buildings were erected in the later decades of the 19th century, though for a long time the place was noted more for its wealth of greenery and the brightness of its flowers than for its architecture. The warm climate encouraged luxuriant growth and roses were the favoured plantings. According to one early traveller, 'every garden, hedge, stoep and even waterfurrow' was festooned with ramblers. Later the famed jacarandas made their appearance: the first two, costing £10 apiece, were imported from Rio de Janiero in 1888. Some 70,000 of these lilac-foliaged trees now grace parks, gardens and about 650 km (400 miles) of its streets. They display their magnificent colours in spring; Pretoria is known as the 'Jacaranda City'.

Pretoria is first and foremost an administrative centre, but it is also the hub of an important rail network, and its advanced industrial complex, originally based on the giant Iscor steelworks just to the south-west, includes engineering, food processing and, principally at nearby Cullinan, diamond mining.

Museums, monuments and landmarks

Pretoria grew up around Church Square, at the intersection of Church and Paul Kruger streets (the city's two principal arteries). The square is dominated by Anton van Wouw's splendid bronze statue of Oom Paul, patriarch, president of the South African Republic (from 1883 until his flight into exile in 1900) and the man regarded as the 'Father of Afrikanerdom'. Church Street, incidentally, is one of the world's longest urban thoroughfares: it measures a full 26 km (16 miles) from end to end.

Among the buildings of note are the Old Raadsaal, or parliament, completed in 1889 in French Renaissance style with a sprinkling of classical features; the graceful Palace of Justice; the South African Reserve Bank (designed by Sir Herbert Baker), and, in sharp contrast, the modern Transvaal Provincial Administration building (in which works by leading artists are displayed; viewing by appointment). Guided tours of the square may be arranged. Along Church Street west of the square is:

KRUGER HOUSE, a modest, single-storeyed building with a wide verandah. The house was presented to Paul Kruger by the *volk* in 1884, and here the old man held open court, receiving his people in informal fashion on the *stoep* for a decade and a half until the guns of the advancing British drove him away. The place has been faithfully restored to something very much like its original character; on view are Kruger's furniture, personal belongings, various memorabilia and, behind the house, his carriage and a stinkwood trek wagon. Open daily.

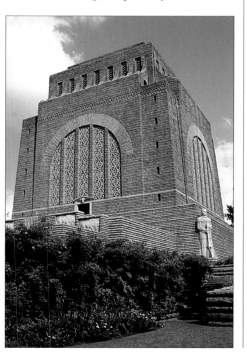

ABOVE: *Jacaranda City, Pretoria, in profile.*
LEFT: *The huge bulk of the Voortrekker Monument.*

THE VOORTREKKER MONUMENT, set on Monument Hill 6 km (4 miles) south of Pretoria, commemorates the Great Trek of the 1830s and is regarded as a shrine by many Afrikaners: a memorial to the founders of their republics and a symbol of Afrikaner identity. Its status within the heritage of the new South Africa is controversial, but it continues to be one of South Africa's top attractions.

The monument was eventually completed in 1949 (although the foundation stone was laid 11 years earlier, during the Voortrekker centenary celebrations in 1938), and comprises a massive 40-m-high (130 ft) block ringed by a *laager* of 64 granite oxwagons. At the monument's entrance is Anton van Wouw's striking bronze sculpture of a Voortrekker mother and children. In the main block are two chambers: the domed, 30-m-high (100 ft) Hall of Heroes, its walls lined by a frieze of 27 marble panels (their combined length is 92 m or 302 ft) depicting the Great Trek's main events; and a lower hall. The latter features a granite cenotaph – so situated that a ray of sunshine falls on the inscription at noon on 16 December each year (the date of the Battle of Blood River) – and a niche holding an ever-burning flame.

There are fine views from the dome and roof parapets, which visitors reach by climbing a circular stairway of 260 steps. Across the road is the Voortrekker Monument Museum, among whose more notable exhibits are costumes, antiques, tapestries, models of Trek scenes and, at the entrance, a Trek camp. Facilities include a restaurant. Open daily.

UNION BUILDINGS Designed by the deservedly celebrated architect Sir Herbert Baker and completed in 1913, this magnificent, crescent-shaped red sandstone edifice looks down over the city from the heights of Meintjes Kop, from where there are panoramic views. Features of note, apart from the graceful architecture, are the statues (of generals Botha, Smuts and Hertzog), the Garden of Remembrance, the Delville Wood memorial and the Pretoria war memorial. The grounds have been beautifully landscaped in terraces.

MUSEUM OF CULTURE (corner of Visagie and Bosman streets). Still being developed at the time of writing. The museum, on the 7 ha (17 acres) site of the old South African Mint, is designed as a showcase of South Africa's archaeological and anthropological heritage.

MUSEUM OF NATURAL HISTORY (Paul Kruger Street). An extensive series of displays, most prominent of which are the 'Life's Genesis' exhibition and the Austin Roberts Bird Hall. The former tells an integrated story of life on earth, while the latter houses a superb array of southern African birds.

The renowned archaeologist Robert Broom and his successors did much of their pioneering work on the man-apes (the Australopithecines, *see* page 47) at the museum; the appropriate displays are fascinating. Special features include informative audio-visual presentations, and an excellent bookshop and coffee house. Open daily. Next door is Melrose House (*see* page 52).

The grounds of Pretoria's elegant Union Buildings, symbol of Boer-British reconciliation.

THE COLOURFUL WORLD OF THE NDEBELE

The Ndebele village near Bronkhorstspruit is one of several 'living' museums of traditional culture you'll find within easy driving distance of Johannesburg and Pretoria. Also well worth a visit is the Botshabelo Museum and Nature Reserve near Fort Merensky, approximately 13 km (8 miles) north of Middelburg.

The Ndebele people are of Nguni (Zulu) stock, though the northern segment have over the decades drawn close to and in some ways been assimilated by their Sotho neighbours. The southern Ndebele, whose historic 'homeland' lies to the north of Pretoria, have remained rather more faithful to their Zulu origins.

Rural Ndebele homesteads are invariably rectangular, thatched, attractively gabled and pedimented (and sometimes turreted) dwellings surrounded by walled courtyards (called *lapas*) and – their most distinctive and world-famous feature – decorated by striking, vibrantly colourful, often geometrically patterned murals.

Originally, natural ochres were used to devise uncomplicated triangular and V-shaped designs; later, more recognizable paintings (stylized animals, birds and so forth) were introduced; and then, with increasing exposure to urban ways and the availability of synthetic paints, the range of both designs and colours expanded to include city scenes and other modern subjects. There is little of the mystical about this Ndebele art form: the pictures are created by the women, who use their fingers to apply the pigments, simply to please the eye. In many instances the women of the village are themselves works of art. The traditional Ndebele have a highly colourful style of dress that embraces beaded blankets and aprons, and never-to-be-removed metal rings that are often piled one upon the other and bound tightly around the ankle, arm and neck.

A Ndebele woman stands outside her hut which is decorated with colourful geometric murals.

MELROSE HOUSE (Jacob Maré Street, opposite Burgers Park). An elegant 19th-century home set in attractive gardens. This was the site chosen for the signing of the historic Peace Treaty of Vereeniging which brought the bloody South African War to an end on 31 May 1902. It is now a museum housing a collection of fine period furniture (though some of the contents were badly damaged by rightwing elements in 1989). It also serves as an occasional venue for chamber music concerts and art exhibitions. It is open every day.

PIONEER OPEN-AIR MUSEUM (Pretoria Street, Silverton). A 3 ha (7 acres) area containing a restored Voortrekker farmstead (house and stables), implements, a horse mill, threshing floor and so forth. It's situated on the banks of the Moreleta Spruit; picnic/barbecue facilities provided. Open daily.

PRETORIA ART MUSEUM (Schoeman Street) contains works by leading South African artists (Pierneef, Van Wouw, Frans Oerder), part of the Michaelis collection of Dutch and Flemish paintings and an art library. Guided tours may be arranged. Open Tuesdays to Sundays.

ANTON VAN WOUW HOUSE (Clark Street, Brooklyn) was the home of Anton van Wouw (1862–1945), arguably South Africa's most highly regarded modern sculptor. Some of his smaller works, less formal and melancholy than his monumental sculptures, are on display here. Open Tuesdays to Saturdays.

PIERNEEF MUSEUM (Vermeulen Street). Jacob Pierneef (1886–1957) is generally acknowledged as the country's most accomplished landscape painter; a collection of his works is on display in this pleasant late-19th-century house, which is open Mondays to Fridays. There is also a tearoom on the premises.

PLACES OF WORSHIP include the Miriammen (Sixth Street, Asiatic Bazaar), oldest of Pretoria's Hindu temples, and the beautiful Muslim mosque, accessible through an arcade in Queen Street. Both places require visitors to remove footwear before entering.

SAMMY MARKS MUSEUM, near Pretoria to the west (off the N4). Grand Victorian mansion built and sumptuously furnished by Marks, a rags-to-riches 19th-century Jewish immigrant entrepreneur, philanthropist and loyal friend of Paul Kruger. The rose garden (old-fashioned varieties) is the centrepiece of the exquisite grounds, which are open to the public. Tours of the house are by arrangement only.

Gardens, parks and reserves

THE NATIONAL ZOOLOGICAL GARDENS are among the largest and best in existence: they comprise 600 ha (1,482 acres) of parkland in the heart of Pretoria. The zoo is home to about 3,500 southern African and exotic animals, including the four great apes, a host of mammals, the rare South American maned wolf, Indian Gaurs and Przgwalski horses from Poland. The zoo's antelope collection is reputedly the world's most comprehensive.

Within the zoo's aegis is the Potgietersrus game-breeding centre (*see* page 89) as well as the 4,000 ha (10,000 acres) game-breeding centre near Lichtenburg in the North-West (*see* page 100), which has successfully bred the scimitar-horned oryx, the addas, the Père David's deer and the pygmy hippopotamus. Indeed, about 20 rare species have been bred under the zoo's supervision, among them the first aardwolf to be raised in captivity.

Much can be seen from the lookout points, which are reached by cable-car. Seals are fed mid-morning and mid-afternoon, carnivores mid-afternoon. Services provided include guided tours (Saturday mornings; booking essential) and courses on ecology and bird recognition. Stalls outside the main entrance offer handicrafts. Next door to, and part of the zoo, is the:

AQUARIUM AND REPTILE HOUSE, in which a great many freshwater and marine species (300 in total) are imaginatively displayed. There are also a splendid sea-shell collection and a variety of snakes, lizards, iguanas and crocodiles.

AUSTIN ROBERTS BIRD SANCTUARY (Boshoff Street, New Muckleneuk) is an 11 ha (27 acres) park that protects about 170 species, many of them waterbirds (blue crane, sacred ibis, heron: there are two well-stocked dams), all of which can be observed from the hide. Also in residence are some small mammals.

PRETORIA NATIONAL BOTANICAL GARDEN (Cussonia Avenue, 10 km/6 miles from the city centre), administered by the Botanical Research Institute, features more than 5,000 indigenous plant species in its 77 ha (190 acres). The displays are sensibly grouped (according to major vegetation and climate type); tours last just over two hours and include a slide show and a visit to the normally inaccessible nursery. Complementing the Botanical Garden is the National Herbarium, a worthwhile port of call for visiting botanists, and indeed for anyone interested in identifying and preserving indigenous flora.

Pretoria's jacarandas bloom in springtime.

WONDERBOOM NATURE RESERVE (situated on Voortrekker Road, 10 km or 6 miles north of the city centre) was established specifically to protect a single 'wonder tree' – a 1,000-year-old, 23-m-high (75 ft) wild fig (*Ficus salicifolia*) which, along with its 13 'daughters' and 'grand-daughters' – the fruits of self-propagation – measures 50 m (164 ft) in diameter. A nature trail wanders through the 90 ha (222 acres) area; there are several pleasant picnic spots near the tree. Open daily.

FOUNTAINS VALLEY NATURE RESERVE (on the Verwoerdburg Road, 5 km or 3 miles south of the city centre). A 60 ha (148 acres) picnic, barbecue and recreational area at the source of the Apies River and highly popular among Pretorians. A further 500 ha (1,235 acres) have been set aside as a game and bird sanctuary. Attractions include two-day hiking trails, several camping and picnic sites, restaurant, swimming pool, small lake (full of swans and other waterfowl), playpark, miniature steam locomotive. Open daily.

MORELETA SPRUIT The stream rises near the Rietvlei Dam to the south-east of Pretoria and later joins the Hartbeest Spruit north of the Derdepoort Regional Park (*see* below). A nature trail follows its course through the city's eastern suburbs, passing through:
• **Faerie Glen Nature Reserve**, a lovely 110 ha (272 acres) area of natural vegetation and home to a large number of bird species. Plants include the cabbage tree ('kiepersol'), wild plum, aloes and proteas. The reserve offers a number of pleasant walks as well.
• **Meyers Park Bird Sanctuary**, a small (7 ha or 17 acres) haven for a prolific avian population.
• **Struben Dam**, a 10 ha (25 acres) park also noted for its birds, among which are some rare species. Fishing is permitted from the small pier.

DERDEPOORT REGIONAL PARK (on the Pietersburg highway) is a 115 ha (284 acres) expanse of bushveld that boasts two dams, picnic/barbecue spots, a restored farmhouse that serves as a delightful restaurant, and a farmyard to which the public has access.

BURGERS PARK (on the corner of Van der Walt and Jacob Maré streets) was established in 1882, named after the South African Republic's second president and remains perhaps South Africa's finest example of a Victorian park. Its florarium is fairly impressive, comprising a complex of separate glass sections each with its own climate and vegetation.

Shopping

Pretoria offers the visitor an inviting variety of general and speciality outlets, shopping malls, arcades and markets.

The principal city-centre complexes are De Bruyn Park (corner of Vermeulen and Andries streets); Sanlam Centre (corner of Pretorius, Andries and Schoeman streets); and the Standard Bank Centre (corner of Church and Van der Walt streets). The major suburban shopping complexes are the Arcadia Centre (corner of Beatrix, Vermeulen and Proes streets); Jacaranda Centre (corner of Michael Brink Street and Frates Road); Menlyn Park (in Atterbury Road); Sunny Park (corner of Esselen and Mears streets); Verwoerdburg City (in Centurion, formerly Verwoerdburg); and Wonderpark (in Wonderboom).

Most, if not all, of these centres have a superb selection of speciality stores of particular interest to foreign visitors: African handicrafts (traditional beadwork, handspun carpets and rugs, pottery and woodwork); hides and skins; ceramics and so forth.

ABOVE: *A Kaiser Chiefs fan celebrates victory.*
OPPOSITE: *One of De Wildt's wild dogs.*

Worth special mention, though, are the crafts on sale outside the entrance to the National Zoological Gardens (*see* page 52). A fleamarket is held each Saturday on the square in front of the State Theatre.

Theatre

Major dramatic, operatic and ballet productions, choral and symphony concerts are staged, principally at the State Theatre complex, by the Performing Arts Council of the Transvaal (Pact). A number of other theatre companies present live shows, in various auditoriums, ranging from the experimentally serious to the light and bright. For details of what's on offer, consult the local newspapers (the *Pretoria News* is the leading English-language daily) or the Pretoria Information Bureau.

The splendid State Theatre complex in Church Street encompasses five auditoriums, good if rather ostentatious restaurants and the Applause coffee bar, from which tours set out each Wednesday (morning and afternoon) and Friday (morning). Bookings through Computicket.

Sport and recreation

Rugby tends to preoccupy much of white Pretoria; the provincial side (Northern Transvaal, known as the Blue Bulls) has often swept the trophy boards in recent years; the provincial stadium is the 85,000-seat Loftus Versfeld on Kirkness Street. First-class cricket matches are played at Berea Park on Van Boeshoten Avenue and at Centurion Park in Centurion. For the rest, the city's sporting amenities are as extensive as Johannesburg's (*see* page 46).

Excursions and tours

Pretoria, like Johannesburg (*see* page 35), is a strategic base from which to explore some of South Africa's prime tourist areas; the city's Information Bureau will have details of all the various packages on offer. The region to the west of the city is covered in the chapter on the North-West (see pages 96–105). For the rest, the surrounding bushveld countryside offers the visitor pleasant self-guided day drives and some points of interest.

BRITS

To the north-west of Pretoria on the R513 is the town of Brits, near which is the:
DE WILDT CHEETAH RESEARCH CENTRE
This centre is renowned throughout the zoological world for its successes in breeding (and studying) cheetah, king cheetah (the only specimens ever to have been bred in captivity), brown hyaena, suni, blue duiker and that most fascinating of hunting animals the wild dog (Africa's most endangered carnivore). Up to the

mid-1990s, over 400 cheetah cubs had been born at the centre, some reintroduced into the wild. Tours by arrangement only on Tuesday and Thursday (10h00), and Saturday and Sunday (08h30 and 13h30).

THE HERBAL CENTRE, on the Pretoria North/ Brits Road, has an intriguing number and variety of medicinal, culinary and aromatic herbs under cultivation. On site is a traditional apothecary's shop, nursery, herbarium, country kitchen (which serves herbal teas and scones), fairy village and small chapel. Herb workshop (cooking, pot-pourri demonstrations and so on) by appointment only. The Herbal Centre is open on Wednesdays. Tours are by arrangement only; day workshops.

IRENE

To the south-east of Pretoria is the village of Irene, near which is situated:

DOORNKLOOF FARM, the family home of renowned Jan Christiaan Smuts, soldier, statesman, politician, philosopher and naturalist. The remarkably modest house, built of wood and galvanized iron (salvaged from a post-First World War military camp), has been restored to its endearingly informal original condition and now serves as a museum in which Smuts's simple furniture and various memorabilia are faithfully displayed. The house and grounds are open daily; among the facilities are several picnic/barbecue spots, a tearoom and a camping site in attractive surroundings.

The endangered cheetah, now bred in captivity.

CULLINAN

This town, 30 km (20 miles) east of Pretoria, was named after Sir Thomas Cullinan who, in 1902, discovered rich volcanic diamond pipes in the vicinity and developed the famed Premier Mine which, in 1905, yielded the massive, 3,016-carat Cullinan Diamond (now part of the British Crown Jewels) and, later, the smaller but very beautiful Premier Rose stone. Many of the original miners' cottages still exist, lending a certain charm to the village; a private outfit lays on conducted tours from Tuesdays to Fridays.

WILLEM PRINSLOO AGRICULTURAL MUSEUM at Rayton, 10 km (6 miles) north of Cullinan, is a well-preserved 1880 farmstead comprising a house, stables, outbuildings, domestic animals and display rooms featuring old implements. Early farming methods are demonstrated on Sundays; also of interest is the Ndebele village and the dam; facilities include picnic/barbecue spots and a cafeteria.

HAMMANSKRAAL

North of Pretoria, this is the centre of the local and usually prosperous maize and groundnut industries. The place is undistinguished except for the nearby Pretoria Salt Pan, the crater of an extinct volcano, and, approximately a dozen kilometres farther north, by the lively and animated Papatso market-place.

ADVISORY: JOHANNESBURG AND PRETORIA

CLIMATE

Summer rainfall region. On most days from December to February, and sometimes into March, thunderstorms begin to build up after lunchtime to produce torrential late-afternoon downpours. The deluge is accompanied by a great deal of noise and fierce flashes of lightning, and occasionally preceded by brief but violent (and destructive) showers of hail.

Summer days tend to be breathlessly hot, the nights less so; winter days are crisp, invigorating; winter nights chilly and sometimes bitter. Pretoria (1,370 m/4,494 ft above sea level) has a somewhat warmer and more humid climate than Johannesburg (1,750 m/5,741 ft); its northern parts are frost-free. Both cities enjoy, on average, nearly nine hours of sunshine a day.

Johannesburg temperatures (Pretoria in brackets): January average daily maximum 26.3 °C/80 °F (28.8 °C/ 84 °F), daily minumim 14.3 °C/58 °F (16,4 °C/62 °F); July average daily maximum 16.5 °C/62 °F (20.2 °C/ 68 °F), daily minimum 4.1 °C/39 °F (2.6 °C/36.5 °F); extremes 35 °C/95 °F (38.2 ° C/100 °F) and -5.6 °C/22 °F (-4.7 °C/23 °F). Rainfall: January average monthly rainfall 137 mm/5.3 in (134 mm/5.2 in), July 11 mm/½ in (9 mm/½ in); highest recorded daily rainfall 100 mm/4 in (125 mm/4.9 in).

MAIN ATTRACTIONS

Johannesburg: The gold mines and Gold Reef City ❑ All the amenities of a modern metropolis ❑ Easy access to the Magaliesberg hills and Sun City to the west ❑ The game reserves and scenic delights to the east.

Pretoria, not far to the north, is also well positioned for expeditions farther afield. It's altogether a quieter and more attractive place, aptly known as the 'Jacaranda City' for its spectacular springtime displays of these lovely trees (October brings them to their full glory).

TRAVEL

Johannesburg is 56 km/35 miles from Pretoria, 334 km/208 miles from Pietersburg, 364 km/226 miles from Nelspruit, 426 km/265 miles from Bloemfontein, 484 km/301 miles from Kimberley, 529 km/329 miles from Messina near the Zimbabwe border, 608 km/378 miles from Durban, 789 km/490 miles from Upington on the fringes of the Kalahari, 983 km/611 miles from Grahamstown, 994 km/618 miles from East London, 1,075 km/668 miles from Port Elizabeth and 1,450 km/901 miles from Cape Town.

Road. The two cities are connected by the N1 national route (M1 out of Johannesburg), and by the more roundabout R21 through Kempton Park and Centurion; both are well served by national and regional highways: good, fast roads link them to all of southern Africa's major centres.

Johannesburg's layout is fairly symmetrical, the streets running roughly east-west and north-south. Finding your way around during the morning and afternoon (16h00–18h00) rush-hours can be difficult: the traffic tends to be dense and slow-moving and there are a lot of one-way streets. Once you escape from the city centre, however, things become a lot easier: the urban freeway system, in particular the M1 North and South and the M2 East and West, is linked to the national bypass freeways.

Parking: On-street parking is at a premium in the central areas. The cities, however, are served by a goodly number of municipal and private parking garages. Johannesburg also operates the Park-and-Ride system, which enables you to leave your car at one of 20 or so city-fringe sites and catch the regular (and frequent) bus service into town.

Bus and coach travel: The municipal services are adequate, though the routes tend to radiate out from the city centre, and cross-suburb journeys can be tricky. Information: Johannesburg tel. (011) 409-6111; Pretoria tel. (012) 313-8330/1. Coach travel is comfortable and relatively cheap; tour operators with offices in Johannesburg and Pretoria offer a wide range of coach and coach/air packages covering the major southern African tourist destinations.

Taxis: The two cities are big and busy enough to warrant fleets of cruising cabs, but they resolutely stick to their ranks. Bookings by phone; consult the Yellow Pages or Hotel reception. The less formal 'black taxis' (mini-buses) ply the main routes in competition for fares: they're cheap, fast (sometimes too fast), crowded and sociable.

Rail. Adequate train services link Johannesburg and Pretoria with many, but by no means all, of the surrounding centres; fast and comfortable trains connect the two cities. Reservations for all train services are best made personally at the respective booking offices or through a travel agent. Information: Johannesburg tel. (011) 774-4469, Pretoria tel. (012) 315-2007.

The renowned Blue Train plies between Pretoria and Cape Town (and other high-profile tourist regions on a sporadic basis), taking in Johannesburg and the Great Karoo en route. Information: Pretoria tel. (012) 315-3354, Johannesburg tel. (011) 774-4470/69 or Cape Town tel. (021) 405-2762. Reservations through the respective station booking offices or a travel agent.

Air. Johannesburg International Airport, located at Kempton Park north-east of Johannesburg and 45 km (28 miles) south-east of Pretoria, serves both cities. South African Airways and many of the major intercontinental airlines operate scheduled services to all five continents. SAA and the private airlines operate frequent scheduled flights to the main domestic centres and tourist destinations (including Sun City and the Kruger National Park). Facilities at the terminal buildings have proved barely adequate in recent years; customs and immigration procedures have drawn considerable criticism from the travelling public. The situation, however, is improving. Information: tel. (011) 975-9963. Reservations: tel. (011) 333-6504. A regular airport bus connects the airport with the two city centres.

Subsidiary airports: Charter airline services operate from Lanseria, located on the Hartbeespoort Dam Road, tel. (011) 659-2997; and Wonderboom, from just off the N1 north of Pretoria; tel. (012) 57-1188. The Grand Central (situated at Midrand, between Johannesburg and Pretoria) and Rand airports also offer a wide range of private services.

ACCOMMODATION

The following is a representative, but by no means exhaustive, selection of hotels. Full details of all types of accommodation can be obtained from Satour and the respective city information authorities.

Select Hotels

JOHANNESBURG: CITY AND FRINGES

The Carlton ***** City centre. Five-star luxury; 169 beautifully appointed rooms; 2 restaurants and 2 bars; conference facilities available for 1,000. PO Box 7709, Johannesburg 2000; tel. (011) 331-8911, fax 331-3555.
Devonshire Hotel ***** Fairly central. 64 rooms, 2 suites; conference facilities available. PO Box 31197, Braamfontein 2017; tel. (011) 339-5611.
Gardens Protea Hotel *** Berea (city fringes). Specialises in hosting sport conference groups; 330 rooms; restaurant; coffee shop; bar; swimming pool; conference facilities for 1,000. PO Box 866, Houghton 2041; tel. (011) 643-6610/1, fax 484-2622, central reservations toll-free 0800 11 9000.
Gold Reef City Hotel **** (pending). This re-created Victorian hostelry boasts authentic period furniture but with all modern amenities; inside the theme park (*see* page 38). PO Box 61, Gold Reef City 2159; tel. (011) 496-1626, fax 496-1636.
Holiday Inn Garden Court: Johannesburg *** City centre. 466 rooms, 26 suites; several restaurants and bars; heated swimming pool; jogging track; squash court; gym; conference facilities available for 900. PO Box 535, Johannesburg 2000; tel. (011) 336-7011, fax 336-0515, central reservations (011) 482-3500.
Holiday Inn Garden Court: Milpark *** About 6 km (4 miles) from the city centre. 246 rooms; à la carte restaurant and lively Irish pub; pool; conference facilities are available. PO Box 31556, Braamfontein 2017; tel. (011) 726-5100, fax 726-8615, central reservations (011) 482-3500.
Karos Johannesburger *** City centre. 363 rooms, 5 suites; carvery restaurant; bar (live entertainment); swimming pool. PO Box 23566, Joubert Park 2044; tel. (011) 725-3753, fax 725-6309.

Mariston Hotel *** City centre. 542 rooms, 2 suites; à la carte and terrace restaurants; 1 lively bar; heated swimming pool; four conference venues available. PO Box 23013, Joubert Park 2044; tel. (011) 725-4130, fax 725-2921.
New Library Hotel ** Central. 30 rooms, 4 suites; à la carte restaurant and bar; conference facilities available for 45 people. 67 Commissioner St, Johannesburg 2001; tel. and fax (011) 832-1551/2/3/4.
Park Lane Hotel *** In cosmopolitan Hillbrow. 129 rooms; à la carte restaurant and several bars; conference facilities for 150. PO Box 17855, Hillbrow 2038; tel. (011) 642-7425, fax 642-3949.
The Parktonian ***** In the city's cultural hub. Close to the Civic Centre and museums; 294 suites; 2 restaurants; bar; conference facilities available for 1,200. PO Box 32278, Braamfontein 2017; tel. (011) 403-5740, fax 403-2401.
The Rand in Johannesburg *** Central. 143 rooms; breakfast room; bar. PO Box 4235, Johannesburg 2000; tel. (011) 336-2724, fax 336-6815.

JOHANNESBURG: NORTHERN AREAS

Ascot *** Small; excellent; 15 rooms. PO Box 95064, Birnham, Randpark 2051; tel. and fax (011) 483-1211.
Balalaika Protea Hotel ***** Sandton. 285 rooms, 40 suites; 2 restaurants; bar; entertainment bar; theatre (musical performances by local artistes); conference facilities available. PO Box 783372, Sandton 2146; tel. (011) 884-1400, fax 884-1463; central reservations toll-free 0800 11 9000.
Capri Hotel *** Close to northern business areas. 50 rooms; à la carte restaurant and tavern; pool; conference facilities for 250. PO Box 39605, Bramley 2018; tel. (011) 786-2250/1/2/3/4, fax 887-2286.
City Lodges No-frills hotels conveniently situated in major centres and offer excellent value. Those in the Witwatersrand area include City Lodge: Edenvale ** (close to the airport), PO Box 448, Isando 1600; tel. (011) 392-1750, fax 392-2644; City Lodge: Randburg ** PO Box 423, Cramerview 2060; tel. (011) 706-7800, fax 706-7819; City Lodge: Sandton Katherine St *** PO Box 781643, Sandton 2146; tel. (011) 444-5300, fax 444-5315; and City Lodge: Sandton Morningside *** PO Box 784617, Sandton 2146; tel. (011) 884-9500, fax 884-9440.
Holiday Inn Garden Court: Airport *** 236 rooms and 6 suites; à la carte restaurant; bar; swimming pool; conference facilities available for 300 people. Private Bag X5, Johannesburg International Airport 1627; tel. (011) 944-6911, fax 974-8097, central reservations (011) 482-3500.
Holiday Inn: Sandton ***** Conveniently situated near Sandton City complex. 248 rooms; à la carte restaurant; buffet; bar. PO Box 781743, Sandton 2146; tel. (011) 783-5262, fax 783-5289, central reservations (011) 482-3500.

Karos Indaba Hotel and Conference Centre *****
25 km (15 miles) from city. Near popular Bryanston shopping centre; 203 rooms, 7 suites; à la carte restaurant with live entertainment; bar; patio (also live entertainment); swimming pool; sauna; sporting facilities; one of the country's largest conference venues. PO Box 67129, Bryanston 2021; tel. (011) 465-1400, fax 705-1709.

Midrand Protea Hotel ***** Between Johannesburg and Pretoria. 177 rooms, 6 suites; à la carte restaurant and bar; swimming pool; conference facilities for 120. PO Box 1840, Midrand 1685; tel. (011) 318-1868, fax 318-2429, central reservations toll-free 0800 11 9000.

Sandton Sun and Towers ***** One of the best, located next to Sandton City. 311 rooms, 23 suites; 6 restaurants; 3 bars; 2 pools; health centre; conference facilities for 1,000. PO Box 784902, Sandton 2146; tel. (011) 780-5000, fax 780-5002, central reservations (011) 482-3500.

Sunnyside Park Hotel ***** In exclusive Parktown. Elegant former residence of High Commissioner Lord Milner; 85 rooms, 12 suites; à la carte restaurant; Irish pub; swimming pool; in garden setting; conference facilities for 650. 2 York Rd, Parktown 2193; tel. (011) 643-7226, fax 642-0019, central reservations (011) 482-3500.

Town Lodge Midrand * Waterfall Park. 116 en suite rooms. PO Box 5622, Halfway House 1685; tel (011) 315-6047, fax 315-6004.

SOUTH OF JOHANNESBURG

Riviera International Hotel & Country Club *****
Vereeniging. 43 rooms, 58 suites; à la carte restaurant and buffet; 2 bars; swimming pool; river cruises; conference facilities available. PO Box 64, Vereeniging 1930; tel. (016) 22-2861, fax 21-2908.

Riverside Sun ***** On the banks of the Vaal River. about 5 km (3 miles) from Vanderbijlpark; 173 rooms; à la carte restaurant and bar; swimming pool; tennis; volleyball; conference facilities for 300. PO Box 740, Vanderbijlpark 1900; tel. (016) 32-1111, fax 32-1348, central reservations (011) 482-3500.

WEST OF JOHANNESBURG

Aloe Ridge Hotel *** Hotel and game reserve in lovely Muldersdrif Valley. About 45 km (28 miles) from Johannesburg; 72 rooms and 4 suites; à la carte restaurant and bar; indoor and outdoor swimming pools; tennis; squash; trout-fishing; game-viewing drives; Zulu village with 'beehive' guest rooms; traditional dancing and crafts. PO Box 3040, Honeydew 2040; tel. (011) 957-2070, ext. 508 for fax.

Heia Safari Ranch *** In private game reserve 40 km (25 miles) from Johannesburg. 28 thatched 'rondavel' rooms; restaurant (à la carte, table d'hôte, buffet); African dancing on Sundays. PO Box 1387, Honeydew 2040; tel. (011) 659-0605, fax 659-0709.

PRETORIA

Arcadia Hotel *** Fairly central. 139 rooms and suites; à la carte restaurant and 2 bars; conference facilities available for 100. PO Box 26104, Arcadia 0007; tel. (012) 326-9311, fax 326-1067.

Assembly Hotel *** Central. 88 rooms and 20 suites; small à la carte restaurant; 7 bars; disco and live entertainment. 390 Van der Walt St, Pretoria 0002; tel. (012) 322-7795.

Boulevard Protea Hotel Central. 74 rooms, 6 suites; à la carte restaurant and terrace (buffet) restaurants; 2 bars (pub lunches); swimming pool; conference facilities available for 300 people. PO Box 425, Pretoria 0001; tel. (012) 326-4806, fax 326-1366.

Cresta Protea Hotel *** Fairly central. 123 rooms; à la carte and buffet restaurants; coffee shop; bar; conference facilities available. PO Box 40663, Arcadia 0007; tel. (012) 341-3473, fax 44-2258, central reservations (012) 341-4440.

Farm Inn *** 42 rooms; à la carte restaurant and bar; pool; horse-riding; conference facilities available for 120 people. PO Box 71702, The Willows 0041; tel. (012) 807-0081, fax 807-0088.

Holiday Inn: Pretoria *** Fairly central. Close to zoological gardens; 241 rooms; à la carte restaurant; small coffee shop; bar; swimming pool; conference facilities available for 400 people. PO Box 40694, Arcadia 0007; tel. (012) 341-1571, fax 44-7534, central reservations (011) 482-3500.

Karos Manhattan Hotel *** Central. 262 rooms, 10 suites; carvery; bar; swimming pool; sauna; conference facilities available for 60. PO Box 26212, Arcadia 0007; tel. (012) 322-7635, fax 320-0721.

Self-catering and budget accommodations

Visitors have a wide range of cottages, chalets, guesthouses, executive suites and apartments to choose from in and around Johannesburg and Pretoria. Contact the appropriate information bureaus for details. A small selection:

Johannesburg: *Don Apartments:* 320 suites in 5 blocks scattered around the northern suburbs; close to amenities; superb; tel. toll-free 0800 115 446, fax 442-8040. *Kyalami Lodge*, situated between Johannesburg and Pretoria: chalets and cottages are available; tel. (011) 464-1237, fax 464-1337. *Vistaero Apartments, Berea (inner suburb):* 162 self-contained and serviced flats; tel. (011) 643-4954, fax 643-3421. *Witberg Executive Apartments, Hillbrow (inner suburb):* self-contained flats; tel. (011) 484-2500, fax 643-4954.

Pretoria: *Clara Berea Lodge (central):* various self-catering units; tel. (012) 320-5665, fax 322-5601. *Orange Court Lodge:* fairly central; 1- to 3-bedroomed apartments; tel. (012) 326-6346, fax 326-2492.

Bed and breakfast: *Central booking office:* 20 8th Ave, Melville, Auckland Park 2006; tel. (011) 482-2206/7, fax 726-6915. *Area booking offices:* Johannesburg/ Midrand tel. and fax (011) 787-3169 and 803-7170; Pretoria tel. and fax (012) 473-597. *United Kingdom representative:* tel. 0787-228-494, fax 0787-228-096.

Select restaurants

Johannesburg and its immediate environs are blessed with a dazzling array of eating houses catering for all culinary tastes, from *haute cuisine* to Cape traditional and other ethnic fare to good, plain steakhouses. Among the latter are members of the Longhorn, Porterhouse, Mike's Kitchen and Squire's Loft chains of eateries, all of which offer value for money. For up-to-date information, contact Restaurant Line, tel. (011) 788-1516 (office hours).

CITY AND FRINGES

Anton van Wouw, Sivewright Ave, Doornfontein. Very South African; good food; tasteful décor; warm atmosphere; tel. (011) 402-7916.

Club Room, Carlton Court. Exclusive; lavish décor; classic and nouvelle cuisine; tel. (011) 331-8911.

Denton's, Marlborough House, Fox St. Lunches only; excellent top-of-the-range Continental cuisine; efficient service; tel. (011) 331-3827.

El Gaucho, Carlton Hotel. South American food, cooked and served on the circular counter; tel. (011) 331-1953.

Fat Frank's Southern Diner, Pavilion Centre, Morningside. Excellent Cajun fare; tel. (011) 807-7055.

Gramadoelas at the Market, Market Theatre Precinct, Newtown. Cape Malay and other spicy dishes from Africa. Customers have included a who's who of notable visitors to the country (Mitterand, Hilary Clinton among them); tel. (011) 838-6960.

Iyavaya, Hunter St, Yeoville. The myriad (and often unusual) tastes of Africa; theatrically ornate décor; exotically dressed staff; tel. (011) 648-3500.

Kapitan's, Kort St. Indian restaurant with an international reputation; tel. (011) 834-8048.

Leipoldt's, Juta St, Braamfontein. A cornucopia of traditional South African dishes, served from an extensive buffet; very popular; tel. (011) 339-2765.

Mamma's Place, La Lanterna, Rockey St, Yeoville. Italian; excellent; young clientele; tel. (011) 648-7201.

Meridians, Parktonian Hotel. Continental cuisine; restful setting; tel. (011) 403-5740.

The Three Ships, Carlton Hotel. Elegant; faultless cuisine, service and appointments; tel. (011) 331-8911.

OUTSKIRTS

The Conservatory, 11th St, Parkmore.Varied vegetarian menu (plus cheeses); delightful Edwardian conservatory setting; take own wine; tel. (011) 783-7418.

Baccarat, Admiral's Court, Rosebank. Buffet; plush and popular; tel. (011) 880-1835.

The Baytree, Prospecta Centre, Linden. Very French; very good; tel. (011) 782-7219.

Casalinga Ristorante Italiano, Mulderdrif Rd, Honeydew. Rural (ask for detailed instructions); most attractively appointed; good Italian fare; tel. (011) 957-2612.

Chapters, Sandton Sun Hotel. Very elegant; emphasis on French cuisine; superb service; tel. (011) 780-5157.

Coachman's Inn and Tippler's Pub, Lyme Park, Sandton. English pub atmosphere, excellent French food; tel. (011) 706-7269.

Coco-de-Mer, Brabazon Rd, Croydon. Imaginative Mediterranean fare; tel. (011) 974-5127.

The Crown, Gold Reef City. Evocative setting; gourmet venison dishes; seafood specialities; tel. (011) 835-1181.

Daruma, Park Gallery, Melrose North. Finest of Japanese foods; beautifully presented; tel. (011) 447-2260.

Delhi Palace, Taj Mahal Centre, Fordsburg. Indian food; strict halal and kosher; no alcohol; tel. (011) 838-6740.

Dickens Inn, Craig Park Centre. Sumptuously English; tel. (011) 787-7219.

Dino's, Bedford Centre, Bedfordview. Inventive menu, comfortable setting; tel. (011) 622-3007.

Falcon Crest Restaurant, Kikuyu Rd, Sunninghill Park, Sandton. All-purpose dining and drinking centre in delightful garden setting; tel. (011) 803-4013.

Front Page, the Mall of Rosebank. Newspaper theme; solid value; tel. (011) 788-8400.

Gatriles, Esterhuizen St, Sandown. Superb; award-winning wine-cellar; tel. (011) 783-4994.

The Herbert Baker, Winchester Rd, Parktown. Smart; outstanding wine cellar; astonishing range of beers; tel. (011) 726-6253.

Hertford Country Inn, Pelindaba Rd, Lanseria. More English than England; tel. (011) 659-0292.

Horatio's Fish Restaurant, 7th St/3rd Ave, Melville. Wondrous variety of seafood served in nautical setting; tel. (011) 726-2247.

Ile de France, Dunkeld West shopping centre. Memorable French provincial dishes; tel. (011) 706-2837.

Jen's Restaurant and Oyster Bar, Bolton Rd, Parkwood. Seafood for the gourmet; tel. (011) 442-9419.

Jos's Place, Grant Ave, Norwood. Delicious home cooking; tel. (011) 483-1246.

Kaola Blu, 7th St, Melville. Thai, Indonesian and other dishes; full of fun; tel. (011) 482-2477.

La Mama's, Videolab Centre, Blairgowrie, Randburg. Range of Italian specialities; tel. (011) 787-2701.

La Rochelle Beer Hall, 6th St, La Rochelle. Portuguese; earthy; fun; tel. (011) 435-3809.

Le Chablis, Sandown Centre, Sandown. English atmosphere; fine French food; tel. (011) 884-1000.

Les Marquis, Fredman Drive, Sandown. *Haute cuisine*; smart; tel. (011) 783-8947.

Lien Wah, Rosebank Hotel. Delicious Cantonese cuisine; tel. (011) 788-1820.

Lord Prawn, 11th St, Parkmore. Lively; seafood specialities; tel. (011) 783-9214.

Lupo's, Dunkeld West. Italian, smart, popular; extensive menu; tel. (011) 880-4850.

Ma Cuisine, corner of 7th & 3rd ave, Parktown. French fare for the gourmet; tel. (011) 880-1946.

Munchner House, Tungsten St, Strydom Park, Randburg. Menu mix a nice blend of German, Austrian and Swiss cuisines; tel. (011) 792-8156.

O'Fado, Hutton Centre, Jan Smuts Ave, Hyde Park. Portuguese; famous for its prawns; tel. (011) 880-4410.

Paros, Rosebank Boulevard. Greek; cheerful; good value; tel. (011) 788-6211.

Pearl Garden, 9th Ave, Edenburg. Chinese excellence; tel. (011) 803-1781.

The Ritz, 3rd Ave, Parktown North. Despite its name, unpretentious; innovative menu; tel. (011) 880-2470.

Sauselito, Linden Rd, Sandown. Very imaginative food and décor; tel. (011) 783-3305.

The Tent, Rivonia Square, Rivonia. Theatrically Middle Eastern; interesting food; tel. (011) 803-7025.

Zoo Lake, Zoo Lake Gardens, Parkview. Outstanding Continental cuisine and wine cellar; complemented by the view; tel. (011) 646-8807.

PRETORIA

Pretoria can't match Johannesburg in the number and variety of its restaurants, but there's more than enough on offer to suit most tastes. Some suggestions:

Allegro, State Theatre, Church St. Elegant setting; ambitious menu; tel. (012) 322-6478.

Caponero, Beatrix St, Arcadia. Good Italian food; family hospitality; tel. (012) 326-4147.

Chez Patrice, Riviera. Creative and delicious French cuisine; tel. (012) 329-4028.

Gerard Moerdyk, Park St, Arcadia. South African food served in beautifully appointed, elegant Cape Dutch setting; tel. (012) 344-4856.

La Madelaine, Esselen St. Charming little Belgian bistro; lovely atmosphere; tel. (012) 44-6076.

La Perla, Skinner St. Continental food at its best; popular for lunch; tel. (012) 322-2759.

Lombardy, Tweefontein Farm, Lynwood Road Ext, Pretoria East. Some distance from the city; a conservative establishment in dignified, tree-shaded surrounds; Continental food; tel. (012) 87-1284.

Ming Woo, Lakeside Terrace, Centurion. Exceptional Chinese dishes in pleasantly unpretentious surroundings; tel. (012) 663-1888.

Oude Kap, Protea Hof Hotel, Pretorius St. Wide variety of dishes (à la carte and a groaning buffet), including Cape fare; tel. (012) 322-7570.

Viktor's, Church St, Arcadia. Continental cuisine; blazon of Chaîne des Rôtisseurs; tel. (012) 326-8282.

USEFUL ADDRESSES AND TELEPHONE NUMBERS

Automobile Association, Johannesburg city offices: 66 De Korte St, Braamfontein; on the corner of De Beer and Bertha streets, Ground floor; tel. (011) 407-1000; Pretoria city offices: 370 Voortrekker Rd, Gezina 0084; tel. (012) 329-1433. Central advisory and emergency services (breakdown; locksmith; international motoring advice; reservations; roads and weather information) dial toll-free 0800 010101.

Computicket, bookings and information services: Johannesburg (011) 331-9991; Pretoria (012) 323-6607.

Embassies, Consulates and High Commissions, Pretoria: Argentina 433-524; Australia 342-3740; Austria 462-483; Botswana 342-4760; Brazil 341-1712; China, People's Republic 342-4194; China, Republic of 436-071; Cuba 346-2215; Denmark 322-0595; Egypt 343-1590; France 435-564; Germany 342-4376; Greece 437-351; Hungary 433-020; India 342-5392; Ireland 342-5062; Israel 421-2222; Italy 435-541; Japan 342-2100; Kenya 342-5066; Korea 462-508; Kuwait 733-351; Lesotho 322-6090; Libya 342-3902; Malawi 477-827; Malaysia 342-5995; Mauritius 342-1283; Mexico 342-5190; Morocco 343-0230; Mozambique 343-7840; Namibia 342-3520; Netherlands 344-3910; Nigeria 343-2021; Pakistan 346-4605; Poland 432-621; Portugal 341-2340; Russian Federation 432-731; Singapore 883-1422; Slovak Republic 342-2051; Spain 344-3875; Swaziland 342-5782; Sweden 211-050; Switzerland 436-707; Tanzania 323-9041; Tunisia 342-6282; Turkey 342-6053; Uganda 342-6031; United Kingdom 433-121; United States 342-1048; Uruguay 432-1541; Zambia 342-1541; Zimbabwe 342-5125.

Emergency numbers National ambulance number (linked to local Metro emergency service) 1-0177. *Hospitals:* Johannesburg 488-4911; Johannesburg northern and north-eastern areas 882-2400; Johannesburg southern areas 435-0022; Pretoria 323-2781; Pretoria west 79-1801. *Poison information centre:* Johannesburg 642-2417/488-3108. *Police flying squad:* 1-0111. *Life Line:* (similar to Britain's Samaritans) Johannesburg 728-1347; Pretoria 343-8888. *Alcoholics Anonymous:* Johannesburg 483-2470; Pretoria 322-6047.

If you experience difficulties with an emergency call, dial 1022.

Johannesburg Publicity Association, Visitors' Information Bureau, situated on the corner of Market and Kruis streets, North State Building, Ground floor. PO Box 4580, Johannesburg 2000; tel. (011) 336-4961, fax 336-4965.

Pretoria Information Bureau, Tourist Rendezvous, Travel Centre, Sammy Marks Complex, corner of Prinsloo and Vermeulen streets; PO Box 440, Pretoria 0001; tel. (012) 313-7980/7694.

Satour (South African Tourism Board), offices situated in International Arrivals Hall, Johannesburg International Airport; tel. (011) 970-1669. *City office, Johannesburg:* as for the Johannesburg Publicity Association above. *City office, Pretoria:* as for Pretoria Information Bureau above.

Welcome Johannesburg, a supplementary visitor information service, also shares premises with the Johannesburg Publicity Association; tel. (011) 29-4961.

MPUMALANGA AND NORTHERN PROVINCE

Mountain and bushveld are the twin and compelling features of the regions far to the east of the Witwatersrand stretching across the great highveld plateau.

The route eastward, to begin with, has little to commend it. The roads lead from Pretoria and Johannesburg to converge near Witbank, 100 km (62 miles) distant and focal point of Africa's largest coalfields. Approximately 75 million tons of the black gold lies just underneath the surface and is exploited, easily and profitably, by the 22 collieries of the region. Much of the coal is exported. This is industrial, not tourist country.

Beyond Witbank, though, the route (now the N4 highway) becomes a lot more interesting as the gently undulating grasslands and scattered rocky outcrops give way to hills, and then to mountains that sweep up in a splendidly imposing ridge, part of South Africa's Great Escarpment and here commonly known as the Transvaal Drakensberg.

A thousand metres high on average, the mountain range runs in a north-south direction for about 300 km (186 miles) from a point north of Nelspruit to the town of Tzaneen and the Wolkberg and Magoebaskloof in the northeast. The heights in these parts are not so dramatically massive as their counterparts to the south in KwaZulu-Natal but, by the same token, are not as intimidating, are accessible to the ordinary and less intrepid traveller and have vistas that are just as lovely.

The Transvaal Drakensberg's eastern faces are especially steep, plunging hundreds of metres to the coastal plain that rolls away through the Kruger National Park and Mozambique to the Indian Ocean.

The plain below is known as the Lowveld: a fierce land, sun-blistered and heat-hazed in the long summer months, dry and dun-coloured for much of the year, but with a beauty and fascination of its own. Here, you really do feel you are in 'the real Africa'.

OPPOSITE: *Two of the Kruger Park's 1,500-strong lion community. The Kruger sprawls over nearly 20,000 km² (7,700 square miles) of Lowveld savanna; among its other residents are leopard and cheetah, elephant, rhino and buffalo.*

THE HIGH COUNTRY

For sheer scenic beauty, very few parts of the southern African subcontinent compare with the Transvaal Drakensberg.

The geological origins of the region are remote, stretching back a full 2,000 million years to the time when the highland plateau, such as it was then, came under colossal seismic pressures, forcing up layers of granite, shale and quartzite; strata which were then covered by immense outpourings of volcanic rock. This igneous matter consolidated, forming a mantle so massive that it bore down on the lower, older levels, tipping their eastern rim upwards to create the Escarpment.

Over the aeons the forces of erosion, the relentless action of wind and rain and river, have created from this geological diversity a spectacular wonderland of massif and buttress, strangely sculpted peak and deep ravine, and verdant valleys along which run the Olifants and the Crocodile rivers and a score and more of their tributaries. One of the latter, the Blyde River, flows through a canyon that ranks as one of Africa's great scenic splendours (*see* below).

This diversity carries through to the vegetation: scattered among the often mist-wreathed hills are yellowwood and black ironwood, cabbage tree and white peach, wild lemon and bastard onionwood, poison olive, notseng, silky bark and bachelor's refuge and much else, all combining to create something of a tree-lover's paradise. The rich woodland green is invariably and attractively counterpointed by the scarlet flash of aloe and the colours of myriad wild flower species. Along the streams and beside the waterfalls are ferns and creepers, conifers and ancient cycads.

This is the indigenous flora, and it is far less prolific than it was a hundred years ago. There has been steady and in places massive encroachment, most notably by the pines, wattles and eucalyptuses of some of the world's largest man-made forests. The plantations are a relatively recent feature of the region, a product of modern commercial initiative – but they are beautiful nevertheless.

THE BLYDE RIVER CANYON
In 1840 a group of Voortrekkers camped on the banks of a small stream that wound its way through and down the uncharted Escarpment. In due course the men set off to explore the

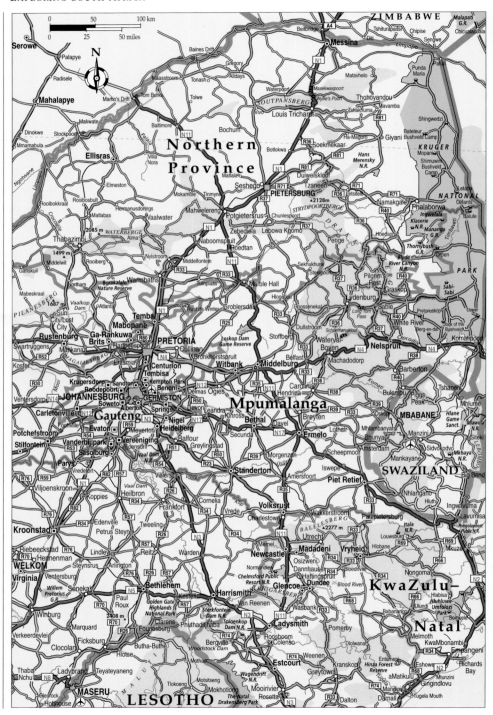

route ahead, but failed to return by the agreed day, so their womenfolk, resigned to widowhood, named the stream Treur (Afrikaans for 'sorrow'). But the men did return eventually, the reunion taking place beside another watercourse. This, in commemoration, they named Blyde, which means 'joy'.

The rivers in themselves are insignificant, but below their confluence is one of the great natural features of the southern subcontinent: the Blyde River Canyon, a majestically massive red sandstone gorge whose cliff faces plunge nearly a kilometre and almost sheer to the waters below.

There are excellent viewing sites overlooking the gorge: Lowveld Lookout, Wonder View, World's End – all easily reached from the main tarmac road (the R532). From these vantage points, you can gaze across the immensity of the lowland plain and, higher and closer, at the formidable Mariepskop massif and the hump-like peaks known as the Three Rondavels, and down at the dizzying depths of the canyon itself. The Three Rondavels are so named because they resemble in shape the circular hut traditional to some African rural communities. Mariepskop takes its name from Maripi, a folk hero of the Pulana group who, in one of the bloodiest battles of the pre-colonial era, held the natural fortress against the repeated onslaughts of a raiding Swazi army.

RESERVE AND RESORT Above the gorge is the Blyde River Canyon (or Blyderivierspoort) Nature Reserve, a lovely stretch of countryside of 27,000 ha (67,000 acres), often rising steeply in sheer quartzite cliffs, which sustains an unusually varied plant life: vegetation ranges from the subtropical bushveld of the lower slopes through grassland and rainforest to stunted mountain cover.

You will not see big game here, although minor characters are prolific: among the antelope here are klipspringer, red and grey duiker, bushbuck, kudu and grey rhebok, oribi, steenbok and Sharpe's grysbok; primates include baboon, vervet monkey, the rare samango monkey and the galagos (bush-baby and nightape), as well as such members of the cat family as caracal and serval, civet, genet and, occasionally, the shy leopard. Among the large and varied bird population (227 species altogether) is the imposing black eagle, the martial eagle, the brown parrot, the purple-crested, Knysna and grey louries and the endangered bald ibis. The Blyde River Canyon Nature Reserve is also the habitat of two rare protea species: the Blyde sugarbush, identified only in 1970, and the Transvaal mountain sugarbush.

Massive red sandstone formations, like the Three Rondavels, rise above the Blyde River Canyon.

THE HUMAN PRESENCE

Long before the colonial era the Escarpment of Mpumalanga had served and sustained both the San (Bushmen) and, much later, groups of Bantu-speaking peoples. The San were hunter-gatherers who used the upland caves for shelter, decorating some of them with their vibrant and timeless art. The Bantu-speakers hunted, too, but also kept livestock and, in simple fashion, cultivated the land. And they were miners, digging the earth for iron and copper. A few years ago archaeologists discovered, at what is known as the 'Head Site' near Lydenburg, a scatter of pottery shards, which they meticulously pieced together. The artefacts – seven sinister-looking masks that evoke images of ancient and nameless rituals – are now on display in the South African Museum in Cape Town, although visitors to Mpumalanga can see replicas at the Lydenburg Museum.

The first Europeans to penetrate the region were Portuguese explorers and traders. They were followed by the path-finding vanguard of the Voortrekkers, hardy people of Dutch descent who reached the Transvaal in the mid-1830s. A few of them, under the leadership of Louis Trichardt, set an eastward course in search for a route to the sea. Trichardt's odyssey ended, tragically, in Mozambique in 1840, but other Boer parties followed hard on their heels.

Then came the pick-and-shovel prospector, in the 1870s, when the purse-strings of diamond-rich Kimberley were steadily being tightened by rich and powerful interests (*see* page 205) and the small man was turning his steps towards the golden lode. The gold was there, found and panned in the streams and creeks of the Escarpment and, later, farther south and lower down at Barberton. But the alluvial deposits were soon extracted and most of the diggers moved west, to the newly discovered and much richer Witwatersrand. Fairly large-scale mining operations did continue at Pilgrim's Rest for three or four decades but here, too, the returns diminished to the point where the companies were forced to look elsewhere for long-term profits.

They found it in the soil, and in the seed of *Pinus patula*, a tree native to South America but suited to Mpumalanga's upland regions. The hills now support 170,000 ha (420,000 acres) of pines and nearly 100,000 ha (247,100 acres) of eucalyptus, a later introduction.

The striking Bourke's Luck Potholes.

The Blyde River Canyon Reserve offers some rewarding rambles and nature and hiking trails (*see* page 93) and, for the horse-rider, pleasant bridle paths. Near the Blyde-Treur confluence, inside the park, are Bourke's Luck Potholes, a fantasia of rock shapes and colours representing one of the stranger results of water erosion and named after early prospector Tom Bourke

(despite the implication of good fortune, he didn't find any gold, though he accurately predicted its presence in the area).

Within the reserve are two resorts, the Sybrand van Niekerk camp on the northern side of the river and the Blydepoort to the south-west. Both are run by the semi-official Aventura organization (*see* Advisory, page 95). In fact they are more like small villages than camps: tarred streets, and modern, solidly built and fully equipped bungalows (bedrooms, bathroom, kitchen, toilet, verandah, carport, a patch of lawn and barbecue facilities). At the Blydepoort there's a supermarket, à la carte restaurant, library, petrol station and airstrip.

PILGRIM'S REST

Gold was discovered in the high Escarpment, early in 1873, in a stream to the south of what is today the town of Sabie, and within days the inevitable throng of hopeful diggers congregated, setting up camps at Spitzkop and Mac-Mac (so called for the number of Scotsmen who had arrived on the scene). Later that year news

Pilgrim's Rest, a charming relic of the gold-rush. The town is now a 'living museum'.

broke of a much bigger strike, made by a dour Caledonian called Wheelbarrow Alec (he carried all his worldly possessions around in a barrow) in a small tributary of the Blyde a little to the north, and within months a gold town had been established and was flourishing. It was named Pilgrim's Rest because here, at last, after so many false trails and faded dreams, the nomadic diggers had found a firm and profitable base – a home.

The place grew: tents and wattle-and-daub shacks were replaced by solid, iron-roofed cottages; women (some of them wives) came to settle; traders and canteen owners set up shop; a school, a church and even a newspaper made their appearance; and the Royal Hotel first opened its welcoming doors to the polyglot and thirsty community.

A lot of gold was discovered including the 6,038-g Reward Nugget, and Pilgrim's Rest, for a time, was a vibrant little frontier settlement that enjoyed itself to the full, mostly peacefully, sometimes eccentrically, occasionally in outrageous style. But before long the alluvial deposits began to run out, the syndicates and companies moved in to dig deeper, to sink shafts and tunnel adits into the hillsides, and the town retired into a quieter and more respectable routine. The last of the mines, the Beta, closed in the 1970s (though, depending on the gold price, some mines could reopen).

Long before then, in the 1920s, the owners had spread their investment, diversifying their interests into large-scale forestry.

Pilgrim's Rest, still a prosperous village of several hundred residents, has a special place in the traveller's itinerary: in 1974 the provincial authorities bought the entire place, lock, stock and barrel, and over the years since then it's been turned into a 'living museum', the buildings meticulously restored to the charming condition they were in during the period 1880 to 1915. Among them are the miners' cottages, the Masonic Church, the old Bank House, the fascinating Miner's House – a perfect period-style re-creation – and the premises of *The Pilgrim's and Sabie News*.

And, of course, the Royal Hotel, which still plays amiable host to residents and visitors. Its pub – whose fittings graced a chapel in far-off Lourenço Marques until 1893, when they were hauled up the Escarpment to serve an entirely different kind of congregation – is well patronized; the rooms you sleep in are very much as they were a century ago, complete with brass bedsteads, quilted covers and pressed-steel ceilings. Also available to guests are some of the miners' cottages, a short way up the hill. There are guided tours around the village, to the old

Reduction Works, to the Diggings Museum (gold-panning demonstrations) and around Alanglade, the early mine manager's home. The house is furnished in art nouveau and art deco style and has been described as 'a showpiece illustrating the opulence of the gold industry'.

GRASKOP

This pretty little forestry village, whose name means 'Grassy Hill', lies just to the east of Pilgrim's Rest. It is perched on a spur of the Escarpment and close to a small indigenous forest called Fairyland, which is much visited by naturalists. Close to town is Kowyn's Pass, a spectacular mountain throughway leading down to the Lowveld and a route well worth taking when you're out on a leisurely drive.

The general area boasts a large number of the Escarpment's most delightful waterfalls (*see* panel, opposite page).

SABIE

This more substantial centre of the forestry industry, and originally a wayside camp for intrepid prospectors and the transport riders

Long Tom Pass, a scenically spectacular route linking Sabie and Lydenburg.

THE ROMANCE OF STEAM

Something of the grand old days of cross-country travel has returned to Mpumalanga with the introduction of Rovos Rail's steam-train safaris. Among the more popular of the excursions (there are several, to various parts of the country and occasionally to points beyond its borders) is the four-day trip from Pretoria to and through the mountains and pine plantations of the Escarpment and then down to the plains below. Here the 46 tour members – which is the maximum the train accommodates – spend at least a night in one of the more luxurious private lodges, and see some of the world's finest big-game country.

On board, passengers enjoy five-star cuisine and service in the most evocative of settings. The dining car dates from 1924 (though its carved wooden arches hint of an earlier time); the compartments are cosily furnished in period style; the best suite has richly panelled walls, a plush little sitting room and a private bathroom; the observation car is glassed in at one end and has a companionable bar at the other. The locomotives, splendid old workhorses that may be changed at various stages of the journey, include an 1893 Class Six ('Tiffany') and three 1938 Class 19Ds.

who followed them to the diggings, lies 25 km (15 miles) to the south of Graskop. Gold was discovered near Sabie in 1895 – accidentally – by a party of picnickers indulging in target shooting (one of the bullets chipped gold-bearing rock) and, during the next 55 years, over a million ounces of the yellow metal was extracted from the seam. But it was the giant mines of the Witwatersrand, and their voracious appetite for timber pit-props, that sustained the settlement over the decades. The Sabie region now supports the biggest single block of man-made forest – and the biggest sawmill – in South Africa, supplying about half the country's needs. When in town, try and make time to

visit the Cultural History Forestry Museum, which displays more than 370 exhibits, including petrified tree-trunks, antique implements and a 'talking tree'. The museum also has six visitors' 'participation areas'.

Long Tom Pass, the most spectacular section of the road linking Lydenburg and Sabie, was named after the huge 150-mm Creusot field gun used during the South African War (1899–1902), by the Boer forces with – for the British – annoying effect during General Buller's advance after the relief of Ladysmith in 1900. The pass is notable for its steep and tortuous gradients, its grand views and for the Knuckles, which are four unusually shaped peaks.

LAND OF WATER

The Escarpment is renowned for its abundant and beautiful streams and cascades, hidden in secret places among the woodland glens. Some of the most charming of these waterfalls are concentrated in the Sabie/Graskop area, and include:
• **The Sabie** Situated within the town's boundary; a chasm of 73 m (240 ft) spanned by a bridge which serves as a viewing platform.
• **The Bridal Veil** Drive 7 km (4.3 miles) north of Sabie, then take a gentle walk through the indigenous forest. The name is evocative of its delicate perfection.
• **The Mac-Mac** Twin cascades, just off the road from Sabie to Graskop; 56 m (184 ft) into a deep-green ravine dense with trees and ferns. A short distance from the falls, and close to the Escarpment's earliest gold diggings, are the Mac-Mac Pools. The name derives from the unusually large number of Scotsmen who arrived on the scene in the 1870s. The pools are in an exquisite setting; there are picnic and barbecue sites, and swimming in clear mountain water (there are changing rooms).
• **The Lone Creek** 10 km (6 miles) west of Sabie; one can drive to the base of the falls, which are 68 m (223 ft) high; the spray nurtures a rainforest.
• **The Horseshoe** About a kilometre beyond Lone Creek, on the same road. The falls are a proclaimed national monument.
• **The Lisbon** Another splendid double waterfall, situated on the western side of the R532 north of Graskop, reached by gravel road. Semicircular in shape – the water collects in pools before spilling over the rim – and in a setting of great beauty. Pleasantly sited picnic spot.

• **The Berlin** Also reached by gravel road off the R532, approximately 3 km (2 miles) north of the Lisbon. One takes a path up to a viewing platform above the falls.

The lovely Lone Creek waterfall.

69

LYDENBURG

The Afrikaans name translates as 'place of suffering', an unhappy epithet derived from the hardships of the eastern Voortrekkers, whose first settlement, Ohrigstad, sited in an unhealthy area 50 km (30 miles) to the north, had been devastated by fever and abandoned by the survivors (it was resettled almost exactly a century later, in the 1940s).

Lydenburg, though, turned out to be anything but a suffering place: it thrived, and is now a substantial and attractive centre. It has, among its other assets, the oldest school building in the former Transvaal (built in 1851) and an interesting little museum. One other small town in the general region deserves a mention, and a visit. If you're a keen angler, try to spend a day or so in Dullstroom.

Make a point of including the Abel Erasmus Pass on your sightseeing drive. The R36 highway runs through it north of Lydenburg, the steepest section twisting its way through thickly vegetated orange and yellow sandstone cliffs (and through the JG Strijdom tunnel) from a point high above the Ohrigstad River down 700 m (2,300 ft) to the Olifants. Again, there are stunning vistas of river and, beyond, the Lowveld. At the bottom of the pass there's a pleasant tree-shaded tearoom.

A short distance off the R36, at the head of the Molopong Valley (this is before you get to the pass on the northward route), are the Echo Caves, an intriguing sequence of formations

Part of the Mount Sheba Reserve.

that includes a cavern fully 100 m (330 ft) long and 50 m (165 ft) high. If you tap some of the dripstone formations (stalagmites and stalactites) they'll echo with disproportionate loudness; hence the name. There are two entrances, though only one is open to the public; the other leads to the gruesomely named and forbidding Cannibal Cave, a large chamber that accommodates millions of bats.

The caves, and others in the vicinity, once sheltered communities of Middle and Later Stone Age people. Relics of their occupation – excavated sites and rock paintings – can be seen at the nearby open-air Museum of Man.

MOUNT SHEBA

One of the loveliest nature reserves in the whole of Mpumalanga is part of a private estate: Mount Sheba, set in a deep green valley and entirely surrounded by the grandness of high hills, a little over 20 km (12.5 miles) west-southwest of Pilgrim's Rest.

To get there, one travels over what is known as Robber's Pass (R533), bearing left at the sign-posted turn-off to continue down a tortuous incline of 11 km (7 miles). The last section of the track is a bit rough, but well worth undertaking: at the journey's end there's a warm welcome at the Mount Sheba Hotel, an elegant cluster of thatched buildings set amid trim lawns and, above and beyond, tier upon tier of magnificently wooded mountain slopes.

The rainforests here are in what is termed 'climax condition' – the trees are left to mature and to die of old age without interference. It's an unusually stable floral community which,

A Kruger lion pride halts traffic.

together with its indigenous fauna (birds and the small animals) form a complete ecosystem. Over a thousand plants and trees have already been identified in the Mount Sheba Forest Reserve, and many more await the exploratory botanist. Some of the yellowwoods are almost a millennium old, and there is a wealth of Cape chestnut, massive cussonias, red pears, and towering, incredibly hard black ironwoods. Signposted paths lead through the forest glades (map and literature are available from the hotel), and many of the individual trees are clearly labelled.

THE KRUGER NATIONAL PARK

South Africa's premier reserve covers an immense slice of Lowveld territory – 20,000 km^2 (7,700 square miles) of it – which is about the size of Wales and larger than the state of Israel. It lies in the savanna-type bushveld between the Crocodile River in the south and the Limpopo River, 350 km (217 miles) to the north (it is South Africa's common border with Zimbabwe). To the east, along the Lebombo mountains, is Mozambique. The park's western perimeter borders on a number of large, private reserves.

The Kruger has no pretensions to exclusivity: it takes an unashamedly popular approach to the business of introducing South Africans to their natural heritage. Comfort and easy accessibility to the superb array of wildlife are the keynotes, and there is very little of the classic African safari about one's holiday here. The park plays host to around 5,000 people daily, and for the inexpensive family vacation it is

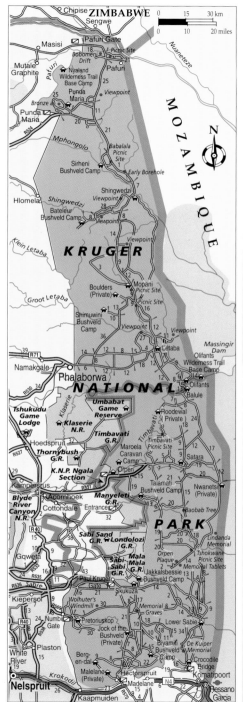

ABOVE: *A lone marabou stork in its nesting tree.*
OPPOSITE: *One of Kruger's 8 000 elephants makes its solitary crossing of the Letaba River.*

probably unsurpassed anywhere. The 22 rest camps, which differ in size and character (*see page 75*), are pleasant, tree-shaded oases in a magnificent setting, linked to each other by a road network covering 2,600 km (1,615 miles). Within leisurely driving distance of each camp are waterholes, viewsites, picnic spots and a wealth of scenic and wildlife splendour.

Despite all this though, the Kruger National Park remains unspoilt. Everything introduced by man – the rest camps, the 'designated areas', the routes and the 'visual bands' that run along either side of them – takes up less than 3% of the total area. The remaining 97% belongs to nature. The camps and viewing roads, as one writer puts it, are 'merely windows looking out into the wilderness'.

The making of a park

The southern African interior, and in particular the grasslands of the northern and north-eastern regions were, not too long ago, one of the world's great treasure-houses of wildlife. Until about the middle of the 19th century huge herds of buffalo, wildebeest and springbok roamed the sunlit veld, free to follow ancient migratory paths, their numbers kept in check only by seasonal drought, by predators, and by the modest needs of the scattered tribespeople.

Then came the white farmer to settle and fence the land, and the hunter with his guns and his lust for the killing sport. Between them they took a devastating toll on the game. Especially destructive, and wantonly so, was the hunter: it is estimated that by 1880 over two million hides had been exported to Europe – a tragic enough figure by any reckoning, but one that does not reflect the true scale of the terrible slaughter. The Victorian 'sportsman' shot indiscriminately, for the highest possible tally, and only a very small fraction of the spoils served any commercial purpose. The remaining, untold numbers of carcasses were simply left on the ground for the hyaena, the vulture and the burning African sun. It eventually became quite clear that something had to be done.

The Transvaal republican government had in fact been conscious of a dwindling natural heritage from the early 1850s, when hunters were officially (and ineffectually) forbidden to kill more than could be consumed, but it wasn't until the 1890s that there was any serious attempt to establish sanctuaries north of the Vaal River. Thereafter, events moved rapidly: on the ageing President Paul Kruger's initiative two reserves were proclaimed – the Pongola (later closed down following an outbreak of stock disease) and the Sabi. Under Warden James Stevenson-Hamilton's firm guidance the Sabi fulfilled its promise, developing into one of the world's largest and finest game reserves. In 1926, when it became the Union of South Africa's first national park, it was renamed in honour of its principal founder.

The park today

The Kruger is a haven for more varieties of wildlife than any other game sanctuary in Africa: 147 species of mammal, 112 species of reptile (including 50 of snake), 49 of fish (not counting an ocean-living shark that has been found in one of the rivers), 34 of amphibian and 230 of butterfly.

For the bird-watcher, especially, the Kruger has enormous appeal: 510 avian species have been recorded, including ostrich, fish eagle, vulture, bateleur, secretary bird, lourie and lilac-breasted roller, oxpecker and woodpecker, owl, francolin, hawk, babbler, hornbill, korhaan and Cape glossy starling. It's a fascinating region, too, for the botanist and lover of trees: there are more than 330 species of the latter, many with evocative names – mountain syringa, live-long, velvet

bushwillow, bride's bush, peeling plane, sumach bean, ironwood and yellowwood, fever tree and mahogany. Not to mention the myriad shrubs, grasses, worts, bulbous plants and aloes.

All these forms of life, together with the uncountable insects and the micro-organisms, combine to create a coherent habitat, a system of gene pools in infinitely delicate balance, and in which the cycle of life is sustained by collective dependence.

The game complement, naturally, includes the 'big five': lion, leopard, elephant, buffalo and rhino (*see* pages 78–79). Most numerous of the larger species are the impala, some 120,000 head in total: medium-sized buck that one sees everywhere (but worth more than a passing glance: they are graceful animals, and remarkable ones in flight – the whole herd moves in beautifully synchronized fashion, leaping prodigiously and in concert over the ground).

Other game figures (approximate ones, since censuses are taken at regular intervals and the numbers change) are: zebra 30,500; wildebeest 13,500; kudu 6,000; giraffe 5,000; waterbuck 3,000; warthog 3,000; hippo 3,000; sable antelope 1,500; reedbuck 800; tsessebe 700; eland 500; wild dog 350.

Details of these and of the scores of other animal, bird and plant species in the Kruger, may be found in a number of excellent publications, available in South African bookshops and at the larger Kruger camps.

VEGETATION Broadly speaking, the Kruger can be quartered according to plant type. South of the Olifants River, which more or less bisects the park, the western section is distinguished by its several acacia, combretum, marula and

A waterhole near Lower Sabie.

red bushwillow species, while to the east are the broad grazing lands of buffalo grass and red grass shaded by knobthorn. Fairly tall, butterfly-leafed mopane trees and the rugged bushwillow dominate the lands north-west of the Olifants and stunted mopane the north-east.

Distinct from all these are the strips of dense riverine vegetation, often graced by sycamore fig and Natal mahogany.

Far to the north, around Pafuri and Punda Maria, the climate and cover changes. This is a unique and, in geophysical terms, quite remarkable region, the meeting place of fully nine of Africa's major ecosystems. Here there is bushveld and wetland, sandveld, grassy plain and green forest, rolling woodland and broad lava flat, granite hill and spectacular gorge. A land of stunning contrasts, the kaleidoscopic elements complemented by a startling variety of animals and birds, bushes and trees. Many species are found in few other areas. Especially notable are the mahogany and ebony trees, and the groves of ghostly fever trees standing pale in the silent riverine jungle; the Mashikiri's giant and ancient baobabs; the massive Lebombo ironwoods, and the diverse and prolific game of the Hlamalala plain.

THE SEASONS The Kruger's climate is generally subtropical. Summer temperatures often reach a high 40 °C (104 °F) and more, though the daytime average is around 30 °C (86 °F), cooling down to just below 20 °C (68 °F) at night.

Summer is also the wet season: on a typical day during the months from November to February the storm clouds, great billowing masses of cumulonimbus, will begin building up from about lunchtime to release their full fury in late afternoon. These thunderstorms are generally brief, but are accompanied by torrential rain and can be of quite frightening proportions while they last. Rainfall tends to be heavier in the southern regions.

Winters are dry, with the days being pleasantly warm and the nights and early mornings cool, often downright cold, the temperature falling to below zero.

All this has its relevance in deciding when to visit the park, though it is difficult to offer an unqualified recommendation. In winter the streams (there are many seasonal watercourses in Kruger) are reduced to a trickle, the wildlife tends to congregate around what water there is, and the vegetation is sparser, so it's easier to see the animals, and see them in greater numbers, in the cooler months. But in many ways the park is at its worst during the winter, the earth parched and dusty, the colours drab.

In startling contrast is the green abundance of spring and summertime, when the rivers flow, the pools fill and the bushveld takes on a rich luxuriance, nurturing the game back to health and vitality and drawing the migrating flocks of birds. Climate, of course, largely determines the nature of the vegetation, which in turn has a major influence on the distribution of wildlife within the park.

Travelling to and in the park

There are eight public entrance gates. They are, clockwise from the south-eastern corner, Crocodile Bridge, Malelane, Numbi, Paul Kruger, Orpen, Phalaborwa, Punda Maria and Pafuri.

The Kruger is open all year, though some low-lying routes may close during the summer rains. There are 2,600 km (1,615 miles) of main (tarred) and secondary (graded gravel) roads.

In the interests of safety – of both the visitor and the animals – travel within the park is restricted to daylight hours. The gates and camps have set opening and closing hours, which vary slightly with the season. There are petrol filling stations at all the gates except Malelane and Paul Kruger, and at all the public rest camps. Speed limits vary between 40 and 50 km/h (25 and 30 mph). Vehicle breakdown services are available at Skukuza and Letaba.

FLYING IN Many visitors to the Kruger Park, and especially those from overseas, prefer to make their way by air, either on a conducted package tour, or by travelling privately. Consult your travel agent for further details. Car and minibus hire services are also available at both Phalaborwa and Skukuza camp.

DAY VISITS For those who really like their comforts and who plan to include visits to the Kruger Park as part of a more wide-ranging Mpumalanga holiday, there are a large number of excellent hotels and country hideaways within fairly short driving distances of one or other of the park's gates (see Advisory, page 95).

The rest camps

The Kruger offers an impressive variety of accommodation, ranging from the simple to the luxurious, in its 22 camps, five of which are small, private clusters of huts and chalets available only on a block-booking basis and one of which is reserved for campers. They are refreshingly restful places, fenced against the animals, neatly laid out, graced by trees and flowering plants and stretches of lawn. Many of the rondavels and bungalows are air-conditioned, surprisingly spacious and attractively thatched. Each camp incorporates a caravan/camping area (with communal facilities).

Camp routine is informal and undemanding, the emphasis on low-cost outdoor living. Visitors usually have to cook their own meals – indoors, if the bungalow has its own kitchen, or on the braai (barbecue) unit just outside. There are also communal field kitchens, and barbecue facilities at the several pleasant designated picnic spots. You can either stock up before you arrive or purchase your supplies at the camp's shop, which will sell you fresh meat, groceries, beer, wines and spirits, dry goods, photographic film, reading matter, curios and oddments.

A pleasant mealtime alternative is the camp's licensed restaurant, a rather casual place that serves adequate food in a friendly atmosphere. Many of the Kruger's restaurants are strategically sited to overlook river or deep valley, and pre-dinner drinks on the terrace, taken as the sun dips low and the golden light spreads, fill a magical hour of the day.

Most comfortable of the different types of units available are the guest cottages, built by private organizations or affluent individuals for their own occupancy but available for hire when not in use. They vary in size and style; some are large (designed for up to nine people) and, usually, beautifully fitted out. There are

JOCK'S BUSHVELD

Until the early decades of the 20th century the Lowveld was savagely inhospitable terrain for both man and his cattle. It had few permanent human inhabitants; settlers were discouraged by the threat of malaria and *nagana*, the 'sleeping sickness' borne by the tsetse fly. As a result, the acacia-thorn and mopane scrubland, with its fertile soil and sweet grasses, was relatively undisturbed, a peaceful refuge for lion, leopard, elephant, rhino and countless head of antelope.

Not quite undisturbed, though, for the risk of fever receded in winter and professional hunters would then embark on safari in quest of ivory and hides, and transport riders would set out across the plains to the coast. At Delagoa Bay they would load their buckwagons with 3,000 kg (6,600 lb) or more of provisions (food, equipment and whisky) and make for the isolated diggings of Barberton and the Escarpment. One of the more notable of these intrepid traders was Percy FitzPatrick, who had arrived at Pilgrim's Rest as a storekeeper in 1884 but tired of the humdrum life and, together with his Zulu driver Jim and his faithful dog Jock, he plied the fever route for two years. Later he recounted his adventures to his children, telling them about the beauty and menace of the Lowveld wastes, describing the rivers and swamps and hidden places, the predators and their prey, and of the eccentric characters he met on his travels. Many of the stories were about Jock, the runt of the litter, who became the bravest of hunters and the most resourceful of companions. In 1907, encouraged by his friend Rudyard Kipling, FitzPatrick published these tales. His book, Jock of the Bushveld, became an immediate bestseller and is today regarded as a classic.

Today a number of commemorative plaques and cairns can be seen along the old transport routes. Most notable of these is on the game-viewing Voortrekker Road that leads from Kruger's Pretoriuskop rest camp south-eastwards and past many early landmarks, including Ship Mountain.

guest cottages at Berg-en-Dal, Letaba, Lower Sabie, Olifants, Pretoriuskop, Satara, Shingwedzi and Skukuza. Bookings should be made at least three months in advance.

There is, however, plenty of less exclusive but adequate accommodation. A typical family cottage is air-conditioned and comprises two 2-bed rooms, bathroom, toilet, small kitchen (gas stove, fridge, cutlery, crockery and utensils) and gauzed-in verandah. Lower down the scale are 1-room 2- and 3-bed units with shower and toilet, and the basic 2- to 5-bed huts (handbasin only, cold water) close to an ablution block.

From the general to the specific. In alphabetical order, the Kruger's camps are:
BALULE On the Olifants River in the central region. A small cluster of 3-bed rondavels, caravan camp and ablution block. Firewood and a communal freezer on site. Shop, restaurant and petrol filling station at nearby Olifants camp, Letaba or Satara (*see* this and opposite page).
BERG-EN-DAL (the Afrikaans name means 'mountain and valley'). A newish, moderate-sized camp whose general layout and architectural style are most pleasing: accommodation units are spaced out in natural bush; there is clever and attractive use of natural building materials. The rest camp overlooks a dam. Conference facilities, swimming pool, petrol filling station, shop (fresh produce), licensed restaurant and laundry. There is a visitor centre and an interpretative trail suitable for the blind.
CROCODILE BRIDGE Sited charmingly on the Crocodile riverbank next to one of the park's two southern gates. Smallish: about 20 3-bed chalets (bath, fridge, no kitchen); shop (limited stock); petrol filling station. This is acacia country, the sweet grasses sustaining large numbers of buffalo, wildebeest, zebra, impala and kudu. Hippo Pool can be found about 8 km (5 miles) along the route to Malelane.
LETABA Beautifully situated above a sweeping bend in the central region's Great Letaba River. Lawns, shade trees (ilala palms, Natal mahogany), aloes, flowering bushes and, for superb game-viewing, well-sited terraces make this one of the park's most attractive camps. It's also strategically placed – at the junction of three major routes – for drives to the north, west and south. Shop (fresh produce), unusually good licensed restaurant, laundromat, petrol filling station, AA garage and workshop.
LOWER SABIE A medium-size camp overlooking the Sabie River; generally regarded as a prime game area; nearby are the Mnondosi and Nhlanganzwane dams. Neat lawns and shade trees are features here. Shop, licensed restaurant and petrol filling station.

MPUMALANGA AND NORTHERN PROVINCE

OLIFANTS Splendid position atop cliffs rising 100 m (330 ft) above the river, with spectacular views to distant hills and the game-rich, lushly evergreen valley below – lovely vistas at all times, magical at sunrise and sunset. There's an especially well-sited viewing point built on a promontory a short distance along the heights. A modern, pleasantly laid-out camp, the accommodation built along rising, aloe-decorated terraces (all with views). Shop, licensed restaurant (self-service), petrol filling station, museum, information centre and amphitheatre (film shows).

MOPANI A newish camp, located between Letaba and Shingwedzi and cleverly designed to blend with the natural surrounds: it's set into a rocky incline, and the views are splendid. The 6-bed cottages and 3-bed huts are of stone and thatch, and they're sited to allow guests a fair degree of privacy. The area is less well endowed with game than the park's more southerly parts, but one can see plenty of elephant, buffalo, zebra, wildebeest and buck. There is a licensed restaurant, pool, shop and petrol filling station.

ORPEN A small, restful camp near the Orpen gate in the west. Pleasant grounds (rock gardens and aloes, tall acacia and marula trees, red bushwillows). Shop and petrol filling station; no restaurant. Nearby, on the banks of the Timbavati River, is the Marula caravan camp.

PRETORIUSKOP Situated 9 km (5.5 miles) from the Numbi gate in the south-west (petrol filling station as well as first-aid station at the gate),

Pretoriuskop is the Kruger Park's oldest and fourth-largest camp. Shop, licensed restaurant, pool (natural rock) and petrol filling station.

PUNDA MARIA Named after the wife of an early ranger and situated in the far north-west, in tropical country not far from the Luvuvhu River. A smallish, rather old-fashioned and unassuming camp in a very pretty setting of rocky hill and evergreen grove with a pronounced wilderness feel about it. Take the short Mahogany loop drive on the evening you arrive: it's an excellent introduction to the area, and the waterhole en route is a gem. Shop, licensed restaurant and petrol filling station.

SATARA The second largest camp, situated in the central region and, though it doesn't enjoy any specially good views, it's popular for its sociable atmosphere, terrace, prolific and attractive birdlife (buffalo weavers, cheeky sparrows and what seems to be a million and more starlings) and its most pleasant self-service restaurant (next to a waterhole). This is lion country, but there's also an abundance of zebra, buffalo, elephant, kudu, impala, wildebeest and waterbuck. Shop, licensed restaurant, laundry facilities; petrol, garage/workshop and information centre.

SHINGWEDZI The largest of the three northern region's rest camps, Shingwedzi is well-known for its spacious grounds, lovely trees (mainly

Olifants rest camp on the Olifants River offers excellent game-viewing opportunities.

THE BIG FIVE

Lion, elephant, rhino, buffalo, leopard – these are at the top of most visitors' game-viewing list, and with patience and a little luck you'll be able to spot the first four in the Kruger.

LEOPARD, the fifth species, is very hard to find: it's a shy, solitary, secretive creature, a nocturnal hunter that hides away during the daylight hours among the rocks of an outcrop or in dense bush or in

A lone lioness.

the branches of a tree. Occasionally it will venture into open ground, but is still difficult to discern: its tawny-yellow body is spotted with black rosettes, creating a colour pattern that enables it to blend beautifully into its surroundings. There are just under a thousand leopards in the Kruger.

In somewhat greater evidence are the Kruger park's 250 or so cheetah, fastest of all land mammals, able to reach sprint speeds of approximately 75 km/h (46 mph) in short, explosively dramatic bursts of movement. Their numbers are few because of competition from the larger predators, and the fact that the Kruger doesn't have too many patches of clear grassland, which this plains-loving species needs in order to run down its prey. It hunts in the open, usually just after dawn or at dusk, so it is more often seen than its cousin. The two are sometimes mistaken for each other, especially in bad light and at a distance, but in fact they're quite dissimilar. Cheetah have longer legs than leopard, smaller heads with rounded ears and, perhaps their most distinguishing feature, 'tear-marks' running from eyes to mouth.

LION The park is sanctuary to about 1,500 of these big cats, territorial animals that live in prides of up to six, though larger groups of a dozen and more are sometimes found. Occasionally, too, one chances upon the hunt and kill, but this is a rare spectacle indeed. Generally the lion is a nocturnal predator, its prey ranging from massive giraffe and buffalo down to the small mammals.

The hunt is a complex process and one in which the female plays the leading role: the male tends to be somewhat indolent. But his strength, when he chooses to use it, is phenomenal. He is the largest of Africa's carnivores, standing a metre high (3.3 ft) at the regally maned shoulder, has a mass of 200 kg (440 lbs) or more and can break a wildebeest's neck with a single swipe of his massive paw. He is also

able to show a remarkable turn of speed, covering 100 m (330 ft) in just four to six seconds. Lion have no natural enemies, but mortality is high among the prides, the biggest toll taken by starvation among the cubs during lean times, and by a number of parasite-borne diseases that affect cubs in poor condition. Lions are also prone to injury during the hunt, often from the horns of buffalo, from the lethal kick of a giraffe and, oddly enough, from too-familiar contact with the humble porcupine – the needle-sharp quills will pierce the flesh to set up an infection that spreads, debilitates and leads to slow death from starvation.

The Kruger's lion are to be found throughout the park but are most common in the central areas, in the general vicinity of Satara camp, and in the south-eastern region, between Lower Sabie and Crocodile Bridge.

ELEPHANTS in the Kruger number approximately 8,000 and are renowned for the size of their tusks – one recent count revealed more than 20 individuals bearing tusks of about 60 kg (132 lbs) in weight. They are scattered throughout the park, usually grouped in herds, and 'tame' enough for you to approach to within a few metres. Herds of 100 or more individuals are often found, but they tend to be smaller in the south of the park, comprising around 30 individuals. Solitary bulls or bull groups can also be seen. Always approach elephants with caution, do not make any unnecessary movement or noise, and be prepared to drive away quickly if any warning signs appear – if, that is, one of the adults turns head on to you, raises its trunk and starts flapping its ears.

Elephant, like lion, have no natural enemies – except man. And in Africa, that's enemy enough. Poaching has been a serious problem throughout the continent in recent years, depleting, and in the case of some countries, seriously endangering the national elephant herds. During the past 15 years Africa's elephant population has dramatically fallen from 1.3 million to about 600,000. The recent international ban on the ivory trade – the Convention on Trade in Endangered Species, signed in October 1989 by 103 nations – should at least slow, if not halt, the tragic decline. Indeed, within three months of the embargo, ivory prices had plunged from US $144 to just $5 a kilogram. The ban itself has been the subject of a lot of heart-searching, and it has its critics among naturalists. Countries like South Africa and its northern neighbour Zimbabwe have an excellent record when it comes to conservation in general and the management of elephant populations in particular, and their elephant herds, far from diminishing over the years, have remained healthy and large, to the point where they have to be periodically culled (reduced in size). Until 1989 ivory from the culled carcasses was sold on the open market and the proceeds devoted to schemes that help preserve the subcontinent's priceless wildlife legacy. That source of income has now disappeared, and the game parks of southern Africa are the poorer for it.

Ivory is a sensitive issue. So too is culling, an unpleasant process but an ecologically necessary one. Elephants can be incredibly destructive: a single adult can consume up to 300 kg (660 lbs) of grass, shoots and stripped bark each day and will topple a tree to get at the few tender leaves from the crown. The consequences for the environment can – if the herd is allowed to become too large for the area to which it is confined – be devastating, posing a threat both to the elephant's wellbeing and to the survival of other species. Surplus animals simply have to be killed off in order to protect the habitat.

BUFFALO This large and powerful relative of the antelope, distinguished by its 800 kg (1,764 lbs) bulk and by the bony boss at the top of the head from which its great horns curve upward, is a common resident of the Kruger National Park. About 25,000 are distributed throughout the park, many of them congregated in herds of well over 200.

Treat the buffalo with the respect he deserves: he may appear to be docile, but hunters regard him as one of the most dangerous and cunning of Africa's game species. Solitary males, exiled from the herd after losing a mating battle and often seen close to

streams and waterholes, can be very bad-tempered and unpredictable. Ordinary visitors to the park, though, are not at risk, provided they adhere to a simple set of rules.

RHINO are relative newcomers to the Kruger – they became locally extinct some decades ago and have only recently been reintroduced to the region.

The first few white rhino were brought in from Zululand in 1961, a translocation that proved so successful that a further 300 were imported 10 years later. Incidentally, the prefix 'white' is misleading: the animal is in fact a dark-grey colour, and the term is thought to be a corruption of the Afrikaans word *wyd*, or wide, a reference to its square-lipped mouth – an evolutionary adaptation to its grazing habits. It could also refer to the animal's appearance after a mud- or dustbath.

By contrast, the black rhino (again the term has little meaning, invented simply to distinguish it from its cousin) is a browser, its pointed mouth well suited to feeding on the leaves and branches that make up most of its diet. It is also the smaller of the two species, reaching a mass of 1,500 kg (3,300 lbs), but should be viewed with caution, especially but not exclusively in the breeding season: it has poor eyesight, is easily provoked by unfamiliar sounds or smells, and has been known to charge without warning. It is also astonishingly agile for its bulk, capable of speeds up to 45 km/h (28 mph) and of wheeling with lightning speed.

One of Kruger's 25,000 Cape buffalo.

The leopard, master of camouflage.

ABOVE: *Shingwedzi camp in northern Kruger.*
TOP RIGHT: *Visitors on one of the Kruger Park's wilderness trails stop to examine animal tracks.*

mopane but also palms) and pink-and-white impala lilies, its somewhat old-fashioned bungalows (though they are quite modern inside) and its swimming pool. Many possible drives, but especially recommended is that to the south-east (towards Letaba), on the secondary road that leads along the Shingwedzi River. The well-patronized Kanniedood Dam is on this route. Shop, licensed restaurant and cafeteria, petrol filling station and information centre.

SKUKUZA In many ways the 'capital' of the Kruger and far more of a thriving little town than just a bush camp, Skukuza is named after the park's first warden (*see* page 72) – the word in translation means 'he who sweeps clean', a reference to Stevenson-Hamilton's ruthless and successful war against poachers.

The camp's focal point is the newly constructed reception and restaurant area, said to be Africa's and perhaps the world's largest thatched building. Accommodation ranges through the spectrum, from self-contained and very well appointed guest cottages through chalets to accommodation specially designed for paraplegics, dormitories for school parties and an extensive caravan/camping area. Amenities and services: supermarket and curio shop, restaurant, 'Train Restaurant' (converted dining and lounge car) and snack bar, post office, bank, airport, Comair and Avis offices, police station, doctor, petrol filling station, workshop and AA service. The information centre houses a good library and an exhibition hall. Well worth visiting is the nursery, which sells baobabs, cycads, palms and other indigenous flora at most reasonable prices.

THE PRIVATE CAMPS There are five of these: secluded, small – the largest can take up to 19 people – but with fully equipped accommodation. They are for groups, and must be booked en bloc. Petrol, shop and restaurant are accessible at the nearest of the larger rest camps.
THE BUSHVELD CAMPS Half a dozen of these small, generally remote and less sophisticated venues cater for the undemanding visitor.

Wilderness trails

Most visitors to the Kruger see the park in comfort, through the windows of the family car or combi. Some, though, want a closer and more intimate experience of one of Africa's most splendid reserves and, for these, seven wilderness trails have been established. These foot safaris are led by rangers who know a great deal about the ways of the wild and are able and most willing to share their knowledge.

There's nothing competitive or challenging about these walks: they are designed simply to stimulate the mind and the eye, to provide enjoyment, relaxation and good companionship, and they tend to be undemanding, go-where-you-will affairs. The ranger will be guided in his choice of route by the character and collective energy of his charges, and he will lead them wherever mood and interest dictate, stopping now and again, perhaps to examine a flower, a tree, an insect, a herd of antelope, or to take in an especially lovely vista, and to talk about the lore of the wilderness. He has an intimate and in-depth knowledge of the countryside, and of its wild creatures.

Accommodation is fairly rudimentary but it has the basics: bedding, food and utensils are provided; visitors must provide their own liquid refreshment. Evenings are usually enjoyably spent in conversation and anecdote, around the camp-fire with the bright stars and the sounds of the African bushveld all around – times to be savoured and remembered.

WEST OF THE KRUGER

The Kruger National Park takes up quite a large portion of Mpumalanga's lowveld region but by no means all of it. Sprawled along the park's western boundaries are Timbavati, Klaserie, Umbabat and the Sabi-Sand reserves, four of the largest privately owned game sanctuaries in the world. Although the fences between these reserves and the Kruger have been taken down and the animals are free to migrate at will, they operate as autonomous enterprises. Beyond them, further to the west, are the foothills of the Escarpment, the pleasant towns of Barberton and Nelspruit, and some of South Africa's most fertile farmlands.

The private reserves

Each of these massive areas comprises a number of farms and independent game properties, some of whose owners have combined their resources to create and operate commercial camps. Each camp is different, with its own distinctive personality and atmosphere, but all are professionally run, supremely comfortable, tend to be quite expensive, and they provide, at a price, the holiday of a lifetime.

Game lodge guests stop to view buffalo.

MALAMALA is perhaps the best known: it offers the ultimate in game-viewing luxury, and its reputation extends far beyond South Africa's borders. The ingredients of its success: a spacious Out-of-Africa (but air-conditioned) bush lodge, excellent cuisine and five-star service; neatly thatched and luxuriously appointed chalets (two bathrooms, fitted carpets) nestling among shade trees and trim lawns, the whole complex set in a wilderness area that boasts the largest concentration of big game on the continent. Special mention should be made of the Sable Suite, a self-contained and ultra-luxurious little complex next to the camp proper, designed for groups of up to 16. It has its own lounge, pool and *boma* (outside dining enclosure), though guests can use all the facilities at the main lodge. Ideal for big-business getaways.

MalaMala has room for about 50 people, and there are 10 rangers to look after them, which, if you work it out, amounts to very personalized service indeed. The rangers are courteous, helpful, knowledgeable, and always with you. The clientele, obviously, falls into the upper income bracket, many of the guests jetting in from Europe and North America for a brief but memorable taste of Africa as it once was.

SABI-SABI, almost as famous as MalaMala, is renowned for its game-viewing but also for its good food and its splendid sociable evenings. A typical menu will offer an impressive selection of fresh salads, four meat dishes (including venison, of course), a 'ranger's platter' of cheeses,

THE PRECIOUS LAND

Fairly expensive though they may be for the average person, the original impetus behind the establishment of the private reserves was not financial gain but, rather, a genuine desire to conserve, and in many cases to restore, the indigenous animal and plant life of the region, to protect the land from the encroachment of alien species and from the depredations of man, and indeed from the very presence of man in destructively large numbers.

The desire is a passionate dedication and life-long commitment in some instances – the Varty brothers of Londolozi, for example, have undertaken what amounts to a crusade to preserve their natural heritage. The job is a tough one, because the countryside is under simultaneous assault from a number of different, though related, quarters. There are the pressures of human population growth, a proliferation of roads, tracks and powerlines, as well as the spread of pollution. The game is confined to specific areas and, despite the enormous size of the reserves, it can no longer move freely with the seasons, a factor which in turn upsets the infinitely delicate balance between predator and prey.

In short, the entire ecosystem is under threat, and to minimize this, to sustain the game, to root out the dense, choking patches of alien bush and return the land to its pristine condition, is a hugely expensive and personally challenging business. Hence the lodges, and the high rates that visitors pay.

There is another element, a new impetus. Land hunger and the voracious appetite of the expanding and generally impoverished rural communities for water, firewood and good grazing pose a growing threat to the environment, and to the integrity of the reserves.

But conservationists are now convinced that the wellbeing of the wildlife and the interests of tourism need not be in conflict with the needs of rural Africans, and recent years have seen the emergence of what is called the 'resource' area – integrated conservancies in which the people of the countryside, instead of being excluded, are brought into the scheme, helping to preserve the habitats, and in return share in its resources – and enjoy the benefits from tourism. It's a win-win rather than a win-lose situation, and it holds real promise for the future.

home-made bread and sherry trifle to finish. It's the traditional braai (barbecue) dinner, though, that one remembers. This is held in the reed-enclosed *boma*, fire-lit and filled with animated chat. The rangers, who join you for the meals, are young and, for all their familiarity with the bush and dedication to their work, full of fun. Shangaan women provide the intermezzo, performing tribal dances and singing with superb gusto. When the dancing is over they resume, somewhat incongruously, their main role and serve food. The atmosphere is informal, cheerful and entertaining; the evenings invariably turn into a roaring party.

Much of one's day at Sabi-Sabi, all but the hottest hours, is spent in a Land-Rover in the company of a ranger-tracker team. These trips provide endless fascination: the team's bushcraft skills are astonishing, the search exacting as one follows, say, the spoor of lion; the climax – first sight of the pride – exhilarating. There are also strategically placed hides overlooking a waterhole and stream and, for the more adventurous, guided walks through the bush.

The other lodges have similar routines, and are equally attractive and hospitable, though each has its own style and special drawcards.

TIMBAVATI RESERVE Ngala, in the southern Timbavati, operates its own three-aircraft charter service to ferry guests to and from camp (others of course arrive by road). M'bali lodge comprises 'habi-tents' overlooking the Nhlaralumi River – canvas-roofed hides built on stilts and reminiscent of Kenya's famed Tree-Tops. Tanda Tula is one of the smallest lodges, an unpretentious cluster of buildings catering for just 14 people at a time, and is run by Pat Donaldson, a man with a 'big' personality, a feeling for the real Africa, and an acute perception of what one wants out of a bush holiday.

LONDOLOZI is world famous for both its excellence and its highly successful efforts to combine tourism with game conservation and good land management. Londolozi's Dave Varty is internationally known for his study of, and films on, the reserve's leopards.

AMONG THE FOOTHILLS

The countryside west of the Kruger and the private game reserves, on the plains proper and on the lower slopes of the Escarpment, is given over to woodland plantations and to intensive farming: the soils are rich, the climate warm, often humid, and the land yields marvellously bountiful harvests of bananas as well as other subtropical fruits, winter vegetables, nuts, tea, coffee and much else.

BARBERTON

Set in the attractive De Kaap valley well south of the Escarpment and close to the Swaziland border, Barberton is the oldest of the region's towns and one of the earliest of South Africa's gold-mining centres.

A prospector named Auguste Robert, better known as 'French Bob', discovered the first reefs in 1883, attracting fortune-seekers in their thousands, among them Graham Barber and his cousins Fred and Harry, who found and worked Barber's Reef and gave it their name.

In its heyday, in the mid-1880s, Barberton was a large and lively settlement, a typical Wild West-type boom town of corrugated iron shanties, music halls and hotels, scores of drinking dens, two stock exchanges and 20,000 people – a citizenry that included almost as many fringe characters as honest diggers. Among them were adventurers, con-artists and various other types of fly-by-night dealers in liquor and fraudulent stock, and the inevitable ladies of pleasure: Florrie, the Golden Dane and the inimitable Cockney Liz, who would of an evening, in the bar of the Phoenix (still a going concern, but now much quieter), auction herself to the highest bidder. In 1885 the rich Sheba Reef was discovered 16 km (10 miles) away and many of the miners moved to the new camp, which they called Eureka City. This, too, boasted its canteens and vaudeville halls and, in addition, had its own racetrack.

Then the 'Barberton Bubble' burst. The gold was solid enough, but too much money had chased the limited resources, and an exodus to the giant, newly-discovered Witwatersrand goldfields (see page 35) began in 1887.

Eureka City is now billed as a 'ghost town', but in reality it amounts to little more than a rather sad scatter of overgrown ruins. Of the old Barberton more remains, and the town is a pleasant place to visit. A must when you're in the area is the Belhaven House Museum, restored and preserved as an especially fine example of turn-of-the-century elegance and good taste. The new Barberton Museum opened its doors in 1994. Among other attractions is a Victorian tea-garden; the Barberton Nature Reserve and its contiguous neighbour, the Songimvelo Nature Reserve covering approximately 56,000 ha (140,000 acres).

The countryside around Barberton is flattish, without too much to recommend it to the casual eye, but the hills are not far away and there are some lovely drives in the area – to the Pioneer Reef, to the waterfall at the Agnes mine, and across the Swaziland border (passports are required, but otherwise the formalities are minimal) to the peaceful woodland magic of Havelock and Pigg's Peak.

The road to the latter is slightly rugged, but it is scenically spectacular; at Pigg's Peak itself there is a luxury hotel and casino complex set in lovely surrounds.

NELSPRUIT

North of Barberton is Nelspruit, capital of Mpumalanga and a pleasant, prosperous-looking place of clean-lined buildings, wide streets and tree-garlanded suburbs. It's the last major centre on the main west-east highway and the jumping-off point for tourists arriving by both road and air (it has a small airport).

There are good hotels and restaurants in and around town and some sophisticated shops; curios, handwoven rugs, carvings and leather goods are on sale in specialist outlets and the larger stores; fresh produce in season is sold by the many farm stalls along the region's roads.

Among Nelspruit's other attractions are the:
LOWVELD BOTANIC GARDENS, one of eight branches of the National Botanic Gardens, sited on the banks of the Crocodile River and haven for a fascinating variety of lowveld floral species – about 600 of them.
LOWVELD HERBARIUM, adjacent to the Botanic Gardens. A walk through the gardens will bring you to the Cascades viewsite, a platform overlooking rock and river.
CROCODILE VALLEY, an immensely fertile part of the beautiful countryside around Nelspruit. It is the second largest of South Africa's citrus-growing regions. Bright green, scented groves of oranges are everywhere. Scattered among them are fields of subtropical fruits, plantations of pine, wattle and eucalyptus and a splendid abundance of other trees and shrubs, indigenous and exotic, to delight the eye, including the lovely Pride of De Kaap (*Bauhinia galpinii*) and the fragrant yellow-blossomed *Acacia karroo*, which blooms just after Christmas.

WHITE RIVER

North of Nelspruit is this pretty little farming centre. It lies in the in-between region as you pass from Lowveld to Escarpment, which encompasses some of the country's richest agricultural land. More than 3,000 smallholders cultivate the soil within a 10 km (6 miles) radius of town, growing, among other things, flowers and tropical fruits. If you are staying in the general area (it has a superb selection of country hotels and guest lodges; see Advisory, page 95), you will find White River both convenient and excellent for shopping.

WATERVAL BOVEN AND WATERVAL ONDER

To the west of Nelspruit, about 70 km (45 miles) along the N4, are these charming twin villages, whose names mean respectively 'above' and 'below' the waterfall. The falls in question are the magnificent cascades of the Elands River, and they are well worth visiting for their splendour and indeed for the scenic beauty of terrain that marks the abrupt transition from the Highveld to the Lowveld.

The area, too, is steeped in railway history. Paul Kruger, president of the land-locked Transvaal Republic in the 1880s and 1890s, was profoundly suspicious of the British at the Cape and in Natal and determined to find his own route to the Indian Ocean. He commissioned a railway line that was finally completed after a decade of setbacks and, for the construction workers, of tragedy, in 1895. It is said that one man died – of fever, drink or from the ravages of wild animals – for every sleeper laid on the track, and of all the sections on the 700 km (435 miles) route this was probably the most difficult. From Waterval Boven the railroad plunges down a dramatic 1:20 gradient (this necessitated a racked, or cogged, line) to the Elands River valley, along which it passes by way of a 213-m-long (700 ft) tunnel.

If you're heading back towards Nelspruit from here, take the secondary road through the enchanting Schoemanskloof Valley. The road loops north and then east before rejoining the main highway after about 60 km (37 miles), and it is a pleasant drive indeed, especially towards early evening when the sun's rays slant gently onto the valley floor and create an infinite subtlety of colour.

SUDWALA CAVES Not far from the junction of the two roads – a little way to the north off the R539 – is a labyrinthine complex of caverns that have been hollowed out of the Mankelekele ('crag-on-crag') massif. The network is thought to burrow its way through the dolomite rock for 30 km (20 miles) and more, but visitors may explore, or be guided through, just 600 m (1,968 ft) or so of the complex – which in fact is quite extensive enough to reveal the caves as a magnificent and justifiable tourist attraction.

The complex comprises a series of inter-linked chambers which are festooned with cream-coloured (although some are reddish or brownish, as a result of iron and manganese in the limestone) stalactites and stalagmites, many with fanciful but highly descriptive names such as The Weeping Madonna, Lot's Wife and The Space Rocket. The most impressive of the chambers is the PR Owen Hall, a natural theatre complete with sloping-floor 'stalls' rising to a 'gallery' 37 m (121 ft) in diameter. The ceiling is dome-like, the acoustics so superb that the hall has been used for choral recordings and public concerts. For some reason, as yet not fully explained, the air within the caves remains at a constant temperature of 20 °C (68 °F), day and night throughout the year.

Sudwala's surrounds are just as impressive: the entrance area and flanking cliff-like slopes are cloaked in evergreen forest and a wealth of colourful indigenous flora, including yellow aloe, white pear blossom and the scarlet kaffirboom to name but a few.

Below the entrance is a pleasant resort offering comfortable accommodation, à la carte fare, tennis, swimming, as well as a healthy and varied selection of nature walks.

Nearby is the Dinosaur Park, an unusual and fascinating open-air display featuring life-size replicas of the giant extinct reptiles that ruled the earth around 250 million years ago. The setting is equally primitive: flora includes the primaeval cycad – the 'living fossil' that resembles both a fern and a palm and whose origins can be traced back 180 million years, to the Mesozoic era. Cycads, of which there are nine genera and about 100 species worldwide, are vigilantly protected in South Africa.

OPPOSITE: *The magnificent Elands River Cascades near the quiet village of Waterfal Boven form part of the region's renowned scenic beauty.*

THE MODJADJI

The best-selling author Rider Haggard based his novel *She* on the legends that wreathe Modjadji – on her powers over man and the elements, and on her immortality. The original Queen, it is thought, was a 16th-century princess of the Karanga people of what is now Zimbabwe. She fled before her enemies southward across the Limpopo to found the Lobedu clan to the north of Tzaneen, part of the Northern Province famed for its giant cycad plants. She and her successors, guardians of the rain-magic, were respected and at one time even feared throughout southern Africa: even the great and powerful warrior King Shaka held her in awe, and she and the Lobedu remained unscathed during the bitter wars of the black peoples in the early 1800s.

There is a Rain Queen still – the title is ritualistically and mystically passed down through the generations – though the image is more romantic than the reality. She lives in seclusion, in her royal residence on the slope of the hill, and she may be visited by the favoured few. In times of drought many people, white as well as black, ask for her intercession.

And her domain still encompasses the cycad forest, where literally thousands of these ancient and now-precious plants thrive; indeed, this is the largest concentration of *Encephalartos transvenosus* (also known as the Modjadji palm) in the world. There are pleasant picnic and barbecue facilities in the forest reserve; cycads may be purchased at a nursery about 5 km (3 miles) to the south.

Part of the Modjadji cycad forest.

THE NORTHERN REGIONS

For ease of description, let's assume you are on a motoring holiday, driving northward along and beyond the Escarpment. The route you'd take is the R36, through the Abel Erasmus Pass (*see* page 70), over the Olifants River – quite wide here, with pools in which hippo and crocodile are often seen – and on, for a long 150 km (95 miles) or so, to the town of Tzaneen, the main commercial centre of the immensely fertile and very lovely Letaba district.

TZANEEN

The town (named after the local baTzaneng people) started as a research station for tropical and subtropical crops, and later became the headquarters of the anti-malaria campaign which, in the 1930s, led to the virtual eradication of the disease, paving the way for the creation of a thriving agricultural economy in the region.

This is largely tea-producing country, the rich, intensively irrigated plantations sprawling to the far distances and the air, in the long harvesting months from September through to May, aromatic with the fresh leaves. Not just tea though: the region has a tropical feel about it, a quality acquired from its position at the foot of the Transvaal plateau, its high rainfall and soils that sustain citrus and avocados, mangoes and bananas, lichis and pawpaws, tomatoes, coffee, macadamia and pecan nuts, cotton and winter vegetables. Flowering trees are everywhere, and huge timber plantations clothe the hills and valleys.

MAGOEBASKLOOF A little to the west of Tzaneen are the misty, thickly-wooded heights of the Magoebaskloof, accessible via a good tarred road, which rises some 600 m (1,968 ft) in a short stretch for 6 km (4 miles). The name is taken from the late-19th-century Batlou tribal chieftain Makgoba, who refused to pay taxes to the white settler administration and led 500 of his people into hiding in the dense upland reaches of the kloof. He was eventually – after more than a year – tracked down by a government-recruited Swazi impi and beheaded. Summary injustice, as it were.

Most of the uplands are the domain of the forestry department, much of it under plantation, but some substantial patches of natural woodland remain. Indeed, the region's largest indigenous forests are in the area.

Harvesting tea near Tzaneen.

WOODBUSH is only a few kilometres to the north of Magoebaskloof's summit (1,370 m or 4,495 ft). It is a short drive to the forest station, but one that offers superb views of the Lowveld to the east. Woodbush is haven to magnificent redwoods, giant 40-m-high (130 ft) ironwoods, cabbage trees, yellow-woods, red stinkwoods. A place for walking and for communing with restful spirits. Just to the east are the:
DEBEGENI FALLS, entrancing in their forest setting and in the surge and clarity of their waters. It's a pleasant spot to picnic. And far-ther east still, close to Tzaneen's town limits, is more water in the attractive shape of the:
TZANEEN DAM (formerly Fanie Botha) and its attendant nature reserve, an expanse covering 1,200 ha (2,965 acres) of lake and grassland sur-rounded by pine plantations. The setting is splendid, more reminiscent of the great North American wilderness areas than of Africa. The dam is popular among anglers for its black bass, tilapia and yellowfish; and among boating enthusiasts and bird-watchers. Altogether, there are some 150 species of bird in the reserve, including tropical waterfowl and the fish eagle.

DUIWELSKLOOF The R36 north of Tzaneen leads through this little village ('Devil's Cleft' or pass) and then, beyond, to the turn-off to Modjadji, realm of the mysterious Rain Queen (*see* panel, opposite page). The principal fea-tures of the area south of Tzaneen are the:
EBENEZER DAM (picnicking, boating, fishing, wind-surfing) in the Letaba River Valley.
GEORGE'S VALLEY George was an early road-builder who loved the hills, and made gratui-tous detours so that travellers could enjoy the finest of views.
NEW AGATHA STATE FORESTS, through which the Rooikat nature trail makes its circu-lar and entrancing way. The forest station serves as jumping-off point for the:
WOLKBERG WILDERNESS AREA, a 22,000 ha (54,000 acres) expanse of peak and valley, forest and grassland which lies a little farther to the south, beckoning the hiker and lover of untouched Africa. The highest point, Ararat, is 2,050 m (6,725 ft) above sea level; the country-side wild and lonely. Game is sparse in the Wolkberg – much of it was shot out years ago by the dagga (cannabis) growers who hid in the valleys, away from prying eyes, and lived off the land – though duiker, reedbuck and klipspringer can sometimes be seen. Leopard and the rare

brown hyaena are also present, as are several types of snake, including the dangerous berg adder, the puff adder and the black mamba.

A lot more rewarding is the birdlife: the reserve is home to a great many species, including Egyptian goose, black eagle, rock kestrel, Goliath heron, white stork and hamerkop.

The last-mentioned is also known as the 'bird of doom', a large, curious-looking creature much feared by the more superstitious of the rural people, though the reason isn't too clear. It may have something to do with its cry, a high-pitched, eerie, tormented whistle.

Hamerkops are commonly seen standing still in shallow water, watchful for the frogs and fish they feed on, or searching the muddy water's edge for smaller fry. But for all its apparent awkwardness, the bird is one of nature's most accomplished architects: its nest is a large and ingenious affair, nothing much to look at from the outside but the dimensions are spacious. The interior is divided into three chambers (the lowest level is a concealed-entrance 'reception area', the middle is the domain of fledglings, the top is for the adults), the whole edifice so strongly built that it can bear the weight of a grown man.

For the rest, the Wolkberg is known for its mists, its clear, cool streams, its rugged mountain slopes and for its many waterfalls. These, and especially the Thabina, are certainly worth more than a passing glance. Visitors to the area need a permit (from the State Forester) and the rules are strict: no fires, no fishing, no soap or detergents in the streams.

HAENERTSBURG

West of Tzaneen, along the road to Pietersburg, lies this hamlet, near which is an especially lovely farm on which azaleas and cherries are cultivated in three large nurseries. In springtime the displays are quite breathtaking, but check the exact flowering period – it varies, depending on how good the rains have been – before visiting. Also a delight to the eye is the Haenertsburg Spring Fair, which coincides with the Cherry Blossom Festival (arts and crafts as well as flowers).

LEYDSDORP

The region to the east of Tzaneen is dominated by the Murchison range of hills, where payable gold was first discovered in 1888. Thousands of claims were pegged, the town of Leydsdorp established and a railway began to snake its way for approximately 330 km (205 miles) north from Komatipoort in the south-eastern Lowveld. But the seams soon gave out, work on the railway stopped (the project, called the Selati line, had in any case been plagued by greed and sharp practice; it was belatedly completed in 1922) and Leydsdorp became a ghost town (though there is still a great deal of mining in the area – of mica and of the largest deposits of the strategic metal antimony in the world). One relic of the old diggers' days, apart from Leydsdorp itself, is the huge, hollow and renowned baobab tree which once served as a pub for the thirsty prospectors. It is recorded that more than a dozen men would huddle *inside* its trunk to take their tipple.

THE HANS MERENSKY RESERVE North of the Murchison range is an island in the Letaba River from which a thermal spring rises at a warm and constant temperature. The river's southern bank is part of the Hans Merensky Nature Reserve, 5,200 ha (12,849 acres) of fairly level terrain (except along the eastern boundary, where leopard hunt in the Black Hills) covered by typical Lowveld vegetation: a mix of mopane, grassland and combretum woodland with scatters of weeping boer-bean, jackalberry and red bush-willow.

The game includes giraffe, the stately sable antelope, zebra, waterbuck, klipspringer, eland, kudu, tsessebe and Sharpe's grysbok.

The river, its hippo pool, the thermal spring and the reserve are a splendid setting for the resort that has been established there and which is called, for obvious reasons, Eiland.

The resort offers excellent accommodation: 100-plus self-contained rondavels (bathroom, fully equipped kitchen, some units with lounge/dining room), all thoughtfully laid out among the tree-shaded lawns to give you a welcome degree of privacy. There are also mineral pools, Hydro Spa, a hotel, a licensed restaurant, entertainment hall, tennis, fishing, horse-riding, shops and, of course, the mineral-rich pools in which you can wallow.

Casual visitors are welcome in the reserve: there are bus tours, guided walks, two- and three-day nature trails, and trips to the open-air museum. This last is a re-creation of a typical Tsonga village, enlivened by demonstrations of pottery-making, weaving, woodcarving and other domestic crafts. The Kruger National Park is an hour's drive away.

THE GREAT NORTH ROAD

A great many South Africans travel up the national highway (the N1) from the Witwatersrand to take their holidays in a part of the country often ignored by the overseas tourist. Some of them go farther, turning eastward to take the route through the culturally fascinating and once – during the apartheid years – independent region of Venda to enter the Kruger National Park through its northernmost gates.

Along the N1 there are pleasant little towns and resort areas, and a lot to see and do.

WARMBATHS

The town, 93 km (58 miles) from Pretoria, is renowned for its curative springs; for water therapy, the Hydro Spa compares with the best in the world. On offer: underwater massage pool; Overspa complex and water playground; hot outdoor pool; restaurants; cosmetic, health and slimming salons. Accommodation ranges from a good hotel and luxurious and fully-equipped chalets to more modest apartments. Some 90 km (55 miles) north on the N1 is the pleasant town of Potgietersrus and its:

The massive 'supertube' slide at Warmbaths.

POTGIETERSRUS NATURE RESERVE, a rather unusual wildlife enterprise. The reserve is part of the National Zoological Gardens, and it serves as a breeding unit for exotic wildlife species – including the blackbuck and hog deer from Asia, banteng wild cattle and mouflon wild sheep, the South American llama and the pygmy hippo – as well as for indigenous South African fauna (including both white and black rhino). Further up the road is:

PIETERSBURG

This town is Northern Province's capital, and a most pleasant place. Features of tourist interest in the area include:
• The art collection at the municipal offices; the open-air exhibition of historical relics (steam locomotive, farming implements and so forth) in Landdros Street; and the open-air display of abstract art at the northern entrance to town. There is also an excellent little photographic museum, housed in the restored and converted Dutch Reformed church.
• Nine kilometres (5.5 miles) south of town, on the Chuniespoort/Burgersfort Road, is the Bakone Malapa Open-air Museum – a kraal in which traditional skills are displayed. Also rock paintings, Iron Age remains, tours and picnics.

FISHING AND HIKING: SOME DO'S & DON'TS

Fishing: The Escarpment and its foothills, and certain parts of the Northern Province, are prime angling areas (yellowfish, tilapia, bream, bass and, above all, trout). There is no closed season, but summer rains tend to discolour many of the streams and pools. The best angling months are from March through to September.

Fixed spool reels are prohibited; artificial non-spinning (trout) flies are mandatory. Licences are obtainable at a modest fee from major sports outlets.

Hiking: This is excellent walking country. Points to remember:

• A large number of the Mpumalanga and Northern Province trails are very popular, so it is advisable to book well in advance.

• Detailed information and comprehensive route maps are available from the South African Hiking Way Board. Satour also publishes a very useful booklet entitled *Follow the Footprints*, which is available from regional offices (*see* Advisory, page 95).

• Take warm clothing (nights can become quite chilly, especially on the Escarpment) and, during summer, rainwear; a good, strong rucksack (but one that does not weigh more than a third of your body mass when packed); woollen socks; strong and well broken-in walking shoes or boots.

• Please do not pick wild flowers (all species are protected), and please do not litter.

• Do not digress from designated routes: you could get lost, with tragic results.

• The Pietersburg Nature Reserve, close to town, is one of the largest municipal sanctuaries in the Northern Province, haven for white rhino, eland, red hartebeest, blesbok, gemsbok, impala, giraffe and Burchell's zebra.

THE CITRUS ESTATES OF ZEBEDIELA, 45 km (28 miles) east of the town of Potgietersrus (south of Pietersburg on the N1). They're the largest such estates in South Africa (more than half a million trees, 500 million oranges). Visit at harvest time: August–October for Valencias; April–June for navels.

THE SOUTPANSBERG range of hills are found in the far north, between the grasslands of the Pietersburg Plateau and the warm savanna plains of the northern bushveld. The uplands are densely wooded with exotic plantations and natural forest (yellowwood, stinkwood, wild fig, Cape chestnut, waterberry tree, cycad, tree fern) and well watered (some parts enjoy 2,000 mm (80 in) of rain a year). The attractive birdlife includes the crowned and black eagles. There are also several lovely scenic drives here, taking in the forest reserve.

In the region south of the town of Louis Trichardt is the Ben Lavin Nature Reserve. Visitor facilities include a rest camp, game drives and walks. Giraffe, zebra, impala, blue wildebeest and prolific birdlife, including Wahlberg's eagle can be observed. Accommodation: 4-bed fully equipped lodges (with bathroom); less sophisticated larger huts; caravan/camping ground; tents and stretchers can be hired.

Towards the west of Louis Trichardt, high on the southern slopes of the Soutpansberg, is Buzzard Mountain Retreat, a small, privately-run enterprise which offers pleasant cottages, scenic beauty, and forest and other trails. Towards the east is the:

HONNET NATURE RESERVE and the Tshipise resort complex, similar to its sister spa in the Hans Merensky Nature Reserve (*see* page 88). Tropical setting: floral features include flamboyant, frangipani, jacaranda, bougainvillea, and a 30- by 20-m (100 by 65 ft) baobab tree estimated to be 4,500 years old.

Among the game that can be observed are giraffe, sable, tsessebe and blue wildebeest. Amenities include a spa, hotel, self-catering chalets, swimming pools, bowling greens, riding stables, game trails and game drives, bus tours and guided horse trails. The Baobab hiking trail winds its way through the reserve.

A little over a kilometre from the resort is the Greater Kuduland Safaris luxury camp, its two bush camps and its 10,000 ha (24,700 acres) private reserve. On offer are guided game trails, hiking trails, game drives, hunting safaris, swimming and canoeing – all in somewhat exclusive style.

MESSINA

South Africa's northernmost centre, set close to the great and grey-green Limpopo River (though greater in Kiplingesque legend than in fact) is a town virtually surrounded by its nature reserve which was proclaimed to protect the huge and ancient baobabs of the area. Other tree species number about 350, some not yet identified. Within the reserve are outcrops of what is known as Sand River Gneiss. The rock strata were formed around 3,825 million years ago – when the earth itself was still comparatively young – and are among the most ancient geological formations in the world.

Some 75 km (46 miles) to the west of Messina, in the Vhembe Nature Reserve at the confluence of the Limpopo and Shahsi rivers, is: **MAPUNGUBWE HILL,** a massive rock feature accessible only by way of a concealed crevice, and a natural fortress that served as sanctuary for the people of the archaeologically important Mapungubwe culture (AD 950–1200). The area is also a magnet for naturalists, the reserve home to lion, leopard, elephant and many other species. Bungalows and tents available.

An ancient baobab tree in the Messina Reserve.

THE COUNTRY OF THE VENDA

Venda, reincorporated into South Africa during 1994, is the smallest of the four former 'homeland' independent states. People visit Venda for the lush, bright beauty of the scenery; for the gambling and fun-filled times to be had at the region's largest and most extravagant hotel, the Venda Sun; for easy access to the renowned Kruger National Park, and for a glimpse of an old culture that remains relatively intact.

THE VHA VENDA The Venda people remain something of a mystery – perhaps because they do not all share a common ancestry. Most of them are thought to have originated in the Great Lakes region of East Africa, moving in gradual migratory waves through the Congo into, and through, present-day Zimbabwe. Some may have crossed the Limpopo as early as

Decorating a pot in traditional style.

the 12th century; others stayed, and shared the power and prosperity of Great Zimbabwe before they, too, moved farther south. These were the Makhwinde group of the Rozwi, who brought with them certain elements of Zimbabwean culture (the stone enclosures, for instance) and imposed their unifying authority on the clans already living in what later became the northern Transvaal regions. Recorded history shows them as a tough and independent people, able to resist Boer incursions (and in one instance to annihilate a large Voortrekker settlement), Swazi, Pedi and Tsonga invasions.

CRAFTS Cottage industries add to the collective income – approximately 3,500 craftspeople ply their trade in Venda – and to the region's attractiveness. The products which they produce are of a high standard and good quality, especially the pottery and woodcarvings. The former is more or less restricted to large, geometrically patterned traditional pots which are ornamental as well as functional. The carvings have greater variety, the range including bowls and dishes, kieries, pots, spoons and walking sticks. For the rest, there is basketry and mat-making (raw materials used here include sisal, cane, reed, bark, and ilala palm leaves), as well as a developing school of ethnic art (painting

and, especially, sculpture). When you are in Thohoyandou, the principal centre, try to set some time aside to visit the Ditike craft centre.

EXPLORING VENDA The region is remarkable both for the variety and beauty of its scenery as well as for the beliefs and legends of its people. Probably the most striking of its natural features is Lake Fundudzi, one of the largest in southern Africa, although technically it is not a true lake but rather the product of a massive landslide that occurred aeons ago. Fundudzi is an intriguing place: swathed in myth (it is reputed to be the lair of the python god of fertility) and sinister in its associations with sacrifice, it is sacred to the people of Venda.

Water, indeed, is the essence of Venda's upland attractiveness. Streams and waterfalls (the Mahovhohovho and the Phiphidi are the most prominent, but there are many lesser ones) nurture the richly-treed hills of the Soutpansberg, which in one section is called the Thathe Vondo. Elsewhere is the Vondo Dam (well stocked with bass; visitors are welcome) and the Sacred Forest, a dense expanse of indigenous woodland that has served Venda's people as a sacrosanct burial place which visitors may look at but are not allowed to explore. Thermal springs are everywhere. One, at Sagole, is the focal point of a small resort, though perhaps the most beautiful is that at Munwamadi, which is remote and difficult for the casual visitor to locate but infinitely worthwhile if one can get there: the water bubbles up through the roots of ancient fig trees, and the setting and atmosphere is magical.

The Nwanedi National Park, approximately 65 km (40 miles) north of Thohoyandou, offers the visitor self-contained chalets, a caravan park, a restaurant and a block of comfortable family rooms. Two of the principal attractions are the twin dams, Nwanedi and Luphephe, where you can angle for yellowfish, barbel, tigerfish and kurper. Game includes white rhino, giraffe, kudu, eland, klipspringer and several other antelope species. The rest camp is shaded by lovely trees; there's a teach-yourself walking trail, and swimming in the natural pool below the waterfall.

Much of what you do and see in Venda is related to the people's spiritual heritage, some of which is only reluctantly revealed to the outsider. There are trained guides to show you around and, if you want to explore the country, you're advised to make use of them.

GETTING AROUND

DAY DRIVES River and waterfall, peak, valley and splendid viewsite – wherever you travel in the Escarpment region you'll find an embarrassment of scenic riches. There is, though, one standard, or at least widely recommended and most pleasant drive called the:

Panorama (or Summit) route, a circular drive with deviations. It varies in its details according to the traveller's preferences and available time, but generally speaking starts from Sabie and takes in: the Mac-Mac Pools and waterfall; the Lisbon Falls; God's Window; the bathing pools in the Blyde River; the Berlin Falls; the flower- and fern-festooned picnic and bathing site at Watervalspruit in the Blyderivierspoort Nature Reserve (*see* page 65); on through the extensive pine plantations to the crossroads at Vaalhoek (petrol filling station; tearoom); northwards to Bourke's Luck Potholes and the Blyde River Canyon; back down to the crossroads, bearing right along the valley of Pilgrim's Creek to Pilgrim's Rest; and on south to Sabie.

For the rest, there are a number of pleasant scenic drives in the Barberton area and truly superb ones around Waterval Boven and the Schoemanskloof Valley in the south-west and, in the north, in the woodland magic of the Magoebaskloof and New Agatha Forest region.

WALKS AND HIKES Mpumalanga and the Northern Province are a walker's paradise, and an impressive number of formal trails of varying lengths have been established.

Among those in the Escarpment region, two are especially recommended for those with energy and time to spare:
• The five-day, 65 km (40 miles) Blyderivierspoort hiking trail starts at God's Window – an unusually formed cleft, at the very edge of the Escarpment, which affords, as its name suggests, a magnificent view over the eastern lowlands – and then leads you northwards along the rim of the 'Berg', taking in the reserve and the gorge and ending at Swadini, near the Sybrand van Niekerk resort, in the Lowveld. Fairly hard going, but worth every step.
• The Fanie Botha trail is slightly longer – about 79 km (49 miles) – and also takes five days to complete. However, there are several pleasant permutations and the less energetic hiker can opt for much shorter routes. The trail meanders from the Ceylon state forest near the lovely town of Sabie, westward to the slopes of Mount Anderson (2,284 m or 7,494 ft) and then further northwards to the Mauchsberg (2,114 m or 6,936 ft), ending up with the Blyderivierspoort trail. Walkers get to see the Escarpment at its best: the path leads through the country's oldest and stateliest of the vast pine plantations, which are interspersed here and there with small patches of lovely indigenous forest. Along the way there are breathtaking vistas and, for the naturalist, a fine floral diversity (this includes tree ferns and entrancing displays of flowering plants), a great many different types of butterfly, and a number of out-of-the-ordinary bird species (among them the white stork and the crowned eagle).
• In the Waterval Boven area: the Elandskrans two-day circular hike and the shorter, one-day nature walk: waterfalls, rock pools, some lovely scenery, labelled indigenous trees, and – rather unusual – a train ride. The Elandskrans holiday resort (chalets, camping) is at the trailhead.

Among the attractive walking options in the northern region:
• In the Hans Merensky Nature Reserve: walks range from the leisurely 1 km (over half a mile) Letaba to the 37 km (23 miles) Giraffe route for the more enthusiastic hiker.
• In the Tzaneen area: the 11 km (7 miles) Rooikat nature trail leads you through the rugged Wolkberg Wilderness (*see* page 87). There is also the fairly strenuous but scenically beautiful Magoebaskloof hiking trail, which is divided into three reasonably long sections.
• In the far northern and border areas: several short rambles in the Ben Lavin Nature Reserve (*see* page 90); as well as in the Soutpansberg (*see* page 90) where a 91 km (57 miles) trail has been established – there are also shorter variations, including an 18 km (11 miles) circular walk.

TOURS A wide variety of attractive packages are on offer. The options and permutations are too numerous to allow any meaningful summary; all one can say here is that both the Escarpment and the Lowveld are well covered, with the emphasis, predictably, on the Kruger National Park. Several tour operators have working arrangements with the prestigious private reserves situated in the big-game country just to the west of the Kruger Park (*see* page 81). Information can be obtained from your travel agent or from the various tour companies. Enterprising local 'black taxi' minibus operators offer a more casual and arguably more interesting service, introducing you to the 'real' Africa.

ADVISORY: MPUMALANGA AND NORTHERN PROVINCE

CLIMATE

Summer-rainfall; hot in summer, very hot in the Lowveld. Thunderstorms in late afternoon last an hour at most. Winter: cold nights and early mornings on Escarpment; cool nights and warm days in Lowveld.

MAIN ATTRACTIONS

Game-viewing ❑ Bird-watching ❑ Scenic drives ❑ Fine fishing – trout, bream, tilapia, yellowfish, bass, barbel ❑ Hiking ❑ Rambling ❑ Horse-riding ❑ Boating in the dams ❑ Rock-collecting, especially in the Murchison range ❑ Swimming: the Escarpment and most Northern Province waters are bilharzia-free; avoid Lowveld rivers and pools; pool bathing at hotels, lodges and resorts ❑ Golf, bowls, tennis, squash: excellent facilities throughout the region.

Hunting. The Mpumalanga Lowveld is splendid big-game country. Year-round hunting facilities at several private reserves. The cooler months (March through September) are the best. There are strict rules, especially in regard to licences and quotas. The services of professional hunters, trackers, skinners and taxidermists are available; a number of firms offer organized hunting safaris. For more detailed information, contact the Professional Hunters' Association of SA (*see* Useful Addresses and Telephone Numbers, opposite page).

TRAVEL

Road. Approximate distances from Johannesburg (Pretoria in brackets): Barberton 368 km/229 miles (357 km/ 222 miles); Graskop 394 km/245 miles (370 km/ 230 miles); Louis Trichardt 441 km/275 miles (387 km/ 240 miles); Lydenburg 323km/201 miles (299 km/ 186 miles); Messina 534km/332 miles (480 km/ 298 miles); Nelspruit 358 km/222 miles (334 km/ 208 miles); Numbi gate (Kruger) 409 km/255 miles (385 km/239 miles); Orpen gate (Kruger) 519 km/ 323 miles (495km/308 miles); Phalaborwa 510 km/ 317 miles (483 km/300 miles); Pietersburg 331 km/ 206 miles (277 km/172 miles); Potgietersrus 274 km/ 170 miles (220 km/137 miles); Punda Maria 581 km/ 361 miles (527 km/327 miles); Sabie 379 km/235 miles (360 km/224 miles); Skukuza 486 km/302 miles (442 km/275 miles); Tzaneen 422 km/262 miles (368 km/230 miles); Warmbaths 156 km/97 miles (102 km/63 miles).

The region has an excellent network of roads. From Johannesburg to Nelspruit and the Escarpment, take the R22 and then the N4 near Witbank. From Pretoria, take the N4 direct. From Nelspruit north into the Escarpment, take the R40, then follow signs. For the northern and north-eastern regions, take the N1 from Pretoria, turn right at Pietersburg on the R71 for the Tzaneen area and the central Kruger (Phalaborwa); for the Venda region and the northern Kruger, turn right at Louis Trichardt on the R524.

Car and minibus hire: There are Avis offices at Skukuza; tel. (01311) 65611.

Coach travel: A luxury coach service operates from Johannesburg to Nelspruit. Consult your travel agent.

Air. Scheduled flights link Johannesburg with Skukuza and Nelspruit. Comair (which maintains its own park lodge) operates large-group excursions from major centres. Many private reserves have their own airstrips.

ACCOMMODATION

ESCARPMENT AREA

Hotel accommodation is available in Sabie and Lydenburg, and there are some pleasant, mostly small, country hotels and lodges within easy driving distance.

Select Hotels

Hulala Lakeside Lodge *** Overlooking Degama lake. Elegant country-house atmosphere and hospitality. PO Box 1382, White River 1240; central reservations tel. (011) 788-1258.

Mount Sheba **** 23 km (14 miles) west of Pilgrim's Rest. Medium-small luxury hotel, time-share; set in forest reserve (*see* page 70). Cottages, suites; conference facilities; outstanding cuisine. PO Box 100, Pilgrim's Rest 1290; tel. (01315) 8-1241, fax 8-1248.

Critchley Hackle Lodge *** Dullstroom. Small (10-suite) stone luxury getaway; cosy; patronized by trout fishermen; cordon bleu cuisine. PO Box 141, Dullstroom 1110; tel. (01325) 4-0145,fax 4-0262.

Cybele Forest Lodge **** Deep forest setting not far from Hulala. Cosy cottage-style rooms; superb cuisine. PO Box 346, White River 1240; tel. (01311) 5-0511, fax 3-2839.

Jatinga Country Lodge Graciously converted farmstead; 'rondavels'; famous cuisine. PO Box 77, Plaston 1244; tel. (01311) 3-1932, fax 3-2364.

KRUGER NATIONAL PARK

Details of the rest camps appear on pages 73–78. Reservations for accommodation and wilderness trails: The Chief Director, National Parks Board Reservations, PO Box 787, Pretoria 0001; tel. (012) 343-1991; or Cape Town: PO Box 7400, Rogge Bay 8012; tel. (021) 22-2810; or southern Cape: PO Box 774, George 6530; tel. (0441) 74-6924/5; or visit the National Parks Board offices in Leyds St, Muckleneuk, Pretoria. Book well in advance, the park is very popular. Indicate your preference for camp or camps, and accommodation. Reduced rates for senior citizens. The Parks Board will send a voucher which should be presented when entering the Kruger and the camp. Rest camp bookings are flexible: one can relocate, after entering the park, through reception.

WEST OF THE KRUGER

Select Hotels

Casa Do Sol **** Hazyview area. Imaginative: as much a small village as a hotel; cobbled walkways, patios, courtyards, fountains, archways, Cordoba-tiled roofs. Plenty for guests; lovely grounds; conference facilities. PO Box 57, Hazyview 1242; tel. (01317) 6811.

Impala Inn *** Close to Phalaborwa gate. 49 rooms; conference facilities for 80. PO Box 139, Phalaborwa 1390; tel. (01524) 5681/2, fax 8-5234.

Malaga Hotel *** In Elands River Valley. Mediterranean-style design; 50 suites; conference facilities; good trout fishing. PO Box 136, Waterval Boven 1195; central reservations (011) 880-4032.

Malelane Sun Lodge **** Luxury hotel on Crocodile River, near Kruger's Malelane gate. 100 rooms, 2 suites; conference facilities for 150. PO Box 392, Malelane 1320; central reservations (011) 482-3500.

Paragon *** In Nelspruit. 45 rooms; conference facilities for 70; pool. PO Box 81, Nelspruit 1200; tel. and fax (01311) 5-3205/6/7/8.

Pine Lake Sun **** Set on lake in White River area. Good sports facilities, golf. En suite rooms; conference facilities for 80. PO Box 94, White River 1240; central reservations (011) 482-3500, fax (01311) 3-3874.

Sabi River Sun **** Close to Kruger gate. Subtropical grounds, 18-hole golf course, en suite rooms; conference facilities available. PO Box 13, Hazyview 1242; tel. (0131242) ask for 160 or central reservations; central reservations (011) 482-3500; fax (01317) 6-7314.

Hotel Winkler **** White River area. Spacious grounds; own farm and dam; unusual architecture; en suite rooms; conference facilities. PO Box 12, White River 1240; tel. (01311) 3-2317/8/9, fax 3-1393.

Private Reserves

Some are described on pages 81–82. Information and bookings: contact the lodges direct, your travel agent or Sights of Africa; tel. (011) 883-4345, fax 883-2556.

NORTHERN REGIONS

The Aventura organization administers the complex at Warmbaths, the resort and hotel complexes of Eiland (Hans Merensky Reserve) and Tshipise (Honnet Reserve). Central reservations: PO Box 720, Groenkloof 0027; tel. (012) 346-2277, fax 346-2293.

Select Hotels

The Coach House Hotel ***** Consistently adjudged South Africa's best country hotel; set above the New Agatha State Forest outside Tzaneen; prides itself on its exclusivity; personal attention is lavished on guests. 35 rooms, all with splendid views of mountain and forest; five-star cuisine. Conference facilities are available. PO Box 544, Tzaneen 0850; tel. (0152) 307-3641, fax 307-1466.

Holiday Inn Garden Court: Pietersburg *** 179 en suite rooms; conference facilities. PO Box 784, Pietersburg 0700; tel. (01521) 91-2030, fax 91-3150, central reservations (011) 482-3500.

Magoebaskloof *** Between Tzaneen and Haenertsburg. Overlooking wooded kloof; first-class; country hotel cuisine. 58 en suite rooms; conference facilities. PO Magoebaskloof 0731; tel. (015276) 42-7618.

Protea Park Hotel *** 28 km (17 miles) to the south of Potgietersrus. 18-hole golf course; en suite rooms; conference facilities. PO Box 1551, Potgietersrus 0600; tel. (0154) 3101/2, fax 6842, toll-free 0800 11 9000.

Ranch *** On the N1 near Pietersburg. Largish and lively hotel; plenty laid on for guests; 2 restaurants; bars; en suite rooms; conference facilities. PO Box 77, Pietersburg 0700; tel. (01521) 293-7180, fax 293-7188.

Venda Sun Hotel and Casino, Thohoyandou. Halfway between Louis Trichardt and northern Kruger. Smaller link in the Sun International chain; tropical setting; splendid pool area; restaurants; animated casino. En suite rooms; four bars; conference facilities available. PO Box 766, Sibasa; tel. (01591) 2-1011, fax 2-1367, central reservations (011) 783-8750.

Private Reserves

Mabula Game Lodge *** 35 km (22 miles) west of Warmbaths. One of the best-stocked, most enterprising and hospitable private game parks' lodges. Game includes the 'big five'. Private Bag 1665, Warmbaths 0480; tel. (014734) 717 or 616, fax 733.

Self-catering

The region is well served by resorts, lodges, self-catering venues and caravan/camping parks, many of which offer chalets and cottages. **Satour** and the local information offices have the details.

Kruger National Park: Superb accommodation in luxury or standard self-catering units and caravan/camping sites. Bookings: Chief Director, National Parks Board, PO Box 787, Pretoria 0001; tel. (012) 343-1991; or PO Box 7400, Rogge Bay 8012; tel. (021) 22-2810.

USEFUL ADDRESSES AND TELEPHONE NUMBERS

Barberton Publicity Bureau, tel. (01314) 2-2121.
Lydenburg Tourist Information, tel. (01323) 2121.
Messina Tourist Information, tel. (01553) 2206.
Pietersburg Tourist Information, tel. (0152) 295-3025.
Pilgrim's Rest Tourist Information, tel. (01315) 81261.
Potgietersrus Tourist Information, tel. (0154) 2244.
Professional Hunters' Association of SA, PO Box 770, Cramerview 2060; tel. (011) 706-7724.
Gauteng Division of Nature Conservation, Private Bag X209, Pretoria 0001; tel. (012) 323-3403.
Tzaneen Tourist Information, tel. (0152) 307-1411.
Warmbaths Tourist Information, tel. (014) 736-3694.

THE NORTH-WEST

The region west of the Pretoria-Johannesburg axis – given political identity in 1994 as the North-West province – is one of the greatest granaries of southern Africa. Here the soils are deep and fertile and, when the rains are generous, hugely productive, yielding a bounty comparable to that from the world's richest food-growing lands. A vast, hot, flattish country of bushveld and thorn, of lonely farmsteads shaded by eucalyptus and bright green willow, of fields of sunflowers and groundnuts, tobacco and citrus, maize, maize and more maize, and villages that sleep soundly in the sun.

Towards the east, though, the horizons change, the land ascending to the heights of the Magaliesberg, a modest but nevertheless attractive and, in places, enchanting range of hills which, each weekend, plays amiable host to thousands of city-dwellers.

To the north of the Magaliesberg there are attractions of a quite different kind: the splendid Pilanesberg National Park and, nearby, the glittering Sun City hotel-casino complex, one of the world's most lavish resorts.

OPPOSITE: *Visitors cool off in the Valley of Waves' giant pool, with its artificial beach, at Sun City's Lost City complex.*
BELOW: *Boaters at the Hartbeespoort Dam.*

HARTBEESPOORT DAM

The dam, fed by the Magalies and Crocodile rivers and a perennial playground of the Witwatersrand's city dwellers, lies among the foothills of the Magaliesberg range 35 km (20 miles) to the west of Pretoria. The waters cover roughly 12 km² (4.5 square miles) of attractive countryside (about 45 km/28 miles of canals irrigate the surrounding farmlands) and the area is a favourite haunt of watersports, angling and boating enthusiasts, weekenders, family day-trippers, caravanners and campers, and the more popular recreational spots can be quite crowded and noisy. However, there are some lovely corners where you can relax in peace; and the views you get from the road that winds around the perimeter, and from the cableway that leads to the eastern Magaliesberg's highest point, are most pleasant. Specific points of interest include the:

HARTBEESPOORT DAM NATURE RESERVE, comprising the dam itself as well as a scatter of small conservation areas, though the indigenous vegetation (mixed bushveld, with white stinkwood, wild olive and other notable tree species) is hard put to withstand the substantial human presence. The Oberon segment is noted for its birdlife and the Kommandonek portion has an enclosed game camp (game includes kudu, bushbuck and zebra). Both these areas have camping grounds, and there are chalets at the nearby Hartbeespoort resort.

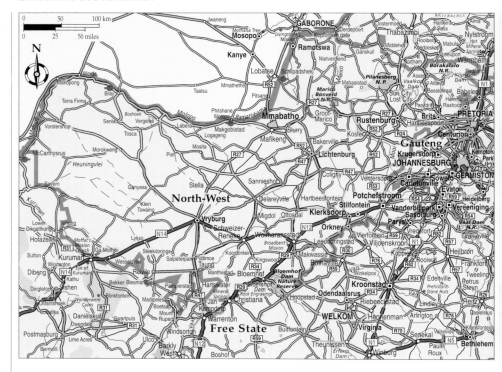

AQUARIUM, 3 km (2 miles) from the dam: local and exotic freshwater fish, performing seals, waterbirds and crocodiles. Open daily.

ZOO AND SNAKE PARK, boasting reptiles and a variety of animals; snake, chimpanzee and seal 'shows' are held on Sundays and public holidays; the zoo serves as the starting point for ferry trips around the dam. Open daily.

TAN' MALIE SE WINKEL (Aunt Malie's Shop), near the dam wall, sells all manner of traditional and specialist goodies, including handicrafts, pottery, curios, preserves and farm food.

THE MAGALIESBERG

The ridge of the Magaliesberg runs from a point near Pretoria due westwards for about 120 km (75 miles) to and just beyond the attractive country town of Rustenburg.

It isn't by any definition a major range of hills – it rises little more than 300 m (984 ft) above the surrounding and rather flattish countryside – but it has a woodland beauty of its own and, in the more precipitous parts, even grandeur. Below the ridge, the land lies at a lower level than that of the Witwatersrand to

the east, and the climate is kind: the air warm and limpid even in winter, and the rainfall relatively high, feeding the many streams and rivulets that tumble down the slopes and into the park-like valleys. The warmth and the water sustain the region's wonderfully rich crops of peaches and oranges, tobacco, subtropical fruits, vegetables and flowers.

The Magaliesberg is one of the last remaining havens of the shy and stately Cape vulture, a species now on the endangered list: the birds depend on the bones of carcasses crunched to digestible size by the strong jaws of the hyaena, and hyaenas have all but disappeared from the North-West, pushed out by the encroaching farmlands. But the vultures may still be seen, wheeling elegantly in the thermals above the hills. They are largely sustained by the 'vulture restaurants' established in the area and, in the breeding season (May to October), by their forays into such game-rich terrain as the Pilanesberg National Park to the north (*see page 101*).

Predictably, the Magaliesberg area is something of a magnet for people who live in the suffocating urban jungles of the Witwatersrand, just an hour's drive away. Some of these visitors come for its strategic position – its western end is conveniently placed halfway between the Johannesburg-Pretoria conurbation and Sun City to the north (*see* page 102), but most are enticed by the tranquillity of the hills and valleys, by the lovely scenic drives and gentle walks, by the charm of the vistas, and by the generally outstanding hospitality of the hotels and lodges of the area. Among the more pleasant of these are Valley Lodge, Hunter's Rest, and Mount Grace Country House, one of southern Africa's most inviting country hideaways.

COTTAGE CRAFTS The peace and beauty of the Magaliesberg and, closer to Johannesburg, the valley of the Crocodile River have attracted a wealth of artistic talent – sculptors and painters, potters and cabinet-makers, cutlers and workers in leather, stone, wood and textiles have settled in the area in their dozens, their cottage-studios yielding a delightful number and variety of highly individualistic and often exquisite products. Much of this can be seen and enjoyed along a popular and informal 'route' known as the Crocodile River Arts and Crafts Ramble: the studios welcome visitors, artists and crafters keep open house during the first weekend of each month, and can provide visitors with a map of the general area showing the specific venues.

RUSTENBURG

A substantial country town at the western end of, and overlooked by, the red-tinged heights of the Magaliesberg range, Rustenburg is a pleasant 112 km (70 miles) drive from Johannesburg, 105 km (65 miles) from Pretoria. The name means 'town of rest' and was well chosen, for this is indeed a relaxing and attractive place. The countryside around is well watered, blessed with an average nine hours of sunshine a day throughout the year, and these elements combine to nurture a marvellous profusion of exotic plants in street and garden: jacaranda and frangipani, hibiscus, poinciana and poinsettia and billows of bougainvillea.

The area has a significant place in the annals of Afrikanerdom. It was here that the two head-strong Voortrekker rivals, Andries Pretorius and Andries Hendrik Potgieter, finally – in 1852 – made their peace with each other. And here, seven years later, under a syringa tree in town (a granite replica of the stump now marks the spot), the Reformed Church was founded as a

body separate from the bigger Dutch Reformed Church. To the former belonged Paul Kruger, patriarch of the Transvaal during the later 19th century. Kruger settled on the farm Boekenhout-fontein in the 1860s, and some 30 ha (74 acres) of the property – on which stand a cottage dating from 1841 (the oldest surviving house in the province), Oom Paul's original homestead and a house the old man built for his son – have been preserved as a museum. Among other features of interest in and around town are:

KWAGGAPAN PARK, on the eastern outskirts: giraffe and buck; lovely views from the lookout tower and picnic spots.

MOUNTAIN SANCTUARY PARK, a lovely scenic area some way to the east of town, attracts the keener naturalist and rock-climber. The area is distinguished by its deep ravines, crystal pools and waterfalls.

OLIFANTSNEK DAM, a 3,000 ha (7,400 acres) lake that irrigates the surrounding citrus and tobacco plantations. The dam wall, 1,344 m (4,400 ft) of 24-m-high (79 ft) concrete, captures the rush of the Hex River as it plunges through a narrow mountain pass. Pleasant teas are served, and the views from the hotel on the banks of the lake are superb; even more splendid views unfold from the Olifantsnek Pass.

RUSTENBURG NATURE RESERVE, a 4,250 ha (10,500 acres) expanse of upland terrain straddling part of the Magaliesberg's northern plateau (it was established on the farm Rietvlei, which also belonged to Paul Kruger). The reserve is distinguished by its striking land-scapes, its steep rock faces, tumbling streams and attractive patches of syringa, acacia and boekenhout. Among the 115 different types of tree and bush are a number of rare species – the succulent *Frithia pulchra* for instance, and *Aloe peglerae*. Among the wide variety of animals to be seen are the oribi, reedbuck, mountain reed-buck, kudu, sable and, if you're lucky, leopard, brown hyaena and black-backed jackal. More than 230 bird species have been recorded, among them the black and martial eagles; a Cape vulture breeding colony has made its home just to the east of the reserve.

For the more energetic visitor, there is the two-day Rustenburg hiking trail; for those who wish to explore at a more leisurely pace there is the 3 km (2 miles), self-guided, circular Peglerae stroll. Other facilities include an information centre, several well-appointed picnic spots and a caravan/camping ground.

MAMPOER COUNTRY

The Marico district extends from the village of Groot Marico to Mafikeng in the west and from a line through the Bakerville area to Zeerust and beyond in the north. The region has been enshrined in South Africa's literary annals by the eccentric genius of Herman Charles Bosman, who lived and worked and set some of his finest stories in and around Marico: it was here, among the lucerne and maize fields, the tobacco lands and orange groves, that the simple, earthy characters of *Mafikeng Road* and *Jurie Steyn's Post Office* played out their whimsical parts, speaking in English but conveying the essence of rural Afrikaans. And it is an area long famed for the quality of its mampoer, a powerful home-brew distilled by the practised hands of the locals from peaches, apricots and other fruit (though not from grapes), and from karee-tree berries, a variety that, said Bosman's Oom Schalk Lourens, 'is white and soft to look at, and the smoke that comes from it when you pull the cork out of the bottle is pale and rises up in slow curves ...'.

A 'mampoer route' has been established, which helps give visitors some sort of focus on the area. This circular tour, starting and ending at the Groot Marico Information Centre, lasts from 10h00 to 16h00. Besides introducing outsiders to the secrets of the distilling process, it takes in a demonstration of whip-plaiting, a traditional lunch at a Marico Kloof farm, and an outing along the Marico River. Contact the Groot Marico Information Centre.

THE FAR WEST

The big country beyond Rustenburg, to the west, tends to be ignored by the holiday-maker and visiting tourist, and perhaps with good reason: it's a sun-blistered, unadorned, functional region, largely the preserve of hardy farmers who do daily battle with a land that is often harsh and unforgiving. In good summers, when the rains arrive on time, the cattle fatten and the maize fields stretch green and pleasant to far horizons, but too often there is drought, and life is a struggle. So tourism doesn't rate too high among local priorities.

Still, for those with time and petrol to spare and a liking for silence, sunlit spaces and sleepy villages, it's certainly worth exploring.

LICHTENBURG

A modern country town, Lichtenburg is notable for its gracious karee-shaded central square, on which stands a striking equestrian statue of General Koos de la Rey, the 'Lion of the North', who fought the British to a standstill in the early part of the South African War and then led his commandos with distinction in the guerrilla campaigns that followed.

The Lichtenburg area, and more specifically the farm Elandsputte to the north, provided the setting for one of the world's last and greatest diamond rushes. News of the first find broke in March 1926 and spread like wildfire, and within months over 100,000 diggers were working the alluvial ground (and scarring it for ever); at the height of the boom more than 30,000 people took part in an official claim-pegging race – a single, frenzied mass scramble for the wealth of the bushveld. Some splendid stones were unearthed, but the madness lasted a bare decade, and by the mid-1930s Lichtenburg had settled back into its older, quieter routines. Displayed in the town's museum are some fascinating relics and mementos of the diamond years.

Lichtenburg also boasts an unusual nature reserve, a 6,000 ha (14,800 acres) area that serves as a breeding centre for the National Zoological Gardens. Among its rare and exotic species are Hartmann's mountain zebra, pygmy hippo, scimitar oryx, Indian water-buffalo, Père David's and axis deer – altogether, 35 species of mammal. There's also a cheetah enclosure, and shallow pans near the reserve's entrance attract a large number and variety of waterbird. Open throughout the year.

Some 80 km (50 miles) to the south-west of Lichtenburg, on the R47, is the:

BARBERSPAN NATURE RESERVE, one of the country's largest waterfowl sanctuaries, central feature of which is an 1,800 ha (4,500 acres) pan nurtured by the Harts River. Here one can see a hugely prolific birdlife – some 350 species in all, including heron, redknobbed coot, egret, wader, wild duck and great flocks of flamingos. Bird-watchers are able to use the hide specially constructed for visitors, or stroll along the prepared trail. There are also several picnic sites and angling spots, and a camping ground.

NORTH OF RUSTENBURG

On the R565 from Rustenburg you'll enter a region that until 1994 was an independent 'homeland' republic, though its autonomy, granted by the apartheid government, wasn't recognized outside southern Africa. It was known as Bophuthatswana, meaning 'that which binds the Tswana'.

The name was carefully chosen: the Tswana people comprise some 60 different groups who speak the same language and, in general, share a cultural heritage but otherwise tend to be clannish. The local Tswana are kinsmen of the people of Botswana further to the north, and of the Sotho of Lesotho far to the south-east.

The region looks poor, and a great many of its inhabitants do indeed live in poverty, but in fact the land is wealthy: it contains much of the earth's prized platinum-group metals. Of these, rhodium, palladium and platinum itself are the most valuable, finding their way into jewellery, electronics, precision instruments, laboratory ware and into car exhaust systems.

PILANESBERG NATIONAL PARK

One of the strangest of southern Africa's geological features rises skywards from the flat northern plains. This is the Pilanesberg range, an aeons-old relic of volcanic convulsion that comprises a series of four concentric mountain rings. The loftiest peak is the Pilanesberg itself, towering 600 m (2,000 ft) above Mankwe Lake. Mankwe is situated at the dead centre of the volcano's bowl, a circular area 27 km (17 miles) in diameter and site of the huge, 55,000 ha (136,000 acres) national park – one of southern Africa's major tourist attractions.

White rhinos in the Pilanesberg National Park.

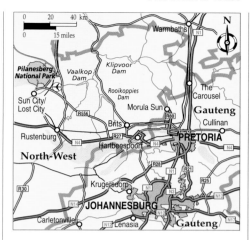

This reserve is the product of 'Operation Genesis', launched in 1979 and among the most successful of the world's game-stocking enterprises. Eland were brought in from Namibia, zebra and waterbuck from Mpumalanga, white and black rhino from KwaZulu-Natal, and elephant and buffalo from the Eastern Cape's Addo Park. Today 10,000 head of game graze, browse, hunt and scavenge on the grasslands and in the bush and wooded valleys of the Pilanesberg. They include, in addition to the animals mentioned, giraffe, hippo, kudu, sable, gemsbok, red hartebeest, tsessebe, waterbuck, warthog, leopard, cheetah, lion, and the rare brown hyaena. The Pilanesberg is one of the few southern African parks that contain a near-complete assembly of the area's original fauna.

Flora includes the rare Transvaal red balloon tree (*Erythrophysa transvaalensis*), of which about a hundred specimens grow in the park and less than 10 elsewhere. There are 100 km (62 miles) of game-viewing roads, hides and picnic spots.

Accommodation includes one hutted rest camp, three bush camps, a caravanning complex which also incorporates permanent accommodation, and a 'dormitory' camp for larger groups. In the middle of the park is the Pilanesberg Centre (excellent restaurant, shop and informative displays), a lovely old building that once served as the local magistrate's court.

The Pilanesberg also embraces two private lodges, Kwa Maritane and Bakubung, which are sited to serve two purposes: they provide comfortable bases from which to enjoy a taste of the bushveld and also to sample the delights of Sun City, just a few minutes' drive away.

SUN CITY AND THE LOST CITY

Sun City is the flagship of the Sun International fleet of hotel-casino resorts, a glamorous pleasure-ground for the privileged that is set, rather incongruously, in one of the bleaker, less developed parts of the country. But for all the contrast, the frivolous splendour among the poverty, it has in fact proved a blessing, generating jobs and a sustained and welcome flow of money into the region.

What Sun City sets out to do – divert, amuse, entertain and spoil the holiday-maker – it does on a grand scale, and in style. Its major components are:
• Four hotels, each designed for different pockets and preferences. They range from the family-orientated Cabanas through the middle-of-the-range Sun City Hotel and the plush Cascades to the new, ultra-sophisticated Palace of the Lost City.

The Cascades is a five-star, 15-storey establishment embraced by exquisite grounds: more than 50,000 m² (540,000 ft²) of the surrounding countryside have been landscaped to produce a sculpted fantasia of lawn, pool, grotto, waterfall, tropical plant and exotic birdlife.

The Palace is the centrepiece of The Lost City, a recent development that elevates the combined complex to the ranks of the world's biggest and most opulent inland resorts. The hotel, an elaborate affair of domes and minarets, columns and curlicues reminiscent (vaguely) of the Raj at its most extravagant, has 350 luxurious rooms and suites, an entrance hall rising three storeys, several excellent restaurants (one of them set on an island girded by cascades of water, another embowered by jungle foliage), a 100 by 60 m (330 by 200 ft) swimming pool with its own beach and 1.8-m-high (6 ft) artificially created surfing waves, and an 'instant jungle', which it shares with the Entertainment Centre (*see* below), of 3,500 trees.
• Indoor amenities. The Entertainment Centre is a vibrant concentration of restaurants, bars, discos, speciality shops, conference rooms, cinemas, slot machines and a massive 200-seat computerized bingo hall. Its core is the Superbowl, used for conventions, banquets (seating for 3,500), extravagant promotions, big-name shows (Frank Sinatra, Liza Minelli, Elton John and Queen have performed there) and international events (title fights, Miss World Beauty Pageant). The Casino, which is part of the Sun City Hotel, offers the standard gaming range plus the ubiquitous slot machines, a salon privé (punto banco and chemmy) for devotees, and the 620-seat Extravaganza Theatre.
• Outdoor amenities. These include tennis, squash, bowls, horse-riding, swimming and tenpin bowling. There is also an animal farm for the children, as well as game-viewing in the Pilanesberg National Park (conducted drives) and in the next-door Letsatsing Reserve. The Gary Player Country Club boasts a top-class 18-hole golf course that has hosted most of the world's greatest golfers and is the venue for the annual Million Dollar Golf Challenge. A second Arizona-style golf course which is a more recent addition forms part of The Lost City complex. Some of the hazards include live crocodiles!

Sun City's grounds are magnificent. The Valley of Waves incorporates 22 different regions of vegetation, from a rocky outcrop of ancient baobab trees to lush tropical jungle. Strollers are also enticed to the Waterscape, a huge arrangement of interlinked pools, a kilometre (3,300 ft) of low weirs and two kilometres (6,600 ft) of walkways that lead through gardens and over, and under, rock formations. The entire area is spectacularly illuminated at night.

A great deal of activity revolves around Waterworld, situated below the Cabanas. This beautiful, 750-km-long (466 mile) man-made lake was designed for both the idler and the sporting enthusiast. Facilities include water-skiing, wind-surfing, parasailing, jet-skiing and so on.

Well worth a visit is the Kwena Crocodile Garden (it's at the entrance gate), a reptile park and ranch distinguished by its dramatically 'ethnic' architecture, its luxuriantly tropical surrounds, and by the giant Nile crocodiles it contains.

OPPOSITE: *The attractively embowered swimming pool of the Cascades Hotel.*
TOP: *The grand Palace of the Lost City is the centrepiece of Sun City's Lost City complex.*
ABOVE: *Putting on the Arizona-style Lost City golf course, designed by Gary Player.*
ABOVE RIGHT: *The Entertainment Centre – hub of Sun City's vibrant nightlife.*
RIGHT: *Eye-catching statuary, like the Temple of Creation, graces the grounds of the Lost City.*
OVERLEAF: *The elaborate entrance hall to the Palace, with its domed ceiling covered with breathtaking murals of Africa's wildlife.*

ADVISORY: THE NORTH-WEST

CLIMATE

Summer rainfall. Climate is similar to Johannesburg and Pretoria (*see* page 57) but generally warmer and, in the west, drier.

MAIN ATTRACTIONS

Sightseeing ❑ Walking, trailing, rock-climbing ❑ Horse-riding ❑ Game-viewing ❑ Bird-watching ❑ Angling ❑ Watersports ❑ Golf ❑ Gambling.

TRAVEL

Road. Good tarred roads to all centres. Approximate distances from Johannesburg (Pretoria in brackets): Krugersdorp 29 km/18 miles (82 km/51 miles); Rustenburg 116 km/72 miles (105 km/65 miles); Sun City 167 km/104 miles (152 km/94 miles); Potchefstroom 113 km/70 miles (185 km/115 miles); Klerksdorp 182 km/113 miles (214 km/133 miles); Lichtenburg 215 km/134 miles (251 km/156 miles); Mmabatho 285 km/177 miles (330 km/205 miles).
Coach travel: Daily trips between Johannesburg and Sun City. Information: book through Computicket; tel. (011) 331-9991, or contact your travel agent for further details.
Air. Sun Air flights from Johannesburg International Airport to Sun City; day excursions. Information: contact Sun International or Sun Air; tel. (011) 970-1623.

ACCOMMODATION
Select hotels

RUSTENBURG AND MAGALIESBERG AREA
Cashane Hotel Rustenberg. 48 rooms; conference facilities. PO Box 1487, Rustenberg 0300; tel. (0142) 2-8541.
Hunter's Rest Hotel Excellent 90-room country hotel; conference facilities. PO Box 775, Rustenberg 0300; tel. (0142) 9-2140, fax 9-2661.
Karos Safari Hotel *** Rustenburg Kloof. 125 en suite rooms; à la carte and buffet restaurants; bar; 2 pools; bowls; tennis; squash; conference facilities available. PO Box 687, Rustenburg 0300; tel. (0142) 97-1361.
Magaliesburg Country Hotel *** In garden setting. 20 en suite rooms; à la carte and carvery restaurants; 2 bars; pool; squash; sauna. PO Box 4, Magaliesburg 2805; tel. and fax (0142) 77-1109.
Mount Grace Country House **** In Magaliesberg. 60 rooms/suites in stone cottages; 2 restaurants; bar; classical music concerts; pool; bowls; conference facilities available. PO Box 251, Magaliesburg 2805; tel. and fax (0142) 77-1350.
Sparkling Waters Hotel *** In Rietfontein Valley. 56 en suite rooms; table d'hôte restaurant; bar; pool; tennis; squash; bowls. PO Box 208, Rustenburg 0300; tel. (0142) 75-0151, fax 75-0190.

Valley Lodge **** 55 thatched en suite cottages and rondavels on river; restaurant; 2 bars; pool; fishing; canoeing; game-viewing; bird-watching; conferences. PO Box 13, Magaliesburg 2805; tel. (0142) 77-1301, fax 77-1306, toll-free reservations 0800 120 777.

THE SUN CITY COMPLEX
Sun City Cabanas On the lake. 380 en suite rooms; steakhouse; self-service restaurants; 3 bars; swimming pool; animal farm; tennis; squash; bowls; horse-riding. PO Box 3, Sun City 0316; tel. (01465) 2-1000, fax 7-4227, central reservations (011) 780-7800.
Sun City Cascades Hotel 233 rooms, 10 suites; 2 restaurants; 2 bars; shops; pool; golf; tennis; squash; horse-riding. PO Box 7, Sun City 0316; tel. (01465) 2-1000, fax 2-1483, central reservations (011) 780-7800.
Sun City Hotel and Casino Five-stars all round; 332 en suite rooms, 8 suites; superb à la carte and buffet restaurants; 7 bars; casino; swimming pool; health spa; conference facilities available. PO Box 2, Sun City 0316; tel. (01465) 2-1000, fax 7-4210, central reservations (011) 780-7800.
Sundown Ranch Hotel *** Close to Sun City. 101 en suite rooms; à la carte restaurant; 2 bars; 100 ha (247 acres) lion park; pool; tennis; horse-riding; conference facilities available. PO Box 139, Boshoek 0301; tel. (0142) 73-3121, fax 73-3114.
The Palace of the Lost City Ultra-luxurious; 322 en suite rooms, 16 suites; superb restaurants; bars; casino; Valley of Waves; Olympic and surf pool; golf and much else. PO Box 308, Sun City 0316; tel. (01465) 7-3000, fax 7-3111, central reservations (011) 780-7800.

Self-catering

The Magaliesberg region is well served by resorts, lodges and caravan/camping grounds (most of which also offer self-catering accommodation). Contact Satour or the Rustenburg Publicity and Tourism Bureau for details.
Lover's Rock Family Resort, tel. (0142) 77-1327/8.
Montana Guest Farm, tel. (0142) 75-0113.
Olifantsnek Country Hotel, tel. (0142) 9-2208.
Omaramba Holiday Resort, tel. (0142) 72-3004.
Rustenburg Kloof Holiday Resort, tel. (0142) 97-1351.
Rustenburg Nature Reserve, tel. (0142) 3-1050.
Utopia Resort, tel. (0142) 75-0352.

USEFUL ADDRESSES AND TELEPHONE NUMBERS

Automobile Association, Rustenburg; tel. (0142) 2-4990/2-0170.
Krugersdorp Publicity Association, PO Box 1575, Krugersdorp 1740; tel. (011) 953-3727.
Rustenburg Publicity and Tourism Bureau, Municipal Offices, Plein St, Rustenburg 0300; tel. (0142) 97-3111.
Sun International Group, Johannesburg Head Office, PO Box 784487, Sandton 2146; tel. (011) 780-1444, central reservations (011) 780-7800.

THE FREE STATE

The province comprises a predominantly flat, mostly treeless and rather bleak 130,000 km² (50,000 square miles) expanse of grassland plains country straddling the east-central portion of the great interior plateau.

A substantial section of the Free State's southern boundary is formed by the Orange River, far and away the country's biggest watercourse and the prime element in an enormous water storage and distribution network. Two of the largest dams in South Africa have been built along its course.

The plains of the central plateau slope gently towards the south-west, bare, desolate and windswept for the most part, the visual tedium only occasionally relieved by dykes and sills of dolerite *koppies* (rocky outcrops). Surface water is scarce, but the soils are deep and rich, the grasses sweet, nurturing great numbers of sheep and cattle.

OPPOSITE: *The long road home: a villager wends his way through eastern Free State countryside.*

By contrast, the land in the east is scenically spectacular, rising in magnificent fashion in a series of picturesquely weathered sandstone hills. This too is a fertile region, kind to the growers of maize and wheat, golden sunflowers, vegetables and fruit (cherries and yellow peaches are prominent harvests).

Indeed, the Free State is one of the wealthier segments of the subcontinent: in addition to its agricultural bounty it has massive mineral resources. Gold, diamonds, platinum and coal are mined in the province; the goldfields, around Welkom, are among the world's biggest; the coalfields supply the world's first viable synthetic fuel plant, established in 1951 at Sasolburg in the far north.

The capital of the Free State, and South Africa's judicial capital, is Bloemfontein, situated at an altitude of 1,392 m (4,567 ft) above sea level and astride the national north-south highway (the N1) that connects Cape Town with Johannesburg, Pretoria and beyond. Of the province's few other major urban centres, the mining city of Welkom is the largest, followed by Kroonstad and Sasolburg and, in the eastern areas, Bethlehem and Harrismith.

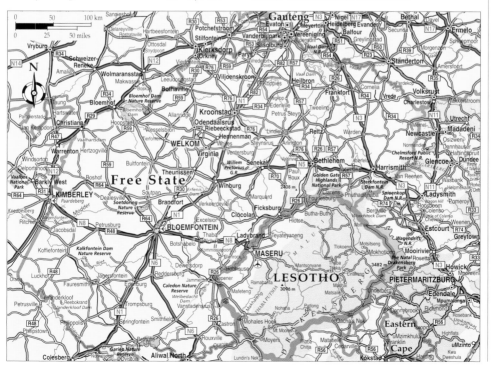

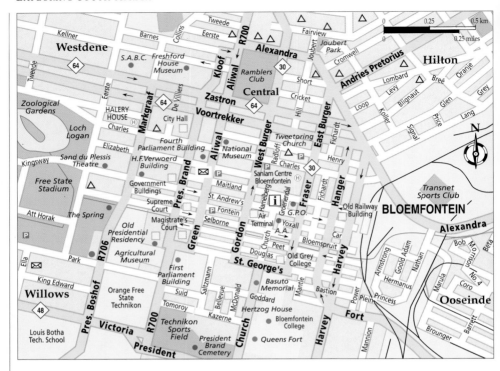

BLOEMFONTEIN

The origin of the city's name is something of a mystery: the obvious explanation is that 'flower fountain' refers to a very attractive spring close to the Modder River, but it seems more likely that it commemorates a cow called Bloem, which was owned by trekker Rudolph Brits, who had settled in the area in 1840. Bloem was in the habit of jumping fences and eventually she paid the penalty: she was caught by a lion. Brits is said to have named his farm after the late, unfortunate and lamented animal.

The property was bought (for just £37.10s) by the local British agent and, in 1854, its modest cluster of houses became the capital of the new Orange Free State republic – and a tiny capital it was: the first village management board met to deliberate on civic matters only in 1859; the first national parliament building, or *raadsaal*, was a small, single-storeyed, thatched structure that had previously served as the village school.

But the place developed, solidly and undramatically, around Naval Hill (so called since the South African War of 1899–1902, when the British soldiers mounted naval guns on its crest). Close proximity to the diamond fields of the Northern Cape and, a short while later, during the 1880s and 1890s, to the then seemingly inexhaustable gold mines of the Witwatersrand, contributed much to Bloemfontein's prosperity; so too did its position on the routes north from the coastal ports, and an array of fine buildings were completed during this period. Excellent examples of this architecture are the new Raadsaal, and the Anglican Cathedral.

By the end of the century a visiting Englishman was able to write that 'the town is one of the neatest and, in a modest way, best appointed capitals in the world. Gardens are planted with trees that are now so tall as to make the whole place seem to swim in green'.

The description is more or less still accurate, though of course the city of Bloemfontein is now a great deal bigger, its growth hugely stimulated by the discovery and exploitation, in the 1950s, of the Free State goldfields 160 km (100 miles) to the north-east and by the massive Orange River irrigation and hydroelectric scheme launched in 1962.

Bloemfontein's baronial-style Old Residency.

Museums, monuments and landmarks

NAVAL HILL There are fine views of the city from the road that winds around the summit. At the top is the Lamont Hussey Observatory, whose staff discovered over 7,000 binary stars (double-star systems) before its American sponsors closed it down in 1972. The buildings have been converted into a cultural centre.

Some 200 ha (494 acres) of Naval Hill have been set aside as the Franklin Nature Reserve, home to eland, springbok, red hartebeest, blesbok and Burchell's zebra.

At the foot of the hill, in Union Avenue's Hamilton Park, is the impressively modern Orchid House, with its transparent domed roof (adjustable for temperature control; internal climatic conditions and the watering of plants are controlled by computer). Inside there are pools, bridges, waterfalls, weathered stone, and over 3,000 lovely orchids.

THE OLD RAADSAAL is Bloemfontein's most venerable structure, site of the Free State's first school, church, social venue and seat of government. The small, dung-floored building, now a national monument, is in St George's Street.

THE FOURTH RAADSAAL, completed in 1893 and the last seat of government of the old Republic, is an exceptional piece of architecture, a dignified building which reflects the classical revival: Greek in detail and Renaissance in form. Inside are vaulted spaces, floors of Devon marble, and an impressive principal chamber, rooflit by coloured glass. Statuary includes busts of the six Free State presidents and Coert Steynberg's representation of Christiaan de Wet, most renowned of the Republic's military sons.

THE OLD RESIDENCY, home of three of the republican presidents, is a splendid edifice in President Brand Street. It now serves as a museum (featuring the trappings of presidential office) and centre for art exhibitions, musical evenings and theatrical performances.

ANGLICAN CATHEDRAL, St George's Street. The foundation stone of the cathedral was laid in 1850 but it wasn't until Sir Herbert Baker came onto the Free State scene, in the first years of the new century, that the building assumed its present, elegantly imposing form. Well worth a visit.

THE NATIONAL MUSEUM, Aliwal Street. Extensive exhibition of fossils; interesting local history and art displays.

MILITARY MUSEUM of the Boer Republics, Monument Road. Devoted to the story of the Boer forces during the South African War (1899–1902): weapons; special displays depicting military, prisoner-of-war and concentration-camp lifestyles; personalia.

NATIONAL WOMEN'S MEMORIAL, on a commanding site in Monument Road. Created in memory of the nearly 27,000 Boer women and children who died (mainly of disease) in British camps during the South African War. The black victims of the camps have not been so well remembered. The monument comprises a 37 m (121 ft) sandstone obelisk and a pedestal supporting statues of two women, one holding a dying child, the other gazing out over the plains of the Free State. The ashes of Emily Hobhouse, the British woman who campaigned so effectively on behalf of the Boer internees, are buried at the base of the obelisk.

Gardens and parks

NATIONAL BOTANICAL GARDENS This is a 45 ha (110 acres) floral sanctuary on Rayton Road, 10 km (6 miles) from the city centre. The gardens, dominated by impressive dolomite outcrops, include formal displays as well as an area of natural vegetation. Other features: a herbarium, an orange-blossom arbour, nursery, summer house, and a petrified tree reckoned to be between 150 and 300 million years old.

Guided walks by arrangement; tearoom; bulbs sold by prior arrangement; open daily. Best months to visit: September through November and February through May.

KING'S PARK, situated along Kingsway and 346 ha (855 acres) in extent, is the city's principal public garden. During the first decade of the century over 125,000 trees were planted, and they're now in their full and glorious maturity. The park incorporates Loch Logan (a largish lake, flanked by a 500 m (1,640 ft) rose pergola and a most pleasant picnic and recreational area); the zoo (animals include a large number of monkeys, and a 'liger' – a cross between a lion and a tiger), and the well-known Rose Garden. The latter was inaugurated by the Prince of Wales (the future King Edward VIII) in 1925 and boasts more than 4,000 rose trees (floribundas, hybrid teas, miniatures, and a special bed of Zola Budd roses, planted in 1985). Best months to see the roses: October and November, during which time the Rose Festival is held. King's Park is the venue for an open-air market, held on the first Saturday of each month.

Theatre

SAND DU PLESSIS THEATRE, in Markgraaff Street, is a modern complex completed in 1985 at a cost of R60 million. Worth visiting for the works of art that contribute to the décor.

THE EASTERN HIGHLANDS

Scenic splendour, a number of important nature reserves, a proliferation of San (Bushman) rock paintings, rewarding day drives and invigorating hikes are the principal attractions of a region that is often, and quite undeservedly, bypassed by tourists. On your way (along the N8), call in at the Maria Moroka Park, which extends over the Thaba Nchu ('black mountain') massif and embraces the Groothoek dam and the sophisticated Thaba Nchu Sun hotel-casino complex. The sweet grasses of the plains, set against a majestic highland backdrop, nurture springbok and eland, red hartebeest and zebra, steenbok and blesbok. Among its 150 bird species is the rare blue korhaan.

OPPOSITE TOP: *Intricate designs make up these wall and window murals in Clarens.*
OPPOSITE BOTTOM: *A traditional Sotho scene near the Golden Gate Park.*
ABOVE: *The strikingly weathered Sentinel Rock in the Golden Gate Highlands National Park.*
RIGHT: *The Golden Gate's Brandwag rest camp.*

GOLDEN GATE HIGHLANDS NATIONAL PARK

An immense 12,000 ha (30,000 acres) expanse of dramatically-sculpted sandstone ridges, peaks, cliffs, caves and weirdly shaped formations, situated south of Harrismith, in the valley of the Little Caledon River and at the foot of the Maluti Mountains. The colours are remarkable: sandstone and iron oxides have combined to create a wonderful array of reds, oranges, yellows and golden browns. The Golden Gate itself is a massive, strikingly-hued cliff face.

The park is mainly a scenic reserve, but grey rhebok, mountain reedbuck, and oribi are long-time residents of the area and other species – eland, blesbok, red hartebeest and zebra – have been reintroduced. Birdlife consists of 160 species, including black eagle, bearded vulture, blue crane and jackal buzzard. Willows grace the riverbanks; the veld is sometimes bright with red-hot poker, fire lily, watsonia and arum lily.

The Golden Gate has two rest camps which offer visitors self-contained accommodation. There is also a caravan/camping ground, two restaurants, a cocktail bar, information centre and curio shop. Recreation activities include some lovely scenic and game drives, various walks (including the two-day Rhebok hiking trail), climbing, scrambling, trout-fishing, horse-riding (mounts may be hired), swimming, tennis and golf.

HARRISMITH

One of the major centres along the national highway (the N3) between the Witwatersrand and the KwaZulu-Natal coastal resorts, the town of Harrismith was founded in 1849 and named after the flamboyant Cape governor and Waterloo veteran Sir Harry Smith. Outside the town hall there is a 150-million-year-old petrified tree. The fifth dinosaur remains ever to be discovered and identified were also unearthed here. The local venison, biltong (sun-dried meat) and trout are famous. The scenically attractive area offers visitors some pleasant distractions. Among them:

HARRISMITH WILDFLOWER GARDENS (formerly Drakensberg Botanic Garden), situated about 5 km (3 miles) from town, at the foot of the Platberg, a well-defined height much favoured by walkers and picnickers. This 114 ha (282 acres) garden is a sanctuary for more than 1,000 plant species occurring on the Drakensberg range to the south. There are picnic spots, two dams and some interesting walks.

MOUNT EVEREST GAME RESERVE encompasses 1,000 ha (2,500 acres) of mountain and plains countryside, and 22 species of game. One may drive or ride (Land-Rovers and horses for hire) or walk (but watch out for the rhino) through the area. Accommodation: luxurious log cabins and an old farmhouse.

STERKFONTEIN DAM, 25 km (16 miles) southwest of town, is a large (7,000 ha/17,300 acres), crystal clear and most inviting stretch of water, popular among trout-fishermen and watersportsmen. Some 18,000 ha (44,500 acres) of the surrounding area has been set aside as a nature reserve. Rather special are the area's yellowwoods and rare tree ferns. Accommodation: fully equipped chalets.

LAND OF THE VAAL

The Vaal River rises on the western slopes of the Drakensberg range and flows south-westwards, forming the boundary between the old Transvaal province and the Free State for 800 km (500 miles) before entering the Northern Cape near Barkly West and, 300 km (186 miles) farther on, joining the Orange.

The total catchment area of the Vaal River is 200,000 km² (77,000 square miles); the mean annual run-off 5.6 billion m³ (200 billion ft³), and it is the Orange's most important tributary, its water intensively exploited for irrigation, for hydro-electric generation, for industry – and for recreation: the Vaal and its willow-shaded banks provide a playground for thousands of holiday-makers and weekenders, most of them from the Johannesburg area.

Along the middle reaches there are resorts, caravan parks, camping grounds and hotels. A few of the latter are of international standard, but generally the area's attractions and amenities have few pretensions to sophistication:

people come for the long, leisurely days of undemanding relaxation in the sunshine, for the watersports, for family-type diversion and entertainment. Pleasant venues on the southern (Free State) side include:

THE VAAL DAM, a 300 km² (116 square miles) stretch of water, 32 km² (12 square miles) of which is ideal for a range of sports. The waters are deep, bilharzia-free and favoured by anglers. On the southern banks of the dam is the Jim Fouché Resort, comprising caravan/camping sites, picnic and barbecue spots, restaurant, shop, tennis courts, pool and stables.

THE FREE STATE GOLDFIELDS

Though geologists suspected the presence of gold in the northern Free State in the later 1930s, it wasn't until April 1946 that an immensely rich seam – what transpired to be an extension of the fabulous Witwatersrand reef far to the north – was unearthed on the farm Geduld. The region now produces about a third of South Africa's vast output of the yellow metal. Its main centre is:

WELKOM

A new, well-planned, fast-developing mining and industrial city of modern buildings, pleasant parks, wide and easily negotiable thoroughfares (there are 23 traffic circles), shopping malls, an airport, good restaurants and a lively theatre.

Highlight of any visit to Welkom must be a surface and underground tour of one of the area's gold mines, some of which are household names within the investment world. Full-day tours are conducted; features of interest incidental to the mining and gold-pouring processes include, curiously and rather charmingly, an underground wine-cellar. Book well in advance.

Among the other points of note are the extraordinarily prolific, and attractive, birdlife of the pans and dams (filled with mine-water, and salty from evaporation) of the area. Notable species include pink flamingo (thousands of them), the sacred ibis, Egyptian goose, maccoa (Muscovy) duck, marsh owl and, most unexpected, a great many seagulls, even though Welkom is around 400 km (250 miles) from the nearest coast.

The two most popular of these stretches of water are the Flamingo Pan (picnic and barbecue spots, lawns, playgrounds, nature trails, and of course bird-watching and bird photography; facilities have recently been upgraded) on the

ABOVE: *Sunflowers are a major crop in the province of the Free State.*
BELOW: *The Gariep Dam's Midwaters resort.*

airport road, and the Theronia Pan, a pristine natural area (again, a marvellous bird-watching venue) within the town's limits.

SOUTHERN FREE STATE

Here there are vast, bare plains that supported millions of head of game until the white farmers and hunters arrived in the 19th century. Sterling efforts are now being made to reintroduce some of the animal species.

The Orange River (*see* panel, page 115), the country's main watercourse, is the dominant natural feature of the region, its waters massively harnessed to meet the growing demands of cities, and of industry and agriculture.

GARIEP DAM

Formerly known as the Hendrik Verwoerd, the Gariep, the country's largest reservoir, has a storage capacity of 6 billion m³ (200 billion ft³) and covers an area of 374 km² (232 square miles).

GARIEP DAM NATURE RESERVE Covering the northern shores of the dam is the 11,237 ha (27,766 acres) nature reserve, home to the country's largest population of springbok, as well as to black wildebeest, mountain reedbuck, blesbok, steenbok, and a breeding herd of Cape mountain zebra.

Springbok are common in Free State reserves.

AVENTURA MIDWATERS RESORT, a pleasant holiday centre of self-contained, well-appointed family rondavels and a shady caravan/camping area on the reserve's western boundary. Fine views of the surrounding water, veld and hills; powerboating, sailing and fishing on the dam; game-viewing; an 18-hole golf course, bowling green, riding stables; a restaurant and shopping centre are all on offer.

To the east, covering a triangular expanse of land at the confluence of the Orange and Caledon rivers, is the:

TUSSEN-DIE-RIVIERE NATURE RESERVE, whose 23,000 ha (57,000 acres) nurtures a number of game species introduced to the area in an impressive relocation exercise launched in the 1970s. The game, now prolific, includes white rhino, Burchell's zebra, blue and black wildebeest, blesbok, kudu, springbok, eland, red hartebeest, mountain reedbuck and gemsbok. Birdlife is varied and interesting (both game and water species are present, the latter mostly on the floodplain to the west). Accommodation is in the form of fully equipped chalets; simple hunters' huts; and a caravan/camping area.

There are several delightful picnic sites, and a network of game-viewing roads and short – 3 to 4 km (2 to 2.5 miles) – nature trails. The farm is open to the general public from September through to April.

OVISTON NATURE RESERVE, 13,000 ha (32,000 acres) in extent (of which about a quarter is accessible to the public) flanks the dam's southern shore. Proclaimed mainly to protect the region's scrub and grassland vegetation (known as the False Upper Karoo ecosystem) and to sustain breeding herds of buck (for relocation to other areas), it offers a guided overnight trail, shorter trails, and about 50 km (30 miles) of game-viewing track.

TAKING TO THE WATERS

One of the more rewarding and intrepid ways to explore the Orange River (indeed, probably the only way to explore it thoroughly) is by canoe, raft or 'rubber duck', as a member of a water-safari group led by an expert guide. Several outfits conduct expeditions, offering four- and six-day trips (all with a wonderful mixture of scenic variety, exercise, some element of challenge, and companionable camp life) at surprisingly cheap rates.

EXPLORING THE GREAT RIVER

The Orange rises in Lesotho's Maluti Mountains to the east and flows for 2,250 km (1,400 miles) across the subcontinent's high central plateau, passing through the magnificent Augrabies Gorge (*see* page 210), close to the Namibian border, before negotiating the last, desolate stretch to the Atlantic seaboard. It is by far the largest river in the country, draining fully 47% of South Africa's total land area.

The river was once known as the Gariep (from the Khoisan word *Garib*, meaning Great River) but was renamed, in 1779, in honour of the Prince of Orange. Its islands, of which there are many, have an especially colourful history: during the 1880s some of them served as suitably inaccessible hideaways for bands of rustlers and brigands, notorious 'river pirates' who were finally, and with difficulty, dislodged by colonial forces sent up from the Cape. The waters of the Orange are erratic, the flow being dictated by seasonal rains. When the summer rains have been generous the river becomes a swift-moving torrent sweeping across the land in a swathe approximately 10 km (6 miles) wide. At other times, in contrast, it is benign, even sluggish.

For almost its entire length the Orange flows through dry, sometimes arid countryside, generally flattish and dun-coloured but enlivened by fringes of strikingly bright greenery along the riverbanks and, increasingly, by irrigated farmlands that yield harvests of cotton, lucerne, dates, raisins and sultanas.

The terrain around the river's lower reaches is rich in semi-precious stones, many of which lie on the surface, literally waiting to be picked up: tiger's eye and amethyst; amazonite, rose quartz, garnet and beryl; tourmaline, agate, jasper and onyx. Diamonds are found, and still mined and panned, in the inland gravels; around the estuary – in the coastal areas of Namaqualand and Namibia – are some of the world's largest alluvial fields (*see* page 265).

Sundowners and sociability on the banks of the Orange, South Africa's largest river.

ADVISORY: THE FREE STATE

CLIMATE

Summer rainfall region. Summers: hot, but the plateau is high and the heat seldom too intense for comfort; thunderstorms bring the rains, but too infrequently in recent years. Winters: bone-dry; cold nights; cool and sometimes warm days.

TRAVEL

Road. Bloemfontein is 175km/109 miles from Kimberley; 108 km/67 miles from Maseru; 411 km/255 miles from Johannesburg; 469 km/291 miles from Pretoria; 614 km/382 miles from East London; 643 km/400 miles from Port Elizabeth; 653 km/406 miles from Durban; 966 km/600 miles from Beit Bridge on the Zimbabwe border, and 1,007 km/626 miles from Cape Town.

Bloemfontein is on the main N1 north-south highway that links Cape Town and the Johannesburg-Pretoria area. Good tarred roads connect the city with all major centres, among the nearer of which are Welkom, Kimberley, Maseru in Lesotho, and East London. Most of the larger car-hire firms have offices in Bloemfontein (city and airport) and Welkom.

Coach travel: Contact Rennies travel for Greyhound bus services to the major centres, Bloemfontein tel. (051) 30-2361 and Translux tel. (051) 408-3242.

Rail. Bloemfontein is a key point on the national rail network; the railway station is in Maitland Street. For principal passenger services contact, Information: tel. (051) 408-2111, Reservations: tel. (051) 408-2941. Welkom, Parys and other larger Free State towns also have efficient rail links with the country's main centres.

Air. Bloemfontein Airport is situated 14 km/9 miles from city centre; tel. (051) 33-1482. Daily flights to and from major South African centres. There is, however, no bus service between city and airport, although taxi services are availabe. Information: SAA. Welkom also has a modern airport; tel. (057) 352-4079.

ACCOMMODATION
Select hotels

BLOEMFONTEIN

Bloemfontein Inn ** In quiet part of city. 33 en suite rooms; à la carte restaurant and breakfast room; 2 small conference venues. PO Box 7589, Bloemfontein 9300; tel. (051) 22-6284, fax 22-6223.

Boulevard Hotel 38 en suite rooms; à la carte restaurant; bar; conference facilities available. PO Box 6907, Bloemfontein 9300; tel. (051) 47-7236, fax 30-6217.

City Lodge: Bloemfontein ** Close to zoological gardens. Largish; no-frills, solid-value hotel; 150 en suite rooms; breakfast room (breakfasts only); bar; pool; conference facilities available. PO Box 3552, Bloemfontein 9300; tel. (051) 47-9888, fax 47-5669.

Holiday Inn Garden Court: Bloemfontein *** In quiet suburb. 147 rooms, 2 suites; restaurant; bar; pool; two small conference venues. PO Box 12015, Brandhof 9329; tel. (051) 47-0310, fax 30-5678, central reservations (011) 482-3500.

Holiday Inn Garden Court: Naval Hill *** Located about 2 km (1 mile) from central area. 143 rooms, 2 suites; up-market à la carte restaurant and friendly bar; pool; conference facilities available. PO Box 1851, Bloemfontein 9300; tel. (051) 30-1111, fax 30-4141, central reservations (011) 482-3500.

CLARENS

Maluti Mountain Lodge Small, comfortable country hotel in scenic region. 10 en suite double rooms, 4 rondavels; à la carte restaurant (regional specialities) and bar; pool. PO Box 21, Clarens 9707; tel. (058) 256-1422.

The Country Lodge Unpretentious; 20 en suite rooms; also self-catering accommodation; pool. PO Box 21, Clarens 9707; tel. (058) 256-1354.

FRANKFORT

Lodge 1896 ** In small town close to Vaal Dam. 10 en suite rooms; à la carte restaurant; bar. PO Box 77, Frankfort 9830; tel. (0588) 3-1080.

HARRISMITH

Harrismith Inn ** 119 en suite rooms; restaurant and bar facilities; pool. PO Box 363, Harrismith 9880; tel. (05861) 2-1011, fax 2-2770.

Sir Harry Motel 48 en suite chalets; superb à la carte restaurant and pleasant bar. PO Box 100, Harrismith 9880; tel. (05861) 2-2151.

KROONSTAD

Toristo Protea Hotel 2 km (1 mile) outside town, halfway between Bloemfontein and Johannesburg. 45 en suite rooms; restaurant; 2 bars. PO Box 871, Kroonstad 9500; tel. (0562) 2-5111, fax 3-3298.

LADYBRAND

Traveller's Inn Hotel ** In picturesque countryside near Lesotho border. 12 en suite rooms; à la carte restaurant; bar; pool room. PO Box 458, Ladybrand 9745; tel. and fax (05191) 4-0191/3.

NORVALSPONT

Glasgow Pont Hotel Near Gariep Dam. 13 en suite rooms; restaurant serves traditional South African dishes; friendly bar. PO Box 5, Norvalspont 5981; tel. (052172), ask for 1022.

PARYS

New Riviera Hotel In attractive little town on Vaal River. 16 en suite rooms; à la carte restaurant; bar. PO Box 1522, Parys 9585; tel. (0568) 2143/4, central reservations (011) 455-5041.

THABA NCHU

Naledi Sun Hotel and Casino A Sun International hotel approximately half way between Bloemfontein and Lesotho. 30 en suite rooms; à la carte restaurant; several bars; pool. PO Box 131, Thaba Nchu 9780; tel. (051871) 5-1061, fax 5-2329.

Thaba Nchu Sun Hotel and Casino Also a member of the Sun International group, situated in attractive private reserve. 116 rooms, 2 suites; à la carte and buffet restaurants; several bars; casino; pool; golf driving range; gym; solarium; sauna; tennis; squash; horse-riding; fishing. PO Box 114, Thaba Nchu 9780; tel. (051871) 2161, fax 2521.

VIRGINIA

Doringboom Hotel In gold-mining centre near Welkom. 30 en suite rooms; à la carte restaurant and bar; pool. PO Box 66, Virginia 9430; tel. (057) 212-5124.

WELKOM

**Golden Orange ** ** 62 rooms (51 en suite); conference facilities available. PO Box 718, Welkom 9460; tel. (057) 2-5281/2/3, fax 2-5281.

Welkom Hotel. * 82 rooms, 5 suites; restaurants and bars; pool; conference facilities for 200. PO Box 973, Welkom 9460; tel. and fax (057) 5-1411.

Welkom Inn * Fairly central (1 km/½ mile) from business and shopping centres). 120 rooms; à la carte restaurant; bar; pool. PO Box 887, Welkom 9460; tel. (057) 375-3361, fax 352-1458.

WITSIESHOEK

Witsieshoek Mountain Resort Hotel An upland retreat beneath the splendour of the high Drakensberg. 25 en suite rooms; restaurant (à la carte and table d'hôte); pub; pool. PO Box 17311, Witsieshoek 9870; tel. (058) 789-1900, fax 789-1901.

ZASTRON

Maluti Hotel * In small farming town beneath the high Maluti Mountains of Lesotho. 19 en suite rooms; pleasant restaurant (à la carte and table d'hôte); gym; sauna; horse-riding; fishing; hiking trails in vicinity. PO Box 2, Zastron 9950; tel. (05542), and ask for 107, fax ask for 379.

Self-catering

The Free State is well served by holiday resorts as well as caravan/camping venues. Satour or the local information offices can be contacted for more details. Of special note are:

Aventura Midwaters Situated on the banks of the Gariep Dam. Particularly popular among watersports enthusiasts; 1-, 2- and 3-bedroomed chalets available. Private Bag X10, Gariep Dam 9922; tel. (052172), ask for 45, fax ask for 135.

Golden Gate Highlands National Park has two rest camps offering visitors self-contained chalets; other types of accommodation also available. For further information and bookings contact the National Parks Board, PO Box 787, Pretoria 0001; tel. (012) 343-1991, fax 343-0905. Cape Town: PO Box 7400, Rogge Bay 8012; tel. (021) 22-2810, fax 24-6211.

Willem Pretorius Game Reserve is situated to the north-east of Bloemfontein. The resort at the western entrance offers visitors 2-bed, self-contained rondavels; other types of accommodation also available. For further information and bookings contact the Nature Conservator, PO Willem Pretorius, via Ventersburg 9450; tel. (01734) 4168; or the Manager, Aventura, at the same address; tel. (01734) 4229.

USEFUL ADDRESSES AND TELEPHONE NUMBERS

Bethlehem Publicity Office, Civic Centre, Muller St; PO Box 551, Bethlehem 9700; tel. (01431) 3-5732; after hours: (01431) 3-1795.

Bloemfontein Tourist Information, Hoffman Square (between Maitland and St Andrew's streets), PO Box 639, Bloemfontein 9300; tel. (051) 405-8489, fax 473-859.

Clarens Tourist Information, tel. (058) 256-1406.

Harrismith Tourist Information, tel. (05861) 2-3525.

Kroonstad Tourist Information, tel. (0562) 2-2601.

Parys Tourist Information, tel. (0568) 2131.

Satour, Shop No 9, Sanlam Parkade, Charlea St; PO Box 3515, Bloemfontein 9300; tel. (051) 47-1362, fax 47-0862.

Sasolburg Tourist Information, tel. (016) 76-0029.

Welkom Publicity Association, Clock Tower, Stateway; PO Box 2030, Welkom 9460; tel. (057) 352-9244, fax 352-9501.

DURBAN, THE EAST COAST AND ZULULAND

KwaZulu-Natal – known as Natal until 1994 – is arguably the most beautiful of South Africa's provinces, a well-watered, fertile region of rolling green hills and a magnificent Indian Ocean coastline stretching approximately 600 km (375 miles) from the Transkei region of the Eastern Cape in the south to Kosi Bay and the Mozambique border in the north. Extending elegantly over the northern coastal plain and the lush, north-eastern interior is the historic territory known as Zululand.

Inland, the country rises to the foothills and then, precipitously, to the massive heights of the Great Escarpment, called here the Drakensberg and, in Lesotho farther to the west, the Maluti mountains.

Pietermaritzburg, set in the hills some 90 km (55 miles) from the sea, is the provincial capital, but by far the biggest urban concentration is in and around Durban, South Africa's third city, leading seaport and premier holiday destination.

DURBAN

The city, 300 km² (116 square miles) in extent, sprawls along the coast to the south and across the Umgeni River to the north, and, inland, up the Berea, a ridge of hills overlooking the business district, the beachfront and the harbour.

At the top of the ridge is the Durban campus of the University of Natal, a prominent landmark and, for orientation purposes, a useful point of reference. The city's most distinctive topographical feature, though, is the bay itself: it is vast, virtually landlocked, its southern waters bounded by an 8-km-long (5 miles) and 250-m-high (820 ft) wooded headland known as the Bluff, its northern by a narrower lower-lying sandy spit called the Point. Within the bay is Salisbury Island, which is joined to the Bluff by a causeway carrying both a road and a railway. Beyond the Berea ridge, to the west, is suburbia, and beyond that a plateau that rises some 500 m (1,640 ft) above sea level, high enough for the inhabitants of its fashionable residential areas – Kloof, Hillcrest, Gillitts, Westville – to escape the worst of the summer heat and humidity.

Durban-Pinetown is said to be the world's fastest-growing conurbation, its population expanding faster than those of Calcutta and Mexico City – but expanding for much the same reasons. The armies of the poor are leaving a countryside that can no longer meet their minimum needs, and are congregating in their thousands around Ntujuma, Umlazi and Embumbula and other settlements on the western city fringes. Their integration into the urban mainstream, the provision of houses, schools and clinics, the creation of jobs – these constitute Durban's real priority, and the contrast between that reality and the image the city projects – that of a playground for the privileged – is marked indeed. But then, when one comes down to it, it

OPPOSITE AND BELOW: *The Golden Mile, Durban's main leisure area, extends along 6 km (4 miles) of subtropical seafront and offers just about everything the holiday-maker could wish for.*

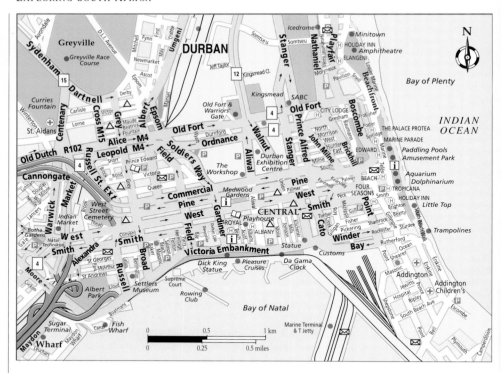

is only by exploiting its considerable natural assets to the full – by offering the ultimate in frivolous pleasure – that Durban can remain prosperous enough to cope with the future.

Greater Durban is also home to quite a large number of Indian people, some of whom are the direct descendants of the indentured labourers brought in from India during the 1860s to work the sugar plantations of the region. The community, a generally prosperous one, has cherished its cultural heritage, retained its religions, languages and customs, its music, dress and food, and it is an attractively prominent part of the city scene.

The Golden Mile

The city's 6 km (4 miles) strip of glittering ocean frontage, known as the Golden Mile, has just about everything the heart of the hedonist could wish for: a pleasure-seeker's extravaganza of sound and light, of amusement parks, pavilions, piers and pools, round-the-clock restaurants and nightspots, glittering entertainment centres, emporiums and colourful markets, wide white beaches, emerald lawns, fountains, graceful walkways and broad thoroughfares

that lead past some of the world's most elegant hotels. Among the points of special interest are: **SEA WORLD,** the renowned aquarium and dolphinarium at the bottom of West Street. On display are tropical fish in great number and of

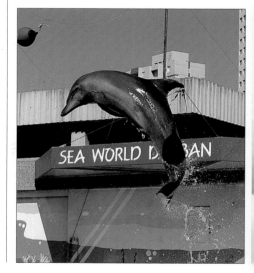

exquisite variety, stingrays and turtles, seals, dolphins, penguins, a collection of sharks and a colourful fantasia of live corals, anemones, seashells, octopuses and lobsters. Divers enter the main 800,000 litre (176,000 gallons) tank to hand-feed its residents; the sharks are fed three times a week (Tuesdays, Thursdays and Sundays); daily highlights are the fascinating dolphin, seal and penguin shows.

Sea World is open each day of the week from nine in the morning to nine at night.

THE FITZSIMONS SNAKE PARK, on Snell Parade opposite North Beach, houses a variety of snakes and an intriguing collection of other reptiles – crocodiles, leguaans (iguanas), tortoises, terrapins and so forth. There are also some exotic species, which are kept in thermostatically controlled cages. Demonstrations are held five times a day; snakes are fed on Saturdays and Sundays, the crocs daily.

THE AMPHITHEATRE, on Marine Parade opposite the Elangeni Hotel, is a most pleasant retreat from the noise and bustle, a sunken area graced by lawns and flowers, fountains and pools, footbridges and summer-houses. A rather splendid fleamarket is held here each Sunday; there are also 'international theme' days on which traditional dancing is performed and exotic food served.

THE WHEEL, perhaps Durban's most lively shopping and entertainment complex, a kaleidoscope of speciality shops (about 140 of them), restaurants, bars and cinemas (around a dozen of these) that opened its doors in Gillespie Street and Point Road at the end of 1989. The place takes its name from a colossal revolving Ferris wheel ringed by ornamental Indian howdah gondolas and mounted on the building's façade above a jewel-encrusted elephant's head. The Oriental theme is carried through into the interior, some of which (on the second floor) makes out as a casbah, though for the most part the mood is nautical – flags, rigging, spars and lifeboats are everywhere to be seen; ship's railings separate the shops; the floor is a planked deck, the walls are bulkheads.

THE RICKSHAS, parked outside the Tropicana Hotel on Marine Parade, have been a familiar sight to generations of locals and visitors. The lightly-built man-pulled carts originated in Japan and were introduced to KwaZulu-Natal by the sugar magnate Sir Marshall Campbell in the 1890s. They proved an immediate success: by 1903 a full thousand and more of them were

OPPOSITE: *One of Sea World's dolphins.*
ABOVE: *A Golden Mile ricksha and its elaborately costumed 'driver'.*

plying Durban's streets, with many more in Pietermaritzburg, Cape Town, Pretoria and even Rhodesia (now Zimbabwe). The early ones were plain-looking, functional affairs, but with the passage of time and increasing competition for custom they and their handsome Zulu 'drivers' took on a much more decorative look: man and carriage were elaborately decked out with beadwork, furs and streamers. Only in Durban, though, did they survive the onslaught of petrol engine and electric trolley, and only as a tourist attraction. Just 20 or so are left, and even these are likely to disappear before long, so ride while you may.

Oriental Durban

Wander a short way to the south of Durban's central business district and you will find yourself in a different world, in a colourful, vibrant, exotic and wonderfully attractive environment fashioned by the city's Indian community. Here the air is aromatic, filled with the pungent scents of spice and sandalwood, incense and rose, noisy with the semi-tonal sounds of the

ABOVE: *Spices on sale in an Indian emporium.*
BOTTOM: *The gold-domed Jumma Mosque in Grey Street – largest in the southern hemisphere.*

tanpura and the beat of Eastern drums, and with the languages of Bombay and Calcutta, Delhi and Madras. The streets and alleyways are crowded; bright saris mingle with the more prosaic styles of the west. In Grey Street stands the southern hemisphere's largest mosque, an imposing building of golden domes that catch and reflect the sunlight and, next door, the Madressa Arcade, a place of bargains and barter and of shops crammed to their low ceilings with both the ornamental and the functional: ceramic, ivory, bronze, brass (a great deal of this), silver and wood; sumptuous silks and satins; exquisite jewellery; craftware and curios; bangles, beads and baubles; fabrics and foods; shoes, shirts and shampoos.

Focal point of this enticing part of Durban, though, is the Victoria Street market, an extensive area bounded by Victoria, Russell and Queen streets and by Cemetery Lane.

The old Indian Market, one of the city's principal tourist attractions for 63 years, was burnt down in 1973. The large fraternity of traders – the market provided a living for approximately

10,000 families, many of whom lost all that they possessed in the massive blaze – eventually moved to 'temporary' and rather nondescript premises in Warwick Avenue. Here the Indian Market remained for 11 years before moving into the new building in July 1990. Modern though the market-place is, the traders and community have been able to re-create much of the enchantment of the past.

Some 80 stallholders sell spices, herbs and other products on the spacious ground floor; above them are 50 or so shops; a walkway leads you to the separate 'wet' meat and fish markets. There's underground parking in the basement area; the whole domed complex (it has 11 domes, each recalling a notable building in India) is a marvellous kaleidoscope of sounds, smells and clashing colours, and an absolute must for the visitor.

There is, of course, a great deal more to Durban's Indian cultural heritage, much of it devotional, sacrosanct and hidden from outsiders. But not all: accessible and of special significance are:

THE JUMMA MOSQUE, mentioned earlier, is in Grey Street; tours by arrangement only; contact the Islamic Propagation Centre.

HINDU TEMPLES Foremost among these is the Hare Krishna Temple of Understanding at the Chatsworth Centre, south of Durban: a striking mix of Eastern and Western architectural styles, the marble-floored building is noted for its splendidly golden interior, its soaring towers,

GANDHI: MAN OF PEACE

The most celebrated of Durban's earlier residents was, without doubt, Mohandas Gandhi, ranked among the 20th century's most influential leaders and father of modern India.

Now better known as the Mahatma ('Great Soul'), Gandhi arrived on Natal's balmy shores in 1893 as a bright young lawyer to take up a private brief – and stayed on, for two eventful decades, to fight for Indian rights in South Africa.

After founding the Natal Indian Congress (in 1894) Gandhi began refining his philosophy of 'passive resistance', or *satyagraha*, which proclaimed that love and truth would eventually and inevitably prevail. His campaigns – for social and political reform and against the harsh immigration laws of the time – involved protest marches and massive strikes that were to lead to several spells in prison. None of this, though, created personal bitterness: he remained serene throughout, and indeed even managed to sustain a relationship of mutual respect with his principal political opponent, General Jan Smuts (for whom he once, while languishing in jail, crafted a pair of sandals – a gift Smuts treasured all his life).

His humanity was not only confined to the immediate cause: at the outbreak of the savagely fought Anglo-Boer War in 1899, for instance, he joined the medical corps to serve as a 'body-snatcher' – as stretcher-bearers were called in those days – on the bloody battlefields of Colenso and Spioenkop.

In due course Gandhi and Smuts reached an agreement on Indian rights – an accord that produced the Indian Relief Act of 1914 – and the Mahatma returned to his native land to embark on the long, hard and ultimately successful struggle for Indian independence.

Visitors to the the city of Durban can view reminders, and reflect on the life, of Gandhi at the Ramakrishna Centre (*see* main text, below).

its surrounding moat and lovely gardens. It was designed and built by the International Society of Krishna Consciousness. Open daily (remove shoes before entering); guided tours; gift shop; audio-visual presentation; restaurant. Other temples, in which intricate religious festivals are celebrated, include:
• **Durban Hindu Temple**, Somtseu Road: significance of shrines, statuary and rituals are explained by the resident priest.
• **Shree Shiva Subrahmanya Alayam**, in Sirdar Road, Clairwood: an especially well-patronized temple complex.
RAMAKRISHNA CENTRE, north of Durban (take the Mount Edgecombe turn-off), is a non-denominational spiritual retreat; open daily.

Phoenix Settlement, next to Kwa Mashu township (off the N2), is a centre for quiet prayer, an ascetic place containing relics and reminders of Mohandas Gandhi, modern India's founding father and, in his early career, a dedicated campaigner for Indian rights in South Africa (*see* panel, above.) He founded the farm at Phoenix in 1903.

Museums, exhibitions and landmarks

For a young and often brash-seeming city, Durban has a surprising amount to offer in terms of serious interest. It has a particularly fine public library (at the City Hall; special arrangements for visitors); excellent theatre, ballet, opera, orchestral music, a sprinkling of monuments and statuary (the equestrian sculpture of Dick King, 'Kwazulu-Natal's Paul Revere', is probably the most impressive; it stands at the bay-end of Gardiner Street, Victoria Embankment) and a varied selection of museums, galleries and exhibition centres, most prominent of which are:
NATURAL SCIENCE MUSEUM, on the first floor of the City Hall: rich displays of indigenous birds, mammals, reptile and insect life; fish; an impressive dinosaur model; a geological collection; an Egyptian mummy (with an X-ray of its skeleton), and the skeleton of a dodo, the now-extinct flightless, Indian Ocean island bird. Special sections include the KwaZuluwazi ('place of discovery') multi-media centre and an electronic 'Journey through Time'. Guided tours and film shows by request.
LOCAL HISTORY MUSEUM, in the Old Court House, Aliwal Street: an insight into KwaZulu-Natal's often turbulent past, into old Durban (the Durban Room houses re-creations of early trader and settler life) and an array of period costumes. There is a museum shop with curios.
KILLIE CAMPBELL MUSEUM, in Muckleneuk: the original home of sugar magnate Sir Marshall Campbell on the corner of Essenwood and Marriott roads, has three main components: the

Africana library (rare books, pictures, maps, manuscripts); the William Campbell furniture collection; and the splendid Mashu collection of Zulu art and craft, together with 400 'ethnic' (mainly costume and regalia) paintings by Barbara Tyrrell, who spent 20 years travelling and studying in search of the authentic.

Lovely bougainvillaea grace the grounds of Muckleneuk. Open daily except Sundays; guided tours by appointment.

PORT NATAL MARITIME MUSEUM, includes the tugboat *JR More* and the naval minesweeper *SAS Durban*, berthed at the small crafts basin: an intriguing insight into the seafaring past; the museum's land components include the small tug *Ulundi* and Sea View Cottage, a re-created early settler home (with souvenir shop). Open Tuesday to Friday, and on Sunday.

WARRIORS' GATE (Old Fort Road): relics of the many battlefields of the region; medals, badges and other pieces of militaria. Open from Sunday to Friday.

WHYSALL'S CAMERA MUSEUM at 33 Brickhill Road: splendid displays tell the story of photography from 1841; 3,800 exhibits; open daily.

DURBAN ART MUSEUM, City Hall, features permanent exhibitions of South African contemporary and overseas works, including paintings by Utrillo, Corot, Lely and Constable, plus fine displays of indigenous crafts in which Zulu beadwork and basketwork are prominent. Also modern graphics, Oriental art, numerous *objets d'art* and visiting exhibitions. Open daily.

DURBAN EXHIBITION CENTRE, conveniently central, accessible from both Aliwal Street and Walnut Road: an extensive exhibition complex and arena, and a busy venue for a wide range of shows, exhibitions, sports, special (indoor and outdoor) events, including the famed Durban Tattoo (in October). The arena (boxing, show-jumping, fashion shows) can accommodate up to 7,000; permanent exhibitions, in hall four, include the audio-visual 'Durban Experience' presentation (every hour on the hour). The open-air South Plaza hosts a lively Sunday flea-market. Restaurants, bars, plenty of parking.

Gardens, parks and reserves

Despite the pressures of rapid population growth and urban development, Durban has been able to maintain a remarkable number and variety of green spaces, small reserves and other conservation areas. And there are more to come: 13 new reserves have been earmarked for

ABOVE: *A colourful corner of the Botanic Gardens' orchid house. The gardens also have a cycad collection and herbarium.*
OPPOSITE: *Basketware at a street market.*

development in the greater Durban area. All in all, it's an impressive environmental success story, for which a lot of the credit is due the Metropolitan Open Space System (Moss). Among the more prominent venues are:

BEACHWOOD MANGROVES NATURE RESERVE (north of Durban, access via Leo Boyd Highway). One of the last of the area's mangrove swamps. The term 'mangrove' is a loose but convenient group name for trees which are able to thrive in the salty or brackish fringes of tropical bays and river estuaries. Worldwide there are some 60 species of mangrove, belonging to 22 genera of a number of mostly unrelated plant families (many of which, in fact, cannot abide life in a swamp). Eight species occur along the KwaZulu-Natal coast, in swamps that are ecologically valuable: they serve as nursery areas for commercially important fish, and as self-renewing barriers against tropical storms that would otherwise destroy the fragile estuarine ecosystems.

BOTANIC GARDENS (Lower Berea). Indigenous flowering trees, tropical plants, birds; special features include an orchid house, a herbarium, a fine cycad collection, a garden for the blind. There's a pleasant tea-garden and waterlily pond.

BURMAN BUSH NATURE RESERVE (Morning-side). A most pleasant place for rambling and bird-watching (it comprises 45 ha/111 acres of indigenous woodland; trees bear their National Tree List numbers). There are also troops of vervet monkeys to be seen. Information centre; picnic spots; open daily.

JAPANESE GARDENS (Tinsley Road, Virginia). A charmingly designed area of arched wooden bridges, winding pathways, Torii gateways and stone lanterns.

SILVERGLEN NATURE RESERVE (Clearwater Dam, Silverglen). A large (220 ha/544 acres) area of beautifully preserved indigenous coastal grassland and bush which serves as home to forest fever berry, Natal camwood, velvet bush-willow and other trees, and to some 145 bird species. Some of the plants in the reserve are much sought after, for their real and supposed medicinal properties, by African traditional healers, and a protective nursery has been established to minimize the threat of theft.

UMGENI RIVER BIRD PARK (access is from Marine Parade via Umgeni River Bridge). The Umgeni is, apparently, rated the third finest of the world's bird parks: a world of waterfalls,

pools, enormous walk-through aviaries built into the cliff-face and filled with macaws, colourful parrots, cockatoos, lorikeets, great Asian hornbills, rare pheasants, toucans, flamingos, cranes and so on – altogether, about 300 exotic and local species, many with magnificent plumage. Home-made refreshments and light lunches are available.

KRANTZKLOOF NATURE RESERVE (to the north-west of the city; take the turn-off from the N3 at Kloof). A 535 ha (1,322 acres) area definitely worth visiting for its deep gorge, its lovely forest, streams and waterfalls and for its wildlife, which includes some rare plant and bird species (cycads and crowned eagles) and buck, bushpig and vervet monkey. There are approximately 20 km (12.5 miles) of meandering pathways, a pleasant picnic site, and an interpretative centre.

Local tours

The visitor to Durban is exceptionally well looked after by tour operators. Some of the highlights include coach trips around the city's Oriental areas, scenic drives around the gardens and nature reserves, around the harbour and along the coasts, as well as to the Valley of a Thousand Hills (see page 128). Court Helicopters offer scenic trips around the city and coasts. Various ventures lay on harbour and deep-sea cruises; launches are available for private charter (champagne, luncheon, night and deep-sea excursions). For railway enthusiasts there's the Umgeni Steam Railway, which regularly puffs its way between New Germany and Sarnia. The sugar industry (Huletts) welcomes visitors to its giant terminal on Mayden Wharf.

Shopping

Among the bigger and more popular shopping complexes and malls are the Victoria Street market (mainly but not exclusively Indian, and a mandatory port of call for visitors to Durban, see page 122), the enterprising Game City (in Stamford Hill Road, guaranteed lowest prices) and La Lucia Mall (in William Campbell Drive, La Lucia). Others worth a visit are:

THE WORKSHOP in Pine Street, an enormous Victorian building that once served as a railway workshop and has now been transformed into a lively shopping/browsing/eating/entertainment/fun showpiece and 'theme centre'. It houses something over 120 speciality shops, many of them replicas of, or at least reminiscent

of, British-Natal colonial houses complete with 'old world' fanlights, wrought-ironwork and brass trimmings. Victorian-type barrow stalls do business in the central ground floor area, which has been planted with fully-grown trees.

FLEAMARKETS do a brisk trade in the vicinity of The Workshop, in the Amphitheatre (*see* page 121), on the South Plaza of the Durban Exhibition Centre and on the beachfront on the second and last Sundays of each month. Under development is the Pinelands Junction craft market, a venue that will re-create the art, craft and lifestyles of the past.

THE ARCADE, opposite the Pine Parkade and fronting on West, Field and Pine streets, houses about three dozen up-market speciality shops.

THE AFRICAN ARTS CENTRE, in the Guildhall Arcade off Gardiner Street, is, according to the Transvaal Institute of Architects, 'one of the real treasures of Durban'. It is a non-profit enterprise (initiated by the Institute of Race Relations as a self-help project), a part-gallery part-shop that caters for discerning collectors of Zulu arts and crafts (bead-, wood- and grass-work, pottery, sculpture, fabrics and graphics). Well worth a visit.

Theatre, music and entertainment

The entertainment scene is lively and very changeable: consult Durban Unlimited or the local newspapers for the specifics.

Focal point of Durban's performing arts is the stylish and historic:

THE PLAYHOUSE COMPLEX in Smith Street. Once a brace of cinemas, one Tudor-type and the other elaborately Moorish (this was the old and much-loved Colosseum), the building has been converted to provide five venues – used variously for drama, intimate theatre, orchestral music, ballet and opera. The foyers and wood panelling of the cinemas have been retained; everything else is very modern.

MUSIC Choral, orchestral, jazz and pop performances and the very popular Sunday afternoon concerts are presented at the City Hall (watch the local press for notices as concerts are irregular); brass-band music in some of Durban's parks on Sunday afternoons; musical soirées; chamber and jazz recitals at the Little Abbey Theatre; there is a wide range of musical and dramatic offerings from the universities of Natal (celebrity and lunchtime recitals) and Durban-Westville (the acclaimed Oudemeester Master Concerts, featuring visiting artists). Especially recommended is the The Nederburg Theatre, an elegant building attached to Stellenbosch Farmers' Winery at New Germany (soirées and individual recitals).

WINING AND DINING The Durban area is a gourmet's delight, full of outstanding eateries, and it's difficult to present a fair picture in such limited space. A select list of restaurants appears on pages 142–143.

OPPOSITE: *The Playhouse complex, a major venue for theatre and music.*
ABOVE: *Board-sailing off the Golden Mile.*

Sport and Recreation

Durban is world-renowned for its wide white beaches, and especially for those along the Golden Mile (*see* page 120). Sunbathers, swimmers and surfers flock to them in their tens of thousands during the long hot summer. Durban's Golden Mile can become uncomfortably crowded, especially during the Christmas school holidays when the beautiful and far less congested beaches farther afield beckon.

For the rest, Durban offers many splendid opportunities for walking, bird-watching, sailing and other watersports, golf, bowls, tennis and the standard range of spectator sports; ask Durban Unlimited for details.

AROUND DURBAN

In 1828 the great Zulu warrior-king Shaka led an impi down the south coast in a raid against the Pondo people, rested for a while on the lower reaches of a river, drank its cool water, and remarked appreciatively: *Kanti! amanzi a mtoti.* The words mean 'So, the water is sweet', and from them were derived the modern names of both the river and the settlement that grew up on its banks.

AMANZIMTOTI

The settlement, some 25 km (16 miles) south of Durban and a substantial town in its own right (though for practical purposes the two can be grouped together: many of its residents are city commuters), is now one of the most popular of KwaZulu-Natal's coastal resort areas. Among its attractions are superb beaches, a lagoon (easy-to-handle boats for hire), safe swimming (shark nets provide protection), surfing, sun-worshipping, rock- and beach-angling, entertainment, fun in the sun, hotels, bars and plenty of good holiday accommodation.

ILANDA WILDS, a few minutes' drive from the centre of town, is a beautiful and richly varied 14 ha (35 acres) riverine haven for more than 160 bird species, 120 kinds of tree and shrub. There are several popular nature trails along the river banks and picnic sites.

JAPANESE-STYLE GARDENS, along Fynn Road, are a joy; one can laze on a sundeck overlooking the pond and watch the birds. The gardens are open at all times.

UMDONI BIRD SANCTUARY, a smallish expanse of indigenous forest, is home to a wide variety of bird species, including giant and pygmy kingfishers, green-backed herons and, in a special section, exotic and indigenous species, many of them waterfowl; the peacocks are the feature. Many of the trees and plants are labelled for identification. Bird-watching hides, one short trail, information centre, cream teas at weekends.

UMHLANGA ROCKS

This North Coast counterpart of Amanzimtoti, though rather nearer (18 km/11 miles from the city centre), is smaller, more up-market and especially noted for its four luxury hotels (one five-star), three large resort complexes, apartment blocks, holiday homes and the residential suburb of La Lucia. It has a fine beach; swimmers, surfers, paddleskiers and ski-boaters are protected by shark nets (only in the waters north of the distinctive red-and-white lighthouse) and the Natal Sharks Board maintains its headquarters on a low hill overlooking the town (lectures, demonstrations and audio-visuals are regularly presented; booking advisable).

UMHLANGA LAGOON NATURE RESERVE This small (26 ha/64 acres) patch of river-mouth, now rare dune forest and lagoon, attracts a large number and variety of birds (among them the fish eagle and the crested guinea-fowl), as does the adjacent, larger and privately owned Hawaan Forest. Buck species include blue and red duiker and bushbuck. Both reserves can be explored, the former by way of an established nature trail.

Villagers of the Valley of a Thousand Hills, only half an hour's drive from Durban.

VALLEY OF A THOUSAND HILLS

Undoubtedly the region's most striking natural feature, the majestic valley follows the course of the Umgeni River for some 65 km (40 miles) from a flat-topped sandstone hill to the east of Pietermaritzburg called Natal Table Mountain, to the Indian Ocean in the east.

The mountain is 960 m (3,150 ft) high and its plateau-like summit is graced by a profusion of wild flowers. Those who climb to the top (the best route begins on the Pietermaritzburg side) are rewarded with breathtaking views stretching to the sea on one side and the distant Drakensberg on the other.

The valley itself is incredibly hot in summer, heavily populated in parts (it is home to the Debe people, many of whom live in traditional beehive huts and some of whom still wear traditional dress), ruggedly wild in others, and everywhere luxuriant with lilies (arum, fire and snake), Mexican sunflowers and flowering aloes. One can drive along much of the southern rim of the valley.

To get there from Durban takes a pleasant half an hour; follow the N3 to Hillcrest and then turn right; there are farm and craft stalls and tea-gardens on the way. Points of interest within the valley include the unusual, capacious, vaguely Tudor-style Rob Roy Hotel (with delicious cream teas and carvery lunches eaten on the terrace) and slices of 'authentic' Africa tailor-made for tourists:

PHEZULU The word means 'high up', the place comprises a Zulu village featuring Zulu lifestyles, Zulu dancing (a superbly pulsating spectacle), bone-throwing witchdoctors, demonstrations of African cooking, thatching, spear-making and beadwork. There are also an art gallery, curio shop (baskets, clay pottery, beadwork and wood carvings are some of the souvenirs on offer), nature trail, tearoom and sundeck. Somewhat similar, and also a prime tourist drawcard, is: **ASSAGAY SAFARI PARK**, which features crocodiles, snakes, a natural history museum, a Zulu village (the resident performers are the Gaza Zulu Dancers), a botanic garden, a colonial-style restaurant, picnic areas, a curio shop and, to keep children entertained, a treasure-trove.

THE SOUTH COAST

A balmy tropical climate, lovely wide expanses of beach, the warm, intensely blue waters of the Indian Ocean, a lushly evergreen hinterland, fine hotels, a score and more of sunlit towns, villages and hamlets, each with its own, distinctive personality and its own attractions – these are the ingredients that combine to create one of the southern hemisphere's most entrancing holiday regions.

The southern shoreline is divided into two segments (an arbitrary division really, since there is no essential difference between them, but those who promote and write about the region find it a useful distinction): the stretch from Amanzimtoti – about 26 km (16 miles) from the city of Durban and discussed above (*see* page 127) – to Mtwalume is known as the Sunshine Coast; the stretch from Hibberdene to Port Edward along the Eastern Cape's border is called the Hibiscus Coast.

KINGSBURGH

This 8-km-long (5 miles) municipality along the Sunshine Coast encompasses five seaside holiday resorts that are very popular among visitors for their white beaches and shark-protected off-shore waters.

UMKOMAAS

Fourteen kilometres (9 miles) farther south, the small town of Umkomaas boasts a championship golf course, an indigenous tree park and a floodlit tidal pool.

SCOTTBURGH

This substantial and very pleasant town is one of the Sunshine Coast's most popular resorts. Scott Bay is the main beach, a quite charming expanse of sand overlooked by lawned terraces at the mouth of the Mpambanyani River (which translates as 'confusion of birds', a reference to its twisting course). Scottburgh's attractions include safe bathing and fine angling, a fine golf course, bowling greens, a huge saltwater pool (with supertube), the renowned miniature railway and, 4 km (2.5 miles) to the north, Crocworld. This last comprises a wildlife museum, a snake pit and 'snake tunnel', nature trails, a Zulu village (Zulu dancing on Sundays) and, of course, crocodiles. Nearby is the:
VERNON CROOKES NATURE RESERVE, a lush and hilly, 2,190 ha (5,410 acres) sanctuary for various antelope species. The reserve has nature trails and drives, picnic sites and, if you're staying over, accommodation in 4-bed rustic huts.

PORT SHEPSTONE

The 80 km (50 mile) shoreline from Mtwalume to Port Edward (known as the Hibiscus Coast) is studded with small resorts, not easily distinguishable from each other at first glance – they all offer sun, sea and sand in abundance – but, as the locals and regulars will tell you, highly individual places once you get to know them.

Port Shepstone, sited at the mouth of the Umzimkulu River, is the largest of southern KwaZulu-Natal's watercourses, navigable by small craft for about 8 km (5 miles) upstream. For holiday-makers, there are bowling greens, an 18-hole golf course that ranks among South Africa's finest, part of the Country Club (which plays amiable host to visitors), tree-shaded parks, beaches and tidal pools. About 20 km (12.5 miles) inland from Port Shepstone is the:
ORIBI GORGE NATURE RESERVE, a 1,837 ha (4,539 acres) expanse of magnificently rugged hill and deep valley, stream, waterfall, forest and emerald-green grassland and, its most striking feature, the spectacular canyon carved from the sandstone layers by the Umzimkulwana River. The gorge is 24 km (14.5 miles) long, around 5 km (3 miles) wide, 366 m (1,200 ft) deep, and the vistas, including that from the extraordinary overhang called Hanging Rock, are unforgettable. Set aside at least a morning for the scenic drive through the gorge.

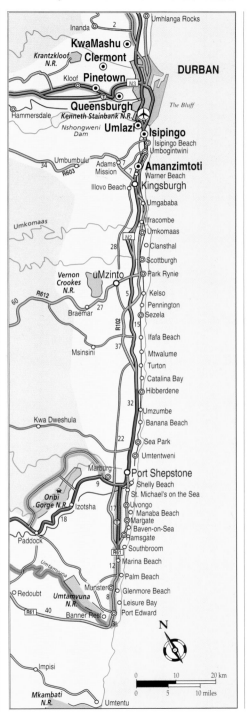

The Mbezane (or Blue) Lagoon at Ramsgate – a paradise for boating enthusiasts and fishermen.

The reserve's wildlife comprises 40 mammal species, including the shy samango monkey, baboons and various antelope, though not the graceful and now quite rare oribi, from which gorge and reserve take their name. Nearly 270 species of bird have been recorded in the area; of special note are the raptors (jackal buzzard, crowned, longcrested and black eagles). There are trails, pleasant picnic sites, fishing spots (permits are required) and, for those wishing to stay overnight, a hotel and a hutted camp run by the Natal Parks Board.

MARGATE

Like the popular English seaside town after which it is named, Margate – large, lively and crowded – is the 'capital' of the Hibiscus Coast, offering all the standard holiday attractions but with a flair and an uninhibited *joie de vivre* that lifts it far above the ordinary. Among its tourist

assets: lovely beaches, good fishing, safe bathing, an Olympic-standard pool, an 18-hole golf course, bowling greens, an amusement park, hotels, apartment and self-catering complexes, shops and supermarkets, speciality restaurants, discos and three cinemas. It is also a residential town with a substantial business base and an airport (KwaZulu-Natal's second largest).

RAMSGATE

Ramsgate, situated 4 km (2.5 miles) farther along the coast, is renowned for its magnificent Mbezane Lagoon, a mecca for wind-surfers, and for its long beach, which it shares with the next-door and rather exclusive community of Southbroom. The Frederika Nature Reserve, which protects the coastal forest, separates the beach from the short (but demanding), rather splendid and very busy 18-hole golf course. Among Ramsgate's other drawcards is the Crayfish Inn, which serves marvellous seafood and is crammed with seafaring relics of one sort or another, and the many antique, craft and other 'browsing' shops that line the main street.

PORT EDWARD

This is the final stopover before you reach the Umtamvuna River (the Eastern Cape border), across which is the famed Wild Coast Sun Hotel/Casino Complex (see page 177).

Port Edward's pleasant beach is overlooked by the wooded slopes of Tragedy Hill, site of the 1831 massacre, by the Zulu, of a party of whites – what was later acknowledged to have been a tragic misunderstanding,

To the south is the:

UMTAMVUNA NATURE RESERVE, a place of forest, gorge, steep hill, rich plant life (over 700 floral species, among them 35 types of orchid) and great scenic beauty. Self-guided trails; no accommodation (though there is plenty just along the coast, of course).

THE NORTH COAST

The Dolphin Coast, stretching 100 km (62 miles) north from Durban to the Tugela River mouth, is noted for its seaside resorts – not as numerous as those along the South Coast but just as pleasant in their own, rather quieter way: small clusters of holiday homes, hotels, luxury apartment blocks built beside river-mouth lagoons and overlooking the warm and generally kindly Indian Ocean. The sands are broad and white, the shoreline tropical, graced by ilala palms, Madagascar casuarinas, hibiscus, bougainvillaea and other strikingly colourful flowering shrubs and trees. The coastal highway – the M4 from Durban to Ballito, where it joins the N2 toll road north – is called Shaka's Way, and it provides a splendid scenic drive from Durban.

An alternative route is the old North Coast Road. Running a few kilometres inland and parallel to the N2, this follows the old trade route, once used by the hunters of elephant and traffickers in ivory and skins, and by the Zulu impis on their way south to do battle with the Pondo. It now serves the vast sugar-cane plantations and 'sugar towns' of the region, and is busy with the passage of cane trucks.

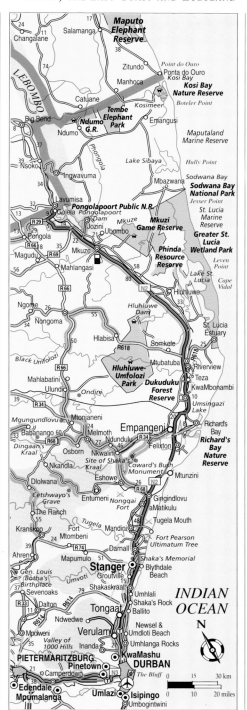

TONGAAT

This is a substantial town with a large Indian population and an attractively tropical feel about it: avenues and gardens and embowered with jacaranda and poinsettia and bamboo; street stalls sell luscious fruits. Bordering town is the headquarters of the giant Tongaat sugar group, whose buildings are designed in Cape Dutch style and beautifully furnished with antiques. The river from which the place takes its name (*thongathi* is the word for the trees that line its banks) runs into the ocean at:

WESTBROOK BEACH, an especially lovely stretch of sand. The quiet little resort comprises seaside cottages in a setting of casuarinas, two hotels and a large tidal pool. Upriver is:

CROCODILE CREEK, a ranch devoted to the breeding and conservation of the Nile crocodile. Guided tours are on offer. Much further along the old road and 8 km (5 miles) inland is:

STANGER

Stanger is the main centre of another large sugar-producing district. It was established as a colonial outpost in 1873, at the site on which Shaka built his maze-like capital Dakuza (the word translates, roughly, as 'the place of the lost person') and where he was murdered, in 1828, by his half-brothers Dingane and Mhlangana. In the centre of town, marking the exact spot (occupied at the time by a grain pit, into which the king's body was thrown) is a small memorial garden. Farther north along the coast is:

BALLITO

Ballito is a popular holiday centre 40.5 km (25 miles) north of Durban. Shark-protected bathing; tidal pool. Nearby is the older and quieter Willard Beach, just inland the Umhlali Country Club, which has one of the country's finest golf courses. Shaka tested the bravery of his warriors by making them leap from the headland overlooking Thompson's Bay.

TUGELA MOUTH

HAROLD JOHNSON NATURE RESERVE This 104 ha (257 acres) sanctuary, on the steep south bank of the Tugela River, preserves a patch of coastal forest, some attractive orchid species, and relics of the brutal Anglo-Zulu conflict including Fort Pearson and the Ultimatum Tree. An intriguing excursion is the Remedies and Rituals Trail (one of three self-guided walks), which introduces you to trees that are significant in traditional (and white settler) medical and spiritual belief.

ZULULAND

The territory extending from the Tugela River north to the frontiers of Swaziland and Mozambique is known as Zululand – a historical rather than a formal name, and one which had a more precise meaning in the 19th century. The far northern subsection, a beautiful region of hills, savanna plains, wetlands and high coastal dunes, is called Maputaland.

This is a luxuriant land, one that nurtures a proliferation of wildlife. Indeed, the northern conservancies are among the most impressive in the world: warmth, moisture and lush vegetation provide ideal habitats for a large variety of animals and birds. The Hluhluwe section of the Hluhluwe-Umfolozi Park, for instance, is little more than one-twentieth the size of the Kruger National Park but contains almost 70% of the total number of the Kruger's species.

Among the many other attractions this lovely country has to offer are a myriad fascinating cultural venues, splendid walks and wilderness

BELOW: *Traditional Zulu 'beehive' and rondavel homes dot the KwaZulu-Natal landscape.*
OPPOSITE: *A Zulu vendor displays her wares.*

trails, bathing and skin-diving (be careful to stick to the safe areas), and superb opportunities for photography, hunting and fishing.

ESHOWE

Established in 1860 by the Zulu king-in-waiting, Cetshwayo, on a ridge of hills 36 km (22 miles) inland and 75 km (47 miles) north-west of the Tugela River mouth, Eshowe was burnt to the ground by the retreating Zulus in the 1879 war with the British. The extensive royal 'residence' has been faithfully reconstructed, and an informative cultural centre and museum established, at Ondini near Ulundi. It's an attractive little town, notable for Vukani (in Main Street: Zulu arts and crafts), for its romantic-looking colonial fort, for the Zululand Historical Museum it contains and for the:

DLINZA FOREST NATURE RESERVE, a 200 ha (494 acres) patch of unspoilt indigenous woodland that occupies the centre of town. Dlinza's fauna includes rich birdlife, vervet monkey, wild pig, blue and red duiker and bushbuck. There are half-a-dozen pleasant picnic spots, a

central clearing known as Bishop Seat (venue for church services and the occasional nativity play) and a network of short trails.

ZULU LIFESTYLES The Nkwaleni Valley, along the road between Eshowe and Melmoth, is the location for three excellent and increasingly popular Zulu 'living museums' that offer visitors day-long and overnight 'kraal experiences'. Biggest is Shakaland, which was built for the TV epic *Shaka Zulu* and now comprises a hotel, a kraal of 120 beehive huts (with en suite bathrooms); specialities include Zulu delicacies, dancing, praise-singing, fascinating displays by spirit mediums (sangomas) and herbalists, basket-weaving, pot-making and hut-building.

RICHARDS BAY AND EMPANGENI

Richards Bay is a relatively recent deep-water port – it came on stream in 1976 – and, despite the fact that its harbour isn't the biggest in the country (that ranking belongs to Durban), it's the busiest in terms of cargo volume handled. The coal terminal is the world's largest.

ZULU HERITAGE

In traditional Zulu society the women cultivated the land, cared for the children, saw to the family's water, food and firewood needs; the young boys herded cattle; the men hunted and made war. Zulu homes were beehive-shaped and positioned around a central cattle-kraal, which was considered a sacred place, accessible only to the daughters of the house. Cattle served as the accepted measure of wealth, and on marriage were used for the bride-price (called *lobola*) which the groom's family paid.

The customary clothing materials were hides and pelts, adorned in various ways by the fighting men to distinguish each of the age-graded regiments, the regimental 'uniform' completed by plumes and patterned oxhide shields. When the first white traders came onto the scene in the early 19th century they found a ready market among the Zulu for their coloured beads. These were stitched together in intricately ornamental designs, each colour taking on symbolic significance. The principal Zulu musical instrument was the cowhide drum – and the human voice, used with magnificent effect on ceremonial occasions, and as a prelude to battle. The Zulu language is complex, subtle, expressive, full of imagery, and punctuated by 'click' sounds borrowed from San (Bushman) speech.

The Zulu were intensely aware of the spirits in the world around them. Animistic belief credited a rock, a pool, a tree, or a river with a personality of its own, and it was believed that a very powerful force, called Nkulukulu ('great, great one')
watched over the people. It was the ancestral spirits, however, who were responsible for the day-to-day welfare of their descendants.

The fourth element in the body of traditional Zulu belief are the diviners, or *sangomas*, who act as intermediaries between the ancestral spirits and their living descendants, and are able to predict, divine and heal a multitude of ills, usually psychological and social. They are recruited to their calling by the ancestors, and receive rigorous training under an already qualified diviner.

Today the majority of Zulu are both westernized and urbanized, most belong to the Christian faith (though traditional convictions are still influential), and the old ways are fast dying. Ancient custom and ritual are at their most evident in the more remote rural areas.

Zulus at Shakaland (see page 133).

This all might sound rather industrial and unattractive, but in fact Richards Bay and, especially, the coast and countryside surrounding it have a fair amount to offer the visitor. Not only are the recreation facilities outstanding, but the lagoon of the Mhlatuze River, around which the town has grown, is a successful conservation area, as are some 400 ha (990 acres) of shoreline. The beaches are being developed for tourism (the region has the only officially-approved safe bathing beach in Zululand).

Approximately 20 km inland is Empangeni, a thriving centre for the lucrative sugar, cotton, timber and cattle industries.

THREE INVITING RESERVES Conveniently accessible from both these towns are a number of superb conservation areas. Of these, by far the most prominent are:

• **Enseleni:** A tropical sanctuary set aside for wildebeest, zebra, hippo, crocodile and various species of antelope. Highly recommended is the self-guided Swamp Trail.

• **Umlalazi:** This lovely reserve embraces a very popular beach area; the birds, butterflies and monkeys are an absolute delight. The mangrove swamps in the area are the habitat of crabs and other creatures, as well as the land-living mudskipper fish. The visitor amenities in the reserve include log cabins.

• **Windy Ridge Game Park:** A splendid conservation area of indigenous woodland and riverine expanses nurtures the white rhino, giraffe, leopard, various species of antelope, crocodile and some magnificent birds. The visitor amenities within the park include two pleasant rest camps and a network of game-viewing roads.

ABOVE: *Boating and fishing at St Lucia, part of the magnificent Greater St Lucia Wetland Park.*
BELOW: *A section of the St Lucia wetlands, destined to become a World Heritage Site.*

THE GREATER ST LUCIA WETLAND PARK

One of the biggest and most remarkable land, lake and marine wilderness areas on the continent of Africa, this 250,000 ha (618,000 acres) complex comprises a number of separate but closely interrelated components, among them river estuary, game reserve, forest, lily-covered pan, lake/lagoon, high dune (the highest in the world) and, of course, the sea.

Central feature is the 36,000 ha (89,000 acres) lake formed 60 million years ago, when the ocean receded to leave a sandy flatland, parts of which were low enough to retain both sea and fresh water. The lake and its immediate surrounds are a proclaimed game park.

THE LAKE is really a cluster of lagoons extending up from the estuary and is widest (20 km/ 12.5 miles) in the north, where its eastern portion is known as False Bay (22 km long/14 miles and 2 km wide/1 mile). The waters are shallow (average 90 cm/35 in), and home to 800 hippo (often seen grazing around the estuary), to crocodile and to large numbers of fish, crustaceans, insects and other nutritious creatures that attract vast numbers of birds. Among the latter are a breeding community of fish eagles, thousands of white pelicans, 12 species of heron, flamingos, saddlebills, spoonbills, Caspian terns. Near St Lucia village in the south is the fascinating Crocodile Centre.

ST LUCIA PARK, a thin (1 km/½ mile) belt running along the lake's shores and covering 12,545 ha (31,000 acres) of reedbed, woodland and grassland. The birdlife is prolific; mammals include nyala, reedbuck, bushbuck, duiker, suni, steenbok, bush-pig, vervet monkey.

TEWATE WILDERNESS AREA, formerly called Cape Vidal Forest, is a 12,000 ha (30,000 acres) tree-mantled dune area much favoured by birdwatchers and hikers. Among the resident animals are black rhino, buffalo and kudu.

ST LUCIA MARINE RESERVE This, together with the Maputaland coastline and offshore strip to the north, extends for roughly 150 km (93 miles) and covers 84,000 ha (208,000 acres), which makes it Africa's largest marine conservancy. The St Lucia segment runs from Cape Vidal to a point north of Sodwana Bay; prominent features are the coral reefs (the world's southernmost), a wealth of tropical fish, beach-nesting leatherhead and loggerback turtles (once endangered, now successfully protected) and superb beaches from which beautiful cowrie shells can be garnered. Access by four-wheel-drive; no camping; no bottom fishing, though spear, line and ski-boat are acceptable.

SODWANA BAY NATIONAL PARK A small (1,155 ha/2,854 acres) coastal area that plays host to large numbers of summer vacationers; amenities include campsites, log cabins, a supermarket, community centre, fish weighing points and freezers. For all that, though, Sodwana has its beauty, its wildlife and its serenity. The beach-fringed bay is protected by reef and point; the swamps and lakelets of the hinterland are home to a variety of animals and to a fine array of birds; the waters of the bay are clear and the

offshore reefs lovely, beckoning the scuba-diver and the snorkeller. This is one of southern Africa's finest game-fishing areas: remarkable catches of blue and black marlin, sailfish and tuna are routinely recorded. The Natal Parks Board conducts night-time 'turtle tours'.

ABOVE: *A nesting leatherback turtle, a rare and endangered species, attracts attention.*
BELOW: Crinum *species are among the wild flowers that grace the St Lucia area.*
OPPOSITE: *One of St Lucia's white pelicans.*

MKUZI GAME RESERVE, some way inland extends over 37,985 ha (93,860 acres) of savanna parkland and riverine and sycamore forest. The reserve is bisected by the Mkuze River and Nsumu Pan, home to the ghostly fever tree, crocodile and hippo, and a splendid variety of water-related birds – wild geese and duck, pink-backed pelican (Nsumu Pan is now their only South African breeding site), fish eagle and squacco heron, hamerkop and woolly-necked stork. Among the mammals are white and black rhino, giraffe, blue wildebeest, kudu, eland, mountain reedbuck, nyala, waterbuck and bushbuck. Mkuzi's amenities are especially attractive: there's a pleasant rest camp (choice of cottages, bungalows, rest huts; cooks and helpers make life comfortable); caravan/camping ground; thatched hides beside pan and waterholes; game-viewing drives, trails (including a 57 km/35 miles auto-trail), a 'vulture restaurant', shop (assorted frozen foods) and petrol outlet. There's also the splendid Nhlonhlela bush camp, set beside a bird-rich pan (the viewing platform-cum-dining enclosure is a magical place). Information and bookings: Natal Parks Board (*see* Advisory, page 143).

FALSE BAY SECTION covers around 2,247 ha (5,552 acres) of dune forest, woodland and bush to the west of the lake's False Bay. Here there's a small rest camp, campsite, picnicking, bird-watching (150 species, including the pink-backed pelican), various buck species, and, at Lister Point, some immensely ancient fossil beds.

OTHER AREAS To the south of St Lucia Estuary are the Mhlatuze and, a little farther west, the Dukuduku forests, the latter a large (6,000 ha/14,800 acres) and precious stretch of coastal lowland trees. The environmentally fragile and threatened (by human encroachment) area sustains several endangered bird species. The forest itself is one of the few coastal ones that are self-sustaining; attractions include floral wealth, lovely butterflies and picnic spots. Beware the rare baboon viper.

ST LUCIA'S AMENITIES The wider wetland area offers splendid opportunities for game and bird viewing, walking and hiking, angling, game-fishing, scuba-diving and outdoor living.

ST LUCIA VILLAGE offers private hotels, holiday apartments, self-contained accommodation (prices vary, but off-season rates are unusually attractive), time-share, shops, garages, eateries,

The highly endangered white, or square-lipped, rhino has flourished in Hluhluwe-Umfolozi Park.

swimming beach, tennis and boat-hire. A lake excursion on the *Santa Lucia* launch is a must (there are three trips daily; crocodile and hippo are among the many sights). The Monzi Country Club welcomes visitors. Worth calling in at is the mNandi Arts and Crafts Centre in the main street. There are also guided tours to Hluhluwe-Umfolozi and its neighbouring reserves. Holidaymakers with four-wheel-drives can drive for about 7 km (4 miles) along the broad white beach.

The Natal Parks Board runs a large and popular resort at the village: three caravan/camping grounds, boat tours, a small game park, and, for those who are interested in studying the habits and habitats of *Crocodilus niloticus*, there is the St Lucia Crocodile Centre, considered one of the finest of its kind in the world.

PARKS BOARD ACCOMMODATION and camp-sites are also available in the False Bay park, at Charter's Creek and Fanie's Island (western lakeside); Mapelane, on the Mfolozi River south of St Lucia estuary (wonderful bird life), in the Tewate conservancy and at Sodwana Bay.

HLUHLUWE-UMFOLOZI PARK

These two formerly separate but neighbouring areas are the oldest of South Africa's game sanctuaries. Both were proclaimed in April 1895 – three years before the Kruger National Park began life as the Sabie Reserve. Until the early 1990s they were divided by a narrow corridor, over which the animals moved at will, but have since been consolidated and are now administered as a single entity.

THE UMFOLOZI SECTION extends over nearly 50,000 ha (123,500 acres) of rolling hill and floodplain between central Zululand's White and Black Mfolozi rivers. The name in Zulu translates (roughly) as 'zigzag', a reference to the convoluted course it takes through the hills before dividing into its two colourful offsprings. The area – covered by warm, well-watered, lush, sweetly grassed savanna – was home to teeming populations of game long before the inevitable encroachment of man. Much of the game, though, disappeared during the years after 1921, when the authorities launched a massive, sustained, misguided and, in the event, disastrous game extermination programme designed to eradicate the tsetse fly that plagued the surrounding ranchlands. Altogether, more than

138

100,000 animals were slaughtered before finally, in 1945, the killings mercifully were abandoned in favour of chemical controls.

The Umfolozi made an excellent recovery and today serves as a haven for white rhino, of which there are about 1,800 in the combined reserve – a surprisingly healthy figure, because the species faced extinction until the Natal Parks Board launched an ambitious and deservedly publicized programme (it captured world headlines) during the 1960s. Still endangered elsewhere, the white rhino breeds very well here: surplus animals are regularly translocated to areas throughout and beyond South Africa.

Now its smaller black cousin is in similar decline, the victim of horn-hunting poachers. Two decades ago, the continent-wide population of black rhino stood at over 60,000; today fewer than 3,500 remain, an estimated 400 of them in KwaZulu-Natal.

Among the area's other game species are blue wildebeest, buffalo, giraffe, elephant, leopard, zebra, waterbuck, steenbok, mountain reedbuck, kudu, impala, nyala, spotted hyaena, wild dog, black-backed jackal and warthog. Cheetah have also been introduced. The lion population numbers something over 40, which in many respects is quite remarkable: these predators, prime targets of the 19th-century white hunters, had been regionally extinct for nearly six decades until a lone male made its erratic and elusive way from Mozambique to Umfolozi (a distance of 400 km/250 miles) in the late 1950s, to be joined, later, by a small group of females and the resultant prides flourished. Birdlife: approximately 400 species have been recorded, among them Wahlberg's eagle, night heron, wood stork, black-bellied korhaan and Temminck's courser.

Umfolozi is well geared for visitors: accommodation – at the two hutted camps and the two bush camps – ranges from the fairly luxurious to the basic; there is a wilderness trail, an auto-trail, several walks and an extensive system of game-viewing roads. The nearest shop is at Mtubatuba, 50 km (30 miles) to the south, though petrol, cooldrinks, books and curios are available at the camps.

THE HLUHLUWE SECTION, about half the size of Umfolozi, is stunningly beautiful: a rich land of sometimes misty mountain forest, grass-covered slope, dense thicket, enchanting river (the Hluhluwe, which takes its name from the lianas, or monkey ropes, that festoon the riverine forest) and of an incredible diversity of plant and animal life. Included among the 84 different mammals are white and black rhino, elephant, giraffe, buffalo, blue wildebeest, Burchell's zebra, nyala, lion and cheetah (though both these are elusive, especially in summer), samango monkey, baboon, wild dog, spotted hyaena and waterbuck. There are crocodile, hippo and leguaan in the riverine areas. Bird species number about 425, and include the bateleur, the marabou stork and the white-backed vulture.

Accommodation comprises chalets, simplexes and duplexes at the large and modern Hilltop camp. There are walking and auto-trails, nearly 90 km (56 miles) of game-viewing roads, viewing hides, a Zulu village museum, a restaurant, a superette and a petrol-filling pump. There are also two delightful bush camps.

Other Zululand Reserves

NDUMO GAME RESERVE A smallish 10,000 ha (24,700 acres) area in the far north (it flanks the Mozambique border), renowned for the superb richness of its riverine life: the reserve lies on the floodplain of the Pongolo River, and the watercourse and the pans sustain a great many water-related birds (altogether 416 species have been recorded, among them Pel's fishing owl and the southern banded snake eagle) as well as bream and barbel, tiger-fish and tilapia, hippo and crocodile. The last-mentioned had once been reduced to the point of local extinction by hunters and by the proliferation of barbel (which destroyed the crocodile's food source) but now, thanks to the hatcheries, they're fully restored in number and condition.

Ndumo has a pleasant rest camp of 2-bed cottages (cooks and helpers are in attendance), game-viewing roads and hides. Guided tours in open vehicles are available.

LAKE SIBAYA The country's largest freshwater lake, Sibaya – nearly 30 m (98 ft) deep, blue and clear – extends over 70 km² (27 square miles) of coastal plain north of Sodwana Bay, the eastern shores separated from the sea by a high belt of wooded dunes. Attractions: crocodile, hippo, reedbuck, side-striped jackal and birds (280 species; hides have been established); boating (craft available for hire); walking trails and tranquillity. Basic accommodation at Camp Baya (bring your own food); no other facilities.

KOSI BAY NATURE RESERVE This, the northernmost of the parks, comprises 11,000 ha (27,000 acres) of lakes and mangrove swamps which, like Sibaya, are separated from the sea by dunes. Turtles – the famed loggerheads and leatherbacks – breed in the area; the lake supports hippo and crocodile. Accommodation: luxury lodges (well-appointed, fully staffed), caravan/camp site. Attractions: game trails, turtle-viewing trips and fishing.

ITALA GAME RESERVE Not generically related to the other Zululand reserves, and rather off the beaten track, its 30,000 ha (74,000 acres) lie along the Pongolo River (which here forms the provincial border) and is reached via Vryheid. Some 75 species of mammal inhabit the hilly grasslands and bushveld, among them white and black rhino, elephant, giraffe, zebra, cheetah, brown hyaena and numerous antelope (including eland, kudu and the rare roan). Basic accommodation in the three bush camps and at the caravan/camp site; there are trails and a guided day walk. The sophisticated and quite beautifully designed Ntshondwe rest camp, comprising luxury lodge, self-contained thatched chalets, shop, restaurant, swimming pool, conference venue, all in a magnificent cliff-face setting, is one of KwaZulu-Natal's showpieces.

PRIVATE GAME LODGES A number of privately-run game ranches have been established in various parts of KwaZulu-Natal and Zululand. Accommodation varies from the economical and self-contained to all-found luxury comparable to the best on offer from Mpumalanga's private reserves (*see* page 81). Obvious attractions include excellent game-viewing opportunities,

walking, bird-watching, personalized service and a sociable camplife. Some of the venues specialize in trophy-hunting safaris during the winter months.

• **Bonamanzi Game Park**, near Hluhluwe village. The place offers attractive accommodation in picturesque A-frame tree-houses and in the conventional thatched-hut camp and luxury lodge. Guests are encouraged to walk the several free-ranging wilderness trails and strolls.

• **Bushlands Game Lodge.** Also in the Hluhluwe area. On offer are air-conditioned, self-contained log cabins raised above the ground, connected by elevated wooden walkways; full-service restaurant (venison a speciality); guided game drives around the Hluhluwe-Umfolozi Park and the Greater St Lucia Wetland Park.

• **Phinda Resource Reserve.** This 15,000 ha (37,000 acres) expanse of recently stocked land between the Mkuzi Game Reserve and Sodwana state forest is an up-market 'eco-tourism' showpiece developed with two aims in mind: to provide visitors (mainly from overseas) with a wilderness experience without parallel, and to share its considerable resources with the local rural communities – an integrated approach that benefits everyone. For guests, there are guided game-drives through widely differing ecosystems (savanna, bushveld, palm veld, rare sand forest, wetland) and exploratory forays farther afield to take in the varied land, lake and marine splendours (including the lovely coral reefs) of Maputaland, bird-watching (about 360 recorded species) and luxury accommodation.

Part of Itala's superb Ntshondwe camp.

ADVISORY: DURBAN, THE EAST COAST AND ZULULAND

CLIMATE

Kind to holiday-makers throughout year, though the humidity can be ferocious in high summer (between January and March), especially in the northern coastal areas. Summer rainfall area; some winter rainfall: Durban January average 109 mm/4 in, July average 28 mm/1 in, annual average 1,008 mm/40 in. Durban average temperature: January max. 27.2 °C/80.1 °F; January min. 20.5 °C/69 °F; July max. 27.2 °C/80.1 °F; July min. 10.9 °C/52 °F.

MAIN ATTRACTIONS

Durban: Sun, sea and sand ❑ The kaleidoscopic Golden Mile ❑ Day-drive's to KwaZulu-Natal's renowned game parks and nature reserves ❑ Fine hotels, restaurants, shops, tourist amenities ❑ Excellent sporting facilities, especially swimming, fishing, golf.
South Coast: Sun, sea and sand ❑ Angling, golf, scubadiving ❑ The Oribi Gorge and nature reserve.
North Coast and Zululand: Splendid game and nature reserves ❑ Sun, sea and sand ❑ Angling ❑ Zulu history and culture.

TRAVEL

Road. Durban: 79 km/49 miles from Pietermaritzburg; 608 km/378 miles from Johannesburg; 640 km/398 miles from Bloemfontein; 655 km/409 miles from East London; 664 km/413 miles from Pretoria; 764 km/475 miles from Kimberley; 901 km/560 miles from Port Elizabeth; 1,654 km/1,028 miles from Cape Town. National highways, generally in excellent condition, link Durban with all major South African centres. The N2 leads south and then east through Port Elizabeth to Cape Town; the N3 takes you north-west through Pietermaritzburg and Harrismith to Johannesburg. Coach services link Durban with major centres.

There is a daily bus service between Durban railway station and Pietermaritzburg; tel. (031) 302-2989. Scheduled bus services between Durban and Wild Coast Sun: contact Durban Unlimited for more information. A bus service connects Durban city centre with La Lucia Mall.
Rail. There is a rail service along the south coast. Intercity services connect Durban with all major centres. Information (arrivals/departures): tel. (031) 361-7609. The main railway station is on the Umgeni Road, some way to the north of city centre.
Air. Scheduled services connect Durban with major centres. Durban Airport is off the Southern Freeway (the South Coast road), 15 minutes drive from city centre; a bus service operates between the terminal (corner of Smith and Aliwal streets) and the airport.

Flight information: tel. (031) 42-6111; bookings: tel. (031) 305-6491. Charter services and private aircraft: Virginia Airport; tel. (031) 84-4144. There are daily Comair flights from Johannesburg to Richards Bay. Court Helicopters; tel. (031) 83-9513.

GETTING AROUND DURBAN

City bus and taxi services; the Mynah minibus service is excellent; local tour operators offer sightseeing trips; major car-hire companies have offices in the city, as do local car-, camper- and caravan-hire firms.
South Coast: Linked to Durban by the N2 highway as far as Port Shepstone, thereafter by the R61; both in good condition. Inland roads can be a bit rough.
North Coast and Zululand: Main road is also the N2, parallel to, but out of sight of, the coast until it gets to the general vicinity of Richards Bay (about two-and-a-half hours' drive from Durban), then sweeps inland to the Swaziland border. Excellent condition. Major Zululand roads are tarred; most minor ones (including those in the reserves) are gravel.

ACCOMMODATION

Durban and the South Coast are among South Africa's principal leisure areas; visitors have a choice of hotels, guest houses, holiday apartments, resorts and caravan/camping grounds. Book in advance for the summer months, and especially for the Christmas period.

Select hotels

GOLDEN MILE
Beach Hotel Good value; 103 rooms; conference facilities are available. 107 Marine Parade, Durban 4001; tel. (031) 37-4222, fax 368-2322.
Blue Waters Snell Parade. 264 rooms; conference facilities are available. PO Box 10201, Marine Parade 4056; tel. (031) 32-4272, toll-free reservations 0800 31 2044.
City Lodge Durban *** In attractive garden setting. 160 rooms. PO Box 10842, Marine Parade 4056; tel. (031) 32-1447, fax 32-1483.
Elangeni Sun **** Snell Parade. Large and luxurious; conference facilities are available. PO Box 4094, Durban 4000; tel. (031) 37-1321, fax 32-5527, central reservations (011) 482-3500.
Holiday Inn Garden Court: North Beach *** 243 rooms, 23 suites; conference facilities are available. PO Box 10592, Marine Parade 4056; tel. (031) 32-7361, fax 37-4058, central reservations (011) 482-3500.
Holiday Inn Garden Court: South Beach *** 380 rooms; small conference facilities. PO Box 10199, Marine Parade 4056; tel. (031) 37-2231, fax 37-4640, central reservations (011) 482-3500.
Holiday Inn: Marine Parade **** Large and luxurious; 344 sea-facing rooms; conference facilities available. PO Box 10809, Marine Parade 4056; tel. (031) 37-3341, fax 32-9885, central reservations (011) 482-3500.

141

Karos Edward Hotel **** Seafront elegance. 101 rooms; conference facilities are available. PO Box 105, Durban 4000; tel. (031) 37-3681, fax 32-1692.

Palace Protea Hotel *** 76 self-contained units; à la carte restaurant; conference facilities. PO Box 10539, Marine Parade 4056; tel. (031) 32-8351, fax 32-8307, toll-free reservations 0800 11 9000.

Seaboard Protea Hotel *** 45 rooms; conference facilities. PO Box 10555, Marine Parade 4056; tel. and fax (031) 37-3601, toll-free reservations 0800 11 9000.

Tropicana Hotel 160 rooms, 7 suites; conference facilities available. PO Box 10305, Marine Parade 4056; tel. (031) 368-1511, fax 368-2322, toll-free 0800 11 9000.

UMHLANGA ROCKS

Beverly Hills Sun ***** 79 rooms, 5 suites; conference facilities are available. PO Box 71, Umhlanga Rocks 4320; tel. (031) 561-2211, fax 561-3711, central reservations (011) 482-3500.

Cabana Beach *** 217 self-contained cabanas; 2 restaurants; 2 bars; conference facilities. PO Box 10, Umhlanga Rocks 4320; tel. (031) 561-2371, fax 561-3522, central reservations (011) 482-3500.

Oyster Box Hotel *** Garden setting. 90 rooms, 7 suites; conference facilities. PO Box 22, Umhlanga Rocks 4320; tel. (031) 561-2233, fax 561-4072.

Umhlanga Rocks Hotel 96 rooms. PO Box 2, Umhlanga Rocks 4320; tel. and fax (031) 561-1321.

Umhlanga Sands *** 237 suites; conference facilities. PO Box 223, Umhlanga Rocks 4320; tel. (031) 561-2323, fax 561-4408, central reservations (011) 482-3500.

SOUTH COAST

Bedford Inn 10 pleasant en suite rooms; 2 restaurants. PO Box 1656, Port Shepstone 4240; tel. (0391) 2-1085, fax 2-4328.

Blue Marlin 93 en suite rooms. PO Box 24, Scottburgh 4180; tel. (0323) 2-1214, fax 2-0971.

Brackenmoor Hotel 16 rooms, 2 suites; chapel; 2 restaurants; bar. PO Box 518, St. Michaels-on-Sea 4265; tel. (03931) 5-0065, fax 7-5109.

Crayfish Inn Small; self-catering; à la carte restaurant; bar. PO Box 7, Ramsgate 4285; tel. (03931) 4-4410.

Cutty Sark Protea Hotel Lovely garden setting. 49 en suite rooms; à la carte and table d'hôte restaurants; bar. PO Box 3, Scottburgh 4180; tel. (0323) 2-1230, fax 2-2197, toll-free 0800 11 9000.

Karridene Protea Hotel *** 23 en suite rooms; self-catering units; à la carte restaurant; coffee shop; bar. PO Box 20, Illovo Beach 4155; tel. (031) 96-3332, fax 96-4903, toll-free 0800 11 9000.

Margate Hotel 69 en suite rooms; restaurant; 2 bars. PO Box 100, Margate 4275; tel. (03931) 2-1078.

Marina Beach Hotel 26 rooms. PO Box 9, Marina Beach 4281; tel. (03931) 3-0022.

Oribi Gorge Hotel Near gorge and reserve. 12 rooms. PO Box 575, Port Shepstone 4240; tel. (0397) 9-1753.

NORTH COAST AND ZULULAND

Hluhluwe Hotel Near game reserve. 63 en suite rooms; restaurant; bar. PO Box 92, Hluhluwe 3960; tel. and fax (035) 562-0251.

Ghost Mountain Inn ** Near game reserves. Garden setting; 38 en suite rooms; à la carte restaurant; bar. PO Box 18, Mkuze 3965; tel. and fax (035) 573-1025.

Karos Bayshore Inn ** Next to Richards Bay marina. 100 en suite rooms; restaurant with carvery and buffet; bar. PO Box 51, Richards Bay 3900; tel. (0351) 3-1246, fax 3-2335.

Karos Richards Hotel *** Family hotel just outside town. 88 en suite rooms; à la carte restaurant, carvery, buffet; bar. PO Box 242, Richards Bay 3900; tel. (0351) 3-1301, fax 3-2334.

Marina Lodge 63 rooms, 2 suites, 2 penthouses; à la carte and buffet restaurants. PO Box 10105, Richards Bay 3901; tel. (0351) 3-1350, fax 3-1361.

Salt Rock Hotel and Resort On the beachfront. 64 en suite rooms; à la carte restaurant, carvery, buffet; bar. PO Salt Rock 4391; tel. (0322) 5025, fax 5071.

Shakaland Zulu 'living museum' and cross-cultural centre (*see* page 133). 28 thatched 'beehive huts'; traditional dancing; crafts on view. PO Box 103, Eshowe 3815; tel. (03546) 912, fax 824.

Trade Winds Hotel ** Next to sea and the Umlalazi reserve. 28 en suite rooms; restaurant (Portuguese); bar. PO Box 100, Mtunzini 3867; tel. (0353) 40-1411, fax 40-1629.

Zululand Sun Lodge *** In private game reserve. 65 en suite rooms; superb carvery, buffet, barbecue meals. PO Box 116, Hluhluwe 3960; tel. (035) 562-0241, fax 562-0193.

Self-catering and budget

The region offers a wide choice of resort and other self-catering holiday accommodation and caravan/camping options (mostly along the coasts). Durban Unlimited and the local tourism information offices have the details. The larger game sanctuaries have well-appointed rest camps; contact the Natal Parks Board. For budget accommodation: Bed 'n Breakfast; tel. and fax (031) 764-6354.

Select restaurants
CITY AND SURROUNDS

Captain's Seafood Restaurant, Cowey Park. Soothing atmosphere; seafood delights; tel. (031) 28-3297.

Colony, The Oceanic, Sol Harris Crescent. Dishes from the best of local ingredients; tel. (031) 368-2789.

Incognito, Overport. Atmospheric; cosmopolitan cuisine with French undertones; tel. (031) 26-4795.

La Dolce Vita, Durdoc Centre, Smith St. Imaginative menu; Italian influence; tel. (031) 301-8161.

Le Creole, Fedlife Building, Smith St. Mauritian dishes (and others); charming décor; tel. (031) 304-2470.

Loafer's, Windermere Rd. Coffee-and-cake shop in a class of its own; open until 16h00; tel. (031) 23-2100.

Oliver Twist, Boland Bank House, West St. Victorian English in food and décor; tel. (031) 37-4055.

Rick's Cafe Americain, The Playhouse. Wonderful Cajun fare; tel. (031) 304-3297.

Roma Revolving Restaurant, Victoria Embankment. Panoramic views from the turning top; finest quality fare; tel. (031) 37-6707.

Royal Grill, Royal Hotel. Cosmopolitan; as inviting is the next-door Royal Steakhouse; tel. (031) 304-0331.

Saagries, Coastlands, West St. The very best of Indian cuisine; tel. (031) 32-7922.

Squire's Loft, Florida Rd, Berea. Sophisticated steakhouse; à la carte (seafood, game dishes) and value-for-money set menu; tel. (031) 303-1110.

Swiss Chalet, Tinsley House, Musgrave Rd. What its name suggests; freshwater fish; tel. (031) 21-7922.

Ulundi, Royal Hotel. Indian fare; tel. (031) 304-0331.

Upstairs, Hermitage St. Delectable Thai-Singaporean food in unpretentious surrounds; tel. (031) 306-2707.

GOLDEN MILE

Aldos, Gillespie St. Italian flair; tel. (031) 37-0900.

Frangipani, Holiday Inn Marine Parade. Sumptuous buffet; South African specialities; tel. (031) 37-3341.

Grapevine, Karos Edward Hotel. Imaginatively cosmopolitan menu; tel. (031) 37-3681.

Joe Kool's, Lower Marine Parade. Bewildering variety of food; South African specialities; superb sea views; tel. (031) 32-9697.

Mandarin Room, Karos Edward Hotel. Chinese; sophisticated; superlative service; tel. (031) 37-3681.

Pick and Shovel, Seaview Place, North Beach. Seafood; grills; Oriental dishes; tel. (031) 21-7922.

Punchinello's, Elangeni Sun Hotel. Gourmet seafood (and much else); elegant; tel. (031) 37-1321.

SOUTH OF DURBAN

Commodore, Wild Coast Sun. All-round excellence; tel. (0471) 5-9111.

Trattoria la Terrazza, Umkobi Lagoon. Italian cuisine; seafood specialities; tel. (03931) 6162.

NORTH OF DURBAN

Al Pescatore, Ballito. Seafood and Mediterranean fare; tel. (0322) 6-3574.

The Cabin, Beverly Hills Sun Hotel, Umhlanga. *Haute cuisine*; tel. (031) 561-2211.

Chiquita's, Cabana Beach Hotel, Umhlanga. Wonderfully Mexican; tel. (031) 561-2371.

Gordon's Prawn, Lagoon Drive, Umhlanga. Fine seafood; tel. (031) 561-1596.

Lazy Lizard, Umdloti. Mediterranean and East Asian; tel. (031) 568-1317.

New Original French Café, Main Beach, Umhlanga. The name says it all; delightful; tel. (031) 561-4388.

Razzmatazz, Cabana Beach, Umhlanga. Seafood and venison specialities; tel. (031) 561-5847.

INLAND AND PIETERMARITZBURG

Da Vinci, Pietermaritzburg. Variety of southern European and South African dishes; tel. (0331) 45-6632.

Els Amics, Pietermaritzburg. Stylishly Spanish; lively and friendly atmosphere; tel. (0331) 45-6524.

Falcon Crest, Botha's Hill. Simple; very good country fare in spacious surrounds; tel. (031) 765-5300.

La Buca di Bacco, New Village Market, Westville. Superb Italian menu; friendly people; lively atmosphere; tel. (031) 266-0444.

Le Trouquet, Cowies Hill. French Provençale cuisine; bistro atmosphere; tel. (031) 86-5388.

Seasons, Gillets. International food; cosy atmosphere; tel. (031) 75-1518.

Shortens Country House, Ballito. Victorian homestead; quality food; tel. (0322) 7-1140.

Station Tavern, Kloof. Delectable dishes; steam-railway décor; tel. (031) 764-1312.

White Mischief, Pietermaritzburg. Colonial African setting; fine food; tel. (0331) 642-4579.

USEFUL ADDRESSES AND TELEPHONE NUMBERS

Addington Hospital, tel. (031) 32-2111.

Alcoholics Anonymous, tel. (031) 301-4959.

Amanzimtoti Information Bureau, Inyoni Beach Complex, 95 Beach Rd, PO Box 26, Amanzimtoti 4125; tel. (031) 903-2121.

Automobile Association, (breakdown service); tel. (031) 301-0340.

Computicket, tel. (031) 304-2753.

Dolphin (North) Coast Publicity Association, PO Box 534, Ballito 4420; tel. (0322) 6-1997. The Association runs an information office on the link road from the N2 to Ballito (next to the BP garage).

Durban Unlimited, 19th Floor, The Marine Building, 22 Gardiner St, Durban 4001; tel. (031) 304-4934, fax 304-6196. The Beach Office is on Marine Parade.

Emergency numbers: *National Ambulance Number:* 1-0177; *Fire Brigade:* 309-3333; *Police:* 32-2322 (charge office); *Police flying squad:* 1-0111; *Life Line:* (equivalent to British Samaritans) 23-2323; *Sea Rescue:* 81-5851. If you experience any difficulty getting through to an emergency number, dial 1022.

Natal Parks Board, PO Box 1750, Pietermaritsburg 3200; reservations: tel. (0331) 47-1981, fax 47-1980; general enquiries: tel. (0331) 47-1891, fax 47-1037.

Natal South Coast Publicity Association, Margate beachfront; tel. (03931) 2-2322, fax 2-1886.

Satour, (South African Tourism Board) 160 Pine St, Tourist Junction, First Floor, Durban 4000; tel. (031) 304-7144, fax 305-6693.

Teletourist, (a 24-hour tourist information service): tel. (031) 305-3877 (English-language).

143

THE KWAZULU-NATAL INTERIOR AND THE DRAKENSBERG

Lovely red-brick Victorian buildings; cast-iron railings and store-fronts; luxuriant parks and gardens bright with roses and azaleas; cobbled alleyways, cozy coffee-houses, antique shops and bookstores, and an ambience that draws much from a very colonial past – this is Pietermaritzburg, the capital of KwaZulu-Natal and its second largest city (population: around 200,000 and still growing), nestling among green and sometimes misty hills just under 100 km (62 miles) west of Durban and a place which, to quote the traveller and writer HV Morton, 'wears its air of grace and quality with becoming ease'.

Pietermaritzburg has a lot to offer the discerning visitor: it is an ideal base from which to explore the KwaZulu-Natal interior.

The roads north – the national route for those in a hurry; the old and charming R103 for the leisurely traveller – lead you past and through pleasant and hospitable towns, each with its own distinctive character and its modest array of attractions. Those in the far northern parts – Newcastle, Dundee, Ladysmith and Vryheid – tend to be rather industrial, but they have a special place in the annals: it was on the great grassland plains of the region that Boer, Briton and Zulu played out the bloody dramas of the 19th century, and military enthusiasts come from afar to wander the killing fields and to reconstruct the battles. To the west is the immensity of the Drakensberg, towering 2,000 m (6,600 ft) above foothills that beckon the hiker, the rambler and the lover of solitude.

PIETERMARITZBURG

The eastern prong of the Voortrekkers founded Pietermaritzburg in 1838, just prior to their victory over Dingane's Zulu army at Blood River, as their fledgling Republic of Natalia's seat of government, naming the place in honour of two of their leaders – Gert Maritz and the ill-fated Piet Retief, done to death on KwaMatiwane, the bloody 'hill of execution', earlier that year. The republic, though, lasted only until 1843, when the British annexed the territory and built Fort Napier to reinforce the new authority.

OPPOSITE: *The foothills of the Drakensberg, here overlooked by the distinctive Amphitheatre.*

The Crown Colony of Natal was later granted responsible government – in 1893 – at which time a fine new assembly was added to Pietermaritzburg's already graceful skyline.

Landmarks

Much of Pietermaritzburg's heritage, Trekker and colonial, has been preserved, justifying its ranking as 'one of the most important high-character cities in Africa'. Visitors are introduced to its history-laden charm via the self-guided Town Trail (details from Publicity House, next to City Hall). Of special note are:

CITY HALL, across the square, was built in 1893 and is the southern hemisphere's largest all-brick building, an impressive affair of domes, stained glass, a clock tower that rises 47 m (154 ft) and a splendid pipe-organ.

CENTRAL LANES This charming network of narrow pedestrian alleys – bounded by Longmarket, Timber and Church streets and Commercial Road – was once the city's legal and financial centre: it encompassed four different stock exchanges between 1888 and 1931 and, because of its proximity to the Old Supreme Court, a number of lawyers' chambers. Of particular interest to visitors are the small speciality shops and the elegantly Edwardian Harwin's Arcade.

Museums and galleries

Among the recommended ports of call are:

THE NATAL MUSEUM, in the city centre and very well worth visiting, houses a fascinating number and variety of natural history exhibits, and has sections devoted to geology, palaeontology and ethnology. The Hall of Natal History features Victorian Pietermaritzburg; among the displays is a reconstruction of an early street scene. Open daily.

TATHAM ART GALLERY, old Supreme Court. On display are works by European artists (Picasso, Degas, Renoir, Sisley, Corot, Chagall and Henry Moore, as well as the Bloomsbury Group) and by some leading local painters.

COMRADES MARATHON HOUSE, situated in Connaught Road, is a meticulously restored Victorian home honouring the intrepid runners who have covered the 90 or so gruelling kilometres between Pietermaritzburg and Durban since Arthur Newton inaugurated South Africa's premier ultra-long-distance event in 1921. Newton entered and won the second race, in 1922, maintaining such a pace that officials at

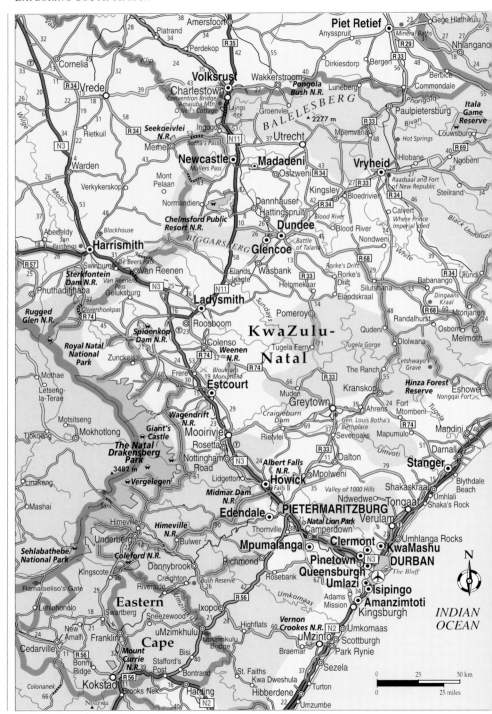

The charmingly elaborate Victorian bandstand in Pietermaritzburg's Alexandra Park.

the finish line were entirely unprepared to receive him – and this despite his short break en route for a sustaining glass of brandy at the Star and Garter Hotel. On display is an interesting collection of photographs, trophies and fascinating race memorabilia.

Gardens, parks and reserves

Pietermaritzburg is known as the 'city of flowers', and deservedly so. It is at its best in springtime; the annual flower show is held in September.

Green Belt walking trails, each clearly marked and involving a gentle two hour walk, enable visitors to enjoy some of the lovely countryside that fringes the city. Attractions are the wild flowers, at their spectacular best during spring and early summer. There are three major routes: the World's View (which follows a portion of the Voortrekkers' road), the Ferncliffe (indigenous and exotic vegetation) and the Dorpspruit (historical). Seven other trails lead walkers to superb viewpoints.

The trails complement the city-centre Town Trails (*see* page 145); comprehensive brochures and maps are available from the Publicity Association in the city centre.

BOTANIC GARDENS A must for visitors: the 22 ha (54 acres) 'international section' is devoted to exotics, and is famed for its springtime displays of azaleas and camellias, and for its lovely mature trees (Moreton Bay fig, swamp cypress, and one truly impressive camphor). The magnolias and the plane avenue are also notable features. The 24 ha (59 acres) Indigenous Garden contains many KwaZulu-Natal mist-belt specimens. There's also a peaceful lake, and a pleasant tearoom.

ALEXANDRA PARK, along Park Drive, is a 65 ha (160 acres) oasis of rock garden (wonderful in wintertime) and azalea, scatters of yellowwood, jacaranda, Cape chestnut, aloes, bougainvillaea and an avenue of stately plane trees. The park also boasts a charming pagoda-style pavilion, Victorian bandstand and Mayor's Garden of formal beddings, rose section and conservatory. The grounds are used for a grand art exhibition held each May. Open daily.

QUEEN ELIZABETH PARK, 8 km (5 miles) north-west of the city, is 93 ha (230 acres) in extent and serves as the Natal Parks Board's headquarters. Aloes, proteas, some game animals (including white rhino), snake-pits, aviaries, self-guided and conducted walks, picnic spots, as well as monthly wildlife film shows, a curio shop and a nursery that sells indigenous plants.

147

CEDARA STATE FOREST extends over 670 ha (1,650 acres), has been planted with a variety of exotic trees (part of an experiment launched in 1903) and includes species from China, the Himalayas, the Mediterranean, North Africa, Australia, Northern Europe, Japan, Mexico and the United States. There's a picnic and barbecue area, fishing in the dams and a forest trail.

AROUND PIETERMARITZBURG

There's plenty to see and do in the general area; especially worth exploring are:

NATAL LION AND GAME PARK, only 22 km (14 miles) from the city off the N3 highway to Durban. On view are elephant, lion, white rhino, giraffe, ostrich and other species. The animals roam freely. Orang-utans, chimpanzees and parrots are residents of the Zoological Gardens opposite the park. There's also a curio shop that stocks hides, skins and souvenirs.

THE ALBERT FALLS, on the Mgeni River 22 km (14 miles) from the city on the Greytown Road; worth visiting more for the lake and the beauty of the countryside than for the cascades themselves, which are only 7 m (23 ft) high. The lake is a popular fishing and boating venue; the 3,000 ha (7,400 acres) nature reserve in which it is set is a pleasant place for bird-watching and picnicking. Accommodation: chalets and rondavels, caravan/camping site. Facilities: picnic sites, pool, game-viewing drives and walks. Information and bookings: Natal Parks Board (*see* Advisory, page 159).

HOWICK

The town was named by Earl Grey, the eminent 19th-century statesman and Colonial Secretary, after his stately home in Northumberland. It's a bustling, friendly, attractive place, unusually well geared to receive visitors. Among its welcoming hostelries is the Howick Falls Hotel,

BELOW: *The 95 m (312 ft) Howick Falls on the Mgeni River. Visitors have a choice of viewsites.* OPPOSITE: *Hot-air ballooning is becoming an increasingly popular sightseeing option.*

built in 1872 and one-time host to distinguished Americans Mark Twain and the newsman-explorer Henry Morton Stanley of 'Dr Living-stone-I-presume' fame. In close proximity to the town are the:

HOWICK FALLS, which plunges some 95 m (312 ft) into the Mgeni River and is much photographed. Other cascades in the area are the Shelter and the 105 m (345 ft) Karkloof.

KARKLOOF FALLS NATURE RESERVE, about 20 km (12 miles) from Pietermaritzburg, is a privately owned wildlife complex which combines conservation and luxurious hospitality with signal success. Once a rather neglected area, the Karkloof is now haven to Cape buffalo, the rare sable and roan antelope and many other animals and to a superb array of avifauna (experts rank the area as one of the region's finest birding locations). The reserve is also a scenic joy, its most striking feature the beautiful 106 m (348 ft) Karkloof waterfall. Guests are accommodated in the 30-bed, four-star Game Valley Lodge, a complex of luxurious thatched cottages. On offer is a range of conducted and self-guided game drives, walks and trails.

UMGENI VALLEY NATURE RESERVE, situated below the falls east of Howick: a noted conservation education centre, its 656 ha (1,621 acres) comprising a variety of habitats. Wildlife includes giraffe, a variety of antelope and over 200 bird species. There is a broad selection of self-guided and conducted trails, and some lovely picnic spots.

MIDMAR PUBLIC RESORT AND NATURE RESERVE This popular resort, 24 km (15 miles) from Pietermaritzburg, 7 km (4.5 miles) from the town of Howick and a favourite among watersports enthusiasts, has been established around the 1,822 ha (4,502 acres) Midmar Dam. For visitors the range of recreational attractions includes tennis and squash courts,

bathing in the dam (the water is bilharzia-free) and swimming pool and fishing (notably for carp and bass). Other facilities: boat-hire, shop, camping ground and the Midmar Historical Village, which features among other attractions a wood-and-iron Hindu temple, a Zulu homestead, blacksmith's shop and the retired steam-tug *JE Eaglesham,* now moored in the dam's fresh water after a long and honourable working life in Durban harbour.

The adjacent reserve is home to zebra, wildebeest and a variety of antelope and prolific birdlife (of note are the waterfowl and the kingfishers, which include both the giant and the pygmy species). Among visitor facilities are chalets and a network of game-viewing trails. Information and bookings: Natal Parks Board (*see* Advisory, page 159).

NORTH OF PIETERMARITZBURG

The highway that leads from Pietermaritzburg northward through Howick, Nottingham Road, Mooi River, Estcourt, Frere, Colenso and across the Tugela to Ladysmith takes you through the Midlands, the country that lies between the extremes of humid coastal woodlands to the east and the monumentally craggy, often ice-capped heights of the Drakensberg to the west. It is a lovely, misty land of deep river valleys, hill upon rolling hill, and sweet green grasses that once sustained great herds of migrating antelope.

The beauty and the peace, though, are deceptive: for a hundred years this region served as southern Africa's great battleground. It was here, in 1818, that Shaka's armies erupted in all their disciplined magnificence to spread fire, assegai and famine among the neighbouring peoples; here that the eastern Voortrekkers fought and sometimes lost to the impis – at Bloukrans, Bushmans River and Italeni – before breaking the power (though not the pride) of the Zulu nation at Blood River.

Thereafter, for the following three decades, black and white men managed to coexist in tolerable harmony until, in 1879, British Imperial ambition provoked new warfare and Isandlwana, Rorke's Drift and Ulundi took their places in the bloody annals of KwaZulu-Natal. And here, too, along and close to the banks of the Tugela, were fought some of the most bitter and bloody battles of the South African (Anglo-Boer) War, when, in the early months of hostilities, the parade-ground British regiments were

THE BATTLEFIELDS ROUTE

A fascinating excursion that holds enduring appeal for visitors with a sense of history and an interest in matters military takes in the killing fields of 'Victoria's little wars' — the 19th-century confrontations during which Zulu, Boer and Briton fought for territorial supremacy in Natal.

Among local battlefields with especially evocative names are Blood River (1838; Zulu-Boer); Majuba Hill (1881; Boer-British); Talana, Elandslaagte, Tugela Heights, Colenso, Ladysmith and Spioenkop (Anglo-Boer War; 1899–1902). Noted personalities who were involved in some of the engagements are France's Prince Imperial, last of the Bonaparte line (who was killed in a Zulu ambush in 1879), Winston Churchill (who was captured near Estcourt in 1900, later making a daring escape), and the great Mohandas Gandhi, who helped raise a medical unit in 1899.

Of the many fire-fights which occurred here, the relatively minor one at Rorke's Drift was especially notable for its heroism: it was here that troops of a small British detachment, garrisoned in the Lutheran mission station, stood ground against the repeated onslaughts of a 4,000-strong Zulu impi. No less than 11 Victoria Crosses were handed out after the engagement – which did something to restore British pride after the humiliation of Isandlwana (where a much bigger force of red-coats had just been massacred). The mission station still stands today and welcomes visitors; worth a good look-round is the nearby African Craft Centre, where you can buy a selection of handwoven rugs and tapestries, exquisite hand-printed fabrics and some good examples of traditional Zulu pottery.

The Battlefields Route extends all the way from Estcourt in the south to Volksrust in the north and then east to Vryheid. A number of organized tours are laid on, and a regular Greyhound coach service covers the area.

Independent motorists should arm themselves with some of the excellent booklets, brochures and maps supplied by the various local publicity associations; an essential ingredient of the information package is the Natal Battlefields Chronicle, which gives a detailed overview of the major military events. An intriguing optional extra is the 'Walk 'n Talk' series of audio-cassettes available for hire.

cut to ribbons by the well-armed Boer riflemen under the command of General Louis Botha. In a word, the Midlands have a great deal to offer those with a military interest (*see* panel, left). For those who do not, the countryside has gentler enticements, among them the Midlands Meander, an inviting (and scenically charming) arts-and-craft route around the Nottingham Road area. Details from the Pietermaritzburg Publicity Association. Prominent places to the north include:

LADYSMITH

Of the three garrison towns invested by the Boers in the early months of the South African War, Ladysmith suffered the most: many of the British troops, deprived of food and medical supplies, died during the 115-day siege. The museum recalls those grim but sometimes glorious days. Other military sites in the area include Wagon Hill, Caesar's Camp, Umbulwana Hill and Lombards Kop. Also of interest is the Gandhi memorial (in the town gardens.)

Spioenkop, the hill over which Boer and Briton fought so furiously in January 1900 (and so pointlessly: it had no real strategic importance; more than 2,000 troops were killed or wounded on the bloody slopes before the British, inexplicably, retired) lies to the southwest; a resident historian shows visitors over the killing ground. Of more recent vintage is the Spioenkop Resort, Nature Reserve and Dam, popular among watersports enthusiasts. The adjacent 400 ha (988 acres) game park is home to white rhino, eland, kudu, wildebeest, giraffe, zebra and other species. Facilities include game-viewing walks, horse-riding, picnicking and boating, chalets, a camping ground at the resort and a small war museum.

NEWCASTLE

This large industrial centre revolves around its textile, steel, synthetic rubber and cast-iron plants, all of which visitors may tour by arrangement. The town has some pleasant hotels, a 500-seat convention centre, a small airport and an impressive colonial-style Town Hall. The Carnegie Library houses an art gallery; Hilldrop House, once the home of author Rider Haggard, and the Fort Amiel Museum are also worth visiting. Several factory shops, associated with the town's textile plants, invite bargain-hunters, as do the Ozisweni Handicraft Centre (a selection of woven goods and basketry), the Mother Earth Pottery and The Weavery. For more information call in at the Publicity Association in the Town Hall (Scott Street).

DUNDEE

The town, centre of the region's giant coal-fields, is worth visiting for its Talana Museum, a splendid collection of Victorian edifices built on the site of the Anglo-Boer War's first battle. On display are some fascinating militaria plus sections devoted to coal-mining, glass- and brick-making. The local Publicity Association is housed in the museum. Other features in the wider area include the MOTH Museum (Anglo-Zulu War) and numerous war memorials and relics. To the north-east is the site of the Blood River battle where, in 1838, the Voortrekkers crushed the Zulu army and where the original 64-wagon laager has been impressively (and now controversially) reconstructed in bronze.

THE DRAKENSBERG AND ITS FOOTHILLS

The formidable range of mountains called the Drakensberg is part – the loftiest and most splendid part – of the Great Escarpment which, rather like a gigantic horseshoe, runs down, across and then up southern Africa's U-shaped perimeter, dividing the relatively narrow coastal plain (or, more technically, the 'marginal zone') from the great plateau of the interior. The range is at its highest in Lesotho, where it is known as the Maluti Mountains, but in visual terms is at its most spectacular in the east, where the heights fall practically sheer for a full 2,000 m (6,600 ft) down to the green and pleasant uplands of KwaZulu-Natal.

The range is, geologically speaking, a young one, formed about 150 million years ago by seismic convulsions that deposited stupendous quantities of basalt lava onto the sandstone

The Tugela, South Africa's third most important river, with the Amphitheatre as backdrop.

plains. The 'wall' so created – 4,000 m (13,000 ft) above sea level, 200 km (124 miles) wide – was then, over the aeons, eroded by rain and river, elements that carved the deep ravines and sculpted the Drakensberg's extraordinary fantasia of cliff, buttress and dragon-tooth ridge, cave, ledge and balancing rock. The massifs and their peaks have evocative names: The Sentinel, The Amphitheatre, Mont-aux-Sources, The Organ Pipes, The Chessmen, Champagne Castle. To climbers, they represent a profound challenge; for everyone else, they are grand beyond description, a joy to behold.

To people who have only heard of the Drakensberg, the region conjures up intimidating images of frozen peaks and snowbound isolation. And the high country can indeed be a formidable environment, beset in winter by blinding blizzards that descend in a matter of minutes, literally out of the blue, and in summer by stupendous thunderstorms. But the places one actually stays at – the resort hotels – generally enjoy a remarkably benevolent climate. They're on the much lower, much gentler slopes, where summer nights are pleasantly cool, the days warm, sometimes hot, subject to morning mists and early-evening thunderstorms. Winter days are generally mild, the nights cold and occasionally bitter, best enjoyed with family or friendly company in the warmth of a scented log fire.

ABOVE: *Horseback trailists take in the grandeur of the Drakensberg and its foothills.*
OPPOSITE: *Injasuti camp, with Champagne Castle and Cathkin Peak in the background.*

The 'Berg has a great deal to offer the visitor. Those drawn to the uplands come not for the more sophisticated pleasures (though these are available), but for the unparalleled scenic beauty, for the fresh, clean mountain air, for the rambles and the horseback trails, the hikes and climbs, for the trout in the streams, the animals and birds of the reserves and for undemanding relaxation in a casual atmosphere.

If you look at the map, you will see that there are three fairly distinctive areas of tourism development: in the Mont-aux-Sources area in the north, around Cathedral Peak and Champagne Castle in the north-central section and, thirdly, below Sani Pass in the south. The last-mentioned, 3,200 m (10,500 ft) above sea level, accommodates the only roadway (restricted to four-wheel-drive vehicles) over this 250 km (155 miles) stretch of the KwaZulu-Natal Drakensberg. Between Cathedral Peak and Sani are a number of important conservation areas, most notable of which is probably the Giant's Castle Game Reserve.

The northern and north-central segments are served by the attractive little centres of Bergville and Winterton, from which roads radiate in all directions; the southern region is served by the even more appealing and picturesque ones of Himeville and Underberg.

As the crow flies, the three areas aren't very far apart, but the connecting roadways are rather rugged and to travel comfortably from one to the other involves a loop route, east to the N3 highway and west again towards the mountains.

Mont-aux-Sources area

The lofty geological formation known as Mont-aux-Sources acquired its name from two adventurous French missionaries who trekked in from the west, across the hostile 'Roof of Africa' – the Lesotho highlands – in the early 1830s. On the precipitous eastern side they observed the rising of an unusual number of rivers and streams, and called it the 'mountain of springs'.

Included among these many watercourses are the Elands and Tugela rivers. The latter initially follows a spectacular course along its 322 km (200 miles) journey from the Drakensberg and across KwaZulu-Natal eventually to reach the Indian Ocean: it rises at the western end of the Mont-aux-Sources plateau, finds its way to and then plunges over the Amphitheatre's rim in an 850-m-long (2,800 ft) series of cascades and falls, one of which drops a sheer 183 m (600 ft), making it the country's highest waterfall. In mid-winter the uppermost cascade freezes to a stalactite-like sheet of ice. The smaller Elands River runs northwards, falling about 1,200 m (3,900 ft) to join the Vaal, tributary of the westward-flowing Orange. Five other rivers are born on Mont-aux-Sources.

Prominent among the peaks are The Sentinel (3,165 m/10,384 ft and difficult to climb), The Eastern Buttress (3,009 m/9,873 ft) and Devil's Tooth (3,282 m/10,768 ft), a jagged feature attempted by only the most experienced and intrepid of mountaineers.

THE ROYAL NATAL NATIONAL PARK This is an 8,000 ha (20,000 acres) sanctuary for various antelope and some 200 different species of bird,

including the rare and endangered black eagle, the Cape vulture and the lammergeier (also known as the bearded vulture).

Botanists come from afar, especially to investigate the lichens of the area. There are at least four easily accessible San (Bushman) sites; the paintings are impressive.

The park, though, is popular principally for the scenic magnificence of its mountains, cliffs and rolling grasslands, and for its outdoor attractions: there are over 30 recommended walks and hikes ranging from the gentle 3 km (2 miles) Otto trail to the 46 km (29 miles) route that takes you to the Mont-aux-Sources plateau, the last stretch involving a chain-ladder ascent up the sheer eastern face. But it's worth it when you reach the top: the vistas are quite breathtaking. There are rewarding excursions, too, to the

ABOVE: *Some of the myriad San rock paintings of the Giant's Castle area.*
BOTTOM LEFT: *The bearded vulture, a handsome resident of the high Drakensberg.*
OPPOSITE: *Eland graze in Giant's Castle Reserve.*

Tugela Falls (*see* page 153), to the river's pools and, if you're a fisherman, to its dam. The park's trout hatchery is the largest in KwaZulu-Natal.

Accommodation: at the Mont-aux-Sources Hotel on the eastern boundary and at the hotel within the park (*see* Advisory, page 159), or at one of the two camps, which offer bungalows, cottages and, at Tendele, a luxury lodge. There's a campsite at Mahai, in a setting of trees and splendid sandstone hills. The Rugged Glen Nature Reserve, virtually part of the park, has a caravan/camping ground and riding stables.

Cathedral Peak area

The peak, rising 3,004 m (9,856 ft) above sea level, is one of a complex of pinnacles, much favoured by mountaineers, that includes the Bell (2,918 m/9,574 ft), one of the country's most challenging climbs, the Pyramid (2,914 m/ 9,561 ft), and the Column (2,926 m/9,600 ft), detached from the main buttress and also difficult; Cleft Peak (3,281 m/10,765 ft) and the Organ Pipes or *Qolo la maSoja*, meaning 'ridge of soldiers'. To climb Cathedral Peak itself does not demand a great deal of experience, but the ascent, which takes a day, is rather strenuous.

Lesser features are the curiously-formed Mitre and Chessmen and, further down, the Rainbow Gorge, Mushroom Rock, the Doreen, Albert and Ribbon falls, and the deeply green and mysterious Oqalweni fern forest. There are many delightful picnic spots in the area.

To walk from the Cathedral Peak ridge (or, more correctly, the Mponjwana ridge) to:
CHAMPAGNE CASTLE, to the south, involves a two- or three-day hike along the foot of the high escarpment, through quite splendid countryside.

Champagne Castle was named by two very British Victorian officers who took a bottle of good bubbly on their climb, found it half empty when they stopped to rest and, rather than accuse each other, politely laid the blame on the mountain itself. The Castle is one of the Drakensberg's easier climbs; its slopes are criss-crossed by a network of foot- and bridle-paths.

Other peaks are more striking and present greater mountaineering challenges. Most prominent among them is probably the 3,194 m (10,480 ft) Cathkin, detached from the main formation and looming majestically over dense forest plantations. Here the Sterkspruit rises to descend to a wide and fertile valley, its middle reaches distinguished by an especially fine waterfall and by some attractive pools.

Below Cathkin Peak is the renowned:
DRAKENSBERG BOYS' CHOIR SCHOOL, founded in the 1960s with a complement of just 20 pupils, now over 100 strong, divided into three choirs that have acquired a reputation for excellence well beyond South Africa's borders. They perform for the public on Wednesday afternoons.

The land between Cathedral Peak and Champagne Castle is protected within the extensive Mlambonja and Mdedelelo wilderness areas. Within these lies the:

NDEDEMA GORGE, the name meaning 'place of rolling thunder', which is apt enough, since some of the 'Berg's noisier storms occur in the area. The gorge, though, is more famed for the 150 or so caves and rock shelters that were once haven to the long-vanished San (Bushman) people of the region. These gentle folk, the greatest of the prehistoric artists and among the finest of all time, found protection in the deep, cavern-studded ravine, both from the elements and from the depredations of their more aggressive fellow-men.

Ndedema and its surrounds are the location for 17 'galleries' holding over 4,000 paintings in all, many of superb quality. One cave alone, the Sebaaieni, holds over 1,000 individual subjects; in another, the Elands Cave in the nearby Mhlwazini Valley, there are over 1,600.

Great numbers of paintings may also be found in the Giant's Castle region to the south (*see* below); together, the two areas hold about 40% of all known southern African rock art.

There are about 15,000 art sites in the sub-continent, ranging in age from 27,000 years (this is pre- or at least proto-San) to a very recent 200. Most of them are less than 1,000 years old; all show the remarkably advanced foreshortening technique associated with the culture: a three-dimensional approach that gives vibrant reality to the animals, to the hunt and the ritual and dance depicted. Movement, flow and power are all there in the leap of an antelope, in the surge of a buffalo. The colours, too, are striking, their essence the mineral oxides of the earth: manganese for black, zinc for white, iron to produce the deep browns, the reds and yellows.

Sadly, many of the paintings have suffered grievously from the passage of time, damaged over the centuries by seepage and by soot from the cave fires of the San's less creative successors – and by the downright vandalism of the moderns. Nevertheless, a great deal of the original beauty remains.

Giant's Castle and other reserves
Originally established to provide sanctuary for eland, this mountainous, beautiful 35,000 ha (86,500 acres) reserve, part of the wider Drakensberg Park, now holds a round dozen species of antelope – together with an impressive variety of birds. The raptors in the reserve include the lappetfaced, hooded, white-backed, Cape, Egyptian

and bearded vulture (lammergeier), the martial, black, crowned and the two types of snake eagle. There is a special hide – the only one of its kind in the world – from which visitors may observe the lammergeier.

A large proportion of the Drakensberg's 800 species of flowering plants occur in the area.

The reserve's southern parts are dominated by the enormous dark basalt wall of the Giant's Castle buttress, the north-western arm by the Injesuthi complex, whose dome rises a full 3,410 m (11,188 ft) above sea level. The area offers a comprehensive network of hiking trails (the crest of the Giant's Castle formation can be reached fairly easily). There are guided horse-trails, three- and four-day mountain rides (for the experienced) and fishing for brown trout in the Bushmans and Little Tugela rivers.

As we've noted, the area is famed for its pro-liferation of San art; there are two site museums within the reserve's boundaries. Accommoda-tion is available in three camps and includes lodges, bungalows, cabins, rustic huts, camping sites and in rather isolated mountain huts. Information and bookings: Natal Parks Board (see Advisory, page 159).

THE SMALLER RESERVES Among the foothills are three especially attractive reserves. The Kamberg (2,230 ha/5,510 acres) is known for its handsome yellowwoods, tree ferns and other eye-catching flora, for its 13 km (8 miles) of trout-angling waters and its Mooi River trail (suitable for the physically disadvantaged). The Loteni (4,000 ha/10,000 acres) also offers spendid fishing, together with a prolific bird life (including eagle and stork species), a 'set-tler's museum', horse-riding facilities and the circular Eagle trail. Similar but smaller is the Vergelegen Reserve. All three areas have pleas-ant cottage accommodation; for further infor-mation contact the Natal Parks Board.

Southern Drakensberg

The sole route breaching the Drakensberg to link KwaZulu-Natal and the mile-high Kingdom of Lesotho runs over the Sani ('Bushman') Pass, a rugged road that follows the course of the Mkhomazana ('Little Mkomazi') River along the cascades and tumbling rapids of its upper reaches.

The mountain-and-valley scenery of the Sani Pass is breathtaking; the dizzy hairpin and switchback ascent – and certainly the final stretch – really too steep for anything but four-wheel-drive vehicles and the pack-mules and

donkeys of the Sotho transport riders. There is a police post halfway up. At the summit there is a customs post (passports are needed for entry into Lesotho) and the Mountaineers Chalet, a small hostelry (it is licensed but visitors are required to do their own cooking); at the bot-tom is the 22,751 ha (56,220 acres) Mzimkul-wana Reserve (home to antelope and some magnificent raptors) and the Sani Pass Hotel, a large, rambling, nicely-appointed, rather colo-nial cluster of buildings set in spaciously attrac-tive grounds (facilities include a golf course, spa complex and horse-riding) beneath the Twelve Apostles, Hodsons Peak and Giant's Cup.

Access to Sani Pass is via:

HIMEVILLE, a charming place, notable for the old jail, which started life as a stockade and now serves as a fascinating little museum, for its superb hotel (13 rooms and a pub for con-noisseurs) and for the 105 ha (260 acres):

HIMEVILLE NATURE RESERVE, something of a paradise for trout fishermen. It has two lakes, and there are boats for hire. Also waterfowl, some antelope, and a camping ground.

Beyond Himeville, back along the route towards Loteni, the foothills have large num-bers of beautiful trees, most of them exotics: cypress and birch, oak and maple, ash and poplar, tulip and crab apple. They were planted by Kenneth and Mona Lund, a farming couple and passionate lovers of nature (they also creat-ed an enchanting little reserve of artificial lake and selected tree species on their property which they call Hazelmere).

Just off the road that leads towards the south-east and to Pevensey is:

THE SWAMP NATURE RESERVE This small, 220 ha (540 acres) expanse of countryside, of which about a quarter is given over to wetland, serves as home to numerous waterfowl. Of spe-cial note is the rare wattled crane.

To the south of and twinned with the village of Himeville is:

UNDERBERG, a slightly larger place that hugs the grassy slopes beneath the high Hlogoma ('place of echoes'). At one time there was a lot of quarrelsome and unforgiving rivalry between the two settlements, but eventually the Lunds (see above) healed the wounds by giving oaks to any-one who agreed to plant a few along the linking road, and the avenue of stately trees became an attractive and enduring monument to renewed friendship. Underberg, too, is a long-standing favourite among trout fishermen.

The Drakensberg is superb hiking country.

COLEFORD NATURE RESERVE, approximately 22 km (14 miles) to the south of Underberg, is a 1,300 ha (3,200 acres) area bisected by the Ngwangwana and Ndawana rivers, and anglers are drawn from far and wide to the rainbow trout in their waters. Other attractions include several types of antelope (including wildebeest and oribi), game-viewing hides, splendid upland scenery, walking and riding trails, rest-huts and cottages. For more detailed information and bookings contact the Natal Parks Board (*see* Advisory, page 159).

Back on the route connecting Himeville with Pietermaritzburg (the R617), one passes Lundy's Hill and Bulwer, with its welcoming Tavern Inn and its all-timber Holy Trinity Yellowwood Church, and some quite spectacular countryside; the pleasant valley of the Mkhomazi River, the lovely Rainbow Falls, the deep-green magic of the Orchid Forest, Devil's Cavern and the tiny yellowwood and mural-decorated church of the Reichman Mission.

GETTING AROUND

DAY DRIVES There is an inviting choice of routes throughout the Midlands and Drakensberg regions. The southern Zululand reserves are also within comfortable driving distance of Pietermaritzburg. It's worthwhile investing in a good map and a detailed regional guide. Meanwhile, a couple of general pointers:

Towards the southern 'Berg: travel from Pietermaritzburg to Howick and on to the R617, continuing west through Bulwer to Underberg, Himeville and the Sani Pass Hotel, where transport can be arranged, given some advance warning, to the top. Return to the Himeville area and north-east on an extension of the R617 to Nottingham Road, and then via the old road (R103) to rejoin the N3 just north of Howick.

Towards the northern 'Berg: take the old highway, the R103, north of Howick through Nottingham Road, Mooi River and Estcourt to Frere. There is an optional arts-and-crafts digression: the Midlands Meander (*see* page 150). After Frere, take the R615 north-west through Winterton and Bergville to the Mont-aux-Sources area, back down the R615, digressing westwards – towards Cathedral Peak, Champagne Castle and so forth. The roads are good gravel and very well signposted. Rejoin the R103. These areas are covered on pages 149–156.

WALKS AND HIKES: The Midlands and the Drakensberg foothills are superb walking country.

Each of the game reserves, nature reserves and wilderness areas covered in this chapter has its own network of trails – Royal Natal Park's, for instance, extends over 130 km (81 miles), Giant's Castle's over 50 km (30 miles).

ADVISORY: THE KWAZULU-NATAL INTERIOR AND THE DRAKENSBERG

CLIMATE

Equable throughout except in the high Drakensberg, where climbers have to be wary of winter blizzards and sudden summer thunderstorms. In the higher areas – the escarpment's foothills – summer days are warm, nights cool; winter days are sunny, the nights crisp, often chilly, occasionally very cold. The mountain air has a champagne quality.

This is a summer rainfall region; the upland areas are prone to mist. Pietermaritzburg average rainfall: January 241 mm/9 in, July 14 mm/½ in, yearly average 928 mm/36½ in, highest daily 214 mm/8½ in. Pietermaritzburg temperatures: average daily maximum January 27.1 °C/80.8 °F, July 21.2 °C/70 °F, extreme 40 °C/104 °F, average daily minimum January 16.6 °C/61.8 °F, July 6 °C/42.8 °F, extreme 1 °C/33.8 °F.

MAIN ATTRACTIONS

Pietermaritzburg: Charming Victorian buildings ❏ Museums and art galleries ❏ City and country walks ❏ Lovely parks and gardens ❏ Modern city amenities ❏ Convenient base for exploring.
Midlands: Charming countryside ❏ Historic sites ❏ Game and nature reserves.
Drakensberg: Delightful scenery ❏ Game and nature reserves ❏ Walks and trails ❏ Climbing ❏ Fishing ❏ Horse-riding ❏ Golf.

TRAVEL

Road. Pietermaritzburg: 79 km/49 miles from Durban; 529 km/329 miles from Johannesburg; 585 km/264 miles from Pretoria; 1,595 km/991 miles from Cape Town; 842 km/523 miles from Port Elizabeth; 561 km/349 miles from Bloemfontein; 596 km/370 miles from East London.

The N3 national highway links the city with Durban to the east and Johannesburg to the north-west. More scenically interesting is what used to be the old main road, the R103, which runs parallel to the N3, taking in Nottingham Road and Estcourt before becoming the R615 near Frere. The R615 is the northern Drakensberg's principal access route.

Coach travel: Scheduled services link Pietermaritzburg with Durban and Johannesburg (and other centres).

Car hire: Facilities are available in Pietermaritzburg and major Midland and northern centres.

Rail. Passenger services link major centres and many of the minor towns.

Air. Scheduled daily flights connect Pietermaritzburg with Johannesburg International Airport. (*See also* air services to and from Durban, page 141.) Comair operates to and from Margate; tel. toll-free 080 131 4155.

ACCOMMODATION
Select hotels

PIETERMARITZBURG
Imperial Hotel *** In the city centre. 61 en suite rooms; à la carte restaurant; 2 bars; conference facilities are available. PO Box 140, Pietermaritzburg 3200; tel. (0331) 42-6551, fax 42-9796.
Karos Capital Towers Centrally situated. Busy; 103 rooms as well as executive suites; breakfast room; conference facilities are available. PO Box 198, Pietermaritzburg 3200; tel. (0331) 94-2761, fax 45-2857.

CENTRAL AND NORTHERN KWAZULU-NATAL
Crossways Country Inn ** Hilton, just north of Pietermaritzburg. 19 en suite rooms; à la carte restaurant and bar; swimming pool; conference facilities are available. PO Box 16, Hilton 3245; tel. (0331) 3-3267.
Etna Hotel Dundee. 30 en suite rooms; restaurant; bar. PO Box 586, Dundee 3000; tel. (0341) 2-4191.
Fern Hill Hotel *** Situated close to the Midmar Dam, Howick. 25 en suite rooms; à la carte and carvery restaurants; bar; action bar; swimming pool; tennis; croquet; superb trout-fishing; conference facilities are available. PO Box 5, Tweedie 3255; tel. (0332) 30-5071, fax 30-2781.
Granny Mouse's Country House Lidgetton, on the banks of a river near Balgowan. Superbly appointed country inn; 16 rooms; 2 dining rooms; charming Victorian tea-lounge; pub. PO Box 22, Balgowan 3275; tel. (03324) 4071/4532, fax 4429.
Griffins Hill Lodge Near Estcourt. In lovely farmland surrounds; 14 en suite rooms; superb à la carte restaurant; lively bar; swimming pool; conference facilities are available for 30 people. PO Box 101, Estcourt 3310; tel. (0363) 2-4720.
Holiday Inn Garden Court: Newcastle *** 168 en suite rooms; breakfast room and bar; swimming pool; conference facilities are available for 180 people. PO Box 778, Newcastle 2940; tel. (03431) 2-8151, fax 2-4142, central reservations (011) 482-3500.
Old Halliwell Country Inn **** A charming 1830s post-house along the old wagon route close to Howick. 15 en suite rooms; restaurant serving excellent country cuisine; bar; swimming pool; conference facilities are available for 20 people. PO Box 201, Howick 3290; tel. (0332) 30-2602, fax 30-3430.
Rawdons Hotel *** Gracious country house in superb setting near Nottingham Road, 40 km (25 miles) to the north of Pietermaritzburg. 25 rooms, 3 suites, lake cottage; table d'hôte restaurant; English pub; swimming pool; gym; sauna; bowling green; tennis; trout-fishing. PO Box 7, Nottingham Road 3280; tel. (0333) 3-6044.
Royal Hotel *** Ladysmith. 71 en suite rooms; à la carte restaurant; several bars; swimming pool; conference facilities are available for 180 people. PO Box 12, Ladysmith 3370; tel. and fax (0361) 2-2176.

NORTHERN DRAKENSBERG

Cathedral Peak Hotel *** 90 en suite rooms; lovely table d'hôte restaurant; bar; swimming pool; gym; tennis; fishing; horse-riding; conference facilities are available for 200 people. PO Winterton 3340; tel. and fax (036) 488-1888.

Cayley Lodge *** Pleasant blend of homeliness and sophistication; unusual (but effective) architecture; restaurant which serves delicious country cuisine; bar; bowls; horse-riding; sunset trips on dam. PO Box 241, Winterton 3340; tel. and fax (036) 468-1222.

Champagne Castle Hotel Old-fashioned country hospitality; splendid views; 47 en suite rooms, luxury suites; restaurant; swimming pool; tennis; bowls; horse-riding. Private Bag X8, Winterton 3340; tel. (036) 468-1063, fax 468-1306.

Drakensberg Sun Hotel **** Cathkin Peak area. Luxurious and attractive; 114 rooms, 4 suites; buffet restaurant; 2 bars; pool; tennis; bowls; fishing; boating; conference facilities are available. PO Box 335, Winterton 3340; tel. (036) 468-1000, fax 468-1224, central reservations (011) 482-3500.

Karos Mont-aux-Sources Hotel *** Beneath the Amphitheatre. Lovely garden setting; 70 rooms; 6 suites; carvery restaurant; bar; pools (one heated); bowls; conference facilities are available. Private Bag 1, Mont-aux-Sources 3353; tel. and fax (0364) 38-1035.

Little Switzerland Mountain Resort & Hotel *** Mont-aux-Sources area. 45 thatched-cottage en suite rooms; self-catering accommodation; à la carte restaurant; bar; pool; tennis, bowls; squash; croquet; horse-riding; conference facilities are available. Private Bag X1661, Bergville 3350; tel. and fax (036) 438-6220.

Royal Natal National Park Hotel Mont-aux-Sources area. Situated within the park; family-orientated; 60 en suite rooms and cottages of various kinds; restaurant; bar; pool; tennis; bowls. Private Bag 4, Mont-aux-Sources 3353; tel. (036) 438-6200, fax 438-6101.

SOUTHERN DRAKENSBERG

Everglades Hotel, & Conference Centre *** Located in the foothills. 46 rooms, suites; restaurant; bar; swimming pool; tennis; bowls; golf; horse-riding; 3 conference venues are available. PO Box 27, Dargle 3265; tel. (03324) 4025, fax 4286.

Sani Pass Hotel & Leisure Resort Below the famed pass. 100 en suite rooms; splendid table d'hôte restaurant; bar; swimming pool; sauna; jacuzzi; golf; bowls; tennis; squash; conference facilities are available for 200 people. PO Box 44, Himeville 4585; tel. and fax (033) 702-1320.

Self-catering and budget

The region offers the visitor a wide variety of resorts and other types of self-catering accommodation, as well as a large number of caravan/camping options (the game and nature reserves are especially well served). The Drakensberg Publicity Association, Satour and the various local tourist information offices will have the details; *see* below.

For budget accommodation: Contact Bed 'n Breakfast; tel. (0332) 30-3343 (Midlands areas) and tel. (03431) 5-1915 (northern areas).

USEFUL ADDRESSES AND TELEPHONE NUMBERS

Drakensberg Publicity Association, The information offices are located close to Durban (Shell Ultra City) as well as at the municipal buildings in the towns of Bergville and Winterton; PO Box 1608, Estcourt 3310; tel. (036) 468-1440.

Dundee Publicity Association, Private Bag 2024, Dundee 3000; tel. (0341) 22121, ext. 264; Talana Museum; tel. (0341) 2-2654/2-2677.

Howick Tourism Association, PO Box 881, Howick 3290; tel. (0332) 30-5305.

Ladysmith Tourism Association, PO Box 1307, Ladysmith 3370; tel. (0361) 2-2992.

Natal Parks Board, PO Box 1750, Pietermaritzburg 3200; bookings: tel. (0331) 47-1981, fax 47-1980; enquiries: (0331) 47-1891, fax 47-1037.

Newcastle Publicity Association, Private Bag X6621, Newcastle 2940; tel. (03431) 5-3318.

Pietermaritzburg Publicity Association, PO Box 25, Pietermaritzburg 3200; tel. (0331) 45-1348/9; visitor information: Publicity House, 177 Commercial Rd; fax (0331) 94-3535.

Satour (South African Tourism Board), Shop 1, The Marine, 22 Gardiner St; PO Box 2516, Durban 4000; tel. (031) 304-7144; fax 305-6693.

159

THE EASTERN CAPE

The region, for the purposes of this chapter, extends eastwards along the Indian Ocean from Cape St Francis through Algoa Bay (Port Elizabeth) and beyond, along the lovely Wild Coast shoreline to the KwaZulu-Natal border. Inland, it covers the country stretching northwards from Port Elizabeth, and westwards from the Transkei area, to the Drakensberg foothills and the semi-arid edges of the Great Karoo.

This is a vast expanse of terrain, multi-faceted, a kaleidoscope of contrasts, the local areas strikingly different in climate and character and in the nature of their attractions. In fact probably the only unifying element is to be found in the colonial past: this was frontier territory until the later years of the 19th century, often violently disputed, an arena in which white settler and black clansman fought bitterly for possession of the land.

Inevitably, after a number of one-sided 'frontier wars', the better-armed white colonists prevailed, the process of conquest and organized territorial expansion beginning in earnest with the importation of shiploads of British immigrants in 1820.

These families – about 4,000 people in all – landed at Algoa Bay (the location of the future Port Elizabeth), were immediately dispatched inland to occupy and settle the newly created Albany border district, and in due course they and those who followed them managed to 'pacify' the countryside.

The Xhosa, for their part, were progressively pushed back into the eastern seaboard region and its hinterland between the Great Fish and Mtamvuna rivers, a region divided into two distinct and now defunct 'homelands': Ciskei and Transkei, separated from each other by a narrowish strip of 'white' territory still known as Border country. The latter's principal centre is the small river-port city of East London.

PORT ELIZABETH

South Africa's fifth city and third largest port, Greater Port Elizabeth (encompassing nearby Uitenhage) is the economic heart of the Eastern

OPPOSITE: *Hobie cats of the Port Elizabeth Yacht Club cluster in colourful profusion on one of the city's splendid beaches.*

Cape, a conurbation with approximately 1,000 factories and a preoccupation with the motor manufacturing industry: Ford established the country's first assembly plant here during the mid-1920s (in Grahamstown Road: it employed 70 people and turned out 12 Tin Lizzies a day); General Motors set up shop about two years later, and the city is commonly referred to as the 'Detroit of South Africa'. It is also a major tourist centre, and in this guise likes to be known as the 'Friendly City' (yet another, and less flattering, soubriquet is 'Windy City', but in fact it's no gustier here than along any other part of the southern coast). Its principal attractions are its wide, open beaches, the renowned oceanarium and snake park, historic buildings and architecture, a fine selection of shops, sophisticated hotels, restaurants and its strategic position as a base for exploring the coastline to either side and the surrounding, often attractive and always interesting countryside.

Historic places

Port Elizabeth owes its origins to the 4,000 or so British settlers who landed on the deserted shores of Algoa Bay in 1820 (although the colonial authorities had built a fort there nearly 20 years earlier). Sir Rufane Donkin, then the acting governor of the Cape, arrived to welcome the disembarking newcomers personally, and decreed the establishment of a township, which he named Port Elizabeth in memory of his beloved young wife who had died of fever in India two years before.

Growth in the region was slow but steady, the impetus provided, initially, by the increasingly prosperous farms of the hinterland: the port served as a principal outlet for the region's beef, butter, mutton and above all for the products of the merino sheep and angora goat.

Among the city's attractions are:

THE CAMPANILE, situated in Jetty Street at the entrance to the docks. This is the site of the 1820 Settler landing and it was inaugurated in 1923 in memory of the British immigrants. Its 204-step spiral staircase leads you up to a platform (there are superb views of the city from here); the 23-bell carillon rings changes on 10 bells three times a day.

DONKIN RESERVE is an open area from which visitors can survey the beautiful bay. It was created by Sir Rufane Donkin as a shrine to his dead wife; its pyramid bears a moving inscription to 'One of the most perfect human beings,

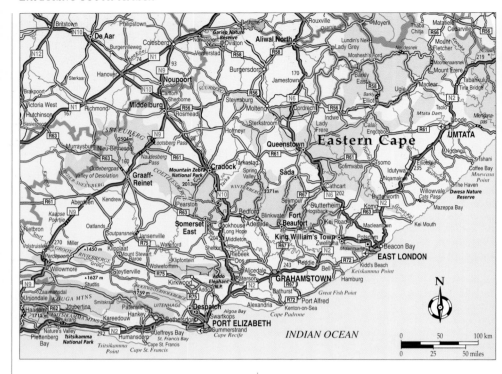

who has given her name to the city below' and mourned by 'the husband whose heart is still wrung by undiminished grief'. Neighbouring the reserve is an old lighthouse which currently serves as a military museum (badges, medals and other militaria of local interest are on public display). Open daily.

CITY HALL Most notable for the replica of the *padrão* (cross) erected by Bartolomeu Dias in 1488, on the headland on which he landed. He was the first European to set foot on what is today South Africa. In front of City Hall is Market Square, where oxwagons once assembled for the long journey inland, and where farmers sold their wares.

HORSE MEMORIAL Fewer than a third of the more than half-million horses in service with the British forces during the South African (Anglo-Boer) War of 1899–1902 survived; a British general told the Royal Commission afterwards that he had 'never seen such shameful abuse of horseflesh in my life'. At the junction of Port Elizabeth's Russell and Cape streets there is a fine memorial to these hard-used animals, erected by public subscription in 1905 and one of only two such monuments in the world.

Museum complex

On the seafront at Humewood and a prime tourist drawcard, the museum comprises an extensive collection of indoor and outdoor areas whose multiplicity of enticements include:

THE OCEANARIUM, particularly well-known for its dolphins, caught in Algoa Bay and trained to play to the gallery, which they do quite delightfully twice a day in the huge pool. Cape fur seals also get into the act. Jackass penguins, and a wide selection of other marine life such as sharks, rays, turtles and fish of all kinds are on display in two large tanks.

THE SNAKE PARK, one of the country's leading reptile repositories and research centres.

On view (behind glass) are snake species of both southern African and exotic origin; there is also a host of crocodiles, alligators, leguaans, lizards, tortoises, otters, meerkats and a bevy of brightly coloured parrots.

Incorporated into the park is the Tropical House, an imaginative and modern exhibition concept: the building encloses a sculpted landscape of jungle-like vegetation, pool, stream, waterfall and an artificial 'mountain'; the resident wildlife includes some lovely birds.

THE MAIN MUSEUM features both cultural and natural history exhibits; among the various components are a costume gallery (fashionable clothing from the Edwardian era to the 1940s), a bird hall and a maritime hall (shipwrecks). Early humanoids (Boskop Man) and other fossils, and Algoa Bay's marine life, are also on display.

Gardens, parks and reserves

The city has some most attractive open areas, three of the more prominent of which are:

ST GEORGE'S PARK is 73 ha (180 acres) in extent and headquarters of the country's first cricket club and venue of provincial matches. It is worth visiting for its outstanding floral displays of orchids and other plants is the adjacent Pearson Conservatory. Elsewhere in the park is a 28 ha (69 acres) garden noted for its massed annuals and perennials and its mature trees, some of them rare. The monthly 'Art in the Park' market is an invitingly colourful feature.

SETTLERS' PARK NATURE RESERVE, on How Avenue, is a 54 ha (133 acres) expanse of indigenous *fynbos* (heath), coastal forest, grassland and Karoo vegetation. The park is bisected by the Baakens River, which meanders through a cliff-lined valley; there are broad lawns, riverside walks, water features, exotic woodland,

ABOVE: *Port Elizabeth's Donkin Street is lined with charming 19th-century terraced houses.*
BELOW: *Dolphins at play in the Oceanarium.*

colourful cultivated displays (best time to visit: November) and a resident buck population – all close to the city centre.

HAPPY VALLEY A delightful recreational area at Humewood Beach, popular for its gardens, including some designed for young visitors (they have nursery-rhyme themes), lawns (for picnickers), ponds, a river (the Shark), riverside footpaths, palm trees and for its giant open-air chess board. The gardens are illuminated, in colour, on summer nights.

163

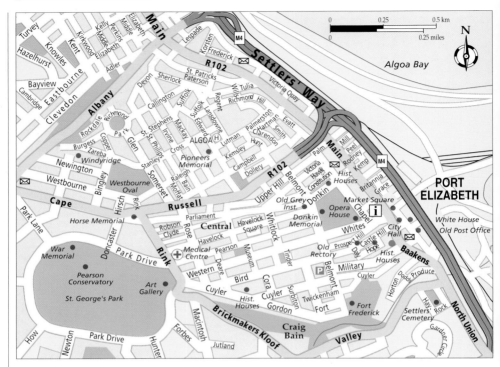

Shopping

The principal shopping areas in Port Elizabeth's central business district are Market Square and Main Street; along the western parts of Main Street are several buildings with upstairs malls; Traduna Mall lies off Market Square; there is a range of inviting speciality shops in Rink Street, Parliament Street and at Walmer Park. Greenacres, in the suburbs, is the third-largest roofed centre in the country.

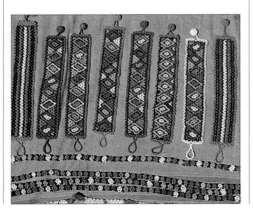

The Publicity Association provides details of the various craft, cottage-industry and street markets that are held in the city.

Theatre and music

Principal auditorium is the splendid, 690-seat, two-level Opera House in Donkin Street (it dates from 1892, has been renovated, and is a national monument). Concerts, opera, ballet and drama are staged by professional and local amateur companies. Other venues include:

• **The Feathermarket Hall**, near Market Square. Built in 1882 as auction premises for the ostrich-feather industry, it now serves as an auditorium for Music Society celebrity performances and an exhibition centre.

• **The Mannville open-air theatre**, in St George's Park, stages Shakespearian productions; the annual festival is well supported.

• **The Savoy Club**, Gilbert and Sullivan, of course, but classical operetta and modern musicals are also staged.

• **Ford Little Theatre**, has shows presented by the Port Elizabeth Musical and Dramatic Society.

• **St Mary's Collegiate Church**, Main Street. Beautiful sacred music.

Wining and dining

There's a varied selection of eating houses, both classic and ethnic, to choose from; the seafood is generally quite excellent. Some specific suggestions appear on page 181.

Sport and recreation

Beaches and watersports feature strongly. The coasts in both directions are distinguished by wonderful stretches of golden sand; the waters of the Indian Ocean are warm (22 °C/72 °F in summer); the bathing is safe; the rollers, in many places, ideal for both casual and competitive surfing; scuba divers and snorkellers revel in the clear waters. Algoa Bay is sometimes storm-tossed but more often calm enough to attract yachtsmen and anglers. There's also good angling from rock and surf and game-fishing in the open sea.

The standard range of sports is also on offer; clubs welcome visitors; details are available from the Port Elizabeth Publicity Association.

OPPOSITE: *Colourful beadwork accessories at a Port Elizabeth beachfront market.*
BELOW: *A group of Addo elephants, last of the once-great Cape herds.*

AROUND PORT ELIZABETH

SUNDAYS AND SWARTKOPS RIVERS The broad alluvial valley of the Sundays River, extending from the shores of Algoa Bay through Kirkwood to Lake Mentz some 100 km (62 miles) to the north, is wonderfully fertile, especially along the middle reaches, and produces about two-thirds of the country's citrus fruit together with a huge volume of fruit juices. To drive up the valley from Port Elizabeth in October, when the trees are in blossom and the air heavy with their scent, is a delight indeed. Flowering plants – bougainvillaea, frangipani, poinsettia and poinciana – are everywhere. The Pearson Park resort is situated at the rivermouth.

Much closer to the city (10 km/6 miles away) is the Swartkops estuary. There are some splendid beaches in the area; the river is navigable for 18 km (11 miles) upstream, and the waters attract yachtsmen, windsurfers and canoeists.

ADDO ELEPHANT NATIONAL PARK This 54,000 ha (133,000 acres) reserve, in the bush country 72 km (45 miles) north-east of Port Elizabeth, was established in 1931 to preserve the last,

FOR RAILWAY ENTHUSIASTS

Port Elizabeth's station building dates from 1875, when the first line came into operation. Part of the terminus has been carefully restored; the cast-iron roof supports are of Victorian vintage.

The Humerail Railway Museum houses some fascinating exhibits – narrow-gauge equipment, steam engines, early passenger coaches and so on. The busy railway repair workshop welcomes visitors. Steam locomotive excursions are popular and include:

• **The Apple Express.** A diminutive, apple-green, squeaky-clean steam loco pulls the Express on the 283 km (176 miles) narrow-gauge (61 cm/24 in) line between the city and the fruit-growing centre of Loerie in the Long Kloof. The line has been operating since 1906. En route the train passes through charming mountain and forest country, and over the 125-m-high (410 ft) Van Stadens River Gorge bridge (highest of the world's narrow-gauge bridges). The train makes its run every second Sunday, more frequently in December.

• **The Dias Express.** Another delightful and old-fashioned steam-pulled narrow-gauge train, but on a much shorter route: this one plies between the Port Elizabeth harbour and King's Beach, calling in at the fascinating Humerail Railway Museum on the way.

The local and very hospitable Steam Enthusiasts Society welcomes like-minded visitors; the organization is contactable through the Publicity Association (*see* Advisory, page 181).

ABOVE: *The dung-beetle, one of nature's more ingenious creatures.*
OPPOSITE TOP: *The pleasantly embowered rest camp in the private Shamwari Game Reserve.*
OPPOSITE BOTTOM: *Custom-built vehicles take Shamwari guests on game-viewing drives.*

The park is also home to black rhino, buffalo, eland, kudu and a number of other bovids, and to 170 species of bird. The latter tend to be quite elusive (much of the vegetation is too thick for good visibility) but an observation point has been established. The elephant and other large game are a lot easier to locate and study: there are game-viewing roads and viewpoints at the watering places.

Accommodation in the park comprises self-contained 2-bed (plus bunk) rondavels, 6-bed family cottages and a pleasant caravan/camp site. There is also a licensed restaurant, shop and a petrol pump.

ZUURBERG SECTION

The Zuurberg National Park was amalgamated into the Addo Elephant National Park in 1995. Situated in the Winterhoek mountain range 12 km (7.5 miles) north of the older part of Addo and until recently a state forest, it was proclaimed a park in 1985 to preserve the region's three types of transitional vegetation. The scenery is spectacular, the prolific birdlife notable for its black eagles. The area is being restocked with game.

This is a place for the hiker, the backpacker and the lover of peace. Facilities are still being developed. The nearby Zuurberg Inn is a pleasant place from which to explore the area (it offers swimming, horse-riding, tennis, bowls and croquet).

tiny remnant of the once-prolific herds of Cape elephant. A decade earlier the elephants had almost been wiped out: they were causing havoc in the cultivated lands and the farmers, losing patience, hired a professional hunter to exterminate them. Between 90 and 100 elephants were shot before the survivors – 16 of them (later reduced to 11) – escaped into the dense tree-and-creeper tangle of the Addo bush and there, in what was described as 'a hunter's hell', they were protected from further persecution by the difficult terrain, and by outraged public opinion. They now number a healthy 185.

The Addo bush consists largely of spekboom (*Portulacaria afra*) and other plants that elephants relish, and the park supports a population three times denser than any other reserve in Africa.

WEST OF PORT ELIZABETH

Well worth exploring is the coastal region on either side of the national highway (the N2) that leads to Cape Town. Of note is:

ST FRANCIS BAY

Extending from Cape Recife (near Port Elizabeth) in the east to Cape St Francis in the west and incorporating the popular Jeffrey's Bay area, St Francis Bay is distinguished by its sandy beaches and by a number of attractive resorts, including Skoenmakerskop, Seaview, Sardinia Bay, Aston Bay and Paradise Beach. The Gamtoos River discharges into the bay 50 km from Port Elizabeth, and its estuary offers good fishing (kob, grunter and silvie). The waters off Cape St Francis are greatly favoured by anglers for their large (22 kg/48 lb) yellowtail.

There are a number of attractive nature reserves along or close to the 100 km (62 miles) of the bay's shoreline.

SHAMWARI GAME RESERVE

Close to the Addo Elephant National Park, 72 km (45 miles) north-east of Port Elizabeth, this 10,000 ha (24,710 acres) private reserve is home to black and white rhino, lion, elephant, leopard (rarely seen), buffalo and 18 antelope species. Day and night drives are offered.

THE VAN STADENS RIVER AREA

The region, just over half an hour's drive from Port Elizabeth, is famed for its scenic splendour and for the large, dune-enclosed lagoon at the estuary. The river is navigable (to small boats; good fishing for musselcracker and steenbras) up to the gorge, which is crossed by a 350-m-long (1,150 ft) bridge. Motorists look down a drop of no less than 125 m (400 ft) to the river below.

You reach the bridge and gorge via the spectacular and very lovely Van Stadens River Pass, just before which is a signpost directing you to the wild flower reserve, a 500 ha (1,235 acres) area (60 ha/148 acres under cultivation) that protects an unspoilt countryside of heath and Alexandra forest. The flowers (erica, protea and watsonia) are attractive between April and September, and especially so at the height of spring. Facilities include a network of paths, picnic spots and an information centre.

JEFFREY'S BAY

On the shores of St Francis Bay some 45 minutes' drive from Port Elizabeth, and one of the world's most notable surfing areas: the rollers off a number of beaches, within easy walking distance of the town, attract international competitors as well as large numbers of local sportsmen.

As renowned are the seashells, found along a 3 km (2 miles) stretch of sand: huge numbers of tropical Indo-Pacific and temperate Cape species that attract collectors from afar. Searching the tide-line is a favourite (and rewarding) pastime among holiday-makers; a museum in town houses unusual and enchanting shell displays. Jeffrey's Bay has excellent visitor facilities.

SETTLER COUNTRY

This is the name by which most white South Africans know the territory that stretches from Port Elizabeth east to the Great Fish River and inland up the valley of that river: a countryside more or less permanently occupied by the Xhosa (together with a handful of hardy Boer frontier families) until the arrival of 4,000 British immigrants in 1820.

The influx represented a major chapter in the politically (and morally) complicated story of colonial expansion in the Eastern Cape, a saga that properly began with the eruption of the first 'frontier war' in 1779. Altogether there

would be eight more major confrontations over the next hundred years (a tragic clash of cultures that saw many of the black clans dispossessed, and the Cape Colony's border moved progressively eastwards), the most significant of which was probably the fifth, in 1819, when the 9,000-strong Xhosa army mounted a direct attack on the military outpost of Grahamstown. This was repulsed, but the event convinced Lord Charles Somerset, the strong-willed Cape governor of the day, that only massive white immigration – from Britain, since 'anglicization' was part of official policy – could bring a semblance of stability to the border areas. Hence the landings at Algoa Bay in the following year.

This is a region of historic little towns, many with Settler connections and rather British in character, surrounded by hills and valleys graced by aloe and euphorbia and by sheep pastures and farmlands that yield wheat and lucerne, beef, milk, butter, cheese, fruit, and timber.

GRAHAMSTOWN

An elegant place situated 60 km (37 miles) from the coast and set among green hills 535 m (1,755 ft) above sea level, Grahamstown is known both as the 'Settler City' and, because of the number of churches within its bounds (around 40 places of worship in all), as the 'City of Saints'. It's also a leading academic and cultural centre, home to Rhodes University, St Paul's Theological College, a number of fine schools, the 1820 Foundation and the acclaimed National Festival of the Arts.

Grahamstown's past is attractively discernible in the original Settler homes that have been preserved and in the rather more imposing Victorian edifices erected during the later and more prosperous years of the 19th century.

Museums, landmarks and memorials

The early British immigrants (and other English-speakers who followed) are commemorated by the grandly modern Settlers Memorial, situated on Gunfire Hill above the city. The monument, built in 1974, consists of exhibition halls, a 900-seat conference centre, a splendid 920-seat auditorium, function rooms, entertainment and recreation areas and so forth. Among its showpieces is the Memorial Court, a place full of symbols representing the British contribution to South Africa's cultural heritage. The auditorium

Part of Rhodes University in Grahamstown.

is used for, among other things, the annual (winter – held in July) National Festival of the Arts, during which an imaginative programme of drama is staged, music heard, dance performed and paintings and sculpture displayed. Among other points of interest are:

THE SETTLERS WILD FLOWER RESERVE, which covers most of Gunfire Hill. This is a 61 ha (151 acres) expanse of ground that stretches from the university to the monument and encloses the town's former botanic gardens. Features include a stone-walled lily pond, flora indigenous to the areas of early British settlement and other local species (proteas, cycads, and aloes) and the Old Provost, a military prison. Altogether a most attractive place.

ALBANY MUSEUM, which focuses on Settler history (*see* below), but more prominently – in its main building on Somerset Street – on natural history, ethnology and anthropology (the history of humankind), African artefacts and musical instruments, as well as exhibitions of traditional Xhosa lifestyles. There's also a wildlife gallery for children.

THE 1820 MEMORIAL MUSEUM, also in Somerset Street (below the Monument) and part of the Albany complex, houses a collection of Settler family treasures (jewellery, silver and porcelain), firearms and military memorabilia, furniture and implements, costumes and accessories and a photographic essay on Grahamstown's growth.

OBSERVATORY MUSEUM, Bathurst Street, is significant for its place in the story of South Africa's diamond industry: it was here that Dr William Atherstone identified Hopetown's 'Eureka' stone in 1867, so prompting the first great diamond rush. He was also noted for his medical work: he pioneered the use of ether as

an anaesthetic, founded the Albany Hospital in 1858, the Grahamstown Lunatic Asylum in 1875 and South Africa's first medical research laboratory. Other interesting features of the museum include its Victorian furniture, its attractive herb garden, its Meridian Room (where astronomical time was calculated) and the country's only camera obscura – a darkened chamber into which coloured images were projected from the outside by an ingenious system of lenses and mirrors (a novelty much enjoyed by wealthy Victorians in the age of nascent photography). Open daily.

ARTIFICERS' SQUARE, around the junction of Cross and Bartholomew streets; distinguished by its charming early Settler homes (these are now privately owned).

ANGLICAN CATHEDRAL of St Michael and St George, an imposing building whose bells, lectern, pulpit, rood screen and organ hold special interest, and whose spire rises almost 50 m (164 ft) over a town square fringed on the southern side by pleasant Victorian façades (all are now national monuments).

HISTORIC HOTELS Two of these are of note:
• **The Cathcart Arms** welcomed its first guests in 1825 (the original deed of sale is displayed).
• **The Grand,** in High Street, has been the site of a hostelry for the past century and now boasts the country's largest private wine cellar (open weekdays and Saturdays; tastings on Saturday mornings).

PORT ALFRED

To the south of Grahamstown, at the mouth of the Kowie River on what is known as the Sunshine Coast, lies Port Alfred, one of the Eastern Cape's fastest-growing resorts.

The Kowie is navigable for 21 km (13 miles) upstream, and at one time – in the mid-19th century – unsuccessful efforts were made to develop the harbour and the place is now noted principally for its 18-hole golf course (one of the country's finest), its proximity to the lively Fish River Sun hotel-casino complex (28 km/17 miles along the coast) and for its pleasant beaches and their seashells (1,800 different kinds have been found, including some rare species). There's safe bathing and excellent fishing (deep-sea, surf, rock and freshwater) in the area; bathing, canoeing and other watersports are enjoyed in and on the river. Among the attractions are the two-day Kowie canoe trail along the lovely valley and the 8 km (5 miles) hiking trail through the 174 ha (430 acres) Kowie Nature Reserve (birdlife includes the fish eagle).

BATHURST

Situated on the road between Port Alfred and Grahamstown: a charming place embowered by giant wild figs and coral trees and set in a countryside renowned for its splendid pineapple harvests. Among the area's features of interest are:
SUMMERHILL FARM, which boasts a traditional Xhosa village, mini-farm, tractor rides, walks, restaurant and charming pub.
THE PIG 'N WHISTLE HOTEL, which started life in 1821 as a blacksmith's forge and an inn, survived the 'frontier' troubles (it was looted, burned and then rebuilt) and still plays amiable host to the thirsty traveller.
THE AGRICULTURAL MUSEUM Early farm equipment and implements on view; closed on Wednesdays and Saturdays.
HORSESHOE BEND NATURE RESERVE, 7 km (4 miles) west of Bathurst and so named for the remarkably convoluted course of the Kowie River. The area is graced by a range of lovely trees and flowering plants, among them aloes, crane flowers, gazanias, euphorbias, crassulas and mesembryanthemums.

SALEM

An attractively preserved village, 13 km (8 miles) from Grahamstown on the road to Port Elizabeth. It was founded by the largest (344-strong) of the Settler groups; of interest is the fortified Wesleyan chapel, and some of the surviving

early houses, double-storeyed and designed for defence. A plaque on a nearby hill commemorates the courage of Richard Gush, a Quaker whose soft words turned away a Xhosa war party. The name of Salem is derived from the Hebrew word for peace (Psalm 76); cricket has been played on the village green since 1844.

To the north of Salem is the Thomas Baines Nature Reserve, a 1,013 ha (2,503 acres) sanctuary for 42 mammal species, including white rhino, buffalo, eland, black wildebeest, bontebok, mountain reedbuck and 171 different types of bird and 24 of reptile.

THE NORTHERN AREAS

Longer excursions from Port Elizabeth and Grahamstown lead you across the Great Fish River Valley, towards and through the rugged Winterberg range of mountains and beyond, through increasingly dry country to the fringes of the Great Karoo.

FORT BEAUFORT

A substantial and pleasant town on the banks of the Kat River and a major centre of the citrus-farming industry, Fort Beaufort was founded as a military post in 1822, and successfully resisted a Xhosa onslaught in 1851. Its Military Museum, once the garrison officers' mess, and its Martello Tower house some intriguing militaria. In Durban Street is the Historical Museum, devoted to items of less aggressive origin: early household implements, documents, and some paintings of local interest by Frederick I'Ons and the prolific (and much underrated) Thomas Baines. To the east of the Grahamstown-Fort Beaufort road lies the Great Fish River Reserve, originally a smallish haven for kudu but expanded to bring the conservation area up to 45,000 ha (111,200 acres) and more. Wildlife includes the kudu, of course, but also white rhino, Cape buffalo, eland, steenbok, springbok and 184 bird species (a checklist is available at the gate). Of particular note is the dense, 2-m-high (6.5 ft) semi-succulent vegetation (known as Fish River Valley Bushveld) which covers large parts of the terrain, and a euphorbia 'forest'. Facilities are being developed. Other features include a network of game-viewing roads, walks, observation hides, pleasant picnic and fishing spots and a reception centre.

The historic Pig 'n Whistle in Bathurst.

SOMERSET EAST

The town, a fairly substantial one, nestles at the foot of the attractive Bosberg in a fertile, well watered area of streams and waterfalls. The Glen Avon Falls are especially worth visiting (permission required); also recommended is the 10 km (6 miles) Auret mountain drive and the pleasant wood-and-ravine walks.

Somerset East is noted for its attractive gardens, its excellent golf course, its museum (church history, but also early wedding gowns and exquisite period dolls), the Walter Battiss Art Gallery and for the 2,000 ha (4,942 acres) Bosberg Nature Reserve (with mountain zebra, antelope, and hiking trail).

CRADOCK

Founded in 1813, on the upper reaches of the Great Fish River 260 km (162 miles) north of Port Elizabeth, Cradock is now a largish and fairly attractive Karoo town – though the fertile Fish River Valley countryside, with its orchards and pastures and fields of lucerne, is quite unlike the Karoo proper. Its Van Riebeeck Karoo Garden is worth visiting for the indigenous plants and the tranquillity; its Ilex oak trees are thought to be the largest of their kind in the world. Among the historic buildings is a restored cottage that was once home to the noted author and feminist Olive Schreiner, who wrote her best-known book, *The Story of an African Farm*, while working as a governess in the area. Not too far away, off the R32, are the popular and allegedly curative Karoo Sulphur Springs (chalets and walking trails).

MOUNTAIN ZEBRA NATIONAL PARK

This wilderness area, 24 km (15 miles) southwest of Cradock in a great amphitheatre of the Bankberg range, was established in 1937 to preserve the last remnant of the once-numerous Cape mountain zebra (which are distinct from the familiar Burchell's variety). The exercise proved highly successful: about 200 of the animals now graze on the hillsides of the 6,500 ha (16,000 acres) reserve, about the optimum number for the area. Surplus animals are periodically translocated to other sanctuaries.

The park is home to 57 other mammal species, including eland, black wildebeest, mountain reedbuck, springbok, African wildcat,

TOP: *Home-made windmills on sale in Cradock.*
ABOVE: *Renovated Victorian homes – this one embellished by a vintage cart – provide tourist accommodation in Cradock.*

black-footed cat, black-backed jackal, Cape fox, bat-eared fox and aardwolf. Dassies (also known as rock-rabbits) are a common sight. Over 200 bird species have been recorded, among them some of the more notable raptors (black, martial and booted eagles, the splendid Cape eagle owl and the chanting goshawk).

For visitors, there is pleasant accommodation in 18 2-bedroomed chalets and in the restored Victorian Karoo farmhouse 'Doornhoek'. There's also a caravan/camping ground and two trail-huts. Amenities include a conference centre for 40 people, à la carte restaurant, shop (groceries and fresh meat), petrol pump, pool, riding stables, picnic areas and, for the energetic, the three-day Mountain Zebra hiking trail.

THE CISKEI REGION

The wedge-shaped Ciskei area, until recently an 'independent' homeland and now an integral part of the Eastern Cape province, lies between the Great Fish River in the west and the Great Kei River in the east (the name, given by the early white colonists, means 'this side of the Kei', to distinguish it from nearby Transkei). The 8,500 km² (3,282 square miles) region is home to more than a million people, most of whom are of Xhosa stock though there are substantial Mfengu and Thembu minorities. All three belong to the Nguni group.

The region has a lot of tourist potential, its most enticing assets the superb scenery, pleasant climate and the 65 km (40 miles) of warm Indian Ocean shoreline whose golden, gently-shelving beaches, estuaries and lagoons remain largely unspoilt. Inland there are attractive mountain and forest areas, some impressive game and nature reserves, challenging hiking trails and a sprinkling of lodges, hotels, resorts and hotel-casino complexes.

THE CISKEI COASTAL AREA

The Fish River mouth is distinguished by its extraordinary geological formations – the maze of caves, tunnels and blowholes sculpted out of the headlands by wind and wave – and by its birdlife: the estuary and lagoon teem with waders and waterfowl, among them Egyptian and spurwing geese, yellowbilled ducks, stilts and wimbrels and breeding pairs of Cape teal.

This is the start of the popular and rewarding Shipwreck Trail, a 64 km (40 miles) route along sand and rocky shoreline to the mouth of the Ncera River, which can be walked, by anyone who is reasonably fit, in three to four days. Attractions along the way include the wrecks

themselves of course (over the centuries this part of the southern African coast has functioned as something of a maritime graveyard), and the stretches of lovely golden beach, the dense coastal bush, the prolific birdlife and, for those lovers of the outdoors who camp out near one of the resorts (you're allowed to make camp anywhere along the beach for a small fee), angling, spear-fishing and scuba-diving, boardsailing, surfing and canoeing.

The more prominent resorts include the:

FISH RIVER SUN, a largish (300-bed) addition to the well-patronized Sun International hotel-casino empire; the amenities are predictably varied and excellent and include Polynesian-style buildings, casino, à la carte restaurant, cocktail bars, 18-hole golf course (designed by Gary Player), pool, squash and tennis.

MPEKWENI SUN MARINE RESORT, another Sun International enterprise, on the beachfront, overlooking the lagoon (safe swimming) just along the coast. Caters for the luxury-loving family; the emphasis is on watersports; also river-cruises, bowls, tennis and squash.

BIRA COASTAL RESORT, a holiday 'township', also rather up-market; lagoon, lovely surrounds, a popular place among bird-watchers and watersports enthusiasts.

THE CISKEI HINTERLAND

Prime attraction for nature-lovers are the three forest reserves – the Cata, Mnyameni and Zingcuka – on the slopes of the lofty and lovely Amatola range in the north, the region's principal coastal-belt rampart. The indigenous forests are dense, distinguished by their yellowwoods,

TOP LEFT: *A young Xhosa boy relishes the nectar from an aloe plant.*
BELOW: *Hogsback's enchanting oak avenue.*

XHOSA HERITAGE

Of Nguni stock, the Xhosa comprise a diversity of Eastern Cape (former Ciskei and Transkei) clans, the main groups being the Gcaleka, Ngika, Ndlambe, Dushane, Qayi, Ntinde and, of Khoisan (San or Bushman and Khoikhoi) origin, the Gqunkhwebe. The language contains three different types of click sound, borrowed from the Khoisan tongues when the southward-migrating Xhosa began to settle the region sometime before the 17th century.

The Xhosa were, and still are, known for the magnificence and variety of their beadwork. Traditionally, their garments and ornamentation reflected the stages of a woman's life: a certain headdress was worn by a newly-married girl; a different style by one who had given birth to her first child, and so on. Marriages – the Xhosa are polygamous (though today only the wealthier men have more than one wife) – involved protracted negotiations between the families of bride and groom over the payment of the bride-price (*lobola*). The Xhosa man fulfilled the roles of warrior, hunter and stockman; the woman looked after the land and the growing of crops.

A clan comprised a number of groups, each led by a chief, or Inkosi, who owed his position to his mother's status (the society, however, was a patriarchal one in which women weren't formally accorded political authority).

The land was communally held; and great emphasis placed on giving according to need: everything was shared, in bad times as well as good; Xhosa families still routinely help one another with such tasks as hut-building.

The body of Xhosa lore has much in common with that of the other Nguni peoples (*see* Zulu Heritage, page 134); animism, and recognition of the presence and power of ancestral spirits and of a supreme authority, are basic elements of belief. Misfortune and illness are attributed to unnatural or supernatural influences (such as the *tokoloshe*, a hairy and potentially malevolent goblin); other figures are the huge lightning bird (*impundulu*), and the gentle *aBantu bomlambo*, human-like beings believed to live in rivers and the sea, and who accept into their family those who drown.

Initiation rites differ markedly between the various African peoples; with increasing urbanization many groups have abandoned circumcision altogether. Among the Xhosa, the youths whiten their bodies, and wear a white blanket or sheepskin to ward off evil; during the ceremonies, enlivened by energetic dances, they wear costumes made from reeds, and at the end of the lengthy initiation period – spent in isolation from the rest of the community – the specially-built huts in which the young men have been living are ceremoniously burned.

LEFT: *Xhosa youngsters in the hilly Katberg area herd cattle on horseback.*
ABOVE: *Xhosa initiates during their ritual transition to manhood. In many areas of rural South Africa circumcision remains a painful part of the growing-up process.*

white stinkwoods and Cape chestnuts. There are also plantations, and patches of high macchia and grasslands decorated with wild flowers.

Winding a 104 km (65 miles) course through these forest areas is the outstanding Amatola trail, attractive both to hikers and climbers.

HOGSBACK, on the northern edge of the Ciskei region (and accessible via either Stutterheim or the Ciskei centres of Bisho and Alice), is a resort area comprising a scatter of permanent homes, three hotels (the Hogsback Inn is recommended), holiday bungalows, a caravan park, and an exquisitely shaded camping ground, all set in the loveliest countryside imaginable. Hikers and ramblers along the country lanes and fern-fringed woodland paths enjoy breathtaking views (of four peaks, including the Hog's Back) and waterfalls (notable are The Madonna and Child, The Swallowtail, The Kettle Spout and The Bridal Veil). One of the more pleasant strolls leads to the Oak Avenue site, where open-air services are held at Christmas and Easter. Nearby is St Patrick's-on-the-Hill, one of southern Africa's smallest churches.

TSOLWANA GAME PARK, south of Tafelberg and abutting the Swart (black) Kei River in the former northern Ciskei, is a quite magnificent, 17,000 ha (42,000 acres) mountain reserve run with both conservation and 'resource management' in mind: the local inhabitants benefit from cheap fresh meat and from the jobs on offer, so poaching and other habitat-damaging practices such as fence- and tree-cutting are kept to the minimum.

Principal features of the park are the river valley, the Tsolwana Mountains, and the region's mix of Karoo scrub and temperate-zone vegetation. On view: white rhino, giraffe and a large number and variety of bovids. Several exotic species have been introduced, including

Barbary and mouflon sheep, fallow deer and Himalayan tahr. Tsolwana caters well for the hunting fraternity (both rifle and – again unusual – bow); professional guides are available; trophy-seekers tend to go for the exotics.

There are guided walking and pony trails, game-viewing roads (vehicles may be hired), trout-fishing spots (rods are also available for hire) and winter-time hunting safaris. Accommodation: self-catering lodges, luxury hunting lodge, caravan/camping site.

THE 'BORDER' REGION

The territory stretching from the far-eastern Cape seaboard inland, through the narrow corridor between the Keiskamma and Kei rivers to Queenstown and beyond, is known as Border, a hangover from the colonial and rather turbulent past: the region, for long occupied by the Xhosa, lay at the extreme limits of white encroachment until the mid-1800s, when East London was founded and immigrants – many of them German – brought a degree of stability and permanence to the tentatively-settled land. The Xhosa were in due course confined to their 'homelands' across the two rivers.

EAST LONDON

This is a fairly substantial city and South Africa's only major river-port: it's situated at the mouth of the Buffalo, which rises in the high Amatola Mountains to the north-west.

East London's attractions are of the more quiet, undemanding, family-orientated kind: it has fine beaches, pleasant parks and gardens, good hotels and restaurants, and some fairly entertaining nightlife in the summer months along the seafront.

The principal thoroughfare is Oxford Street, along which you'll find modern shops and office blocks (though glitzy high-rises are conspicuous by their absence), the post office and the City Hall. Satour, and the air terminal, are in nearby Terminus Street. Features of interest include:

EAST LONDON MUSEUM, in Oxford Street, houses the first coelacanth (*Latimeria chalumnae*) – a primitive fish that lived in the Mesozoic period some 250 million years in the past and was thought to have become extinct 60 million years ago – to have been caught in modern times. The unusual mauve-blue fish was landed near East London in 1938 and shown to Professor JLB Smith of Rhodes University, Grahamstown, who described it as a 'living fossil'. The museum also boasts the world's only known dodo's egg; the last of these large, turkey-sized, flightless birds, once common on Mauritius, died in about 1680, though related species survived on other Indian Ocean islands until the 1790s.

Other more general displays are devoted to ethnology, prehistory and local history; of special note is the fine collection of Karoo reptile fossils; the exhibition of Xhosa beadwork and other items traditional to African ornamentation, custom and belief. Part of the museum complex is Gately House, a fine period home.

QUEEN'S PARK BONANICAL GARDENS along Settlers' Way and Beaconsfield Road displays attractive indigenous flora; among the 1,000 animals at the park's zoo is an endearing bear called Jackie; the children's zoo has pony-rides.

BEACHES AND RESORTS East London's three beaches are renowned. The Orient is the nearest to the city and most popular; bounded by the

OPPOSITE: *The grand hills of the Great Winterhoek range, north of Fort Beaufort.*
BELOW: *Leisure craft dot East London's harbour.*

2 km (1.25 miles) Esplanade, its attractions include the promenade pier, Orient Theatre (plays and reviews) and restaurant. Nahoon and Eastern beaches are also wide and golden, and ideal for safe surfing (the former is a venue for international contests). East London has two freshwater swimming pools and, on the Esplanade, an attractive little aquarium which houses 400 marine species, including seals and penguins (the daily seal shows are very popular with children).

Along what is known as the Romantic Coast to the south-west and north-east of the city are a number of inviting resorts offering a range of outdoor recreation and accommodation from the simple rondavel to the fairly sophisticated hotel. Two of the more prominent places are:
• **Kidds Beach**, at the mouth of the Mcantsi River abutting the Ciskei region to the south-west. There are holiday cottages and three caravan parks; bowling green, tennis courts and a splendid expanse of sand. Fishermen favour nearby Kayser's Beach, Christmas Rock and Chalumna Mouth.
• **Gonubie Mouth**, 25 km (15 miles) north-east of East London, has first-class tourist amenities and an enchanting bird sanctuary.

East London's coasts are a rock-angler's dream.

The tiny (8 ha/20 acres) Gonubie Nature Reserve, proclaimed as a waterfowl haven, hosts more than 130 bird species, including summer-nesting cranes. Among the visitor facilities are observation points, a boardwalk, footpaths and an information centre. In the reserve is a garden of medicinal plants used by herbalists.

KING WILLIAM'S TOWN

On the banks of the Buffalo River some 50 km (30 miles) west of East London, King William's Town started life as a mission station in 1825. The town is steeped in military and political history: it became the capital of the short-lived Province of Queen Adelaide (1835–1836: the area was settled by 'loyal' Xhosa to act as a buffer zone between their more hostile cousins and the whites) which was destroyed in 1836 and resurrected in 1847 to serve as the 'capital' of British Kaffraria, another, but stronger, buffer zone. Among the town's attractions is the:

KAFFRARIAN MUSEUM, one of the best in the country. It was founded in 1884 by the Natural History Society and is now the repository of more than 40,000 African mammal specimens. Of less academic interest are the mounted remains of Huberta, the itinerant hippo that enchanted the public during her 1,000 km (621 miles) wanderings between 1928 and 1931, when she was accidentally shot. Other displays focus on Xhosa culture and ornamentation, and on German and English immigrant lifestyles, costumes, and militaria. Open daily.

QUEENSTOWN

The town, which was named in honour of Queen Victoria, was founded on the Komani River in 1853 and laid out around a hexagonal centre from which the streets radiate (the authorities at the time insisted that the townspeople be responsible for their own defence, and the hexagon arrangement served as both a laager and a means of rapid exit). It is a fairly large railways, cattle- and sheep-farming and educational centre and is famed for the roses that are grown in its gardens. The main road from East London enters Queenstown through the Walter Everitt sunken garden, a charmingly landscaped place of lawns, ornamental trees, ponds, waterbirds, and quiet picnic spots. On the slopes of Madeira Mountain just to the north of town is the J de Lange Nature Reserve, crossed by a superb scenic drive. Among the game animals that can be seen are springbok; the flora includes acacia species, aloes, cycads; the reserve's red- and yellow-blossomed tamboekie thorn, *Erythrina acanthocarpa*, is found nowhere else. There are some pleasant picnic spots. The nearby Xhosa Carpet Factory is noted for its Persian-style rugs.

THE CRUEL SEA

Little now remains of the former Transkei region's Port Grosvenor, a 19th-century attempt to establish a harbour on an especially rugged section of the Wild Coast. The 'port' was named after the ill-fated *Grosvenor*, a treasure-ship that came to grief on the rocky shore in August 1782. Only 15 of the 123 people on board the ship were drowned but most of the survivors, lacking food, fresh water, trading goods and weapons, either perished or simply disappeared (some were absorbed, it is thought, into the black communities) on the long trek west to Cape Town. The *Grosvenor* had been laden with gold, jewels, plates, coins and other precious cargo (including treasure associated with the legendary Peacock Throne of Persia); ambitious and ingenious recovery schemes have been launched by a number of salvage companies, and many individual divers have meticulously explored the turbulent wreck-site, but, although some fascinating and quite valuable odds and ends have been found, the principal prize remains buried beneath the sands of the sea-bed.

More than two centuries earlier, in 1552, another fine ship, the Portuguese vessel *São João*, ran aground on the rocks some way farther down the coast. The survivors – a total of 440 men (some of them of noble rank), women and children – set out on what was to become one of the most tragic odysseys of the pre-colonial era. Their route took them northwards to Lourenço Marques in Mozambique, an incredible journey of about 1,600 km (994 miles) from the scene of the wreck and, again, nearly all died along the way. Just eight Portuguese and 17 slaves eventually managed to stagger to safety.

THE TRANSKEI REGION

The territory, situated between the Great Kei and Mtamvuna rivers, is the traditional home of sections of the southern Nguni peoples, who speak dialects of the Xhosa tongue (isiXhosa), though different groups – the Gcaleka in the south, the Pondo, Mpondomise, Cele and Xesibe in the north, and the Thembu and Bovana in the central parts – preserve their own customs, clothing and ornamentation. The old ways, however, are in decline, even in the remoter rural areas.

Transkei was the first of the 'national states' to be granted independence (in 1976), though its republican status was never recognized outside southern Africa. It is a largely agricultural region of rolling grass-covered uplands dotted with homesteads (most of them of the rondavel type and many, curiously, built with their doors facing east) and bounded in the south-east by a magnificently rugged coastline, its principal tourist drawcard.

Gravel feeder roads lead from the N2 to the coastal resorts. Drive carefully as the lesser roadways tend to be convoluted, and cattle and goats regard them as their own domain.

THE WILD COAST

Transkei's 280 km (174 miles) of beautiful (but sometimes treacherous) Indian Ocean shoreline is a holiday-maker's and hiker's paradise, an unsurpassed stretch of unspoilt wilderness famed for its scenic variety. Here there are sandy bays, lagoons and estuaries, imposing cliffs and rocky reefs that probe, finger-like, out to sea and, in the immediate hinterland, green hills and dense woodlands.

WILD COAST HIKING TRAIL One can explore the sandy beaches, lagoons and estuaries, cliffs, coves and caves, rock-pools and wrecks, forests and mangrove swamps of this most dramatic 280 km (174 miles) coast via the established trail. The full course, marked by white footprints, takes from 14 to 25 days to complete (duration is a matter of personal preference and capability) and is divided into five manageable 3- to 6-day sections.

WILD COAST SUN One of southern Africa's premier hotel, casino and resort complexes is set beside a tranquil lagoon on the northernmost portion of the splendid shoreline. On offer is the full range of sporting and recreational facilities (superb golf course; bowls, tennis, and squash; rock, surf and deep-sea angling; ski-boating; freshwater and sea bathing; water-skiing, canoeing and sailing at Waterworld); gaming rooms; restaurants, a theatre that hosts international entertainers, and two explosively live-show bars.

Not too far away is the Umtamvuna River and its fine waterfall, and the Mzamba River mouth where, at low tide, petrified trees and other fossil remains can be seen. The nearest

The Transkei region's Hole-in-the-Wall.

town is Bizana, known for the herbalists that do brisk pavement business. The hillsides around are aflame with aloes in June.

Farther along the coast, between the Msikaba and Mtentu rivers, is the:

MKAMBATI NATURE RESERVE A pleasant expanse of grassland and subtropical country-side sliced through by perennial streams and by the forested ravines of the Msikaba and Mtentu rivers. The Mkambati has been stocked with eland, hartebeest, blesbok, gemsbok and blue wildebeest; birdlife is prolific (recommended for the more energetic ornithologist is a canoe trip up the Msikaba River: Cape vultures nest on the gorge's sheer cliffs).

Of interest to botanists are the Pondoland palms, or the mkambati coconuts, which are unique to the area. Facilities include cottages and rondavels, a main lodge (five double rooms, guest lounge, table d'hôte restaurant), and the Club House à la carte restaurant (delicious veni-son and seafood specialities). A good network of pathways takes you along the scenically spec-tacular shoreline and through stretches of inland countryside graced by some exquisite wild flowers (watsonias, gladioli, ground orchids and daisies in grassland; wild frangipani and arum lilies in swamp forest).

PORT ST JOHNS

The settlement, which takes its name from the renowned wreck (*see* panel, page 177), lies at the Umzimvubu River mouth in a stunning set-ting of majestic headland, forest, golden sand and blue sea, and it is perhaps the most pleas-ant of the Wild Coast's holiday areas.

The river, navigable for approximately 10 km (6 miles), is ideal for boating. Its valley nurtures lush plantings of subtropical fruits and path-ways lead through dense woodland to some exquisite beauty spots. There are three splendid beaches, two good hotels, the excellent Second Beach 'cottage colony' resort, clusters of holi-day bungalows, caravan/camping sites, a fine nine-hole golf course, bowling greens, tennis courts, and, in town, a small museum, a public library, several garages and general dealers and nine purveyors of patent medicines. Roadside stalls sell bananas, lychees, pawpaws, mangoes, avocados and an attractive array of rugs and basketware. The climate is superb, the sea safe and warm enough even for mid-winter bathing. Quite a few artists, writers and discerning refugees from the concrete jungle have made their home here.

Just to the south is the small and enchanting Silaka Nature Reserve, set in a wooded valley and haven for blue wildebeest, zebra, blesbok, for some elusive forest animals and birds, and for a kaleidoscopic variety of orchids, lilies, mosses, lichens and red-hot pokers.

HLULEKA NATURE RESERVE, a small, especially attractive expanse of countryside some 30 km (20 miles) south of Port St Johns, noted for its patches of evergreen forest, its prolific birdlife, for the antelope and zebra that browse on the grassland reaches of the Hluleka River, and for its rocky coastline, a paradise for fishermen (catches include kob, blacktail and shad). Accommodation in 6-bed chalets.

COFFEE BAY

Similar to Port St Johns in the magnificence of its cliff and mountain setting, Coffee Bay, situated between the estuaries of the Nenga and Mbomvu rivers, is a tranquil little holiday village that offers two comfortable hotels, caravan/camping sites, excellent fishing and surfing, safe bathing and, for light aircraft owners, a 750 m (2,460 ft) landing strip.

HOLE-IN-THE-WALL An hour-and-a-half's walk south of Coffee Bay and an hour's drive inland (there is no coastal road), this is probably the most distinctive – and certainly the most photographed – of the Wild Coast's natural features, a massive detached cliff that stands island-like in the sea, and through whose huge arched opening the surf thunders. Its flat top, extensive enough to accommodate several football fields, is mantled in greenery. The structure is known to the locals as esiKhaleni, or 'place of the noise'. Two kilometres away (1.25 miles), situated above a small bay, is the Hole-in-the-Wall Hotel and holiday village.

QORA MOUTH

The small resort at the Qora River estuary, near the town of Willowvale, offers a fine beach, a lagoon that is ideal for bathing and boating, and some excellent rock, surf and freshwater fishing spots, all within easy walking distance of the Kob Inn (cottage-style bungalows, family rooms, airstrip, marvellous seafood dishes, and a bar set on the edge of the rocks). There is good fishing for kob throughout the year; anglers come from afar to participate in the annual (July/August) 'pignose grunter run'.

DWESA AND CWEBE NATURE RESERVES These adjoining wilderness areas, separated by the Mbashe River, are of similar character – an attractive mix of evergreen forest and open grassland that sustains a wide variety of birds and small mammals, and of rocky shorelines interspersed by mangrove communities, secluded bays and long stretches of golden sand. Shell collectors find the area enchanting. Accommodation is in self-catering chalets and in The Haven resort hotel, known for the quiet comfort of its bungalows, its views of sea, shoreline and forest, and for its seafood dishes and companionable poolside barbecues.

MAZEPPA BAY

Here there are three broad, palm-fringed beaches and an excellent resort hotel (its seafood is famed) linked to its own island by a small suspension bridge. All in all, a most pleasant place for rambling through coastal dune and forest, bathing, snorkelling, scuba-diving and fishing in the sea. Especially fishing: the area's hammerhead sharks, some weighing an impressive 450 kg (990 lb) and more, present a splendid challenge to serious anglers. Other catches include barracuda, galjoen, bronze bream, blacktail, kob, yellowtail, shad, garrick, musselcracker, mackerel and queenfish.

QOLORA MOUTH

Another small estuary resort with a fine beach, three hotels, including the well-known Trennery's, and excellent caravan/camping facilities. In the general area is the lovely pool of Nongqause, the young Xhosa prophetess who, in 1857, claimed to have seen a great vision. This vision, as interpreted by her ambitious uncle Mhlakaza, foretold that a powerful wind would spring up, bringing with it ancestral spirits who would drive the white colonists into the sea. But before this could happen, Mhlakaza said, the Xhosa must first destroy all their grain and slaughter their cattle, and after this 'cleansing' the fields would again stand ready for reaping, the byres would be full, illness and old age would disappear, and the white settlers would be no more. The events that followed represent perhaps the most tragic chapter in the story of southern Africa: an estimated 300,000 to 400,000 head of cattle and most of the grain and garden harvests were destroyed, leading to wholesale starvation, to a huge decline in population, and to the demise of the Xhosa nation as a military power.

ADVISORY: THE EASTERN CAPE

CLIMATE

The Eastern Cape is in the transitional zone between the 'Mediterranean' winter-rainfall and the subtropical summer-rainfall regions: it becomes warmer, and the summers are wetter, the further north-eastwards one travels. Cold, clear winter days in the north-eastern Cape interior; hotter and drier towards the west.

Port Elizabeth enjoys a daily average 7½ hours of sunshine all year. Temperatures: average daily maximum January 25.4 °C/77.7 °F; July 19.5 °C/67.1 °F; minumum January 16.3 °C/61.3 °F; July 7.1 °C/44.8 °F; extremes 40 °C/104 °F and -0.3 °C/31.5 °F. Rainfall: average monthly January 30 mm/1 in, July 51 mm/2 in; highest daily 103 mm/4 in.

MAIN ATTRACTIONS

Port Elizabeth, East London and vicinity: Sun, sea and sand ❑ Sailing, fishing and watersports ❑ Scenic drives ❑ Port Elizabeth Oceanarium ❑ Museums and places of historical interest.
Settler Country: Historic sites ❑ Scenic charm.
Ciskei and Transkei: Magnificent coast ❑ Pleasant resort hotels ❑ Bathing, fishing, hiking and birding.

TRAVEL

Road. Approximate distances from Port Elizabeth: Jeffreys Bay 79 km/49 miles; Grahamstown 124 km/77 miles; Somerset East 152 km/94 miles; East London 310 km/193 miles; Bloemfontein 680 km/423 miles; Cape Town 785 km/488 miles; Durban 952 km/592 miles; Johannesburg 1,115 km/693 miles.

Well-maintained national highways and main roads link Port Elizabeth and East London with major centres; the N2 leads to Cape Town (west) and Durban (northeast); the R32 regional highway links Port Elizabeth with Cradock. Ciskei and Transkei coastal resorts are accessible via subsidiary (gravel) roads leading off the N2. Beware potholes, hairpin bends and stray animals.
Car hire: Major rental companies in Port Elizabeth, East London, Bisho, Umtata and other Eastern Cape centres; consult the Yellow Pages or hotel reception.
Rail. Port Elizabeth's Apple Express for steam fans (*see* page 166). Passenger services link the city with major centres; the railway station is at the harbour entrance; passenger services information: tel. (041) 507-2111. East London: passenger services link the city with major centres; the station is at the corner of Fleet and Station streets; for information tel. (0431) 44-2719.
Air. Daily scheduled flights connect Port Elizabeth and East London with major centres; Port Elizabeth's terminal is in North Union Street; the airport is 10 km (6 miles) from city centre; tel. (041) 507-7204 for information; tel. (041) 34-4444 to make reservations. Private airlines also operate scheduled services.

ACCOMMODATION
Select hotels

PORT ELIZABETH
City Lodge: Port Elizabeth *** Overlooks beach. 150 en suite rooms; no-frills value; pool. PO Box 13352, Humewood 6013; tel. (041) 56-3322, fax 56-3374.
Holiday Inn Garden Court: King's Beach *** Seafront. Sophisticated; 131 rooms and 5 suites; lovely restaurant; residents' bar; pool; conference facilities. PO Box 13100, Humewood 6013; tel. (041) 42-3720, fax 55-5754, central reservations (011) 482-3500.
Marine Protea Hotel *** Beachfront. 73 en suite rooms; à la carte restaurant, buffet; 2 bars; conference facilities. PO Box 501, Port Elizabeth 6000; tel. (041) 53-2101, fax 53-2076, toll-free 0800 11 9000.

EASTERN CAPE COAST
Savoy Protea Hotel *** 37 en suite rooms; à la carte restaurant; breakfast room; bar; tavern; conference facilities. PO Box 36, Jeffrey's Bay 6330; tel. (0423) 93-1106/7, fax 93-2445, toll-free 0800 11 9000.
Victoria Protea Hotel *** 26 rooms; 2 à la carte restaurants; 2 bars; conference facilities available. PO Box 2, Port Alfred 6170; tel. (0464) 4-1133, fax 4-1134.

GRAHAMSTOWN
Cathcart Arms ** South Africa's oldest licensed premises; 14 rooms; à la carte; conferences. PO Box 316, Grahamstown 6140; tel. and fax (0461) 2-7111.
Graham Protea Inn ** 26 en suite rooms, 4 suites; à la carte; pub; conference facilities available. PO Box 316, Grahamstown 6140; tel. (0461) 2-234, fax 2-2424.
Settlers' Inn *** Close to Monument. 52 en suite rooms; à la carte restaurant; bar; pool; conference facilities. PO Box 219, Grahamstown 6140; tel. (0461) 2-7313.

EAST LONDON
Esplanade Hotel ** Overlooking main East London beach. 75 en suite rooms; à la carte restaurant; bar; conference facilities. PO Box 18041, Quigney 5211; tel. (0431) 2-2518, fax 2-3679.
Holiday Inn Garden Court: East London *** On Promenade. 173 rooms, 2 suites; à la carte restaurant; bar; pool; conference facilities available. Cnr John Baillie and Moore st, East London 5201; tel. (0431) 2-7260, fax 43-7360, central reservations (011) 482-3500.
Kennaway Protea Hotel *** On beachfront. 83 rooms, 5 suites; à la carte restaurant; bar; conference facilities. PO Box 583, East London 5200; tel. (0431) 2-5531, fax 2-1326.

EASTERN CAPE INLAND RURAL
Eagle's Ridge Country Hotel Amatolas, near Stutterheim. 22 rooms and suites; à la carte restaurant; bar; teagarden; pool; tennis; conference facilities. PO Box 127, Stutterheim 4930; tel. and fax (0436) 3-1200.

Hogsback Inn ** Charming country hostelry operating since the 1850s; 32 rooms in garden setting; table d'hôte restaurant, bar; swimming pool; conference facilities available for 55 people. Main Rd, Hogsback 5721; tel. (045) 962-1006.
Pig and Whistle * Bathhurst. Built in 1821 as forge and inn; 16 rooms; restaurant; pub. PO Box 39, Bathurst 6166; tel. (0464) 25-0673, fax 25-0688.

CISKEI REGION
Fish River Sun Hotel, Casino and Country Club On the coast. 119 rooms, 1 suite; 2 restaurants; 3 bars; casino; swimming pool; golf; tennis; squash; bowls; fishing; conference facilities available for 200 people. PO Box 232, Port Alfred 6170; tel. (0505) 66-1101, fax 66-1115.
Mpekweni Sun Marine Resort Overlooking lagoon. 93 rooms, 1 suite; à la carte restaurant; 2 bars; swimming pool; tennis; squash; bowls; fishing; watersports. PO Box 2660, Port Alfred 6170; tel. (0505) 66-1026, fax 66-1040.

TRANSKEI REGION
Hole in the Wall Hotel and Holiday Village Close to Coffee Bay. Timeshare resort; self-catering accommodation; 23 en suite rooms; à la carte restaurant; bar; boat storage; conference facilities. PO Box 13135, Vincent 5217; tel. and fax (0431) 31-2715.
Wild Coast Sun Hotel and Casino Mzamba. Superb hotel-casino complex on beachfront; 393 rooms, 6 suites; 6 restaurants, 7 bars; casino; 2 pools; gym; spa; sauna; golf; tennis; squash; bowls; horse-riding; deep-sea fishing; watersports; conference facilities. PO Box 23, Port Edward 4295; tel. (0471) 5-9111, fax 5-2924/5-2850.

Self-catering and budget
The Eastern Cape offers a choice of guest-houses, self-catering accommodation, and many caravan/camping options (prolific along the coasts to either side of Port Elizabeth). Contact Port Elizabeth Publicity Association, Satour, or the local tourism information offices.
Budget: Bed 'n Breakfast; tel. and fax (041) 33-3716 (Port Elizabeth, coasts); tel. (0461) 2-8001 (Grahamstown and East London areas); tel. (0424) 3-3533 (Eastern Cape, inland).

Select restaurants
PORT ELIZABETH
The Bell, Beach Hotel, Marine Drive. Classic cuisine; favoured by businessmen; tel. (041) 53-2161.
Bella Napoli, Hartman St. Unpretentious, Italian fare; Sunday buffet lunches rather special; tel. (041) 55-3819.
Garden Grill, Holiday Inn Garden Court, Summerstrand. Seafood a speciality; tel. (041) 53-3131.
The Coachman, Lawrence St. Excellent steakhouse; family-run; tel. (041) 52-2511.

Edelweiss, Westbourne Rd (central). Tasty traditional German cuisine; tel. (041) 33-3343.
De Kelder, Marine Protea Hotel, Summerstrand. Seafood is a speciality; various kinds of delicious flambée; pleasant atmosphere; tel. (041) 53-2750.
Little Swallow, Cape Rd, Kabega Park (western suburbs). Chinese cuisine; delicious; tel. (041) 30-7382.
Nelson's Arm, Trinder Square. Early naval-wardroom décor; seafood specialities; tel. (041) 55-9049.
Old Austria, Uitenhage Rd. Continental cuisine and charming atmosphere; tel. (041) 54-1204.
Royal Delhi, Burgess and Zareba st. Oriental excellence; tel. (041) 33-8216.
Sabatinos, Westbourne Rd. Italian seafood specialities; informal; pleasant atmosphere; tel. (041) 33-1707.
Sir Rufane Donkin Restaurant, George St. Homely menu; deliciously prepared food; tel. (041) 55-5534.

USEFUL ADDRESSES AND TELEPHONE NUMBERS
Automobile Association, Port Elizabeth, AA House, Granville Rd (tourist information); tel. (041) 34-1313 (o/h), toll-free breakdown service 0800-010101.
Bathurst Municipality, PO Box 128, Bathurst 6166; tel. (0464) 25-0639.
Ciskei Tourist Information, tel. (0401) 9-3214.
Cradock Municipality, PO Box 24, Cradock 5880; tel. (0481) 2108.
Emergency numbers, *National ambulance number:* 1-0177; *City ambulance:* (041) 33-1177; *After-hours pharmacy Mediscore*: 322 Cape Rd, Newton Park; (041) 35-2366, pager 57-3400; *Port Elizabeth fire brigade:* (041) 55-1555; *Police headquarters:* (041) 33-1748; *Police flying squad:* 1-0111; *Sea rescue:* (041) 520-2716; *Lifeline* (equivalent to British Samaritans): (041) 52-3456.
Fort Beaufort Municipality, tel. (04634) 3-1136.
Grahamstown Publicity Association, Church Square, Grahamstown; tel. (0461) 2-3241.
Greater East London Publicity Association, Old Library Building, Argyle St, PO Box 533, East London 5200; tel. (0431) 2-6015.
Jeffreys Bay Municipality, Da Gama St, PO Box 21, Jeffreys Bay 6630; tel. (04231) 3-1111.
Port Alfred Publicity Association, PO Box 63, Port Alfred 6170; tel. (0423) 93-1111.
Port Elizabeth Publicity Association, Market Square, Port Elizabeth 6000; tel. (041) 52-1315, fax 255-2564.
Queenstown Municipality, Private Bag X7111, Queenstown 5320; tel. (0451) 3131.
Satour, (South African Tourism Board), Port Elizabeth office: 21–23 Donkin St; PO Box 1161, Port Elizabeth 6000; tel. (041) 55-8884. East London office: Old Library Building, Argyle St; PO Box 533, East London 5200; tel. (0431) 2-6015.
Theatre and other bookings, Port Elizabeth. Computicket Information Kiosk, Greenacres Centre; tel. (041) 34-4550/1.

THE SOUTHERN SEABOARD

The Cape Fold Mountains are a long series of sandstone formations that stretch along the beautiful southern coast, from an area some way to the east of Port Elizabeth to False Bay's Cape Hangklip, near Cape Town in the west (and beyond: the series incorporates the Cedarberg, Olifants River and Drakenstein ranges: *see page 269*). At no point do the heights ever quite reach the shoreline: uplands and sea are for the most part separated by a narrow, lushly fertile plain hugely rich in plant species.

To the north is the Swartberg, an imposing 800-km-long (500 miles) chain of mountains lying between the Great and Little Karoos.

The coast and its immediate hinterland – especially the lovely 230 kilometres (143 miles) known as the Garden Route – are prime holiday areas, offering a multiplicity of enticements, superbly developed for tourism.

THE GARDEN ROUTE

This scenically stunning segment of the coastal belt extends from Storms River in the east to Mossel Bay in the west. On one side is the Indian Ocean, its shores a delightful compound of rocky cliff, cove, broad embayment and beach, navigable river estuary, lagoon and lake; on the other are the wooded slopes of the Tsitsikamma and Outeniqua mountains; between the two is the coastal terrace, the aptly named 'garden' of which a French traveller of the 1780s wrote: 'The flowers that grow there in millions, the mixture of pleasant scents which arise from them, the pure and fresh air one breathes there, all make one stop and think Nature has made an enchanted abode of this beautiful place.' François le Vaillant's words are as descriptive today as they were two centuries ago.

For the modern visitor, the attractions are many, various and mostly gentle. There's the charm of the green and pleasant countryside of course; and the kindly climate: plenty of sunshine; rains that fall throughout the year (and, happily, mostly at night-time); modest extremes of heat and cold. There are excellent hotels, resorts, caravan/camping grounds, attractive

OPPOSITE: *The Wilderness shoreline. The lovely southern coastal belt is famed for its Garden Route, and for the splendour of its mountains.*

marinas and good restaurants. The clear blue waters of the ocean are warm in summer, and they invite the bather and surfer, the sailor, the rock angler and the deep-sea fisherman. Marine life is prolific and brilliantly coloured.

THE TSITSIKAMMA AREA

The name is derived from the Khoikhoi (Hottentot) word for the sound of running water, and it's apt enough: the region, extending across the 160 km (99 miles) of coastal countryside between Humansdorp and Knysna, is notable for its high rainfall and for the numerous perennial streams that tumble down the slopes of the Tsitsikamma Mountains. The latter are an eastward extension of the Outeniqua range, with their highest point 1,677 m (5,502 ft) above sea level.

TSITSIKAMMA STATE FOREST RESERVE This 500 ha (1,235 ft) patch of upland was proclaimed to preserve a remnant of the once-vast natural forests of the southern seaboard: dense woodlands of yellowwood and stinkwood, white alder, candlewood, ironwood, assegai and other handsome tree species. The giants among them are the Outeniqua yellowwoods, growing to 50 m (164 ft) and more in height. Among the rather secretive forest residents are bushbuck and duiker, bushpig, baboon and some brilliantly colourful birds, including the Narina trogon and the Knysna lourie.

TSITSIKAMMA NATIONAL PARK This lovely conservancy comprises an 80 km (50 miles) strip of narrow coastal plateau extending from the Groot River near Humansdorp to a point near the Keurbooms River and embracing the sea for a distance of 5 km (3 miles) from the rocky shoreline. The waters of the many rivers and streams that enter the ocean within the park are brown (from the slow decay of vegetation); the land area is richly endowed with a plant life that includes *fynbos* (heath), forest, ferns, wild orchids and a fine array of lilies; among the land animals are the Cape clawless otter, baboon, bushbuck, blue duiker and Cape grysbok. About 280 bird species have been recorded in the area. The rock pools teem with marine life – anemones, sponges and starfish – and whales and dolphins can often be seen sporting beyond the breakers.

Accommodation consists of fully equipped cottages, 'oceanettes' and a caravan/camping ground at Storms River Mouth. There is also a caravan/camping ground at Nature's Valley.

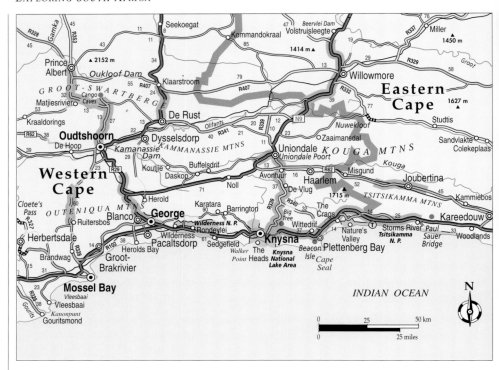

Within the coastal park there are underwater trails for swimmers and divers (only qualified scuba-divers may do the trail as such but snorkellers are always welcome), short land trails, and 30 km (20 miles) of alternative pathways in the De Vasselot area. The park is also traversed by the renowned and much-travelled 41 km (25 miles) Otter Trail.

NATURE'S VALLEY A small village and reserve at the bottom of the Groot River Pass (from the top of which there are stunning views of the valley), in a charming setting of mountain, forest, lagoon and sea.

PLETTENBERG BAY

The town of Plettenberg Bay is probably the most fashionable of this region's coastal resort centres. It's a charming little place just to the west of Nature's Valley, modern and sophisticated for the most part though it does have its history: the bay was known to European seafarers from the earliest days of maritime exploration. Its first 'settlers' were sailors from the *São Gonçalo*, which came to grief off the coast in 1630, and from which some fine Chinese (Ming)

pottery was recovered. The rescued pieces, now known as the Jerling Collection, are on display in the town's municipal buildings.

The bay and its surrounds are spectacularly beautiful; the area is blessed with 320 days of virtually uninterrupted sunshine each year; there are three superb beaches in the vicinity; Beacon Island (linked to the shore by a causeway) supports a fine hotel and timeshare complex; 'Plett time' gives visitors an extra hour of daylight from December to April in which to enjoy the amenities, which include golf, bowls, tennis, horse-riding, beach volley-ball, angling and scuba-diving; boating (the World Hobie Championships are held off Central Beach) and water-skiing (on the Keurbooms River).

ROBBERG NATURE RESERVE extends over a red-sandstone promontory that juts about 4 km (2.5 miles) into the Indian Ocean to the south-west of Plettenberg Bay. The headland ends in a point called Cape Seal; to the north there are almost-sheer cliffs; the southern slopes are gentler. White-breasted cormorants, southern black-backed gulls and black oystercatchers breed in the area, and the surrounding sea is a designated marine reserve. Signs of simple Khoikhoi 'Strandloper' habitation can be seen in the Nelson Bay cave.

OPPOSITE: *Hobiecats line the golden beach in front of Plettenberg Bay's Beacon Island hotel and timeshare complex.*
BELOW: *The 'Heads' flank the sea entrance to Knysna's large and lovely lagoon.*

KEURBOOMS RIVER NATURE RESERVE, some 8 km (5 miles) north-east of Plettenberg Bay, is a pleasant 760 ha (1,880 acres) expanse of riverbank and forest adjoining the larger (3,500 ha/8,650 acres) Whiskey Creek Reserve. Attractions include some lovely rambles, fishing (the Plettenberg Bay Angling Club is based here); bird-watching (among the recorded species are African finfoot and breeding pairs of Caspian terns), and watersports. The Aventura Keurbooms Resort has fully equipped family cottages, a caravan/camping park and an attractive stretch of beach. The Keurbooms Hotel offers two-star accommodation.

KNYSNA

Also a most attractive and highly popular resort town, but bigger than Plettenberg Bay. Knysna's motto is 'This fair land is the gift of God', a fitting testament to the beauty of lagoon, forest and coastal countryside. The local Mitchell's Brewery, which welcomes visitors, produces superb draught ale. Knysna is also famed for its honey, cheese, ham (from Dormehl Farm), trout, oysters (reputedly the best in the country) and its indigenous hardwood furniture.

Knysna was home from 1803 until the death in 1839 of the legendary George Rex, said to be the son of England's King George III. Rex lived – with two common-law wives (although not

concurrently) – the life of a prosperous country squire who entertained a string of distinguished visitors on his extensive estate. His property now forms part of the Knysna National Lake Area that encompasses the town, the lagoon, its two distinctive rocky promontories and its backing of evergreen forest. Though it isn't a proclaimed reserve in the orthodox sense of the term, the area is carefully monitored by the National Parks Board, who ensure that an intelligent balance is maintained between conservation and tourist development.

KNYSNA LAGOON The sea entrance to this magnificent 17-km-long (10.5 miles) expanse of water is guarded by two steep sandstone cliffs known as 'The Heads', the eastern one of which affords splendid views of Knysna and Leisure Island. On the western one is the private Featherbed Bay Nature Reserve, which is open to the public (approachable only by boat; the ferry service is free), and which offers

TOP LEFT: *Rustic holiday chalets grace the densely wooded shores of the Knysna lagoon.*
TOP RIGHT: *Millwood House, translocated from the early goldfields, now serves as a museum.*
BOTTOM LEFT: *One of Knysna's 'big trees'.*
ABOVE: *The handsome Knysna lourie, a common resident of the Garden Route's evergreen forests.*

guided nature trails and memorable gourmet meals – oysters and champagne breakfasts, for example – in the forest restaurant.

The lagoon is a popular arena for sailing, boating (cabin cruisers may be hired), canoeing, water-skiing and fishing. It's also one of nature's treasure-houses, noted for its superb oysters, for the variety of its fish, birds, crabs, prawns, for its 'pansy shells', and for the rare sea-horse (*Hippocampus capensis*). Two local boating companies offer a holiday with a difference: you live aboard one of their cabin cruisers (the crafts sleep between two and eight people);

cruise wherever the fancy takes you; cook your meals in the galley or tie up for a barbecue at one of the lagoon's many secluded spots. The *John Benn* floating entertainment centre – a locally-built 20 ton boat – leaves the jetty each morning (wining, dining and sightseeing).

KNYSNA FOREST When combined with the Tsitsikamma, this forms the largest expanse of indigenous high forest in South Africa, a 36,400 ha (90,000 acres) expanse which is home to the stately yellowwood and ironwood, the kammasie (Knysna boxwood), the stink-wood, the white alder and the blackwood. In its deep-green depths lives the last, tiny remnant of the once-great herds of Cape bush elephant. In fact, of the original group just one female remains, though three elephants were recently brought in from the Kruger National Park.

Forest hikes include the Elephant Walk, a six-hour trek (there are shorter alternative rambles) that starts from the Diepwalle forestry station, just over a kilometre away from which is King Edward's Tree, a yellowwood whose circumfer-ence measures an impressive 7 m (23 ft).

MILLWOOD Site of South Africa's first gold mine, situated in the heart of the Goudveld state forest some 25 km (16 miles) north-west of Knysna. There are plans to reconstruct the original, thriving little settlement. On offer are some most inviting walks and picnic spots among the trees; a yellowwood house built at the original diggings has been re-erected in Knysna, where it serves as a museum (local his-tory and George Rex memorabilia).

The Royal Hotel is rather special. Its original licensee, Master-Mariner Thomas Horn, settled in Knysna in 1847, and during the next century and more the establishment played caring host to an unusually distinguished clientele (early guests included Prince Alfred; among the hotel's later ones was George Bernard Shaw, who spent some weeks here writing his play *A Black Girl in Search of God*).

WILDERNESS

This enchanting resort is set around a lagoon at the mouth of the Touw River, 40 km (25 miles) west of Knysna and the first in a chain of lakes that lie between the two towns. Again, the area falls under the control of the National Parks Board, which helps co-ordinate development. Oddly enough, although the Wilderness lakes are very close together they were not all formed

by the same process. Swartvlei is really a drowned river valley that was originally filled by the rising seas of a post ice-age era; Rondvlei is known as a 'deflation basin', created by the scouring action of wind and later filled with water; Langvlei, like Rondvlei, has no direct con-nection with rivers – it is a low-lying area drowned by rising water levels; Groenvlei, although separated from the sea by just a single tier of dunes, is, surprisingly, a freshwater lake. Other large expanses of water in this area are Island Lake (Eilandvlei) and the Serpentine.

The Wilderness area has excellent tourist facilities, among them some good hotels (one of which is quite outstanding: *see* Advisory, page 198), Parks Board chalets, caravan/camp-ing sites. Swartvlei and Eilandvlei are favoured by watersport enthusiasts, the entire region by hikers and nature-lovers.

GOUKAMMA NATURE RESERVE This is a 2,230 ha (5,510 acres) area east of Wilderness that incorporates Groenvlei and the lower reach-es of the Goukamma River, its estuary, and the rocks, dunes and beaches along 14 km (9 miles) of pristine coastline. Among the reserve's resi-dents are bontebok, common and blue duiker, Cape grysbok, vervet monkey and around 210 bird species, including the African finfoot (this is the western limit of its range). There are 35 km (22 miles) of pathways, pleasant picnic and bar-becue sites and watersports (boating, canoeing) in the estuary.

BUFFELS BAY One of the more inviting holi-day spots; a magnificent beach stretches from the bay eastwards to Brenton-on-Sea.

SEDGEFIELD Another favourite among vaca-tioners, this charming and tranquil village is set on the Swartvlei lagoon.

GEORGE

A largish, most pleasant town set at the foot of the high Outeniqua Mountains, named after England's King George III and distinguished by its broad, oak-lined streets. George is the Gar-den Route's principal urban centre, the sur-rounding countryside devoted to general farming, forestry and the cultivation of hops, used in the brewing of beer (this is the south-ernmost and technically most advanced hop-growing area in the world).

George is linked to Knysna by the main Gar-den Route highway; by the Old Passes Road, which runs through an enchanting countryside of fern forest and woodland (fine views en route: on one side is the 'Map of Africa'; on the other the blue Indian Ocean); and by the:

OUTENIQUA CHOO-TJOE This old (Class 24) narrow-gauge steam train will take you on a memorable day-trip. Essentially a working freight train – though its technical status, revised in 1993, proclaims it as a 'preserved railway' and the country's only 'museum line' – it starts its journey from George at 08h10 and puffs into Knysna at 11h30, giving you time to browse around briefly in the many quaint shops and perhaps have a pub lunch before starting the return trip at 12h55.

GEORGE MUSEUM Housed in the Old Drostdy (magistrate's court and residence, established in 1813), the museum is noted for its fine array of antique musical instruments (it boasts the country's largest collection of early gramophones). Also on display are intriguing exhibits relating to local history and to the timber industry. Open from Monday to Saturday.

THE CROCODILE PARK Situated about 2 km (1.25 miles) from the town's centre; visitors are conducted on tours. Open daily.

The Outeniqua Choo-Tjoe, a Class 24 veteran, puffs its way from Knysna to George.

MOSSEL BAY

The bay, which for centuries was home to the less-advanced Khoikhoi 'Strandlopers' (their staple diet comprised the mussels after which the place was eventually named), was known to the earliest of the white seafarers. In 1501 the Portuguese admiral João da Nova camped out on the shores, staying long enough to construct a small chapel, the first European-type stone building erected in South Africa (nothing remains of the edifice today). Bartolomeu Dias, Vasco da Gama and other navigators replenished their freshwater supplies from the perennial spring. In 1500 one of the Portuguese captains placed his report in the trunk of a large milkwood tree, for collection by the next fleet that passed by; other sailors got into the habit of using the tree for mail delivery, so establishing the country's first 'post office'.

Mossel Bay is a fairly large town: the 1985 census pegged its population at a modest 37,000, but, with the later discovery and current exploitation of offshore oil deposits, the numbers have increased quite dramatically, threatening to transform what was once a quiet fishing village and holiday resort into a busy little industrial and commercial centre.

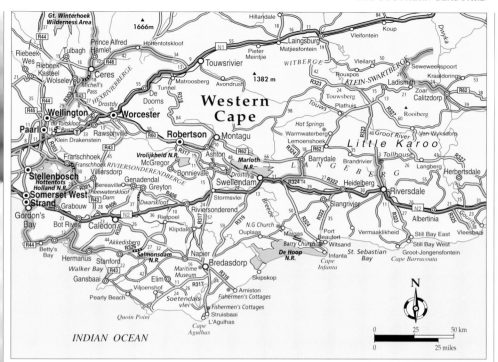

Still, the local beaches are as inviting as ever, the mussels as delicious, and the sea as kind to yachtsmen, windsurfers and bathers.

THE BARTOLOMEU DIAS MUSEUM This complex was established in 1988 to commemorate the 500th anniversary of the great navigator's momentous visit. Among its components are a maritime museum, an arts-and-crafts centre (housed in Munro's Cottages), the original Post Office Tree (*see* opposite page) and a replica of a *padrão*, the cross (of either wood or stone) erected by Portuguese explorers at various points along the southern African coastline.

SEAL ISLAND Home to around 2,000 of these marine mammals. The island may be visited; cruises start from the harbour.

THE LITTLE KAROO

This distinctive and, in some places, ruggedly beautiful region, about 250 km (155 miles) long and 70 km (43 miles) wide, lies between the southern coastal rampart (the Outeniqua and Langeberg) and the Swartberg uplands to the north. There can be few more impressive ranges than the magnificent Swartberg, a spectacular chain of mountain heights sliced through by precipitous passes and deep, tangled kloofs. The wild flowers that are found in this region – the painted ladies, the fire lilies and many more – are quite beautiful, the air sweet and clear and the vistas memorable.

The plain below is part of the Karoo System, but it has its own personality, distinctive and very different from the Great Karoo, its big brother in the north (*see* page 201). Although rainfall averages a low 150 mm (6 in) a year, the countryside isn't dry: there is good water from the streams that flow down from the mountains to join the Olifants River, bringing rich deposits of soil southwards.

The Little Karoo is renowned for its flocks of ostriches, a species that prefers a dry climate and thrives on the emerald-green lucerne that is grown in the area. During the fashion-led ostrich feather boom of the late 19th and early 20th centuries these large birds were the mainstay of the local economy, and indeed they still contribute to the region's wealth. Today, though, farming is a lot more diverse: in addition to the lucerne, the land yields fine crops of wheat, tobacco, walnuts and grapes.

OUDTSHOORN

Set along the banks of the Grobbelaars River south of the Swartberg range, the town is known as the world's 'feather capital', a reference to its pre-eminent position as the centre of the late-Victorian and Edwardian fashion-led ostrich-feather industry.

During those years the bigger farms of the area each accommodated around 600 birds; a breeding pair could fetch £1,000 on the market; London buyers paid up to £112 for a pound of prime white plumes – and some of the local farmers and businessmen made fabulous fortunes. The richest built themselves marble-floored farmhouses, or moved into town and constructed mansions that came to be known as 'feather palaces', hugely ostentatious multi-roomed extravaganzas of turrets and gables and cast-iron trimmings. A little of this lively past has been preserved, and is perhaps seen at its most evocative in the:

CP NEL MUSEUM (High Street). The museum's period-furnished annexe is one of the original feather palaces; the façade of the main building, green-domed and constructed of sandstone, is considered the most superb example of stone-masonry in South Africa. Exhibits include those in the Ostrich Room, which features the bird and the industry in all their aspects; local antiques; feather-boom fashions; and a splendid collection of firearms. Open daily. Other 'feather palaces' that have survived include Foster House, Pinehurst (now part of the local teachers' college), Greystone and Welgeluk.

DE OUDE PASTORIE A shop in Baron van Rheede Street that offers an interestingly eclectic range of goods, including antique furniture, dried fruit and preserves, hand-woven wear, locally made pottery, an art gallery and refreshments in the garden.

OSTRICH FARMS Still very much a feature of the area (the demand is steady; Oudtshoorn is the only place in the world where feathers are still sold at regular auctions). Apart from the feathers – used mainly in the manufacture of fashion accessories and household dusters – the bird is valuable for its meat (ostrich steak and biltong), its eggs (equal, in terms of an omelette, to 24 hen's eggs), and skin (handbags, wallets and shoes). Show farms include Safari and Highgate (open daily; two-hour guided tours; 'ostrich derbies'). The homestead on Safari is one of the most splendid of the 'feather palaces'.

Ostrich-riding near the town of Oudtshoorn. Showfarms welcome visitors.

CANGO WILDLIFE RANCH This complex, just outside town, is home to about 300 crocodiles. Among other features of interest are a crocodile museum, snake park, children's farmyard, tame animals (including Twinkle the otter, Winston the warthog, Claude the camel and some endearing miniature horses), curio shop and tearoom. The ranch also embraces a spacious cheetah enclosure, whose 200 m (660 ft) raised walkway meanders across the bushveld, enabling visitors to observe and photograph these graceful big cats (as well as lions and jaguars) in their natural environment. There are conducted tours by expert and efficient guides.

CANGO CAVES

This vast limestone labyrinth of multi-coloured stalagmites and stalactites, situated in the Swartberg range 29 km (18 miles) north of Oudtshoorn, is ranked among the most splendid of Africa's many natural wonders.

The caves were originally 'discovered' and tentatively explored by a white farmer named Van Zyl in 1780. He gained access to the first

MOUNTAIN DAY DRIVES

There are some magnificent routes through the Swartberg and other Little Karoo mountain ranges. Some suggestions:

• **Robinson Pass** breaches the Langeberg, the direct route from Oudtshoorn to Mossel Bay. There are fine views from its 860 m (2,800 ft) summit; the distance can be covered in an hour.

• **Seven Weeks Poort** (Seweweekspoort), a lovely river pass through the Swartberg north of the road connecting Calitzdorp and Ladismith. Towering over the pass is the 2,326 m (7,632 ft) Seven Weeks Poort Mountain, the Swartberg's highest. The origin of the name is obscure: it may be derived from the time it took the brandy smugglers to complete their evasive route, or from the everlasting 'seven-weeks' wild flower.

• **Outeniqua Pass** cuts through the Outeniqua range to link George with the Little Karoo. Splendid views all along; there is a toposcope 51 km (32 miles) from Oudtshoorn.

• **Swartberg Pass** was constructed by the talented 19th-century road builder Thomas Bain, with the help of convict labour, between 1881 and 1888. It links Oudtshoorn and the Little Karoo with Prince Albert on the southern fringes of the Great Karoo.

There are stunning views, though the gradients along its 240 km (149 miles) length are unremittingly steep and the curves endless. The summit is 1,585 m (5,200 ft) above sea level; the mountain slopes are covered with proteas and watsonias in summer and with snow in winter.

Close to the summit a road branches off to:

• **Gamkaskloof.** Formerly 'The Hell' (or Die Hel), a deep, 20-km-long (12.5 miles) gorge through which the Gamka River flows. The valley served as refuge for a reclusive 19th-century farming community which deliberately shut itself off from civilization. Something of the same isolationist spirit still pervades the valley, which now features in a nature conservation programme. Wheat, grapes, raisins, figs and vegetables are grown on the farm Boplaas, an open-air museum. The area is being restored to its original character.

• **Meiringspoort** follows the main highway from Little to Great Karoo (the R29 from De Rust north to Beaufort West). Splendid vistas unfold along the route. The road, which crosses the Groot River fully 26 times, is flanked by precipitous and often strangely eroded sandstone cliffs. The cleft of Meiringspoort is especially dramatic.

The Swartberg Pass cuts through the grandly imposing Outeniqua mountain range.

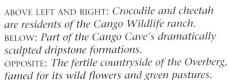

ABOVE LEFT AND RIGHT: *Crocodile and cheetah are residents of the Cango Wildlife ranch.*
BELOW: *Part of the Cango Cave's dramatically sculpted dripstone formations.*
OPPOSITE: *The fertile countryside of the Overberg, famed for its wild flowers and green pastures.*

and one of the most impressive caverns, the 98-m-long (322 ft) chamber now named in his honour. Stone implements and San (Bushman) wall-paintings were later found close to the entrance to the complex which indicated that the site was occupied by human communities in the Later Stone Age (20,000 years to about 2,000 years ago). The caves were also home to countless generations of bats: their petrified skeletons litter an area gruesomely known as the 'bats' graveyard'. The 28 chambers are interlinked by 2.4 km (1.5 miles) of passages, and they are remarkable for the variety of their calcified formations, the whole combining to produce a wonderful array of colours and weirdly

sculpted shapes. The largest chamber is the Grand Hall, measuring 107 m (351 ft) across and 16 m (52 ft) high; Botha's Hall has a column fully 12.5 m (41 ft) high. The temperature within the caves remains at a constant 18.3 °C (65 °F).

In 1970 Cango Two (the Wonder Cave), a beautiful 270 m (886 ft) extension of the original system, was discovered; Cango Three, a sequence stretching for 1,600 m (5,250 ft), was first explored in 1975. Cango Four, beyond and at a lower level than the others, is still being investigated by the experts. There are several other cave systems in the area, at least two of which are larger than the Cango, but difficult access and potentially dangerous passages keep them closed to the public.Open daily except Christmas day; conducted tours (every hour on the hour); restaurant; curio shop and crèche.

CALITZDORP

On the plains of the Little Karoo to the west of Oudtshoorn and also a centre of the ostrich-farming industry: the birds can be seen wandering freely among the lucerne fields. The village, which has a great deal of old-fashioned charm, overlooks the Gamka River Valley; the local church, built in neo-Byzantine style, can seat a congregation of 1,050 and is worth a visit.
CALITZDORP SPA, along the banks of the Olifants River just over 20 km (12.5 miles) from the town, is a renowned health resort centred on thermal springs whose waters emerge at a constant temperature of 51 °C (124 °F). The place is especially popular during winter; the facilities include swimming pools (here the temperatures range between 36 and 40 °C/97 and 104 °F), sauna, restaurant, entertainment complex, fully equipped, attractively sited chalets and a pleasant caravan/camping ground.

Calitzdorp is a developing wine-producing region, with its own wine route (two estate cellars, one co-operative). The grapes have a high sugar content. During your tour you can also sample the region's excellent sun-dried fruit.

THE OVERBERG

The translation of the word is 'the other side of the mountain', and was used by early Capetonians to describe the lands beyond the Hottentots Holland range. This segment of the southern coast is well known for its magnificent spring displays of wild flowers, for the gentleness of its countryside, for its rich wheat and barley fields, its green pastures and its forest plantations.

The ocean, too, can be gentle, but is not always so: it has claimed a great number of ships over the centuries, and their wrecks, some of them visible, most of them hidden beneath the shallow seas of the Agulhas Bank, testify to the ferocity and intensity of the storms that sometimes lash these shores. However, most summer days provide visitors with gloriously balmy weather. The waters are warm and placid and play host to ever-increasing numbers of holiday-makers, fishermen, sailors, surfers and skiers and other watersports enthusiasts.

If you look at the map (*see* page 184), you will notice that the numerous marine resorts – and these are far and away the areas that attract the majority holiday-makers – tend to be rather isolated from each other. There isn't a major, continuous coastal route and, generally speaking, in order to reach any of them one has to take the N2 route, turning south at the appropriate inland town.

STILL BAY

The bay itself, and especially the banks and mouth of the Kafferkuils River, has been pleasantly if rather informally developed for tourism and recreational purposes. The Still Bay area is popular among the local farming communities; it is crowded during the summer holiday season but almost deserted during the rest of the year. The sea is safe for bathing, the beach wide and sandy and there is excellent fishing in both the ocean (rock, surf and deep-sea) and estuary. The river is navigable for about 12 km (7.5 miles) and its eels are famous: many weigh up to an impressive 7.5 kg (16 lb) and, curiously, they tend to be quite tame.

Beachcombers find delight in the unusual quantity and variety of shells, marine seeds and, occasionally, prehistoric (Still Bay Culture) relics found along the shores. Still Bay has a small harbour, and there's a generous range of accommodation on offer. Many of the holiday cottages are built on stilts to cope with the strong spring tides.

LEFT: *A southern right whale and calf.*
ABOVE: *The Malgas pont is still in operation.*
OPPOSITE: *Cape Agulhas, the southernmost extremity of Africa. There is also a lighthouse and a museum, which has many interesting exhibits.*

THE ST SEBASTIAN BAY AREA

A fisherman's paradise: some superb catches have been recorded from both bay and Breede River estuary, where you'll find the popular little resort of Witsand. There's also a small fishing harbour. The area is renowned for its oysters and other shellfish and for:

MALGAS, situated 35 km (22 miles) upstream at the end of the navigable stretch of river. It was once a port of sorts: before the coming of the railway it was used as an outlet for wheat and wool and for the fashionable ostrich feathers of the Little Karoo. Much of the quaintness of the past remains, most obviously discernible in the workings of the quaint vehicle pont, powered by two men and the last working contraption of its kind in South Africa.

DE HOOP NATURE RESERVE, to the west of St Sebastian Bay, is one of the Cape's most important sanctuaries: it protects the region's most extensive remaining expanse of coastal *fynbos* (heath) vegetation. The reserve contains about 1,500 plant species, 50 of which grow only in this particular place, over 70 classed as either endangered or rare.

The proclaimed area, which includes the adjacent marine reserve, extends over some 60,000 ha (150,000 acres). Among the residents are approximatley 70 mammal species (bontebok, Cape mountain zebra, Cape clawless otter and various buck). Of the 13 marine mammals to visit the reserve, the southern right whale is perhaps the most distinguished. An impressive

230 bird species have been recorded. Visitor amenities include a network of game-viewing roads, trails (guided and self-conducted), picnic and barbecue spots and fairly simple accommodation (4-bed rondavels, communal facilities). Inland, just off the N2, is:

SWELLENDAM

The country's third-oldest white settlement (after Cape Town and Stellenbosch), Swellendam was founded in 1746 and named after Cape governor Hendrik Swellengrebel and his wife, Helena ten Damme. Historic sites, of which there are many, include:

THE DROSTDY COMPLEX (Swellengrebel Street), completed to accommodate the *landdrost* (magistrate) in 1747. A magnificent building which now houses a museum exhibiting period furniture, household items, animal-drawn vehicles, and an interesting collection of early paper money. Well worth a visit.

Opposite is a cluster of re-created craftsmen's premises: blacksmith, cobbler, charcoal burner, coppersmith, miller, cooper and so forth. A watermill grinds flour. Within the complex is Zanddrift, an 18th-century house which now serves as a pleasant restaurant.

THE OLD JAILHOUSE, and the thatched-roofed post office next door (the early gaoler also functioned as postmaster).

THE COTTAGE This is an impressive example of Cape architecture of the middle period (it dates back to the early 1830s).

ZUURBRAAK, farther afield, on the way to the scenically outstanding Tradouw Pass and Oudtshoorn, is a 19th-century mission station that now manufactures sturdy cane furniture. The 'Zuurbraak Chairbodgers' use traditional craftsmen's methods.

BONTEBOK NATIONAL PARK, about 70 km (43 miles) to the south of Swellendam, has had a chequered and in some ways remarkable history. In the early 1830s a group of Cape farmers had the foresight to keep the few remaining bontebok in safety on their lands, so sparing the antelope the fate that overtook the blue-buck, a species that once roamed the plains of the southern Cape in huge numbers. A century later the first Bontebok National Park, with a breeding herd of 17 animals, was proclaimed in the Bredasdorp district; 30 years later the reserve was moved to its present location. By then, the bontebok population had grown to 84.

The park, through which the Breede River passes, sustains some 500 plant species, many of them rare; yellowwood, wild olive and milkwood line the riverbanks; in spring wild flowers carpet the ground. Apart from the bontebok, the antelope population includes grysbok, grey rhebok, steenbok and duiker. About 200 bird species have been recorded. Facilities include game-viewing roads, walking trails, picnic areas, a caravan/camping site, a shop, information centre and petrol pump.

CAPE AGULHAS

The cape is the southernmost point of the African continent, its name derived from the Portuguese word for needles – the early navigators found that here their compasses weren't affected by magnetic deviation, but instead bore directly upon the true poles of the earth.

Apart from that, though, the area has little of immediate interest to offer. The cape itself is the southern part of a substantial inland plain which, after the mild interruption of a small range of hills, slips quietly under the sea to become the vast, shallow Agulhas Bank, the most extensive part of southern Africa's continental shelf. A lighthouse (18 million candle-power), built in 1848 and now an intriguing little museum, stands on the headland. Close by is the tiny village and beach resort of L'Agulhas, but the nearest town of any substance is:

BREDASDORP

Centre of a prosperous farming region (wool, grain, dairy products), 24 km (15 miles) north of Agulhas. The town's museum complex (three separate sections) will occupy a fascinating hour or two of your time. Among much else, it features relics of many of the vessels wrecked along the rocky, gale-swept coast over the centuries.

ELIM A Moravian mission station about 37 km (23 miles) south-west of Bredasdorp, founded in 1824. It is a picturesque little place of beautifully thatched, whitewashed cottages, fruit trees and wild flowers (notably the great mass of everlastings that decorate the countryside). Elim's German-made church clock first started ticking in 1764 and still keeps good time; the town's watermill (1828) is a national monument.

ARNISTON

Also known by its more official name, Waenhuiskrans, this is an enchanting little fishing village of thatched and limewashed cottages to the south-east of Bredasdorp. The two names given the place have their interest: the *Arniston* was a British troopship wrecked in the area in 1815, with the loss of 372 lives; Waenhuiskrans translates as 'wagon house cliff', a reference to the huge sea-cavern nearby.

Of interest here and along the coast are the giant pods of the *Entada gigas* sea-bean, and a number of stone fish-traps built by the 'Strandloper' ('beachranger') people in prehistoric times. The local hotel is deservedly renowned.

THE GREYTON AREA

West of Swellendam along the N2 is the small town of Riviersonderend which takes its name from the local river: it rises in the Hottentots Holland Mountains and flows eastward, seemingly (to the early settlers) 'without end'. The area is noted for its natural forests. A minor road (the R406) will take you along the southern slopes of the Riviersonderend range of hills to Greyton, one of the region's most peaceful and charming villages (though, since it has been 'discovered' by press and public, it's become a fashionable getaway among weekenders and its character could be threatened). The village's main street is pleasantly oak-lined, the surrounding countryside scenically pleasing. The Greyton Nature Reserve comprises

2,220 ha (5,500 acres) of spectacular terrain at altitudes ranging between 240 and 1,465 m (787 to 4,807 ft). The renowned Post House, one of Greyton's three hotels, was built in 1860 in the English-country style (with antiques, log fires and a rose garden) and bills itself as 'purveyors of food and lodging to the gentry'.

GENADENDAL This charming settlement, whose name means 'valley of grace', is a little to the west of Greyton. It was South Africa's first mission station, founded by Georg Schmidt, also known as the 'Apostle of the Hottentots', and later taken over by the Moravian missionaries. The place is frozen in the past; of note are the church and its old bell, the parsonage, the early school building and the neat little thatched and limewashed cottages.

CALEDON

The town of Caledon, farther along the N2, was established (its origins go back to 1709) to take advantage of the area's most prominent asset: the superb hot spring, whose radioactive waters are believed to have curative properties. The spring still yields 1.25 million litres (275,000 gallons) a day, at a constant temperature of 52 °C (126 °F) – though it is cooled to 39 °C (102 °F) in the pools. In the decades before the Second World War the place ranked as one of the most fashionable spas in the southern hemisphere, boasting swimming pools, a sanatorium and a fine hotel, but the complex was destroyed by fire. Many visitors, though, continued to 'take the waters', and are now accommodated in the splendid new Overberger Country Hotel and Spa (*see* Advisory, page 199), which opened its hospitable doors in 1989.

CALEDON NATURE RESERVE AND WILD FLOWER GARDEN More officially known as Victoria Park, the garden is widely renowned for its magnificent displays of springtime flowers, among which are fully 135 species of proteaceae. The reserve covers 214 ha (529 acres) of Swartberg hillside; within it there is a 56 ha (138 acres) cultivated section, a masterpiece of landscaping distinguished by its indigenous trees and shrubs and colourful *fynbos* species (including the lovely Caledon bluebell, *Gladiolus spathaceus*), its scenically charming pathways, wooden bridges and picnic spots. The Caledon Wild Flower Show is an annual event (it's held in mid-September) that attracts thousands of visitors.

THE HERMANUS AREA

Hermanus is a fairly substantial centre and the Overberg's premier resort, attractively set between mountain and blue ocean and a paradise for fishermen, crayfish and perlemoen divers, sailors and watersports entusiasts. And for whale-watchers: from July to about November, giant southern right whales make their way into Walker Bay and other inshore stretches along the coast to mate and calve (the whale's gestation period is 12 months). These great sea-mammals can be clearly seen from the backing cliffs; the local 'whale crier' heralds their arrival and announces the best whale-spotting sites.

There are several quite splendid beaches in the area and the sea is safe for both bathing and surfing. The popular Kleinriviersvlei Lagoon is a longish, inviting stretch of placid water that hosts the local yacht club.

The walk along the top of the cliffs, from the harbour to the lagoon at De Mond, yields fine views of the rocky shoreline and its secluded coves; even grander vistas unfold along the Rotary Mountain Way, a scenic drive that cuts through the overlooking uplands.

OLD HARBOUR For over a century Hermanus served as the centre of a thriving fishing (and whaling) industry. The old harbour has been preserved as a museum and a national monument; on view are reconstructed buildings and vintage fishing boats. The fine new harbour accommodates modern craft used by both commercial and sporting fishermen; some of the boats can be hired for deep-sea tunny and marlin fishing expeditions.

ONRUS RIVER On the western side of Hermanus is the hamlet of Onrus River, a peaceful place at the entrance to the lagoon; the Onrus Kitchen, according to the *Cape Times* newspaper, 'just has to be one of the best restaurants in the country'. Nearby are Vermont and Hawston, two pretty little resort areas, and:

GANSBAAI, a tranquil fishing village whose name means 'goose bay'. Freshly caught fish are sold at the harbour. Close by is the well-named Danger Point, off which the British troopship the *HMS Birkenhead* came to grief in February 1852 with the tragic loss of 445 lives. The majority of the dead were soldiers on their way to the Eastern Cape frontier, and they died heroes to a man, standing to rigid attention as the vessel foundered, so allowing most of the civilians to clamber aboard the three serviceable

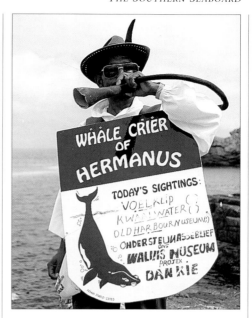

The town crier heralds the whales' arrival.

lifeboats. Their courage, exemplified by the phrase 'women and children first', is honoured both in the annals and in the language: the 'Birkenhead Drill' became descriptive of unyielding discipline in the face of disaster.

Today a lighthouse (which welcomes visitors) guides shipping around the point; nearby is a remarkable 'blowhole' through which the sea jets to heights of 10 m (33 ft) and more. North of Gansbaai is the small village of:

STANFORD, notable for the Evans pottery and local craft centre. Apart from its sturdy glazed-clay products, it also produces copperware, hand-spun jerseys, wooden toys and a selection of traditional rawhide whips.

KLEINMOND, a pretty little resort at the mouth of the Bot River (west of Hermanus). Nearby are the Palmiet River Lagoon and Sandown Bay (where the fishing is good but the swimming is hazardous). Waterbirds in their thousands congregate on the Bot River marshes.

BETTY'S BAY, a short distance to the west of Kleinmond, is yet another peaceful resort area, popular among anglers, lazers-in-the-sun and, especially, nature-lovers. Its 190 ha (470 acres) Harold Porter Botanic Garden is renowned for its layout and the wealth and beauty of its wild flowers, among which ericas are prominent.

ADVISORY: THE SOUTHERN SEABOARD

CLIMATE

Transitional but mainly summer-rainfall region. The uplands enjoy good rains; the Little Karoo has a generally hot, dry climate, though the land is well watered by the streams that flow down from the mountains. Winter nights can be cold. Strong summer winds sporadically assault the coastal areas; the intervening periods are sun-filled and balmy.

Coastal region. Cape Agulhas temperatures: January average daily maximum 23.5 °C/74 °F, daily minimum 17.2 °F/63 °F; July average daily maximum 16.4 °C/61.5 °F, daily minimum 10 °C/50 °F; extremes 36.1 °C/97 °F and 3.9 °C/39 °F. Rainfall: January average monthly 20 mm/1 in, July 54 mm/2 in; highest recorded daily rainfall 126 mm/5 in.

Little Karoo. Oudtshoorn temperatures: January average daily maximum 32.2 °C/90 °F, daily minimum 15.3 °C/59.5 °F; July average daily maximum 18.9 °C/66 °F, daily minimum 10 °C/50 °F; extremes 44.2 °C/112 °F and -3.3 °C/26 °F. Rainfall: January average monthly 10 mm/½ in, July 16 mm/½ in; highest recorded daily rainfall 51 mm/2 in.

MAIN ATTRACTIONS

Garden Route: Scenic variety and beauty ❑ Forest, mountain and ocean ❑ Pleasantly developed coastal resorts ❑ Sun, sea and sand ❑ Plettenberg Bay and the lakes and lagoons of the Knysna-Wilderness area ❑ The wild flowers everywhere.
Little Karoo: Scenic drives through the Swartberg and other ranges ❑ The Cango Caves ❑ Ostrich farms.

TRAVEL

Road. The main N2 national highway runs east-west along the coastal belt from Port Elizabeth to Cape Town; its 230 km/148 mile middle stretch, which hugs the shoreline, is the famed Garden Route. From Mossel Bay it follows an inland course to the Strand-Somerset West area. From the latter stretch, subsidiary routes take you south to the Overberg coastal resorts. Generally good roads lead over the often spectacular mountain passes to the Little Karoo (*see* page 189).

Car hire: Facilities in Knysna, George, Oudtshoorn and other major centres described in this chapter.

Coach travel: An inter-city express coach service operates between Cape Town and Port Elizabeth via the Garden Route and Oudtshoorn.

Rail. Spoornet passenger services connect most centres between Cape Town and Port Elizabeth. A regular steam passenger train service runs between George and Knysna (*see* page 188).

Air. George Airport, 10 km/6 miles from town, is served by national and regional airlines; Plettenberg Bay and Oudtshoorn by regional airlines.

ACCOMMODATION
Select hotels

GARDEN ROUTE

GEORGE
Fancourt Hotel and Country Club 5 km (3 miles) from airport. Built in 1860; a national monument; elegant; 37 rooms; 27-hole golf course. PO Box 2266, George 6530; tel. (0441) 70-8282, fax 70-7605.
Far Hills Protea On the N2 highway. 49 en suite rooms; conference facilities available. PO Box 10, George 6530; tel. (0441) 71-1295, fax 71-1951, toll-free reservations 0800 11 9000.

KNYSNA-WILDERNESS
Brenton-on-Sea Hotel * About 15 km (9 miles) from Knysna. 30 en suite rooms; 13 self-catering chalets and a luxury cottage; conference facilities. PO Box 36, Knysna 6570; tel. (0445) 81-0081.
Fairy Knowe Hotel * On the banks of the Touw River. 42 en suite rooms; conference facilities for 60; buffet and carvery restaurant; pool. PO Box 28, Wilderness 6560; tel. (0441) 9-1100, fax 887-0600.
Karos Wilderness Hotel **** Near lakes and lagoon. 160 rooms; conference facilities; à la carte restaurant; 2 cocktail bars; pools; bowls; tennis; squash. PO Box 6, Wilderness 6560; tel. (0441) 9-1110, fax 887-8600.
Knysna Protea *** Near lagoon. 50 rooms, 1 suite; conference facilities for 200; à la carte restaurant; pool. PO Box 33, Knysna 6570; tel. (0445) 2-3568, toll-free reservations 0800 11 9000.
Wilderness Holiday Inn Garden Court *** On beachfront. 149 rooms; conference facilities; à la carte restaurant with carvery; action bar; pool; tennis. PO Box 26, Wilderness 6560; tel. (0441) 877-1104, fax 877-1134, central reservations (011) 482-3500.

MOSSEL BAY
Eight Bells Mountain Inn *** Below Robinson Pass, 35 km (22 miles) from Mossel Bay. 10 rooms, 8 family suites, 5 Swiss-style chalets; table d'hôte restaurant; pool; bowls; tennis; squash; horse-riding. PO Box 436, Mossel Bay 6500; tel. (0444) 95-1544, fax 95-1548.
Santos Protea *** On the beachfront. 55 rooms; pool. PO Box 203, Mossel Bay 6500; tel. (0444) 91-7103, fax 91-1945, toll-free reservations 0800 11 9000.

PLETTENBERG BAY
The Arches * Set on a hill overlooking lagoon. 20 en suite rooms; conference facilities for 150; à la carte restaurant; disco bar. PO Box 155, Plettenberg Bay 6600; tel. (04457) 3-2118, fax 3-3884.
Beacon Island **** 192 rooms, 8 suites; conference facilities; à la carte and table d'hôte restaurants; several bars; pool; sauna; floodlit tennis. Private Bag 1001, Plettenberg Bay 6600; tel. (04457) 3-1120, fax 3-3880; central reservations (011) 482-3500.

Formosa Inn Country Hotel * Old-established hotel (1870); 38 rooms (chalets in garden setting); conference facilities available for 50; à la carte restaurant; carvery; disco. PO Box 121, Plettenberg Bay 6600; tel. (04457) 3-2060, fax 3-3343.

Hunter's Country House Elegantly appointed; thatched garden suites; conference facilities are available; swimming pool. PO Box 454, Plettenberg Bay 6600; tel. (04457) 3-7818/7858, fax 3-7878.

The Plettenberg Hotel *** On a rocky headland with superb views. 26 rooms; à la carte restaurant; bar; swimming pool; 40 Church St, Plettenberg Bay 6600; tel. (04457) 3-2030, fax 3-2074.

SEDGEFIELD

Lake Pleasant Hotel *** 17 en suite rooms; swimming pool and tennis courts. PO Box 2, Sedgefield 6573; tel. (04455) 3-1313, fax 3-2040.

STORMS RIVER

Tzitzikama Forest Inn * 41 en suite rooms; conference facilities for 60; à la carte restaurant. PO Storms River 6308; tel. (042) 541-1711, fax 541-1669.

LITTLE KAROO

OUDTSHOORN

Holiday Inn Garden Court: Oudtshoorn *** About 30 km (19 miles) from the Cango Caves. 120 rooms; conference facilities available for 20 people; à la carte and carvery restaurants; 2 cocktail bars; swimming pool and tennis court. PO Box 52, Oudtshoorn 6620, tel. (0443) 22-2201, fax 22-3003, central reservations (011) 482-3500.

Riempie Estate Hotel *** Close to centre of town. 40 rooms in thatched chalets; conference facilities available for 120; à la carte restaurant and carvery; swimming pool. PO Box 370, Oudtshoorn 6620; tel. (0443) 22-6161, fax 22-6772, toll-free reservations 0800 11 9000.

THE OVERBERG

ARNISTON (WAENHUISKRANS)

Arniston Hotel *** Long-standing favourite among discerning holiday-makers. 22 en suite rooms, 2 suites; conference facilities available; à la carte restaurant; swimming pool. PO Box 126, Bredasdorp 7280; tel. (02847) 5-9000, fax 5-9633.

BREDASDORP

Victoria * 28 rooms (most en suite); PO Box 11, Bredasdorp 7280; tel. (02841) 4-1159, fax (02841) 4-1140.

CALEDON

The Overberger Country Hotel and Spa *** 98 rooms; conference facilities and convention centre; restaurant; hot spa; health centre. PO Box 480, Caledon 7230. tel. (0281) 4-1271.

GREYTON

The Post House Built in 1860; served as the village post office; 14 en suite Beatrix Potter-style bedrooms; a charming and popular place of roughly-hewn yellowwood ceilings, cosy fireplaces; traditional, lively English pub; Main Rd, Greyton 7233; tel. (028) 254-9995, fax 254-9920.

HERMANUS

Marine *** Excellent hotel; lovely views of Walker Bay; 41 rooms, 14 suites; conference facilities available for 80; table d'hôte restaurant; outdoor and indoor swimming pools; whirlpool. PO Box 9, Hermanus 7200; tel. (0283) 2-1112, fax 2-1533.

KLEINMOND

Beach House on Sandown Bay *** On Sandown Bay beachfront. Has excellent reputation; 23 rooms; conference facilities available for 30; à la carte restaurant (seafood specialities). PO Box 199, Kleinmond 7195; tel. (02823) 3130, fax 4022.

SWELLENDAM

Swellengrebel *** 51 en suite rooms, 1 suite; conference facilities available for 45; à la carte and table d'hôte restaurants. PO Box 9, Swellendam 6740; tel. (0291) 4-1144, fax 4-2453.

Self-catering and budget

The southern seaboard region is well served by guesthouses, resorts and other self-catering accommodation, as well as caravan/camping facilities. Contact the local publicity associations and tourist information offices for further details.

Budget: Contact Bed 'n Breakfast; tel. (0444) 91-3654 during business hours.

USEFUL ADDRESSES AND TELEPHONE NUMBERS

George Publicity Association, PO Box 1109, George 6530; tel. (0441) 74-4000.

Hermanus Tourist Information Bureau, Main Rd, Hermanus 7200; tel. (0283) 2-2629.

Knysna Publicity Association, PO Box 87, Knysna 6501; tel. (0445) 2-1610.

Mossel Bay Tourist Information, The Town Clerk, PO Box 25, Mossel Bay 6500; tel. (0444) 91-2215.

Oudtshoorn Publicity Association, Seppie Greef Buildings, Voortrekker Rd; tel. (04431) 22-2228.

Plettenberg Bay Angling Club, tel. (04457) 9740.

Plettenberg Bay Business & Publicity Association, Kloof St, PO Box 894, Plettenberg Bay 6600; tel. (04457) 3-4065, fax 3-4066.

Satour (South African Tourism Board), 124 York St, PO Box 1109, George 6530; tel. (0441) 74-4000.

Swellendam Publicity Association, PO Box 369, Swellendam 6740; tel. (0291) 4-2770.

THE GREAT INTERIOR

The Great Karoo covers about 400,000 km² (154,440 square miles) of the Western and Northern Cape (and some of the Free State) – which is about one-third of the area of South Africa. Its boundaries cannot be precisely defined because it is the product of a number of elements: the nature of its soil, rocks, topography, climate and vegetation. Generally speaking, though, it extends from the southern rim of the Great Escarpment – the mountain ranges of the coastal region – northwards to the Orange River, and westwards to Namaqualand.

It is a huge, semi-arid country whose name, derived from the Khoisan word for 'thirst', is apt indeed. There are very few villages, and even fewer towns; those that have been established are isolated from each other and remote from the country's major centres, though the roads are generally good, and straight, enabling one to travel quickly from one to the other.

Towards the north, beyond the wide reaches of the Orange River, are the great diamond fields of the Northern Cape, their focus the historic city of Kimberley. To the west of these lies the Gordonia region, also vast and dry, whose principal town is Upington. Its northern limit is the Kalahari Desert and Botswana, its western the young, sparsely populated republic of Namibia. To the north and west of Upington are two splendid tourist showcases: the Kalahari Gemsbok National Park and the magnificent roaring Augrabies Falls.

In the remote wilderness far south of Upington are some of the world's largest 'pans', enormous shallow depressions from which the rare rainwater has evaporated to leave hard sediments of mineral salts – whitish surfaces that reflect the intense sunlight, disturbing the atmosphere to create shimmering mirages and violent little whirlwinds called 'dust devils'. Grootvloer ('great floor'), 40 by 60 km (25 by 37 miles), is the most extensive of these dry 'lakes'; Verneukpan ('deception pan') the best known: it was selected by Sir Malcolm Campbell in 1929 for his near-successful assault on the world land speed record.

OPPOSITE: *The craggy heights of the south-eastern Karoo's Valley of Desolation. Nearby Graaff-Reinet is ranked among the country's most historic, and most attractive, towns.*

THE GREAT KAROO

Geologically, the region is part of what is known as the Karoo System, which extends over a very much wider area. The shale and sandstone strata are horizontal, and large parts of the countryside are flat and featureless, though elsewhere the monotony is relieved by dolerite formations – dykes (or ridges) and sills (*koppies*, or rocky outcrops) – thrust up by millennia of volcanic action and randomly weathered by periodic floods into stark and often even bizarre shapes. Perhaps the most scenically remarkable example of this broken Karoo country is the evocatively and aptly-named Valley of Desolation, which looms over the small town of Graaff-Reinet.

It is a region of distant horizons, of the occasional, lonely farmstead, girded by its windmill and by the green of gumtree and willow, a brave splash of colour in the huge bleakness; of clear and bone-dry air, intense sunshine, blistering summer days and, in winter, bitterly cold nights – and of low rainfall, varying from 375 mm (15 in) a year in the eastern areas to under 50 mm (2 in) in the desolate west.

Predictably, plant cover is sparse, but special in the way it has evolved and adapted to the harsh conditions: the Karoo's succulents – aloes, mesembryanthemums, crassulas, euphorbias and stapelias – are unique, surviving because they are able to store water in their thick fleshy leaves or root systems.

And then there are the desert ephemerals, wild flowers whose seeds remain dormant for years, only germinating and briefly blossoming when the rare rains come.

But there is a surprisingly plentiful supply of underground water running below much of the Karoo – a precious, life-giving resource that is tapped by thousands of wind-pumped boreholes – and this, together with the sweet grasses of the eastern regions, sustains enormous flocks of merino and fat-tailed sheep.

Bisecting the Karoo is the N1 national highway, the Great North Road, that links Cape Town with Johannesburg, Pretoria and points far beyond. Approximately a quarter of the way along it (travelling from Cape Town, that is) is Beaufort West, the 'capital' of the region; the halfway point is the town of Colesberg and between the two, at Three Sisters, one turns off onto the R29 to Kimberley. For the unhurried visitor, the first port of call is:

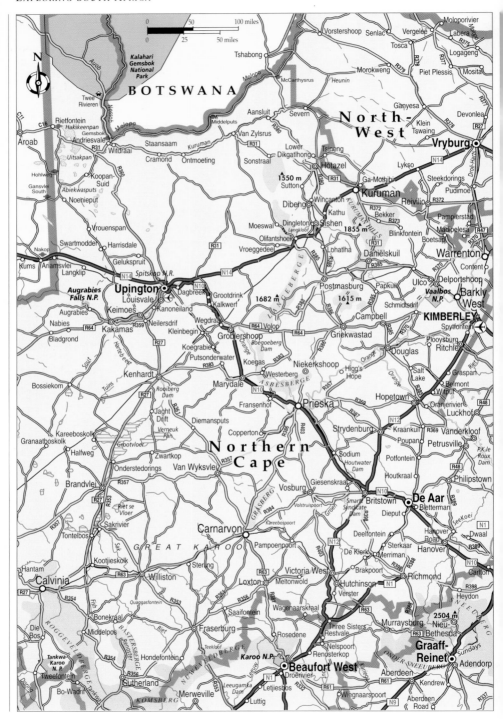

Matjiesfontein's Lord Milner Hotel, centrepiece of a charmingly preserved Victorian village.

MATJIESFONTEIN

An atmospheric and lovely Victorian village that takes its name from a reed (*matjiesgoed*) which is found in the area and which is used in the manufacture of matting. Its small cluster of buildings and railway station are situated in a hollow just off the main highway (there's a scenic view of the place from the road) 250 km (155 miles) from Cape Town.

The place was built (around the station) during the 1880s by ex-railwayman James Douglas Logan, an entrepreneur with flair, impeccable taste and a nagging chest complaint, as a dry-air health resort. Soon enough it attracted a rather distinguished and fashionable clientele which included, among other luminaries, Lord Randolph Churchill, the Sultan of Zanzibar and the noted writer and feminist, Olive Schreiner. It was also, incidentally, the first village in the country to be serviced with electricity and waterborne sewerage.

The village, Victorian down to the street lamp-posts that the 'Laird of Matjiesfontein' imported from England, has been preserved in its entirety by hotelier David Rawdon as a 'living museum'. Features of particular interest are Olive Schreiner's cottage; the tiny museum, crammed to its low eaves with a fascinating array of trivia ranging from weapons to porcelain to household utensils; the village store and coffee shop; the post office; and the Lord Milner, a superbly elegant hostelry that has been adjudged South Africa's best country hotel (*see* Advisory, page 212).

BEAUFORT WEST

The largest town (population 29,000) on the Karoo section of the Great North Road, Beaufort West was founded in 1818 and, 20 years later, was the first municipality to be proclaimed in South Africa (under the new elective laws). It is noted for its pleasant pear-tree-lined streets, and as the birthplace of heart surgeon Chris Barnard, many of whose awards are on display in the local museum. Its newspaper, *The Courier*, has been published without interruption since 1869. Just north of the town is the:

KAROO NATIONAL PARK, a 33,000 ha (81,542 acres) expanse of flattish terrain, was proclaimed in 1979 to preserve the local vegetation, mainly dwarf shrubs, sweet-thorn trees and, along the dry riverbeds, a variety of other hardy flora. Reintroduced game includes Cape mountain zebra (the 120-strong herd is the country's second largest), black rhino, black wildebeest, springbok, gemsbok, steenbok, klipspringer, mountain reedbuck, kudu, duiker, and leopard. There are 170 bird species.

Visitor facilities include game-viewing roads, self-guided trails, picnic and viewing points, the three-day Springbok hiking trail and a main camp comprising fully equipped chalets, a restaurant, a shop, an information centre and

CROSSING THE KAROO IN STYLE

Perhaps the most relaxing way to cross the great, empty spaces of the Karoo is aboard the famed 16-coach, 107-berth Blue Train – a journey that provides one of the world's most luxurious travel experiences. The train, which makes the 1,480 km (920 miles) run between Pretoria (through Johannesburg) and Cape Town in a leisurely 26 hours, offers carpeted and air-conditioned comfort, five-star cuisine and service in its stylishly appointed dining car, lounge area and bar. Compartments and coupés vary in character: the 'B'-type units have private bathrooms; the 'C'-type units have a private shower and the 'D'-type units have shared shower and toilet facilities. There is also a three-roomed suite consisting of bedroom, lounge (with private bar) and bathroom.

The Blue Train (there are in fact two identical trains) also ventures on occasion into other regions of the country, including the scenically superb and game-rich Mpumalanga.

provision for business conferences. Well to the east of the Beaufort West area (take the R61 for approximately 200 km/124 miles) is:

GRAAFF-REINET

Named after Governor (1785–1791) Cornelis Jacob van der Graaff and his wife Cornelia Reynet, Graaff-Reinet is the oldest town in the Eastern Cape, and the third oldest in the Cape region. Known as the 'Gem of the Karoo', it was founded in what was then the frontier – the limits of white settlement – in 1786, and had a stormy childhood: less than 10 years after its birth, its citizenry was in open revolt against the authority exercised from Cape Town by the Dutch East India Company. The tiny republic was forced to capitulate with the installation of the new British regime in 1796, but rebelled again – on three occasions.

Graaff-Reinet nestles in a loop of the Sundays River beneath the double-domed summit of Spandau Kop. It's a neat place of great historical

Graaff-Reinet's Dutch Reformed Church.

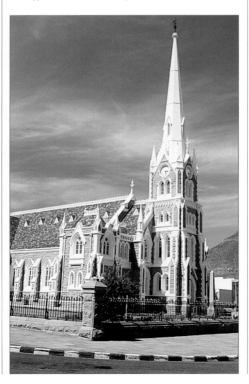

interest. Unlike so many other South African towns that grew in haphazard fashion, it was laid out according to a sensible plan; much of the early construction work was carried out by talented craftsmen; over 200 of its early buildings, ranging from rudimentary, flat-roofed Karoo-style homes to imposing Cape Dutch and Victorian houses, have been restored and declared national monuments. Parsonage Street, between the Drostdy and Reinet House, is being restored in its entirety. Of particular interest to visitors is:

THE DROSTDY, in Church Street; completed in 1806 as the residence and office of the early *landdrost* (magistrate) and one of the finest examples of French architect Louis Thibault's work. Its interior has been carefully restored and the building, together with a mall of 13 renovated cottages, now forms a rather unusual and very beautiful hotel complex (*see* Advisory, page 212).

THE REINET MUSEUM (Church and Somerset streets) is worth a visit for its various contrasting collections. These include permanent displays of clothing dating from 1800; the William Roe exhibition featuring the work of an early (1860) and talented local photographer; superb reproductions of San (Bushman) art, and a collection of fossils dating back 230 million years. The Karoo shales form one of the world's richest sources of fossil saurian remains; the Beaufort Series has yielded significant specimens: too many to mention, but they include the big, thick-skulled reptile Tapinocephalus, one of the oldest of the 'fearful-heads' (the Dinocephalians); and many Dicynodonts ('double dog-toothed' creatures with small bodies and huge heads). The museum houses the information office of the Graaff-Reinet Publicity Association.

THE GROOT KERK, an imposing building at the northern end of Church Street, is modelled on Salisbury Cathedral in England, and houses an unusually fine collection of ecclesiastical silver (on view during office hours).

THE GRAAFF-REINET PHARMACY Opened in 1870 and still going strong.

THE JAN RUPERT CENTRE, in Middle Street, was inaugurated in the early 1980s as a labour-intensive (unemployment-relief) project specializing in spinning and weaving. Local materials (Karoo bush dye and merino wool) are used to manufacture attractive clothing, furnishings and tableware. Open during working hours. Almost surrounding the town is the Karoo Reserve, which also embraces the:

VALLEY OF DESOLATION A fantasia of many wind-eroded dolerite peaks, pillars and balancing rocks that loom over Graaff-Reinet. There are fine views of the Plains of Camdeboo to the south and of the surrounding countryside. The valley is easily accessible from town.

NIEU-BETHESDA

A tiny hamlet in the foothills of the Compass-berg 50 km (30 miles) north of Graaff-Reinet. It is a place of shuttered homes and lovely gardens, and of the Owl House, home of the late and eccentric Helen Martins. She was a sculptor who specialized in bizarre figures – largely but not exclusively of owls; the sculptures are on display in the backyard. A private collection of pre-historic Karoo fossils may be viewed nearby.

DIAMOND COUNTRY

South Africa's first notable diamond was found by 15-year-old Erasmus Jacobs in 1866, near Hopetown on the banks of the Orange River in Griqualand West. He gave it to a neighbouring farmer, Schalk van Niekerk, and in due course it reached Dr William Atherstone, Grahamstown's leading medical practitioner. Atherstone identi-fied what was to be known as the 'Eureka' stone (21.77 carats, valued at £500 at the time).

Three years later, Van Niekerk produced another find: an 84-carat stone given to him by a Griqua shepherd in exchange for 10 oxen, 500 sheep and a horse. This was the 'Star of South Africa'. The new El Dorado, it was now thought, lay north of Hopetown; and the rush was on: diggers poured into Griqualand West and by the end of 1869, 10,000 claims had been pegged along miles of the Vaal River in the vicinity of Klipdrift, later renamed Barkly West.

All this, though, paled to insignificance when several diamond-rich kimberlite 'pipes' were discovered, four of them clustered within an 8 km² (3 square miles) patch of arid country-side 30 km (20 miles) south of Klipdrift, in an area which included the farms Bultfontein and a 9-m-high (30 ft) hill called Colesberg Kopje.

The *kopje* lay on Vooruitzicht farm, owned by the brothers De Beer; it had been discovered in July 1871 by a party of prospectors led by one Fleetwood Rawstorne, and it was full of dia-monds. It was soon to disappear beneath the picks and shovels of what was to become Kim-berley's world-famed Big Hole.

The garden of Nieu-Bethesda's Owl House.

KIMBERLEY

By 1872, when young Cecil Rhodes arrived on the scene, a huge tent-town had spread across the veld; 50,000 miners had congregated; at any given time 30,000 could be found working cheek by jowl in the ever-deepening Big Hole. Instant fortunes were made (and lost); money and champagne flowed like water. At this stage 3,600 claims were being worked, each about 9 m² (97 ft²), most divided and subdivided into even smaller plots. As the men dug deeper into the 'blue ground' many of the paths collapsed, so a confusing network of aerial ropeways appeared, and conditions became increasingly chaotic. Syndicates and small companies were formed, but by 1885 there were still nearly 100 separate operators; confusion grew as mining costs esca-lated and diamond selling prices fluctuated.

Rhodes decided to consolidate the fields and began buying up claims held by the De Beers company. By 1887 he owned the enterprise out-right, and then turned his attention to the even richer Kimberley Mine, owned by the Jewish Londoner, Barney Barnato. In his year-long struggle for possession of the diggings, Rhodes was backed by the wealthy and internationally connected Rothschild family, and in 1888 Barna-to accepted a cheque for £5,338,650 – an almost unheard-of sum in those days.

Thereafter De Beers stabilized the industry, and Kimberley settled into a more orderly way of life, though its peace was shattered during the South African (Anglo-Boer) War: from November 1899 until February 1900 its residents (Rhodes among them) were besieged by Boer forces, suf-fering bombardment and deprivation. The siege was especially tragic for the town's black people.

Kimberley's Big Hole. It yielded about 3 tons of diamonds during its lifespan.

Today four of the area's diamond 'pipes' are still active; several other minerals (iron, gypsum and salt) are mined in the area; and the town (population: 150,000) serves as the principal centre for the region's cattle ranches and irrigated farmlands. The original diggings – long since mined out – are now part of a number of historical sites and exhibits that form the:

KIMBERLEY MINE MUSEUM The museum's centrepiece is the Big Hole, the world's largest man-made crater dug without the use of machinery: by 1914, when it was finally closed, it had reached a depth of 1,097 m (3,600 ft) and yielded a fabulous three tons of diamonds.

Beside the partly-filled Big Hole, and providing an evocative and comprehensive insight into Kimberley's lively past, is a re-creation of part of the early town: lining the cobbled street are shops and cottages, a diggers' pub, Barney Barnato's boxing academy, the private railway coach used by the De Beers directors, and much else. Nearby is the old mining headgear; other components of the museum include:
• **The De Beers Hall** houses diamond displays. Among the glittering exhibits are some fine items of finished jewellery, stones of various and attractive colours ('fancies'), the largest uncut diamond (616 carats) in the world and the 'Eureka' diamond which young Erasmus Jacob picked up near Hopetown (*see page 205*).
• **The Transport Hall**, which holds some splendid Victorian vehicles.
• **The Art Galley**, which profiles the various and fascinating faces of 19th-century adolescent Kimberley. The museum is open daily; there's a tearoom and gift shop (which sells diamonds, among other things).

DUGGAN-CRONIN GALLERY (Egerton Road). The esteemed ethnologist and pioneer photographer, Alfred Duggan-Cronin, settled in Kimberley in 1897 and developed a deep interest in the peoples of the area, in particular San (Bushman) culture. Later (in 1919) he embarked on a systematic, 20-year photographic survey and the results were outstanding. The gallery's comprehensive and fascinating photographic collection also includes some non-ethnic subjects. Rock engravings and African crafts are also on display. Open daily.

DIAMOND DEALERS These include The Jewel Box (Long Street): diamonds are available ex-factory and a goldsmith works while you watch; Kimberley Jewellers (Jones Street); visitors are offered a video presentation and VE de Smidt Jewellers (Jones Street). The curio shop at the Mine Museum also sells diamonds.

DRIVE-IN PUBS Only two are believed to exist anywhere in the world, and they're both in Kimberley. The Halfway Hotel, at the corner of Du Toitspan and Egerton roads, is a hangover – if one may use the word – from the days when patrons arrived, and stayed for a drink or two, on horseback. The Kimberlite Hotel has a similar amiable facility.

THE DIAMOND ROUTE

The semi-arid countryside of the region offers few natural features of immediate interest to the visitor, though it has considerable botanical significance: it's a transitional zone between Karoo, Kalahari and grassland vegetation.

The Diamond Route follows a path between Victoria West through Hopetown, Kimberley and Warrenton to Potchefstroom to the west of Johannesburg. At the entrance to each of these towns is a notice-board briefing travellers on the local sites of interest.

HOPETOWN AND WARRENTON

Hopetown, 130 km (81 miles) south-west of Kimberley, is an isolated little place close to the Gazella Game Reserve (gemsbok, eland, kudu and springbok) and not too far from the extensive Vanderkloof (originally PK le Roux) Dam. In the vicinity of Witput Station a local farmer has established some rewarding one- and two-day trails along the Orange River; hikers enjoy good game-viewing and bird-watching (fish eagle, black eagle, bustard, waterfowl).

Warrenton, situated beside the Vaal River to the north of Kimberley on the R29 road, is the supply artery to the Vaal-Harts irrigation scheme, the southern hemisphere's largest. The countryside is refreshingly lush; diamond mining is still a preoccupation; the semi-precious stone processing factory welcomes visitors; the Warrenton Nature Reserve, rich in succulents, is worth calling in at (best time: May–June). Far to the north-west of Kimberley – about 310 km (193 miles) along the R31 – is the centre of:

KURUMAN

This was the site of one of Africa's most important mission stations, and the base from which many pioneering expeditions, both religious and adventurous, set out in Victorian times. The church and mission buildings are still a functioning complex; the grounds are overgrown, shaded by syringa and fig trees, pears and pomegranates, and they're quite lovely.

Nearby, below a small range of hills, is the source of the local river, a spring that yields about 20 million litres (4.4 million gallons) of sparkling water each day. This is the famous 'eye' of Kuruman: it supplies the town, and around it a most pleasant little park has been created (there are picnic spots beneath the willow trees; and the fat fish of the river expect to be fed). Restful too is the 850 ha (2,100 acres) Kuruman Nature Reserve, sanctuary for rhino, zebra and a number of antelope species.

THE NORTH-WESTERN AREAS

Most of the region comprises Gordonia, named after Cape prime minister Sir Gordon Sprigg (he held office four times between 1878 and 1902) and the country's largest magisterial district: it covers nearly 55,000 km^2 (21,236 square miles) of dry scrubland, semi-desert and, in the Kalahari region to the north, pure desert.

A vast, lonely country, sparsely populated, seemingly barren for the most part – but bountiful nevertheless: Gordonia is bisected by the Orange River, whose waters irrigate fields and plantations that yield marvellous harvests of lucerne and wheat, raisins and sultanas, cotton, vegetable seeds and grapes. Beyond the irrigated areas are huge salt pans, and ranchlands that nurture hardy cattle and karakul sheep.

UPINGTON

A pleasant, fairly substantial, isolated town on the north bank of the Orange, founded as a mission station in 1871 and named after Thomas Upington, prime minister of the Cape Colony from 1884 to 1886. The missionary Christian Schroder established an irrigation scheme that, over the decades, has been hugely expanded and now stretches either side of the river from the Boegoeberg down as far as the Augrabies area. The fertile islands of the Orange are also intensively cultivated; palm trees grow especially well in the region and dates are a prominent crop. The sun shines brightly throughout the year. The terrain tends to be rather featureless, but has its special attractions: diamonds and semi-precious stones (amethyst, beryl, agate, jasper, rose quartz, tourmaline, tiger's eye, ruby) attract fossickers from far and wide.

LOCAL PRODUCTS Visitors are welcomed by the Karakul Research Station; by the South African Dried Fruit Co-operative, the world's second largest; and by the Oranjerivier Wine Co-operative, the country's most northerly and, again, the world's second largest (tours by arrangement); contact the Upington Tourist Information Office: see Advisory, page 213.

OLYVENHOUTSDRIFT is an island resort in the middle of the Orange River – a refreshing place of lawns, a 1,041 m (3,416 ft) avenue of date palms (longest in the world), bowling greens, tennis courts, pool, chalets, caravan/camping ground and facilities for watersports and angling (carp, moddervis and yellowfish).

THE ROARING SANDS is a unique feature of the wider region – a 9-km-long (5.5 miles), 2-km-wide (1.25 miles) 'island' of white dunes set among the red-sand country off the R32, near the village of Groblershoop some 120 km

The desert-adapted black-backed jackal.

(75 miles) south-east of Upington. The dunes are about 100 m (330 ft) high and in dry weather the sands, when disturbed (even slightly, for instance, by running your hand through them), emit an eerie moaning sound that occasionally rises to a muted roar. The phenomenon has something to do with the white sand's granular texture and loose composition, elements that prevent it mixing with the more compacted red sands. Best places to hear the noise are on the southerly faces. Fulgurites – sand fused into threads and tube-shaped lengths by the action of lightning – are sold by the locals as souvenirs. Visitor facilities in the area include hutted accommodation and a camping site.

KALAHARI GEMSBOK NATIONAL PARK

The Kalahari, an area of about 1.2 million km² (463,320 square miles), extends over the eastern parts of Namibia, most of Botswana, a large portion of Zimbabwe, some of Angola and a small segment of South Africa north of the Orange River. Although termed a desert – because of its porous, sandy soils and lack of surface water – much of the region is in fact wilderness, its great plains covered by sparse but sweet grasses that sustain enormous herds of game animals.

This immense, parched-looking and hauntingly beautiful country is the last refuge of the traditional San (Bushmen), only a few clans of whom remain relatively untouched by western culture (see box, opposite).

The Kalahari Gemsbok National Park is a 9,590 km² (3,700 square miles) wedge of sandy territory sprawling between the borders of Namibia and Botswana. Combined with the adjoining Gemsbok National Park in Botswana (there are no fences; game animals are free to migrate, which they do *en masse* – an unforgettable spectacle), the conservation area extends more than 2,046,103 ha (5,056,851 acres), or 79,000 km² (30,500 square miles), which is somewhat larger than the Republic of Ireland and seven times the size of Lebanon. Much of the countryside between the invariably bone-dry riverbeds of the Auob and the Nossob (the latter 'watercourse' flows only about once a century) is rolling red duneland, scantily clad with a variety of grasses. Plantlife, which is more profuse near the river courses, includes camel-thorn, blackthorn and several other acacia species. Summer temperatures often exceed 40 °C (104 °F); winter nights can be freezing.

THE SAN OF THE KALAHARI

By tradition the San (Bushman) people are hunter-gatherers, subsisting largely on game, honey and the roots and fruits of plants. They lived – and in the Kalahari a few still live – in total harmony with nature, posing no threat to either wildlife or vegetation, their semi-nomadic routines governed by the seasons and by the movement of the animals.

That the San once inhabited most of southern Africa is evident from their wonderfully animated paintings on rocks and cave walls, their 'galleries' still to be seen as far afield as the Drakensberg and the southern Cape. But from about 2,000 years ago pastoral peoples began to encroach on the ancient hunting grounds. Some San clans were assimilated by the newcomers (who incorporated two or three of the San 'click' sounds into their own Nguni languages); others moved westwards and northwards until they found land where they could live freely – which, in effect, confined them to areas that were too inhospitable for peoples who were less skilled in the ways of the wild: to the wilderness regions of the north-western Cape, the Kalahari, Namibia and Botswana.

Today, most San groups have abandoned the nomadic lifestyle in favour of a more settled, sometimes even pastoral existence.

The true desert people live today much as their ancestors did many years ago, moving in small clans, each with its clearly defined territory. The women gather roots and edible berries and wild melons such as the tsamma, a source of both food and water. The men hunt with a wooden bow strung with sinew, and arrows which they carry in a skin or bark quiver (they also use clubs or spears if the occasion demands). The arrowheads are tipped with a poison made from insect grubs, a toxin which acts slowly on the prey's nervous system, and the hunters may have to pursue and track the animal for enormous distances before it finally drops.

When the kill is made, the whole group joins in the feast, singing and dancing in a trance-like ritual around the fire. San music is based on an atonal scale and is as unique to these people as their clan language. When game is scarce, the group splits up into smaller parties to glean and garner food (snakes, lizards and even scorpions are included in the diet); during severe, prolonged droughts the women chew the bark of a particular tree: this prevents conception, so limiting the number of mouths to feed.

In especially dry areas, and during times of drought, the San store water in ostrich shells, which they bury deep below the sandy surface of the desert. These they recover with uncanny accuracy, even when no signs of the cache are visible to the untrained eye.

Ostrich shells are also used for making beads; clothing consists of skin karosses, loincloths and aprons. Possessions are very basic, and few: nothing can be owned which cannot be carried. Shelters are rudimentary, comprising structures of sticks which form two-thirds of a 150-cm-high (59 in) circle. Some of the southern clans cover the sticks with mats woven from reeds.

Making a home among the red sand-dunes of the Kalahari.

The park was proclaimed in 1931 to put an end to the indiscriminate slaughter of the gemsbok and springbok herds. Approximately 80 wind-powered boreholes have been sunk deep into the earth to tap the precious underground water, and dams and waterholes attract large numbers of game. Many of the park's animals, though, obtain their moisture from the hardy and ingeniously adapted desert succulents, notable among which are the tsamma melon (*Citrullus lanatus*) and the wild cucumber (*Acanthosicyos naudinianus*).

The park serves as sanctuary for a wide range of large mammals including blue wildebeest, eland, steenbok, red hartebeest, duiker and many smaller mammals – and, of course, for gemsbok and springbok. Among the carnivores are lion, leopard, cheetah, wild dog, spotted hyaena and the rare brown hyaena; avian life (215 species have been recorded) includes the secretary bird, bateleur, martial eagle, tawny eagle and two types of snake eagle.

Visitors to the Kalahari Gemsbok have a choice of three camps: Twee Rivieren, near the confluence of the Auob and Nossob; Mata Mata, on the Auob to the west, and the Nossob, near the Botswana border. All have fully-equipped 4- and 6-bed huts and cottages (with kitchen and bathroom; Twee Rivieren's are air-conditioned) and caravan/camp sites. Groceries and fuel are available; Twee Rivieren offers fresh food (but no bread or milk), a swimming pool, a 'lapa' where informal meals are served, and a landing strip (Avis car-hire available). The game-viewing roads are extensive. Information and reservations: National Parks Board (*see* Advisory, page 213).

AUGRABIES FALLS

About 120 km (75 miles) west of Upington, in a barren and desolate land of sand, scrub and rock, the broad Orange River plunges through a massive canyon in a sudden and dramatic sequence of rapids and cascades. In exceptional seasons and at flood peak the flow rises to about 400 million litres (88 million gallons) a minute, the waters descending through the ravine to breach the rim of the main gorge. Here, 19 separate waterfalls drop, sheer at first and then in a misty tumble of cataracts, to the turbulent, rock-enclosed pool 200 m (660 ft) below. At times of medium flood the flow is confined to a single fall.

The Augrabies – the name is derived from the Korana word for 'big waters' – are ranked among the world's six largest waterfalls. The gorge is 18 km (11 miles) long, 250 m (820 ft) deep in places, and all along its length there are towering, starkly eroded granite cliffs.

THE AUGRABIES FALLS NATIONAL PARK
This was proclaimed in 1966 to conserve just under 10,000 ha (24,710 acres) of rugged river landscape along both banks of the Orange River, and was recently – and greatly – enlarged with the addition of a 70,000 ha (173,000 acres) expanse known as the Riemvasmaak. The expansion will enable the area to be restocked with the larger game species. Currently in residence are black rhino, eland, springbok, klipspringer and steenbok, leopard, caracal, blackbacked jackal and bat-eared fox, baboon and monkey, and about 160 species of bird (among them the martial and black eagles). Visitor amenities include comfortable accommodation in fully equipped cottages and huts (kitchen, bathroom and air-conditioning), camping site, restaurant, shop, petrol pump and information centre. Among other facilities are several pleasant picnic spots, game-viewing roads, walking trails, and the Klipspringer hiking trail (April to October; overnight huts en route).

LEFT: *Hardy gemsbok thrive on the sparse grasslands of the Kalahari park.*
OPPOSITE: *The Orange River makes its way through the Augrabies gorge; at peak flood 19 separate falls cascade into the pool below.*

ADVISORY: THE GREAT INTERIOR

CLIMATE

The country's great interior extends over a large part of the great central plateau. This is a summer-rainfall region, but the rains tend to be infrequent; summer days can be extremely hot, the nights much less so; winter days are blessed by long hours of intense sunshine but there's no cloud cover, the altitude is fairly high, and the nights can be bitterly cold.

Karoo. Beaufort West temperatures: January average daily maximum 32,5 °C/90.5 °F, the daily minimum 16.2 °C/ 61 °F; July average daily maximum 18.1 °C/ 64.5 °F, the daily minimum 4.9 °C/40.8 °F; extremes 41.9 °C/107.4 °F and -5.6 °C/22 °F. Rainfall: January average monthly 23 mm/1 in; July 8 mm/½ in; highest recorded daily rainfall 104 mm/4 in.

North-western areas. Upington temperatures: January average daily maximum 35.2 °C/95 °F, daily minimum 19.7 °C/67.5 °F; July average daily maximum 20 °C/ 68 °F, the daily minimum 4.8 °C/40.6 °F; extremes 42.1 °C/107 °F and -4.7 °C/23.5 °F. Rainfall: January average monthly 16 mm/½ in, July 2 mm/¼ in; highest recorded daily rainfall 119 mm/4½ in.

MAIN ATTRACTIONS

Karoo: Starkly beautiful landscapes, at their best at dawn and sunset ❑ Historic Matjiesfontein village and the town of Graaff-Reinet.
Northern Cape: The Diamond City of Kimberley.
North-western Cape: Kalahari Gemsbok National Park ❑ The Augrabies Falls.

TRAVEL

Road. Approximate distances: Kimberley is 175 km/ 109 miles from Bloemfontein; 484 km/301 miles from Johannesburg; 540 km/336 miles from Pretoria; 764 km/ 475 miles from Durban; 965 km/600 miles from Cape Town and 402 km/250 miles from Upington.

The main highways traversing the Karoo and the northern and north-western regions are in generally good condition, allowing comfortable motoring.

Alternative routes between Johannesburg and Cape Town are: the R29 via Kimberley, which joins the national highway (N1) at Three Sisters in the Karoo, between Richmond and Beaufort West; or the R29 to Kimberley, west on the R64 and R32 to Upington, west again on the R64 to Springbok in Namaqualand and then south along the N7 to Cape Town. This is about 200 km/124 miles longer than the direct route, but the roads are relatively free of traffic.

Rail. Kimberley's railway station is situated on Florence St; tel. (0531) 88-2060 for more information; tel. (0531) 88-2761 to make reservations.

Air. Both Kimberley and Upington have air and rail links with South Africa's major centres.

ACCOMMODATION
Select hotels

KAROO

Central * Colesberg. Halfway house between Cape Town and Johannesburg; 67 rooms; ladies' bar; meals available; swimming pool. PO Box 58, Colesberg 9795; tel. (051) 753-0734, fax 753-0667.

Drostdy * ** Graaff-Reinet. One of South Africa's best country hotels; 51 rooms; à la carte restaurant; bar; pool; conference facilities for 80. PO Box 400, Graaff-Reinet 6280; tel. (0491) 2-2161, fax 2-4582.

**Grand Hotel ** ** Laingsburg. 13 en suite rooms; table d'hôte restaurant (traditional cuisine); swimming pool. PO Box 8, Laingsburg 6900; tel. (02372), ask for 38.

Hotel De Graaff Graaff-Reinet. 23 rooms; à la carte restaurant. PO Box 43, Graaff-Reinet 6280; tel. (0491) 2-4191/2, fax 2-4193.

**Laingsburg Country Hotel ** ** Along the N1. 11 en suite rooms; à la carte and table d'hôte restaurants; pool. PO Box 53, Laingsburg 6900; tel. (02372), ask for 9 or 185, fax ask for 62.

**Lord Milner ** ** Matjiesfontein. Historic (*see* page 203); award-winning country hotel; 33 rooms; table d'hôte restaurant; pool. PO Matjiesfontein 6901; tel. (02372), ask for Matjiesfontein 2.

Merino Inn Motel * ** Colesberg. Convenient halfway stopover between Johannesburg and Cape Town; 70 rooms; conference facilities available; à la carte restaurant; bar. PO Box 10, Colesberg 5890; tel. (051752), ask for 25.

**Oasis ** ** Beaufort West. 49 rooms; 3 bars. PO Box 115, Beaufort West 6970; tel. (0201) 3221/2/3/4.

Panorama Swiss Guest House On Magazine Hill, overlooking Graaff-Reinet. 46 rooms; à la carte, buffet and traditional Cape restaurants; conference facilities available for 300 people. PO Box 314, Graaff-Reinet 6280; tel. (0491) 2-2233.

Swartberg Hotel Prince Albert. Charming surrounds; 17 rooms, 2 suites; table d'hôte restaurant (country cuisine); pool; gym; sauna. PO Box 6, Prince Albert 6930; tel. (04436) 332.

**Van Zylsvlei Motel ** ** Colesberg. 19 thatched en suite rondavels; à la carte restaurant; bar; pool. PO Box 50, Colesberg 5980; tel. (051) 753-0589.

NORTHERN REGIONS

**Colinton Hotel ** ** Kimberley. Quite central; 10 double rooms. PO Box 400, Kimberley 8300; tel. (0531) 3-1471, fax 3-1472.

**Diamond Protea Lodge ** ** Kimberley. 34 en suite rooms; buffet breakfasts. PO Box 2068, Kimberley 8300; tel. (0531) 81-1281, fax 81-1284; toll-free reservations 0800 11 9000.

Halfway House Inn * Kimberley. Historic hotel with 12 en suite rooms; drive-in pub. PO Box 650, Kimberley 8300; tel. (0531) 2-5151.

Holiday Inn Garden Court: Kimberley *** Pleasant garden surrounds, 3 km (2 miles) from Big Hole. 107 rooms, 8 suites; à la carte restaurant; pool. PO Box 635, Kimberley 8300; tel. (0531) 2-6211, fax 2-1814; central reservations (011) 482-3500.

Horseshoe Motel Kimberley. Quite central; 56 rooms; à la carte restaurant; pool; conference facilities for 200. PO Box 67, Kimberley 8300; tel. (0531) 2-5267.

Kimberlite *** Kimberley. 30 rooms; lovely à la carte restaurant; drive-in pub. 162 St George's St, Kimberley 8300; tel. (0531) 81-1967.

Queens * Barkly West. 13 en suite rooms. PO Box 17, Barkly West 8375; tel. (053) 531-0514.

Radnor ** Hopetown. 13 en suite rooms. PO Box 25, Hopetown 8750; tel. (05392), ask for 15.

Savoy Hotel Kimberley. 43 rooms, 2 suites; à la carte restaurant; conference facilities for 200. PO Box 231, Kimberley 8300; tel. (0351) 2-6211, fax 2-7021, toll-free reservations 0800 11 9000.

NORTH-WESTERN REGIONS

Oasis Protea Lodge ** Upington. 32 en suite rooms; breakfast room; bar. PO Box 1981, Upington 8800; tel. and fax (054) 31-1125.

Upington Protea Inn Upington. On banks of Orange River; 53 en suite rooms; conference facilities for 55. PO Box 13, Upington 8800; tel. and fax (054) 2-5414.

Waterwiel Protea *** Kakamas. 25 rooms; à la carte restaurant; pool; tennis; conference facilities for 60. PO Box 250, Kakamas 8870; tel. (054) 431-0838, fax 431-0836, toll-free reservations 0800 11 9000.

Self-catering and budget

This vast region is reasonably well served by guesthouses and, especially in and around Kimberley and in the Kalahari Gemsbok National Park, by self-catering accommodation. Caravan/camping facilities are available in or near a dozen or so centres, including Kimberley, Graaff-Reinet, Colesberg, Beaufort West and Kuruman. Contact Satour or the local tourism information offices for more details.

USEFUL ADDRESSES AND TELEPHONE NUMBERS

National Parks Board Head Office, PO Box 787, Pretoria 0001; tel. (012) 343-1991, fax 343-0905; PO Box 7400, Rogge Bay 8012; tel. (021) 22-2810, fax 24-6211.

Northern Cape Nature Conservation, tel. (0531) 2-2143 (office hours).

KIMBERLEY

Automobile Association, AA House, 13 New Main Rd, Kimberley 8300; tel. (0531) 2-5207 or toll-free 0800-010101 (emergencies).

Car hire, major rental firms represented at airport and in city; consult local directory or hotel reception.

Emergency numbers, Kimberley (code 0531). *National ambulance number*: 1-0177; *local ambulance*: 81-1955; *hospital casualty*: Lyndhurst Rd, 80-9111; *fire brigade*: 2-4211; *police headquarters*: 2-2237; *police flying squad*: 1-0111; *all-night pharmacy*: The Pier Muller Pharmacy, Old Main Rd, 81-1787.

Kimberley Municipal Publicity Office, City Hall, Market Square, Kimberley 8300; tel. (0531) 2-7299

Satour (South African Tourism Board), Flaxley House, Du Toitspan Rd, Kimberley 8300; tel. (0531) 3-1434.

Tour Guide Services, tel. (0531) 2-5842.

OTHER CENTRES

Graaff-Reinet Information Bureau, PO Box 153, Graaff-Reinet 6280; tel. (0491) 2-3241 (the chairman's residence).

Upington Tourist Information Office, Public Library Building, Town Sq, Upington 8800; tel. (054) 2-7064.

CAPE TOWN AND THE PENINSULA

The Cape Peninsula is a slender, 75-km-long (47 miles) promontory which curves into the sea at the extreme south-western corner of the African continent. Popular belief has it that it is the dividing line between the Atlantic and Indian oceans, but the technical separation occurs farther to the east, at Cape Agulhas, the most most southerly point in Africa.

The Peninsula stretches from the Cape of Good Hope and Cape Point northward to Table Bay and the city of Cape Town. It comprises, for the most part, a strikingly beautiful mountain plateau that achieves its loftiest and most spectacular heights in the famed Table Mountain massif overlooking the bay and the city. Its western and eastern shorelines are graced by attractive little (and some not so little) residential and resort centres that are a magnet for summer holiday-makers, boating enthusiasts, scuba-divers, surfers and sun-worshippers.

To the north are the Cape Flats, a region that once – 60 million years ago – lay beneath the sea, so separating what is now the Peninsula from the mainland. Over the millenia the waters receded to expose a low, sandy, flat area known to the early Dutch colonists as 'Die Groote Woeste Vlakte' (the Great Desolate Plain) – a nightmare of drifting dunes. Eventually, during the 19th century, the sands were stabilized by planting out hardy hakeas and wattles and, most of all, Port Jackson willows. These last, imported from Australia, served their purpose only too well: in due course the tenacious plants spread throughout the region and are now regarded as thoroughgoing pests.

Today the northern plain is intensively cultivated in some parts (wheat, vegetables and strawberries) and dense with suburbia in others.

CAPE TOWN

Cape Town is a place of startling contrasts, which strike visitors immediately on the drive in from Cape Town International Airport. In the distance there is the spectacular and distinctively flat-topped bulk of Table Mountain towering over a city that seems as remote from the Third

OPPOSITE: *The familiar shape of Table Mountain and its flanking features, seen from the West Coast town of Bloubergstrand.*

World as Brussels, Bristol or Boston. It is a clean, neat, bustling little metropolis of handsome (sometimes historic) buildings, gracious thoroughfares, glittering shops and a general ambience that has more of Europe in it than Africa.

The metropolitan area fills the natural amphitheatre formed by Table Mountain and its flanking peaks, sprawls northwards over the Cape Flats, and stretches out on either side of the Peninsula and inland, the suburbs hugging the lower slopes of the mountain range and extending southwards along the line of rail (these are the oldest of the residential areas outside the city proper, founded as farms along the Sweet – now the Liesbeek – River by the first of the 'free-burghers' in the later 1650s). The central area is comparatively small, its potential for expansion restricted by sea and mountain.

Popularly termed the 'Tavern of the Seas', Cape Town owed its prominence and prosperity over three centuries and more to its strategic position astride the ocean lanes, and it remains a substantial port city: the harbour is South Africa's fifth busiest and, after Durban, its second biggest; the pre-cooling stores are among the world's most extensive; ship repair is a major industry (the dry dock, well used by tankers in need of maintenance, is the largest in the southern hemisphere). And part of the docks have been magnificently revitalized for leisure purposes (*see* page 226).

City centre

Cape Town's main thoroughfare is the Heerengracht, which starts at the harbour and runs straight as an arrow towards the mountain, changing its name to Adderley Street at about the halfway mark. To stroll from one end to the other takes a pleasant half-hour.

In its broad lower reaches the thoroughfare is flanked by rather stately office blocks; the central island section supports lawns, palm trees, an ornamental fountain and pond and some quite impressive statuary (the war memorial, and Jan van Riebeeck and his wife, Maria de la Queillerie). This area is part of what is called the Foreshore, a 145 ha (358 acres) expanse of land which was reclaimed from the sea, some of it during the 19th century and the rest in the 1930s and 1940s. The enterprise was a spin-off from harbour construction work – the dredging operations produced enormous quantities of sand that had to be disposed of, and the new ground was a bonus for the town planners.

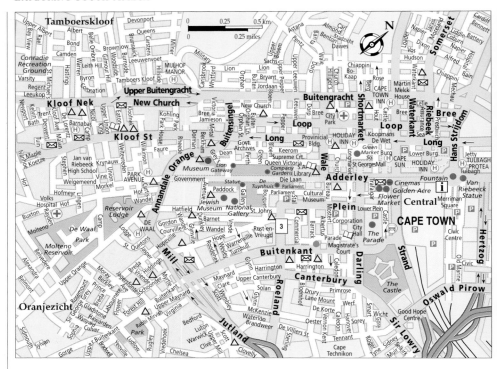

If you position yourself on the intersection of Lower Adderley and Strand streets, facing south, you will see on your left-hand side the mosaic-walled railway station; on the other side of the road is the massive Golden Acre office and shopping complex; beyond and farther away to the left, are the Castle of Good Hope, the Grand Parade and City Hall.

THE CASTLE A massive pentagonal fortress and the oldest occupied building in South Africa: its construction began as early as 1666 and, after some delays, ended during the brief governorship of Johann Bax (1676), at which time it comprised 'five polygons with their gate, sally port, outworks, two ravelins with their counter-scarps and those of the outworks'. The bastions were named after the various titles of the Prince of Orange: Nassau, Oranje, Leerdam, Buren and Catzenellenbogen.

Originally, the Castle's interior was a single large courtyard, but this was later divided in two by a defensive cross-wall, or 'Kat', on which additional cannon were mounted. Later still the wall was used as support for the Kat balcony, an elegantly balustraded feature fronting the large reception room, which in time became the focal point of the Cape governor's splendidly attractive official residence and of Cape Town's aristocratic social life.

Part of the Castle has served as the headquarters of the Western Cape military command; elsewhere it functions as a museum. On display are collections of furniture, carpets, porcelain, *objets d'art* and the principal paintings of the noted William Fehr collection.

Recently added attractions include a reconstruction of the original moat and wooden bridge, and the Good Hope Collection, consisting of a house, a military and a restoration museum (containing artefacts, found during renovations, which date back to the Dutch, British and French occupations of the Castle). A Ceremony of Keys has also been introduced. The Dolphin Pool at the rear of the fortress was 'rediscovered' and officially opened in September 1990. There are daily conducted tours; the entrance is on Castle Street.

Strand Street

This runs down from the slopes of Signal Hill and through the city centre. Principal points of interest along this broad street are:

TOP: *The City Hall overlooks the Grand Parade, used for parking, trading and rallies.*
ABOVE: *Part of the Castle's interior.*

KOOPMANS-DE WET HOUSE, once the home of Maria Koopmans-De Wet (1834–1906), a noted patron of the arts, philanthropist, socialite and passionate Afrikaner. Maria was placed under house arrest during the South African War for her republican leanings and for her efforts to help the women and children of the concentration camps.

Originally built in 1701, the house was enlarged several times by different owners. Today, with its façade attributed to Louis Thibault and Anton Anreith, it stands as a classic example of typical late-18th-century Cape domestic architecture. On display: a priceless collection of Cape and European furniture, Dutch and German glassware, restored murals, Nanking porcelain, Delft ware and *objets d'art*. Open Tuesday to Saturday. Close by is the:
LUTHERAN CHURCH with its splendid pulpit (carved by Anreith). Next to the church is Martin Melck House, once the parsonage and also designed by Anreith. Beautifully restored, it embraces a secluded walled garden as well as the fashionable Hemmingways.

DISTRICT SIX

Once described as 'the soul of Cape Town', and a vibrant inner suburb of 55,000 coloured people, District Six became the focus of national and international attention in the mid-1960s, when the government declared it 'white' under the apartheid laws and began moving its residents to Mitchell's Plain and to other townships on the desolate Cape Flats.

Officialdom argued that the removals were part of a genuine upliftment programme, that District Six had become untenable in terms of the Public Health Act and the Slums Act. And indeed the place was overcrowded and unsanitary, its buildings dilapidated, its warren-like streets crime-ridden. But it had colour, and charm, and above all a powerful perception of community. Remembers one resident: 'When we were evicted, we lost more than our home. We lost neighbours and friends whom we could rely on in times of sickness and other misfortune. The government gave us another home; it couldn't give us a sense of belonging.'

District Six, on the city's eastern fringes, is prime land, yet developers did not move in. It remained a wasteland, mute reminder of a tragic exercise in what its apologists called 'social engineering', and of a heartless system that only recently crumbled. Plans to return the area to the people are well advanced.

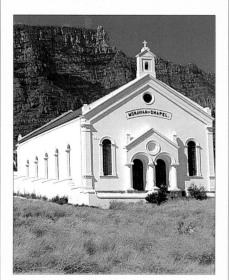

The Moravian Church in District Six.

Adderley Street

Named in honour of Sir Charles Adderley, a mid-19th-century British politician who helped prevent the establishment of a convict colony at the Cape in its early days.

GOLDEN ACRE On the left as you walk up toward the mountain is this vast and glittering complex of department stores and speciality shops, coffee shops and restaurants, cinemas and offices. It is part of an even more extensive underground concourse running beneath Adderley and adjoining streets.

The area is believed to be the site of Jan van Riebeeck's first earth-and-timber fort (which was erected on his arrival in 1652). During excavations for the Golden Acre's foundations, part of a dam, or reservoir, built by Van Riebeeck's successor (Zacharias Wagenaer), was discovered. The architects redrew their plans in order to retain the relics *in situ*, and they are now on display, behind glass.

FLOWER-SELLERS A little way beyond the Golden Acre are Cape Town's famous flower-sellers – raucous and good-humoured, offering exquisite blooms at low prices.

GROOTE KERK This splendid Dutch Reformed Church (NGK) building stands at the upper end of Adderley, though it also fronts onto Church Square (a place lined with historic buildings and worth a look-over). The first stone of the original Kerk was laid in 1678. Of this building, only the soaring steeple remains.

The second church was consecrated in 1841 and is notable for many architectural and sculptured features, including its pulpit resting on a pedestal of lions. Also notable are the teak-and-pine roofing and vast roof-span, and the old gravestones, some of which have been incorporated as paving stones, others into the walls.

CULTURAL HISTORY MUSEUM, situated in upper Adderley Street. Originally the Dutch East India Company's slave lodge (and brothel), the building was converted into government offices between 1809 and 1815, in the early years of the second British occupation, and in 1810 served as the Supreme Court. Certain sections of the building (notably the fine Assembly Room, the Court Room and the judges' chambers) were masterfully designed by the celebrated French architect Louis Thibault. When you are there, take special note of the pediment on the rear façade: yet another creation of the ever-present and mischievous Anreith, it features a caricature of the Royal coat of arms, with the Unicorn showing shocked revulsion for an old and degenerate British Lion. The museum has an interesting archaeological section; other displays include furniture, glassware, weaponry, musical instruments and exhibits relating to the country's postal and currency history. Open from Monday to Saturday.

ST GEORGE'S CATHEDRAL, in Wale Street, round the corner from Adderley. The church became a cathedral when Robert Gray was appointed Cape Town's first Anglican bishop in 1848. Later Victorians condemned the building as too 'pagan' in concept, and architects Herbert Baker and Francis Masey were commissioned to produce a more respectable 'new Gothic' edifice. The lovely classical spire and portico were lost in the process; the most recent extensions, completed in the 1980s, are functional and unremarkable. Of note, though, are the Rose Window (by Francis Spear), the Lord Mountbatten memorial window, and stained glass work by Gabriel Lore of Chartres. The cathedral has been the venue for some no-nonsense 'political' sermons by Nobel laureate Archbishop Desmond Tutu (who resigned his high office in 1996); the meeting place for protest against injustice, and starting point of the first legal mass march in recent years. On a gentler note, the choir, led by Barry Smith, sings like angels, and choral and orchestral concerts are periodically performed.

City centre stroll

Cape Town is one of the few South African cities (two others that come to mind are Pietermaritzburg and Grahamstown) whose central areas are best explored on foot. A great deal of what there is to see is concentrated within ambling distance. Available from Captour is a series of booklets entitled *Cape Town Historical Walks*, which include city pedestrian routes (together with, among others, a harbour route).

The walks are just over two hours, longer if you linger. Alternatively, try an even easier and perhaps less earnestly educational stroll, taking in:
ST GEORGE'S MALL This used to be a six-block traffic-congested city street until closed off for the near-exclusive use of pedestrians. Shops and arcades run up on either side; there are kiosks, umbrella-shaded bistros and vendors along the central pavement area.
GREENMARKET SQUARE, one of the prettiest plazas in Africa, and usually filled by street-traders' stalls. There are intriguing buys and occasionally a genuine antique among the bric-a-brac. A colourful, cheerful place, girded around by graceful buildings, including the:
• **Old Town House,** an elegant late-1750s Cape Baroque structure once used by the Burgher Senate and the Burgher Watch, the city's first

OPPOSITE: *Adderley Street's famed flower-sellers with some of their exquisite wares.*
BELOW: *Bird's-eye view of Greenmarket Square, perhaps Cape Town's most attractive piazza.*
BOTTOM: *One of the square's buskers.*

ISLAMIC CAPE TOWN

Although relatively few in number, Muslims contributed a great deal to the early development of the Cape. The first to arrive were slaves from Java, the Celebes, Bali and Timor and other Indonesian islands and regions, who were immediately valued for their industry, their skills as craftsmen – and for their exotic cuisine, from which such traditional Cape foods as *bobotie*, *bredie* and *blatjang* developed. The slaves were in due course joined by high-born political exiles, men such as Sheik Yusuf and the Rajah of Tambora, who had rebelled against the unwelcome and often-harsh authority of the Dutch East India Company in Java and Ceylon (Sri Lanka), and who brought their families and some of their followers with them.

For almost 50 years, from 1715 onwards, slaves arrived from the East in an almost continuous stream until the community had grown from a handful to several thousand. Many who were not originally of the Islamic faith were converted after their arrival. Among them were skilled silversmiths, excellent tailors, coopers, wainwrights and builders (the famed Cape Dutch gable did not in fact originate in the Netherlands but in the East). With the abolition of slavery in the 1830s, many of these highly respected people settled on the slopes of Cape Town's Signal Hill, in the picturesque Bo-Kaap ('Above-Cape', sometimes but wrongly called the Malay Quarter).

The customs and traditions which the Muslim community has maintained include the Ratiep, originally a sword dance that was part of Islamic religious ceremony. It was performed under a kind of hypnosis, or self-induced trance, during which the dancers, youths and men, pierced their flesh with swords and other sharp metal instruments. These instruments did not cause pain or draw blood, nor was there any sign of a wound when they were withdrawn. Today the dance lacks much of its religious significance and many imams (spiritual leaders) disapprove of the ritual, though it is still performed as a spectacle.

There was little intermarriage with other groups and the community is still very much integrated (though it hasn't confined itself to the Bo-Kaap area) and devoutly Muslim. Its members regularly attend their mosques and many make pilgrimages, not only to the Holy City of Mecca (as is required of every Muslim if he can afford it) but also to the local kramats – the tombs of holy men. There are five kramats on and around the Peninsula and one on Robben Island which, together, form a 'holy circle'.

The kramat – shrine to a holy man – on Cape Town's Signal Hill.

Imposing statuary in the public gardens.

police force. It's now a gallery housing some fine works of art, including the 96 Dutch and Flemish masters donated, in the early 1900s, by Rand financier Sir Max Michaelis (who also funded the noted Michaelis School of Fine Art). Chamber concerts are held here on Friday evenings. Open daily between 10h00 and 17h00.

• **The Metropolitan Methodist Church**, whose entrance is around the corner in Burg Street: a fulsome Gothic building regarded by the Victorians as the country's most splendid place of worship. It has real architectural merit.

LONG STREET, once the vibrant centre of city life. Parts of it are now a bit seedy, but lively enough with its inviting antique shops; well-stocked second-hand bookstores (the best is probably Clarke's: if they don't have what you're looking for they can almost certainly obtain it for you); plenty of restaurants and, especially at the top end, a number of charmingly filigreed Victorian façades.

Of note and of curiosity interest are buildings in Orphan Lane; the Blue Lodge (beautifully preserved exterior); the Palm Tree Mosque, the city's only complete surviving 18th-century house; the Dorp Street Mosque; Carnival Court and the nearby building No. 203; and the Sendinggestig, a fine church museum.

The Gardens area

The humble vegetable patch that the first white colonists planted in the autumn and winter of 1652 (*see* page 20) still flourishes, though over the centuries it has changed beyond recognition, both in appearance and function. It is now one of the world's more attractive, and botanically most interesting, city parks.

Over the centuries the Gardens have been greatly reduced by the encroachment, on the east side (Government Avenue) of the Houses of Parliament, Tuynhuys, the National Gallery, the Old and Great Synagogues and Cape Town High School, and on the west by the South African Museum and the buildings of the former South African College. The South African Library and St George's Cathedral (*see* page 219) are on the north (Queen Victoria Street) side.

For visitors, and especially those with a botanical interest, the Gardens are a must: over 8,000 varieties of tree, shrub, flower and other plants – most of them exotic – can be seen in the grounds. The large conservatory at its upper (mountain) end is known for its fine palm and orchid species. Close to the conservatory is an attractive aviary and a tea-garden.

221

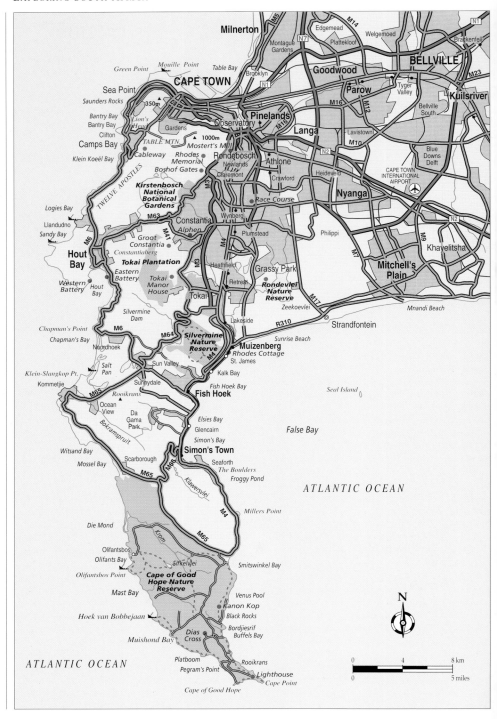

Milnerton
Edgemead
Welgemoed
Brackenfell
Montague Gardens
BELLVILLE
Green Point
Mouille Point
Table Bay
Goodwood
M23
Brooklyn
Parow
Tyger Valley
Sea Point
CAPE TOWN
Kuilsriver
Saunders Rocks
M16
Bellville South
Bantry Bay
Bantry Bay
Lion's Head
Gardens
Pinelands
M12
Blue Downs Delft
Clifton
Observatory
Langa
Lavistown
Camps Bay
TABLE MTN.
1000m
Mostert's Mill
Klein Koeël Bay
Cableway
Rhodes Memorial
Rondebosch
Athlone
Heideveld
CAPE TOWN INTERNATIONAL AIRPORT
Boshof Gates
Newlands
Claremont
Crawford
Kirstenbosch National Botanical Gardens
Race Course
Nyanga
Logies Bay
Wynberg
Llandudno
Constantia
Sandy Bay
M63
Alphen
Plumstead
Philippi
Khayelitsha
Hout Bay
Groot Constantia
M41
Constantiaberg
Tokai Plantation
Heathfield
Grassy Park
Mitchell's Plain
Eastern Battery
Tokai Manor House
Retreat
Rondevlei Nature Reserve
Western Battery
Hout Bay
Tokai
Zeekoevlei
Mnandi Beach
Silvermine Dam
Lakeside
R310
Strandfontein
Chapman's Point
M6
Silvermine Nature Reserve
Sunrise Beach
Chapman's Bay
M64
Muizenberg
Noordhoek
Rhodes Cottage
St. James
Salt Pan
Sun Valley
Klein-Slangkop Pt.
Kalk Bay
Seal Island
Kommetjie
Sunnydale
Fish Hoek Bay
Rooikrans
Fish Hoek
M65
Ocean View
Da Gama Park
Elsies Bay
False Bay
Witsand Bay
Glencairn
Simon's Bay
Mossel Bay
Scarborough
Simon's Town
Seaforth
The Boulders
ATLANTIC OCEAN
M65
Froggy Pond
Klawersvlei
Die Mond
Millers Point
M65
Olifantsbos
Olifants Bay
Sirkelvlei
Smitswinkel Bay
Olifantsbos Point
Cape of Good Hope Nature Reserve
Mast Bay
Venus Pool
Kanon Kop
N
Hoek van Bobbejaan
Black Rocks
Bordjiesrif
Dias Cross
Buffels Bay
Muishond Bay
Platboom
Rooikrans
ATLANTIC OCEAN
Pegram's Point
Lighthouse
Cape Point
Cape of Good Hope

350m

Chapman's Point

Bokramspruit

Krom

M4

M6

M3

M4

M7

M17

M9

N2

M10

N2

N1

N7

M5

N1

M14

N1

0   4   8 km
0   5 miles

HOUSES OF PARLIAMENT Originally built in 1884, the handsome buildings that initially housed the Cape colonial legislature were enlarged when South Africa became a Union in 1910 and extended several times in the decades that followed. The Parliamentary Museum contains the Gallery Hall, housing portraits, busts, and relics (including the Black Rod and mace, and the Speakers' chairs), and a wealth of historical documents. There is public access to the gallery during sessions; guided tours during recess periods (usually July to January).

SOUTH AFRICAN NATIONAL GALLERY, off Government Avenue. The gallery holds over 6,500 works of art; the main hall is used for, among other things, a frequently changed exhibition of modern South African art. Open daily.

GREAT SYNAGOGUE, in Hatfield Street, off Government Avenue. An impressive Baroque building, domed and twin-towered, consecrated in 1905. Next door is the Old Synagogue, the first to be built in South Africa, now housing the historical and ceremonial treasures of the Jewish Museum. Open Tuesdays to Thurdays in the afternoons, by appointment. The Old Synagogue, the Egyptian Building farther up the avenue and the Gymnasium at Paarl are the only major edifices in the country designed in the Egyptian Revival style.

SOUTH AFRICAN MUSEUM, at the upper end of the Gardens (entry via Queen Victoria Street), offers a range of displays in the realms of natural history (marine life and birds), geology, ethnology, archaeology and printing. Of special interest are the San (Bushman) plaster casts, examples of their rock art, and an array of mystical 'images of power' artefacts; the 'Whale Well', and dioramas of the fossil-rich Karoo and its reptiles of 200 million years ago.

THE PLANETARIUM, in Queen Victoria Street, was completed in 1987 as part of the R20 million extension to the South African Museum. Its projectors are able to reproduce the day or night sky over Cape Town at any stage during a 26,000 year period – 13,000 years on either side of the present time. The particular instrument that performs this task is an improved version of the Minolta Series Four star-projector, similar to those used by NASA astronauts during their training. The equipment is capable of simulating panoramic terrestrial landscapes as well as celestial subjects; sound effects complement the visuals. The planetarium shows are changed every three months.

THE CAPE'S FLORAL HERITAGE

The Peninsula is part of the Cape Floral Kingdom, a zone that extends over the winter-rainfall belt running along the country's south-western and southern coasts and botanically quite remarkable: occupying just 0.04% of the earth's total land area, it nevertheless enjoys equal status with the great Boreal Kingdom that extends over North America and most of Europe and Asia.

The Cape Floral Kingdom includes almost 8,600 species; of the 989 genera occurring, fully 193 are unique to a particular area; as many as 121 different species have been found growing within a single 10-m^2 (108 ft^2) patch. Collectively, this floral wealth is known as *fynbos* ('fine bush'), and for the most part it comprises such tough, low-growing, small-leafed, evergreen shrubs as the lovely ericas (a total of 600 species); the proteas (368 species; the king protea is South Africa's national flower); the almost leafless, reed-like *restio* and a great number and splendid variety of bulbous and cormous plants.

Some 3,000 *fynbos* species – rather more than a third of the total – occur on the Peninsula itself. But the numbers are declining and the plants are steadily falling victim to human encroachment and pollution, to competitive alien flora, too-frequent fires and to the predations of the flower industry.

The red disa, or 'Pride of Table Mountain'.

RUST-EN-VREUGD, Buitenkant Street. Not part of the Gardens area (it is some way to the east) but worth a digression: the 18th-century house contains the bulk of the noted William Fehr collection of Africana and watercolour paintings (the remainder of the collection is housed in the Castle). Open daily.

TABLE MOUNTAIN

Flanked by Devil's Peak and Lion's Head, moody and changeable, majestically dominating the Peninsula's northern skyline, the mountain is without doubt South Africa's best-known landmark and premier tourist attraction. Sculpted from sandstone, it rises 1,086 m (3,563 ft) above the bay; its flat summit measures nearly 3 km (2 miles) from end to end and, on clear days, it can be discerned about 200 km (124 miles) out to sea.

Very often, though, the heights are hidden from view. The clouds that billow across its rim to tumble down the massively precipitous northern faces are known as the 'tablecloth', and are the product of the south-easter. The wind, which collects moisture as it blows around False Bay, collides with the mountain barrier and rises, cooling as it does so, the moisture condensing to form a thick cloud cover which then cascades down, dissipating as it reaches the warmer levels. It is a continuous and spectacular process, and a source of endless fascination to watchers in the city below.

Almost every one of the Peninsula's more than 2,000 species of indigenous flora is found on the slopes and on the mountain's heavily-watered central plateau, among them the silver tree and the lovely wild orchid *Disa uniflora*. Hunters long ago exterminated the bigger game, but the uplands and heights are now a protected area and they still sustain baboon, duiker, grysbok, grey rhebok, civet cat, lynx, rock-rabbit (dassie), porcupine, tortoise, and an exotic animal called the Himalayan tahr, which is reminiscent of a goat. The tahrs, descendants of a pair that escaped from Groote Schuur in the 1930s, are a menace to the environment and their numbers have to be controlled.

More than two million people ascend the mountain each year, most of whom take the: **CABLEWAY,** which provides easy, comfortable and safe access to the flat summit. The trip takes just five minutes, and in over 50 years of operation there has never been a serious accident. The cableway operates throughout the year (including public holidays – but always subject, of course, to favourable weather).

OPPOSITE: *Most visitors ascend Table Mountain by cable-car; the journey takes just five minutes.*
ABOVE: *Relaxing on top of Table Mountain. The vistas are panoramic and spectacular.*
ABOVE RIGHT: *A scale model of the Peninsula on the summit of the mountain enables visitors to locate points of interest.*
BELOW: *One of the many rock-rabbits or 'dassies' which have adapted to the steep slopes.*

Until recently visitors had to stand in line for a place on the cable-car, sometimes for hours on end. It is now both possible and preferable to book a place in advance.

The departure area, linked to the lower station by a shuttle bus service, is at the top of Kloof Nek Road. Either drive there, take a taxi, or board the bus that leaves from Adderley Street (outside OK Bazaars) in the city centre.

ON THE SUMMIT there are splendid viewing points, a restaurant, a souvenir shop from which letters bearing the Table Mountain postmark can be sent, a fax machine and three wall plaques that describe the Table Mountain Nature Reserve, the short walks that may be taken from the cable station, and the flora that may be seen in the different seasons. Best time

of the day to make the ascent is probably late afternoon, to catch the sunset and the deepening colours of sky and land.

CLIMBING UP There are over 350 charted paths to the plateau summit, (*see* page 240), some fairly undemanding, others exceptionally difficult – and it's only too easy to lose your way, which can prove disastrous if the mountain's notoriously treacherous weather suddenly takes a turn for the worse. The heights regularly and tragically exact their toll of human life. Arm yourself with a good map and guide-book, available from most local bookshops; choose a route that's well within your physical capacity, and make the climb in the company of someone who knows the route.

LION'S HEAD is the unusual sugar-loaf feature to the right of Table Mountain as you look from the city. The two are connected by the saddle of land known as Kloof Nek.

Lion's Head and its attendant ridge, which ends in the 'rump' of Signal Hill, is said to resemble that animal when viewed from certain angles. One may climb (chain-ladders help with negotiating the most difficult stretches) to the 669 m (2,195 ft) peak of the Head, from which there are lovely views of the mountain and, to the south, the massive buttresses of the Twelve Apostles, and of Robben Island, sea and city.

Signal Hill was once used as a semaphore post for communication with ships at sea, and it is from here that the noon gun is fired each day. One can drive to the top, from where the vistas are also impressive.

DEVIL'S PEAK guards Table Mountain's eastern flank. It too is just over 1,000 m (3,218 ft) high; on its slopes there are three small block-houses, complete with cannon, built by the nervous British during their first occupation of the Cape (1795–1803). The actual peak is accessible only to experienced climbers.

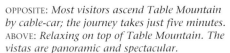

225

THE WATERFRONT

The Victoria and Alfred basins are the oldest part of the city's harbour. And they were, until about 50 years ago, intimately connected with Cape Town and its people, a part of their daily lives. But then, with land reclamation and motorway construction and the dwindling volume of maritime traffic, the links were broken. The leisure beach, the charming old pier and much else disappeared, eventually to be replaced by a wasteland of functional dockyard, ugly buildings, oil storage tanks, fences and a raised highway that stands as a monument to bad planning and bad taste.

But city and sea now have been rejoined, brought together in happy reunion by the hugely ambitious and imaginative Victoria and Alfred Waterfront development scheme.

The multi-billion rand venture draws its inspiration from highly successful harbour 'humanization' projects elsewhere – from Boston's Quincy Market and from San Francisco, from the traffic-free waterfronts of St Tropez and Antibes, from Sydney, Vancouver and New York's South Seaport – but it is tailored to match Cape Town's own needs and unique personality. Among its highlights:

• Many of the more characterful of the old buildings have been converted, and new ones built, to serve as hotels (four of them to date; more, including a floating hotel, are planned); museums, restaurants, umbrella-shaded bistros,

ABOVE: *A section of the Victoria and Alfred Waterfront, the city's premier leisure area.*
OPPOSITE TOP: *A musician in carnival mood.*
OPPOSITE BOTTOM: *The Waterfront's Two Oceans Aquarium: a marine wonderland.*

pubs, craft markets, entertainment centres, a small brewery (superb draught ale) and wine centre. One of the main attractions is the Victoria Wharf, a speciality retail complex of shops, eateries, cinemas, a huge fish market, fresh produce market and parking for around 3,000 cars.
• Open quaysides, graceful promenades and public squares. A walkway and, possibly, a Venetian-style waterway leading into the city are featured among plans for the future.
• A world-class oceanarium with transparent underwater tunnels, which give visitors the sensation of 'walking on the ocean floor'.
• A new up-market leisure-craft basin, beautifully fashioned from the shell of the old, bleakly functional tank-farm.
• The 4,000 m² (13,123 ft²) South African Maritime Museum, which features the world of shipping, wreck salvage and a wealth of maritime memorabilia. Just along the quayside you'll find its two floating exhibits, the historic *SAS Somerset* (the world's only surviving boom vessel) and the steam tug *Alwyn Vintcent*.
• The breathtaking Imax cinematic experience. Pin-sharp, almost three-dimensional images are projected onto a five-storey-high screen (housed

jewellery, basketware, township art, African beadwork and much else is on view (and on sale) in the adjacent Red Shed craft workshop. Another venue worth visiting is the excellent Waterfront Art and Craft Market.

Although the waterfront development is aimed at both locals and the tourist market, it is by no means exclusively a tourist enterprise: it functions as a worked-in, lived-in area as well as an entertainment venue. The graving dock continues to operate, fishing boats still use the basin, and offices and upmarket apartments are beginning to make their appearance.

in the BMW Pavilion) which, in conjunction with powerful multi-speaker sound, produces something akin to virtual reality.

• A spendid array of outlets for the exploratory shopper. The main centre is the cavernous King's Warehouse (part of the Victoria Wharf), which houses a multitude of enticing stores ranging from a biltong (sun-dried meat) bar to the trendiest and most up-market of fashion boutiques. It also offers a cornucopia of produce and fine-food shops. Ceramics, textiles,

PENINSULA: WEST COAST

The western, or Atlantic, shoreline is characterized by rocky indentations, one beautiful stretch of wide beach and charming bays around which cluster some of the Peninsula's more affluent suburbs and villages. The route – Beach Road, which turns into Victoria Drive, or the M6 – begins at Green Point and Sea Point on the city's western fringes and winds its way, ultimately as Chapman's Peak Drive, to Scarborough, some 54 km (34 miles) to the south. The scenery along the way is always attractive, sometimes breathtaking.

The western strip is a prime holiday area. Many sun-worshippers prefer this side of the Peninsula to the east: the water ir icy cold, but the lovely white beaches are sheltered from the prevailing summer south-easter.

SEA POINT

A busy, vibrant, crowded, cosmopolitan seaside suburb. Parts of it have become shabby in recent years – the Victoria and Alfred Waterfront has enticed away trade – but luxurious apartment buildings still line the elegant, palm-graced beachfront and time-share is much in evidence; hotels, delis, restaurants, discos and other nightspots are everywhere. A bright, glitzy, often noisy place, and full of fun and action if you are in the mood.

CLIFTON

The area is known, and well patronized during summer, for its magnificently broad white beaches – four of them, all sheltered from the wind by the bulky mass of Lion's Head and much favoured by the beautiful people. The backing slopes support expensive-looking holiday cottages, houses and small luxury apartments. On your left, for several kilometres as you drive south, are the Twelve Apostles, a series of imposing, often cloud-wreathed peaks that form part of the Table Mountain range.

CAMPS BAY AND LLANDUDNO

Similar to Clifton but larger and perhaps even richer: some stunning houses have been built into the cliffs. There are shops, the lively Theatre on the Bay, a lovely beach, a large tidal pool and an imaginatively conceived hotel called The Bay.

After a winding and dramatically scenic 15 km (9 miles) drive along a by-now virtually deserted coastline you reach Llandudno, a small, exclusive seaside village. It has a quite spectacular setting, hugging the precipitous slopes beneath a peak called Little Lion's Head. From the viewing spot on Victoria Drive the place looks like Toy Town, and is much photographed.

HOUT BAY

An enchanting town and fishing harbour nestling in a wide, green, hill-flanked valley. In translation the name means 'Wood Bay', derived from its value as a source of timber in the earliest colonial days. Tourism and fisheries are now its main industries. It is the headquarters of the Peninsula's crayfishing fleet, though crayfish are not the only sea harvest: in June

OPPOSITE: *One of Clifton's four world-renowned and fashionable beaches.*
ABOVE: *The snoek catch at Hout Bay.*

and July vast quantities of snoek are caught offshore and sold on the quayside; the annual and very popular Snoek Festival is held during this period. Attractions include:

THE HARBOUR, full of fishing boats and yachts in a picturesque setting of sea and mountain. From here one may embark on launch trips around the coast. On the quayside is Mariner's Wharf, an emporium modelled on its namesake in San Francisco (fresh fish and live lobster, nautical gifts and curios, and an atmospheric seafood bistro/restaurant). There are imaginative schemes for further waterfront development.

HOUT BAY MUSEUM in Andrews Road: natural and cultural history of the area from prehistoric times to the modern fishing industry.

KRONENDAL, a Cape Dutch H-plan homestead on Main Road, built in 1800 and now a national monument, housing an excellent restaurant.

THE WORLD OF BIRDS, in Hout Bay Valley. This is the country's largest bird park, attracting upwards of 100,000 visitors a year. The aviaries are beautifully landscaped to simulate natural habitat; you walk through while the inmates (more than 3,000, belonging to some 450 different species) carry on with their busy lives.

The marine route from Hout Bay then continues, in a dramatic and scenic 10 km (6 miles) stretch, over:

CHAPMAN'S PEAK DRIVE Here, the road cuts through different strata of granite and sandstone and the rock faces are attractively multicoloured, red and yellow predominating. At its highest point the drive skirts cliffs that plunge almost sheer to the sea some 600 m (1,969 ft) below, and there are magnificent views, from

the picnic sites and look-out points, of Chapman's Bay and its wide expanse of beach, and of Hout Bay and its distinctive Sentinel peak. You then descend into the flat, low, marshy plain of Noordhoek, until recently a relatively isolated rural settlement but now a fast-developing suburb. The beach here is broad, long, windy, excellent for surfing but not recommended for casual swimming.

Final port of call on the west coast route is:
SCARBOROUGH, a tiny cluster of cottages set in heath-type countryside. Here, you turn inland to reach the entrance to the:

CAPE OF GOOD HOPE NATURE RESERVE

The reserve, about 70 km (43 miles) from Cape Town city centre, covers an area of 7,750 ha (19,150 acres) with a coastline of about 40 km (25 miles), and is noted more for its floral diversity – indigenous *fynbos*, with some annoying and in places seriously threatening alien encroachment – than for its fauna. In springtime (September and October) the wild flowers are a delight. Animals to be seen include bontebok (a type of antelope once threatened with extinction; see page 195), Cape mountain zebra, springbok, steenbok, Cape grysbok, grey rhebok, red hartebeest, eland, duiker, Cape fox, caracal and chacma baboon, of which there are four troops.

These baboons are thought to be unique within the primate world – if, that is, we exclude man himself – in that their diet consists largely of marine foods, which they garner at low tide. They also feed on tourist handouts, which poses something of a problem: they have become too familiar with and dependent on visitors. If thwarted they can be annoyingly persistent and even aggressive (in which case they simply have to be put down). The troop near Cape Point is adept at raiding cars. Don't feed these animals, and lock your vehicle.

Over 160 species of bird have been recorded in the reserve, ranging from the reintroduced ostrich down to minuscule sunbirds. Marine life is interesting: species found along the western coast differ from those of the eastern waters.

Within the reserve, which is open throughout the year, there is an extensive network of roads; picnic spots with barbecue facilities; viewsites; some pleasant walks and trails, and a restaurant and gift shop. There are fairly ambitious (but environment-friendly) plans to upgrade the visitor facilities.

CAPE POINT

The Point part of the reserve is the finest of viewsites. One either walks up (which is hard going) or takes the shuttle bus, and the vistas, from the base of the old lighthouse, are unforgettable: albatross, gannet, petrel and gull wheel over and around the Point; the cliffs fall sheer to the sea, and one can often spot whale, dolphin and seal in the blue depths far below.

It is off Cape Point that the *Flying Dutchman*, the phantom ship with its broken mast and tattered sails, is destined to sail the seas until the end of time. The legend originated in the 17th century, when the Dutch captain Hendrik van der Decken, his storm-tossed ship foundering, swore to round the Point even if it took until Doomsday. Providence took him at his word, and many 'sightings' have been recorded, notably by the future King George V while he was serving as a Royal Navy midshipman.

PENINSULA: EAST COAST

The eastern shoreline is lapped by the warm (summer average 22 °C/72 °F), blue and often wind-blown waters of False Bay, which stretches in a wide arc from Cape Point northward and then eastward to the Hottentots Holland Mountains, a range which projects into the sea at Cape Hangklip. The bay is so named because early navigators, bound for Table Bay, mistook the Point for Hangklip – a costly error: wind and current are perverse, and over the centuries there have been a great many shipwrecks.

The bay is one of the country's main angling, surfing and boating areas (and, incidentally, a treasure-house for marine biologists). It is fringed by a 35 km (22 miles), almost continuous stretch of beach; on its southern shores are a scatter of seaside towns and resort villages linked by rail and by the coastal road.

MUIZENBERG

A rather old-fashioned town, notable for its turn-of-the-century villas, boarding houses and (converted) fishermen's cottages, and until recently one of the southern hemisphere's best-known seaside resorts. Rudyard Kipling loved it ('white as the sands of Muizenberg,' he wrote, 'spun before the gale'); so did the Victorian and Edwardian gentry, Cecil John Rhodes and many of the Rand's holidaying multi-millionaires.

Rhodes spent his last years in Barkly Cottage (now called Rhodes Cottage), on Main Road between Muizenberg and St James. The house, which contains personal relics of the controversial politician and financier, is now a museum.

DE POST HUYS, Main Road, built in 1673 as an observation post and small fort, and today the oldest habitable building in South Africa.

NATALE LABIA MUSEUM, Main Road, named in honour of Count Natale Labia (1877–1936) and his wife Princess Ida Louise (1879–1961). Furniture, works of art; open Tuesday to Sunday.

MUIZENBERG BEACH A gently sloping expanse of sand; no rocks, few pebbles, safe bathing. Muizenberg walkway is a 15-minute stroll along the coast to St James, starting out from the Muizenberg Pavilion.

ST JAMES, directly to the south of Muizenberg overlooking False Bay. The hillside village has a pleasant beach, and is favoured by the quieter type of holiday-maker.

KALK BAY means 'Lime Bay', so named after the kilns where shells were burnt to make lime for painting buildings. This small fishing centre and resort is much photographed by visitors; very busy during snoek season (June/July). Fresh fish sales are a feature of harbour life.

OPPOSITE TOP: *The massive headland of Cape Point, at the southern tip of the Peninsula.*
OPPOSITE BOTTOM: *Colourful bathing huts add to the rather Victorian charm of St James.*
ABOVE: *The sweeping sands of Muizenberg.*

THE KALKBAAIBERG hills that rise behind the shoreline between Kalk Bay and Muizenberg are popular among hikers, ramblers, naturalists and those who like exploring caves, of which there is a profusion in this wild and rocky area.

SIMON'S TOWN

The town, terminus of the Peninsula railway line, was named in honour of Simon van der Stel. The early and accomplished Dutch governor of the Cape explored the bay in 1687 and recommended it as safe winter anchorage. It was the Royal Navy's main South Atlantic base from 1810 to 1957, when the dockyards were taken over by the South African Navy. There are fine beaches and walking trails, including a Saturday morning 1.2 km (0.75 miles) guided Historical Walk. Features of interest include:

SIMON'S TOWN MUSEUM (formerly The Residency) in Court Road features naval and local history displays.
SOUTH AFRICAN NAVAL MUSEUM, on the West Dockyard, also houses intriguing exhibits relating to ships, sailors and the sea.
JUBLIEE SQUARE, in which stands the statue of Able Seaman Just Nuisance, a Great Dane dog who befriended, and was much loved by, British sailors during the Second World War. He was formally attested into the Royal Navy. On his death Just Nuisance was buried with full military honours, 200 officers and men standing to attention as a volley rang out and the Last Post sounded.
THE STEMPASTORIE, the original Dutch Reformed parsonage, is now a museum featuring the story of South Africa's national emblems (anthem, coat of arms and flag).
WARRIOR TOY MUSEUM, in St George's Street, contains an intriguing exhibition of dolls, lead soldiers, miniature cars and trains.
TOPSTONES, off the Red Hill Road leading to the west coast, is a large gemstone factory. Visitors are introduced to the manufacturing

ABOVE: *A jackass penguin makes his way across Boulders Beach. These birds are strictly protected.*
OPPOSITE TOP: *Rhodes Memorial, a monument to 'the immense and brooding spirit'.*
OPPOSITE BOTTOM: *Jogging in the Newlands area.*

and polishing processes, and encouraged to fossick in the 'scratch-patch', a dump containing many beautiful gemstone fragments. What you find you may keep, providing you buy a container from the factory.

THE BOULDERS, a rocky stretch of coastline south of Simon's Town. Here there are numerous inlets, pools, secluded little beaches and a protected colony of jackass penguins.

PENINSULA: INLAND

The central portions of the Cape Peninsula are heavily residential along the suburban railway line but in many other parts and, especially on the mountain slopes, quite beautifully treed. These woodland mantles are at their most attractive around Constantiaberg and Tokai and in the Silvermine Reserve.

The nearest 'suburb' to the city is Zonnebloem, a largely deserted, grass-covered area better known by the colloquial and historic name of District Six (*see* panel, page 217).

RONDEBOSCH

Site of the Dutch colony's first wheat-growing experiment, launched in 1656 near a distinctively round grove of trees (the area was known as 't Ronde Doorn Bosjen at the time); now a major suburb embracing the famed Groote Schuur Estate, bequeathed to the nation by Cecil Rhodes on his death. This sprawls over part of Rondebosch and neighbouring suburbs, on the lower slopes of Table Mountain. The most prominent elements of the estate are:
THE UNIVERSITY OF CAPE TOWN and its teaching hospital, Groote Schuur, where the first heart transplant operation in the world was performed – by Professor Chris Barnard and his excellent cardiac team – in 1967. The university is the oldest in the country (it started life as the South African College in 1829) and probably the most attractive: the spectacular heights of Devil's Peak provide its backdrop and the campus's stately, ivy-covered buildings provide a breathtaking view across to Milnerton on the coastal plain and Table Bay beyond.
GROOTE SCHUUR or 'Great Barn'. The mansion was originally used as a 17th-century granary which was later converted into a house (which burned down) and finally reconstructed for Rhodes by Sir Herbert Baker to create a grand, but essentially simple, home that now serves as the State President's official residence. It was recently renamed Genadendal.

RHODES MEMORIAL, an impressively imperialistic, classical-style 'temple' set some distance up Devil's Peak. The memorial incorporates GF Watts's fine statue, 'Physical Energy', and a large bust of Rhodes beneath which is inscribed part of Kipling's moving tribute to a man who, whatever his faults – and they were many – was undeniably a powerful force in the shaping of the subcontinent during the latter part of the 19th century: 'The immense and brooding spirit shall quicken and control. Living he was the land, and dead, his soul shall be her soul.'

It is a pleasant walk to the memorial, from which there are fine views over the suburbs towards the Hottentots Holland Mountains.
MOSTERT'S MILL, along Rhodes Drive, just below the university campus, is one of Cape Town's best-known landmarks. Built in 1796 as a 'horse' mill, it was restored with the help of the Netherlands government in 1936. The mill is not functional, although there are plans in the pipeline to make it so.

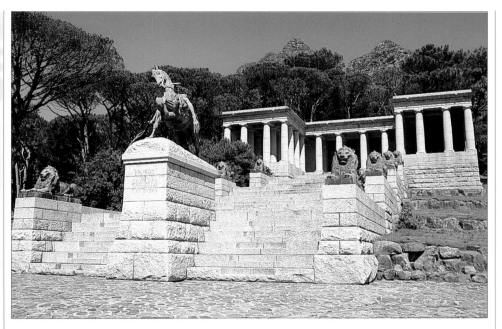

NEWLANDS

A large, fashionable and generally attractive suburb 9.5 km (6 miles) from the city centre, noted among other things for its exceptionally high rainfall (more than 150 cm/59 in per year), for the beautiful homestead that once belonged to the social commentator and letter-writer Lady Anne Barnard and which is now the Vineyard Hotel, and for its famed rugby and cricket grounds, venues for both provincial and international matches.

THE JOSEPHINE WATERMILL is situated at the entrance to the Newlands rugby stadium. Built during 1840, named after the Queen of Sweden and powered by the Liesbeek River, the building and its massive waterwheel have been meticulously restored (by university students and the Historical Society) and is in excellent working order. There are milling demonstrations every day as well as a permanent blacksmithing exhibit. Open from Monday to Friday. Conducted tours from 10h00 to 14h00. The first floor of the mill serves as the:

NEWLANDS RUGBY MUSEUM, the largest of its kind in the world. It houses a fascinating collection of exhibits and mementos dating as far back as 1891, when South Africa entered the international rugby arena for the first time (the

visiting British team, which was captained by WE Maclagan, conceded just one try in the 19 matches played against the local sides). Open from Monday to Friday as well as on those Saturdays for which important matches have been scheduled.

NEWLANDS FOREST The main road past the university (De Waal Drive, which changes to Rhodes Drive, which in turn becomes Union Avenue) is a scenic joy: there are lovely trees everywhere along the route and on the hillsides that rise grandly above, and the verges and centre islands support a profusion of flowering plants. To your right, driving away from the city, is Newlands Forest, a favourite among picnickers, walkers and joggers.

CONSTANTIA

Not so much a suburb as an extensive area of attractive wooded parkland, valley and hill on the northern uplands of the Table Mountain range. Constantia homes tend to be spacious, luxurious and secluded. It is also the location of some of the country's most historic mansions (*see* panel, right).

If you turn right at the intersection of Union and Rhodes avenues (*see* Newlands Forest, above) and follow the route for about 2 km (1.25 miles) on the right will be the entrance to: **KIRSTENBOSCH,** one of the world's leading botanic gardens and headquarters of South Africa's National Botanic Gardens network. It was established in 1913 on yet another parcel of land bequeathed to the nation by Cecil Rhodes: 560 ha (1,384 acres) of lush terrain extending over the mountain slopes to Maclear's Beacon. Here, some 9,000 of the country's 18,000 indigenous flowering plant species are cultivated – mesembryanthemums, pelargoniums, proteas, ericas, ferns, cycads and many others. The Compton Herbarium, within the grounds, has over 200,000 plant specimens.

Part of Jan van Riebeeck's hedge of wild almond, which enclosed the first Dutch settlement and which is now the oldest national monument, can still be seen on the property. Also of interest is the spring, lined with Batavian bricks and shaped like a bird, which is popularly but incorrectly known as Lady Anne Barnard's bath. There are delightful walks along the many pathways; expert guides are available; for the blind, a perfume garden and the Braille walk have been laid out. There's a pleasant restaurant within the grounds which also host Sunday open-air concerts. Open daily.

From the T-junction just beyond Kirstenbosch, Rhodes Drive bears right and winds its way up the slopes to Constantia Nek – a magnificent scenic drive. Above the road is:

CONSTANTIA'S GRACEFUL HOMESTEADS

Groot Constantia, by far the stateliest of the Cape's historic mansions, was originally designed and built, with loving care, by Simon van der Stel, the outstanding early Cape governor and a man of impeccable taste. He lived there until his death in 1712.

In 1778 the estate was taken over by Hendrik Cloete, who added a particularly fine wine-cellar and developed the vineyards to produce wine of legendary quality, sweet and rich vintages that found their way to the royal tables of Europe and whose praises were sung by poets. The Cloete wine-making secrets did not survive the passing of the estate's vintners, but the Constantia Valley continues to produce a range of fine reds, some of them awarded the rare 'Superior' accolade. Constantia wines are much sought-after and tend to be in short supply.

The farmstead, now owned by the government and a national monument, was burned down in 1925 but has been superlatively restored to its former glory. It is notable for its Cape Dutch architecture, splendid period furniture, Chinese, Japanese, Rhenish and Delft porcelain collections, and for its two-storeyed cellar, designed by Louis Thibault.

The cellar's exquisite cherub-adorned pediment is the work of renowned sculptor Anton Anreith. The adjacent museum tells the story of wine and wine-making through the centuries. From the homestead an oak-lined avenue leads to an ornamental pool in which the Augustan owners and their guests once bathed, and where the smiling and berobed ghost of Van der Stel is reported to have been seen. The house, museum and wine-cellar are open to the public daily.

Groot Constantia is one of three functioning wine farms in the Constantia Valley. As attractive in their own, slightly more modest way are Klein Constantia, a lovely old (1796) farmstead rescued from urban assault, neglect and decay by Capetonian Douglas Jooste, who has renovated it beautifully; and Buitenverwachting, also resurrected, the gabled house, stables, cellars and slave quarters faultlessly restored. Buitenverwachting has an especially inviting restaurant. For further details of the Constantia wine route, *see* pages 238–239.

Part of the lovely Kirstenbosch gardens.

CECILIA FOREST is an entrancing place for communing with nature, for picnicking and for taking long walks. There are many winding tracks and paths as well as a circular mountain-biking route. The Cecilia waterfall is worth finding your way to. At the top of Rhodes Drive is the Constantia Nek restaurant, and here the route divides, the road to your right leading down to Hout Bay valley (*see* page 228), that to your left taking you through the lush and fertile wine-producing countryside of Constantia, and to Groot Constantia, its most notable farmstead (*see* panel, opposite). From Constantia Valley a short, pleasant drive north-eastwards will bring you to Tokai Forest (walks and picnic spots) and, nearby, to the:

SILVERMINE NATURE RESERVE, lying to the north of Tokai Forest and accessible via the scenically enchanting, convoluted Ou Kaapse-weg ('Old Cape Road'), a favourite among Sunday drivers. An unspoilt wilderness area that extends from Muizenberg and Kalk Bay on the east coast to Noordhoek Peak in the west, the reserve is very popular among picnickers and ramblers. Grand views unfold from the walk to the heights above the reservoir.

RONDEVLEI NATURE RESERVE, to the east, is a vital waterfowl wetland and ornithological research station, haven to 220 bird species, 70 of which breed within its 137 ha (339 acres) area. The reserve comprises a shallow lake (or vlei), marshland and indigenous bush, a picnic area and interesting small museum, and a number of observation points and waterside hides. A mecca for bird-watchers. Open daily; the best months to visit are January to April.

CITY LIFE

Shopping

The city centre's major retail areas are the Golden Acre and its adjoining concourse, Adderley Street, St George's Mall and, on the seaward fringes, the Victoria and Alfred Waterfront.

BUYING CHEAP If you're bargain-hunting for standard items, you could do a lot worse than go straight to the manufacturer. Pam Black's *A–Z of Factory Shops* is a useful guide. Otherwise, try Pick 'n Pay Hypermarket in Ottery – it stocks just about everything you could possibly need or want, at competitive prices.

SPECIALITY SHOPPING Among the more rewarding venues are (again) the Waterfront, Claremont's Cavendish Square (90 up-market

outlets, restaurants, art exhibitions, concerts; open till late) and the similar but smaller Link complex next door. The city also offers an abundance of art, craft and curio outlets; ask Captour for further details.

MARKETS For fun shopping, there are three major permanent open-air markets: in Greenmarket Square, on the Grand Parade and at the railway station. They offer a great deal of junk, some good buys and a few real bargains. Also permanent but a lot more stylish are the Waterfront's Art and Craft Market and the stalls in its Red Shed (*see* page 227).

Open-air markets are held sporadically at many suburban venues, mostly over weekends and public holidays and mostly under the auspices of the Cape Crafters' Association. Among the best are the Groot Constantia Sunday craft

LEFT: *The Grand Parade, once used for military drills, now serves as a marketplace.*
BELOW: *Open-air music and other shows are a feature of the Victoria and Alfred Waterfront.*
OPPOSITE: *Hundreds of minstrel troupes, each bedecked in its group finery, gather in central Cape Town for the New Year Coon Carnival.*

fair; the Constantia craft market at nearby Alphen, and the Kirstenbosch market (opposite the garden's entrance). Again, a lot of the handwork is rather ordinary, but if you take your time you'll find both the unusual and the exquisite. Captour has full details.

ANTIQUES There is plenty to explore in this field, but beware of tourist traps. Available at hotels and from Captour is Shirley Kelner's booklet on the 'Antique Route'. Long Street (*see* page 221) is a good place to start. Best of the open-air antique fairs is on Church Street.

Theatre and music

Cape Town's two main performing arts venues are the Nico and the Baxter theatre complexes.

THE NICO (DF Malan Street, Foreshore). Three auditoriums: the Opera House (1,200 seats), the Theatre (550 seats) and the Arena (120 seats). Opera and drama, of course, but also some outstanding ballet and oratorio, and lighter presentations (operetta and modern musicals), mostly staged under the auspices of the Cape Performing Arts Board (Capab), which has a resident orchestra. Restaurant; undercover parking.

THE BAXTER (Main Road, Rondebosch). This lively complex is an integral part of the University of Cape Town; 657-seat theatre; 100-seat studio/workshop; 640-seat concert hall. Popular theatre and music but also local and, occasionally, experimental drama. Restaurant.

SMALLER VENUES There are several of these, including the Herschel in Claremont, the Masque in Muizenberg, and the Little Theatre and UCT Arena in Orange Street, Gardens. The leading privately run venues are the Theatre on the Bay, in Camps Bay, which puts on excellent (professional) shows in its 400-seat auditorium, and the Victoria and Alfred and Dock Road theatres at the Waterfront. There are also many intimate cabaret venues, notably Elaines in Observatory and Chaplins in Sea Point.

THE CAPE TOWN SYMPHONY ORCHESTRA performs regular concerts (on Thursdays and Sundays) in the City Hall. The programmes are suitably varied to cater for most tastes in classical music and are published well in advance.

LIVE ENTERTAINMENT The jazz and nightspot scene is attractively animated; much of the activity takes place around Loop and Long streets as well as at the Victoria and Alfred Waterfront. The entertainment scene changes constantly; consult Captour or the relevant section of the local newspapers.

Wining and dining

City and Peninsula have a lot to offer the lover of fine food. Captour brings out an annual *Restaurant Guide*, and there are several intelligently opinionated books on the shelves of most good bookshops. A select list of Cape Town restaurants appears on pages 244–245.

237

Sport and recreation

SUN, SEA AND SAND The Peninsula has nearly 150 km (93 miles) of coastline, much of it ideal for beach leisure, bathing, boating, surfing and fishing. The western waters are chilly but many of the beaches are pleasantly sheltered from the south-easter and favoured by sun-worshippers. Conversely, the eastern (False Bay) side tends to be windy but the sea is warm.

Currents, backwash and the odd rogue break-er put bathers at risk along some stretches. Warning notices will tell you which parts to avoid but, still, if you're a first-time visitor you'd be wise to seek advice from someone who knows. Generally, it's sensible to stick to the more popular areas – those monitored by lifesavers, and patrolled by beach constables.

Some of the region's more pleasant stretches of sand are those at Milnerton, Clifton (four fashionable beaches), Camps Bay, Noordhoek (Long Beach beckons the horseback rider and seeker of solitude), in the Cape of Good Hope Nature Reserve and along much of the eastern (False Bay) coast, most notably at Muizenberg.

For the rest, Cape Town and the Peninsula offer splendid opportunities for sea-angling, scuba-diving, sailing and other watersports, bird-watching, jogging, cycling, golf, bowls, tennis and squash. City and suburbs are also well served by health-and-fitness centres.

ABOVE: *A gentle ride on the wide white sands of Noordhoek's Long Beach.*
OPPOSITE TOP: *Chapman's Peak Drive, between Hout Bay and Noordhoek, is among the Peninsula's most spectacular routes.*
OPPOSITE BOTTOM: *Klein Constantia, a charming venue on the Cape Peninsula's wine route.*

GETTING AROUND

Day drives

The Western Cape is scenically outstanding; nearly every part of the Cape Peninsula, and of the Winelands to the north (*see* following chapter) is worthwhile exploring.

PENINSULA ROUTES The most obvious, and among the most pleasant, of the longer local routes is that which follows the Peninsula's coastline in circular fashion – from Sea Point along Victoria Drive, through Hout Bay, over Chapman's Peak Drive and on to Cape Point, returning via the eastern (False Bay) shoreline. A shorter option is to turn inland at Hout Bay to take in the Constantia estates (*see* below) and the lovely Kirstenbosch Botanical Gardens, returning to the city on the M3.

THE WINE ROUTE around the three splendid Constantia homesteads can either be incorporated into the shorter circular drive or undertaken as a separate journey, with a pub lunch.

• **Buitenverwachting.** Excellent restaurant; gabled and thatched cellar; maiden vintage from the new vines appeared in 1985 and the wines have since won international awards. Cellar tours by appointment, Monday to Friday 11h00 to 15h00; wine sales and tastings: weekdays 09h00 to 17h00, Saturday 09h00 to 13h00. The restaurant is among the country's best; one can also order (in advance) a picnic meal.

• **Klein Constantia.** Beautiful homestead, more private than the other two; no restaurant. After a 49-year break the estate's first wine, the 1986 sauvignon blanc, was adjudged best white at the South African Wine Show. Cellar tours by appointment; wine sales: weekdays 09h00 to 17h00, Saturdays 09h00 to 13h00.

• **Groot Constantia.** Guided tours through the cellars are undertaken hourly, between 10h00 and 16h00; daily wine sales 10h00 to 17h00. A variety of gentle walks along the estate's footpaths; two superb restaurants: the up-market Jonkershuis (traditional Cape lunches and teas) and the more informal Tavern (buffet meals) or simply pack a picnic basket and relax on the shady lawns behind the cellars.

FARTHER AFIELD The many wine routes of the hinterland are renowned, and deservedly so. Those within convenient proximity to Cape Town are the Stellenbosch, Paarl and the Vignerons de Franschhoek (*see* page 251).

However, there is a lot more to the region than its vineyards, and an impressive number of other routes have been established, giving the visitor a choice of general and specialist

interests. They include the Fruit Routes, the Jazz Route, the Wool Tour of the southern seaboard, the Afrikaanse Taal (Language) Route, the Huguenot Route, the Arts and Crafts Route of the Peninsula and the Cape Winelands (maps available from Captour and Satour), the Antique Route of the Peninsula, Somerset West, Stellenbosch and Paarl, the Wreck Route along the south and west coasts, the Whale Route along False and Walker bays ... and so on.

Advice, brochures and maps are available from Captour's Visitors' Information Centre.

TOURS AND TRIPS A great many coach and minibus half- and full-day trips are on offer. Most tour operators cover the west and east coasts of the Peninsula, Cape Point, Constantia and Kirstenbosch, mountain, bay and harbour, and places farther afield – the Winelands, southern seaboard (including the Garden Route) and the West Coast.

Walks and trails

As we've seen, the best way to explore the city itself is to wander the streets on foot: practically everything that's worth seeing is within gentle walking distance. One recommended route is described on page 219, but, if you would like a more detailed and firmer itinerary, ask Captour for information on city walks.

However, a word of caution: there's a lot of poverty in and around Cape Town; crime generally and street crime in particuclar are cause for concern; crime is high, the unwary risk muggings. Take the basic precautions: the main streets and open spaces of the city and of most suburbs are quite safe during the busy daylight hours; at other times it's wise to take your urban ramble in company, preferably in a group. Prime (and safe) walking and hiking areas are along stretches of the west and east coasts; in the Cape of Good Hope Nature Reserve; inland around Fish Hoek, Hout Bay and Constantia, and of course on the many slopes of Table Mountain (the latter should be planned).

ABOVE: *The view from Chapman's Peak Drive, taking in Hout Bay and, at left, the distinctive Sentinel massif.*
OPPOSITE: *Two young climbers gaze across city and suburb from the summit of Table Mountain.*

ADVISORY: CAPE TOWN AND THE PENINSULA

CLIMATE

Mediterranean; winter rainfall. Summers: warm to hot, cooled by frequent and strong south-easterlies. Winters: cold and wet periods interspersed with warmer, sunny spells and, sometimes, by hot 'berg wind' conditions. Best weather: spring (September), autumn and early winter (March–June).

MAIN ATTRACTIONS

The mountain ❑ Sun, sea and sand ❑ The Victoria and Alfred Waterfront ❑ The Constantia wine estates ❑ Cape winelands ❑ Botanical and public gardens ❑ Historic buildings ❑ Fine hotels, restaurants, shops and tourist amenities.

TRAVEL

Road. Cape Town is 1,421 km/883 miles from Johannesburg; 1,479 km/919 miles from Pretoria; 1,776 km/1,104 miles from Durban; 790 km/491 miles from Port Elizabeth; 1,015 km/631 miles from Bloemfontein and 1,500 km/932 miles from Windhoek.

These cities are linked by a network of excellent national highways. The main route northwards to Johannesburg, Pretoria and the Zimbabwe border at Beit Bridge (this was originally the first section of Cecil Rhodes's over-ambitious Cape-to-Cairo highway) is the N1, which passes through the lovely Cape Winelands and, via the toll-gated Huguenot Tunnel, through the high Du Toits Kloof Mountains before entering the arid vastness of the Great Karoo. Other major routes include the N2 eastwards (inland to Mossel Bay, coastal thereafter) to Port Elizabeth, Grahamstown and eventually to Durban and beyond to the Swaziland border, and the N7 that runs up through Namaqualand to Namibia (*see* pages 263–275).

Coach travel: Intercity semi-luxury bus services run between Cape Town, Johannesburg and Pretoria, via Bloemfontein and Kimberley.

Rail. Railway passenger services connect Cape Town with all major centres in South Africa, Namibia, Botswana and Zimbabwe.

Air. Cape Town International Airport: 22 km/14 miles from the city centre, off the N2 highway. Regular services connect all major centres, and there is an increasing number of direct flights to European and other overseas destinations. Passenger services and information: tel. (021) 93-62357. South African Airways central reservations: tel. (021) 403-1111. There is bus transport between the city terminal and airport.

TRAVEL WITHIN CAPE TOWN AND PENINSULA

City and Peninsula rail, bus and taxi services are quite adequate. Major international car-hire companies have offices, as do local car-, camper- and caravan-hire firms. Tour operators offer a choice of one-day and half-day scenic coach, air and sea trips. For more information, contact Captour.

ACCOMMODATION

The Peninsula is a prime tourist area; visitors have a choice of good hotels, guest-houses, holiday apartments and hideaways. Book in advance for December and January, the prime vacation months (when many hoteliers and landlords increase their rates).

The following is a representative but not exhaustive selection of hotels. Full details on accommodation can be obtained from Captour or from your travel agent.

Select Hotels

CITY AND FRINGES

Cape Sun Inter-Continental ***** Strand St. Skyscraper linked to shopping concourse; 350 rooms and suites; restaurants; cocktail bar; conference facilities available. PO Box 4532, Cape Town 8000; tel. (021) 23-8844, fax 23-8875, central reservations (011) 482-3500.

Cape Swiss Hotel *** On the lower slopes of mountain. 40 rooms, 4 suites; restaurant. PO Box 6856, Rogge Bay 8012; tel. (021) 23-8190, fax 26-1795.

Capetonian Protea Hotel **** Off Heerengracht. Near theatre, harbour and city centre; 169 rooms; à la carte restaurant; breakfast and buffet/luncheon restaurant; five 100-seat conference venues. PO Box 6856, Rogge Bay 8012; tel. (021) 21-1150, fax 25-2215, toll-free reservations 0800 11 9000.

Holiday Inn Garden Court: De Waal *** Gardens. 127 rooms, 3 suites; à la carte restaurant; bar; pool; conference facilities. PO Box 2793, Cape Town 8000; tel. (021) 45-1311, fax 461-6648, central reservations (011) 482-3500.

Holiday Inn Garden Court: Greenmarket Square *** Central. Pleasant piazza setting; 171 rooms; à la carte restaurant; terrace meals; bar. PO Box 3775, Cape Town 8000; tel. (021) 23-2040, fax 23-3664, central reservations (011) 482-3500.

Holiday Inn Garden Court: St. George's *** Central. 137 rooms; restaurant; conference facilities available. PO Box 5616, Cape Town 8000; tel. (021) 419-0808, fax 419-7010, central reservations (011) 482-3500.

Mount Nelson ***** Gardens area. One of the world's most elegant hotels; personal service and exquisite cuisine; 159 rooms and suites; 2 pools; tennis; extensive conference facilities. PO Box 2608, Cape Town 8000; tel. (021) 23-1000, fax 24-7472.

Town House Hotel **** Central. Close to Parliament; 104 rooms; lovely à la carte restaurant; bar; heated pool and health club. PO Box 5053, Cape Town 8000; tel. (021) 45-7050, fax 45-3891.

Tulbagh Protea Hotel *** Central. 49 rooms, 4 suites; à la carte restaurant; 2 bars; conference facilities. PO Box 2891, Cape Town 8000; tel. (021) 21-5140, fax 21-4648, toll-free reservations 0800 11 9000.

WATERFRONT

Breakwater Lodge Old prison area (imaginatively converted) alongside the Graduate School of Business. 330 en suite rooms; à la carte and self-service restaurants; bar; conference facilities. PO Box 41465, Sea Point 8060; tel. (021) 406-1911, fax 406-1070.

City Lodge: Victoria & Alfred Waterfront ** Waterfront. Good value; 160 en suite rooms; breakfast room (many restaurants nearby); pool. PO Box 6025, Rogge Bay 8012; tel. (021) 419-9450; fax 419-0460.

The Portswood 58 twin rooms, 35 doubles, 9 suites; restaurant (buffet breakfasts/à la carte), terrace meals; bar; pool; conference facilities. PO Box 6221, Rogge Bay 8012; tel. (021) 418-3281, fax 419-7570.

Victoria & Alfred Hotel **** In harbour. 68 rooms; historic, renovated; mountain views; à la carte restaurant; bar; conference facilities. PO Box 50050, Waterfront 8002; tel. (021) 419-6677, fax 419-8955.

RIVIERA

Ambassador Hotel and Executive Suites **** Overlooks sea. 69 rooms; à la carte restaurant (seafood); bar; pool; conference facilities. PO Box 83, Sea Point 8060; tel. (021) 439-6170, fax 439-6336.

Karos Arthur's Seat Hotel **** Sea Point. 117 rooms, 6 suites; à la carte restaurant; 2 bars; swimming pool; conference facilities available. Arthur's Rd, Sea Point 8001; tel. (021) 434-1187, fax 434-9768.

Peninsula All-Suite Hotel **** Luxurious; prime seafront position; 1- to 3-bedroom suites; à la carte restaurant; terrace meals; bar; 2 swimming pools, gym, sauna. PO Box 17188, Regent's Rd, Sea Point 8061; tel. (021) 439-8888, fax 439-8886, toll-free reservations 0800 22 4433.

Ritz Inn Sea Point. 216 rooms, 6 suites; revolving restaurant; bar; pool, jacuzzi; conference facilities. PO Box 27224, Rhine Rd, 8050; tel. (021) 439-6010, fax 434-0809, toll-free reservations 0800 11 9000.

The Bay ***** Camps Bay. Elegant; 65 rooms, 5 suites; 2 restaurants; bar; swimming pool; conference facilities available. PO Box 32021, Camps Bay 8040; tel. (021) 438-4444, fax 438-4455.

Winchester Mansions Hotel *** Seafront. 51 rooms; à la carte restaurant; bar. 221 Beach Rd, Sea Point 8001; tel. (021) 434-2351, fax 434-0215.

SOUTHERN SUBURBS

Alphen Hotel **** Historic (1753) and beautiful Constantia Valley homestead and wine estate; 29 rooms; antiques everywhere; excellent restaurant; also pleasant lunches under oaks; swimming pool; conference facilities available. PO Box 35, Constantia 7848; tel. (021) 794-5011, fax 794-5710.

The Cellars-Hohenort Country House ***** Top-of-the-range hotel situated next to the Kirstenbosch Botanical Gardens. 29 rooms, 1 self-catering flatlet sleeping 4, 3 suites and 8 luxury double rooms; table d'hôte and à la carte restaurant (English, French, traditional Cape cuisine); 2 swimming pools; tennis; 2 small conference venues. PO Box 35, Constantia 7848; tel. (021) 794-2137, fax 794-2149.

City Lodge: Mowbray Golf Club *** Overlooking golf course in near-central suburb. Value-for-money; 130 rooms; restaurant; pool. PO Box 124, Howard Place 7450; tel. (021) 685-7944, fax 685-7997.

Holiday Inn Garden Court: Eastern Boulevard *** Conveniently situated on city fringes (Woodstock suburb). 279 rooms, 2 suites; à la carte and carvery restaurant; pool; conference facilities. PO Box 2979, Cape Town 8000; tel. (021) 47-4060, fax 47-8338, central reservations (011) 482-3500.

Holiday Inn Garden Court: Newlands *** Close to Newlands rugby and cricket grounds. 145 rooms, 5 suites; steakhouse; bar; gym; conference facilities available. Main Rd, Newlands 7700; tel. (021) 61-1105, fax 64-1241, central reservations (011) 482-3500.

Vineyard Hotel **** Historic country house in Newlands area. Built in 1799 and now one of the country's finest hotels; lovely grounds; 124 rooms, 5 suites; excellent à la carte restaurant; coffee shop; bar; pool; gym; conference facilities. PO Box 151, Newlands 7725; tel. (021) 683-3044, fax 683-3365.

EASTERN SEABOARD (FALSE BAY)

Lord Nelson Inn *** Simon's Town. Overlooking harbour; colonial/naval décor; 10 rooms; 2 restaurants; bar (pub meals). 58 St George's St, Simon's Town 7995; tel. (021) 786-1386, fax 786-1009.

Shrimpton Manor ** Muizenberg. Exclusive; hospitable; 21 rooms; excellent restaurant (seafood); conference facilities. 19 Alexander Rd, Muizenberg 7951; tel. (021) 788-1128/9, fax 788-1129.

Self-catering and budget

Cape Town, its suburbs and the wider Peninsula area are extremely well served by guest-houses as well as executive apartments and other self-catering accommodation. Captour has all the details.

Budget: For full information contact Bed 'n Breakfast; tel. (021) 683-3505, fax 683-5159.

Select restaurants:

CITY AND FRINGES

Anatoli, Napier St. Excellent Turkish food in dramatic Middle Eastern surrounds; tel. (021) 419-2501.

The Balkan, Shortmarket St. Eastern European culinary delights; folk music; hospitality; tel. (021) 24-9337.

Buccaneer, Gardens area. Award-winning steakhouse; plus Swiss and other specialities; tel. (021) 24-4966.

Champers, Deer Park Drive. Low-key; friendly; rather formal; cuisine moderne with classic undertones; superlative salads; tel. (021) 45-4335.

Floris Smit Huijs, Church St. Modern and unusual décor; fine food; tel. (021) 23-3414.

The Grill Room, Mount Nelson Hotel, Gardens. Cape Town's most famous hostelry; now impressively restyled. Continental classic-type food in modern setting; light music for dancing. The Garden Room next door is baronial and graceful; attractively conservative menu; impeccable service; tel. (021) 23-1000.

Guido's Alpenstrube, Kloof St, Gardens. Outstanding German, Austrian and Swiss cuisine; tel. (021) 23-5412.

Kaapse Tafel, Queen Victoria St, Gardens. Authentic Cape cooking of the highest order; tel. (021) 23-1651.

Kotobuki, Mill St, Gardens. The very best of Japanese cuisine; tel. (021) 462-3675.

Maria's, Barnett St. Tiny restaurant serving delicious Greek fare; casual and atmospheric; tel. (021) 45-2096.

Nelson's Eye, Hof St, Gardens. Cosy; nautical-pub atmosphere; seafood and delicious meat dishes; charmingly served; tel. (021) 23-2601.

Old Colonial, Barnett St, Gardens. Exceptionally hospitable; restfully old-fashioned décor; varied menu; though there are German and Cape traditional undertones; altogether quite excellent; tel. (021) 45-4909.

Pagoda Inn, Bree St. Cantonese; tel. (021) 25-2033.

Sukhothai, Hof St, adjoining Helmsley Hotel. Thai food that lingers in the memory; tel. (021) 23-4725.

Tastevin, Cape Sun Hotel. Imaginative menu; extensive wine-list; tel. (021) 23-8844.

Rozenhof, Kloof St, Gardens. A quiet and dignified place that serves you the very best; tel. (021) 24-1968.

34 Napier Street. Quiet; tasteful décor; cordon bleu cuisine; tel. (021) 25-1557.

WATERFRONT

Alabama 2000, Waterfront. Floating restaurant; buffet; traditional Cape fare; tel. (021) 419-3122.

Bertie's Big Easy, Fish Quay. Informal; popular; varied menu; live entertainment; tel. (021) 419-2727.

Café San Marco, Victoria Wharf. Joyous Italian food; tel. (021) 418-5434.

Cantina Tequila, Quay Five. Mexican; tel. (021) 419-8313.

Charly's Waterfront Cafe, Victoria Wharf. Mediterranean and health dishes; tel. (021) 418-5522.

The Edge, Pier Head. Seafood; tel. (021) 21-2583.

The Greek Fisherman, Waterfront. What its name suggests; delightfully informal; tel. (021) 418-5411.

The Green Dolphin, Pier Head. Menu for all tastes; jazz while you eat; tel. (021) 21-7471.

Horizons, Fish Quay. Upstairs from the less formal Bertie's Big Easy (*see* separate entry). Cosmopolitan menu; seafood specialities; tel. (021) 419-2727.

Morton's on the Wharf, Victoria Wharf. Cajun and Creole fare in New Orleans-style; tel. (021) 418-3633.

Musselcracker, Victoria Wharf. Buffet with variety of South African seafood dishes; tel. (021) 419-4300.

Nando's Tasca, Shop 154. Portuguese food and décor; most enjoyable; tel. (021) 21-5820.

Panama Jack's, Eastern Mole Rd, Harbour. Treasure-house of seafood; down the road from the fashionable Victoria and Alfred Waterfront; tel. (021) 47-3992.

Peers, Pier Head. International cuisine in memorable setting; tel. (021) 21-7113.

Quay 4. Busy downstairs tavern and upstairs restaurant; seafood specialities; tel. (021) 419-2008.

Sports Café, Victoria Wharf. Generous helpings of good food; TV sportscasts; tel. (021) 419-5558.

Waterfront Cafe, Victoria & Alfred Hotel. French cuisine; nautical setting; tel. (021) 419-6677.

RIVIERA

Andy's Bistro, Sea Point. Just what it sounds like: cheerful, friendly – and good; tel. (021) 439-2470.

Bayside Café, Camps Bay. Superb steaks and seafood; very popular; tel. (021) 438-2650.

Blues, Camps Bay. Varied menu; quality fare superlatively served; tel. (021) 438-2040.

Chaplin's Theatre Restaurant, Sea Point. Charlie Chaplin theme; cabaret; tel. (021) 434-8409.

Delmitchies, Sea Point. Fabulous seafood buffet for set price; tel. (021) 434-6500.

Europa, Sea Point. An elegantly converted old house; seafood specialities; tel. (021) 439-2820.

Jackson's, Peninsula All-Suite Hotel, Sea Point. Top of the range food and décor; tel. (021) 439-8302. The Cafe Bijou terrace restaurant alongside (seafood marvels) is just as inviting; tel. (021) 439-8888.

La Perla, Sea Point. Extremely popular; large menu; tel. (021) 434-2471.

The Round House, the Glen, Camps Bay. Stylish; imaginative fare; lovely setting; tel. (021) 438-2320.

San Marco, Sea Point. Popular; true Italian cuisine; beautiful tableware; tel. (021) 439-2758.

Tarkaris, 305 Main Rd, Sea Point. Indian food at its best; rich décor; tel. (021) 434-4266.

Top of the Ritz, Ritz Protea Hotel, Sea Point. Imaginative *haute cuisine* enjoyed in sky-scraping, revolving room; tel. (021) 439-6010.

SOUTHERN SUBURBS

Africa Café, Lower Main Rd, Observatory. The exotic tastes of Africa, from Malawi to Mali: a memorable experience; tel. (021) 47-9553.

Barristers, Newlands. Standard range of dishes; beautifully prepared and served; popular and often crowded; tel. (021) 64-1792.

Cellars, Cellars-Hohenort Hotel. French country cooking at its best; tel. (021) 794-2137.

Clementine's, Wynberg. Popular; with a youngish clientele; innovative menu; tel. (021) 797-6168.

Constantia Uitsig, In the Peninsula's wine belt. Cuisine draws inspiration from Provence and northern Italy; lovely setting; tel. (021) 794-4490.

The Courtyard, Vineyard Hotel. Outstanding menu; beautiful dining room; tel. (021) 683-3044.

Fisherman's Cottage, Plumstead. Delightful menu; honest food exquisitely prepared; tel. (021) 797-6341.

Jake's, Kenilworth. A friendly place with an innovative menu; tel. (021) 797-0366.

La Scala, Cavendish Square, Claremont. Bistro-type Italian restaurant; lively atmosphere; excellent food. tel. (021) 61-3252 or 61-2394.

La Vita, Newlands. Very popular; Continental cuisine; tel. (021) 685-2051.

Pancho's Lower Main Rd, Observatory. Mexican menu; casual; inexpensive; youthful clientele; fun; tel. (021) 47-4854.

SOUTHERN PENINSULA

Alphen Restaurant (The 1703 Room), Alphen Hotel, Constantia. Formal; gracious; quiet; classic menu and excellent cuisine; tel. (021) 794-5011.

Black Marlin, Miller's Point, near Simon's Town. Enterprising à la carte in Victorian house; on the way to Cape Point; seafood a speciality; tel. (021) 786-1621.

Brass Bell, Waterfront, Kalk Bay. Casual; a favourite among surfing fraternity; seafood features prominently; barbecues on the terrace; tel. (021) 788-5456.

Buitenverwachting, Constantia. Stately home overlooking Constantia Valley (*see* panel page 234); opulent restaurant; superlative cuisine; tel. (021) 794-3522.

Gaylords, Muizenberg. Indian cuisine at its tastiest; tel. (021) 788-5470.

Jonkershuis, Groot Constantia Estate. Superb Cape cuisine in a 300-year-old setting; tel. (021) 794-6255.

Kronendal, Hout Bay. Elegant Cape Dutch homestead; modern dining room; smallish menu; classic dishes; tel. (021) 790-1970.

Shrimpton's, Muizenberg. Emphasis mainly but not exclusively on seafood specialities; excellent sauces; delicious; tel. (021) 788-1128.

Wharfside Grill, the Harbour, Hout Bay. Seafood in atmospheric setting; tel. (021) 790-1100.

NORTHERN AREAS

Blue Peter, Blue Peter Hotel, Bloubergstrand. Fine food; French influence; overlooking sea; dinner dances Friday and Saturday; tel. (021) 56-1956.

Dale's Place, Table View. Excellent and varied menu; South African specialities; tel. (021) 557-4212.

Ons Huisie, Bloubergstrand. Early 19th-century fisherman's cottage; seafood; excellent; tel. (021) 56-1498.

On the Rocks, Bloubergstrand. Continental; shoreline setting; views of Table Mountain; tel. (021) 56-1988.

USEFUL ADDRESSES AND TELEPHONE NUMBERS

Automobile Association, tel. (021) 21-1550 (general); toll-free 0800 010101 (breakdown service); tel. (021) 21-1550 (touring information); fax 419-6032.

Captour, Tourist Rendezvous Travel Centre, Adderley St; tel. (021) 418-5214/5. Other bureaux: Municipal Building, Atlantic Rd, Muizenberg; tel. (021) 788-1898 (southern Peninsula); Shop 007, Tyger Valley Shopping Centre, Bellville; tel. (021) 948-4993 (northern areas); Johannesburg office: Shop 123, Rosebank Mall, 50 Bath Ave, Rosebank; tel. (011) 442-4707.

Captour accommodation: tel. (021) 418-5216. Also assists in booking local tours and car hire reservations. Captour produces some very useful maps, booklets and brochures covering accommodation, restaurants, shopping and special-interest tours.

Satour (South African Tourism Board), information offices at the Tourist Rendezvous Travel Centre (*see* Captour above). Private Bag X9108, Cape Town 8000; tel. (021) 21-6274, fax 419-4875.

Theatre and other bookings, through Computicket. No telephonic reservations; tel. (021) 21-4715 for information, fax 418-3409. Offices throughout city, suburb, Peninsula and northern areas; telephone for directions, or ask Captour or hotel reception.

Table Mountain Cableway, no telephonic reservations; bookings must be made in person at the Tourist Rendezvous Travel Centre (*see* Captour above), the Waterfront Information Office, or the cableway itself (lower station). A bus service plies between Adderley St (outside OK Bazaars) and the cableway station.

Emergency numbers: *National ambulance number*: 1-0177; *hospital casualty:* Groote Schuur 404-4141 or 404-9111; Somerset Hospital (Green Point) 482-6911; Tygerberg (northern areas) 938-5235; Red Cross Children's Hospital (Rondebosch) 658-5175; poisoning centre: Red Cross Children's Hospital 689-5227; *fire brigade:* 461-5555; *police headquarters:* (Caledon Square) 461-7282; *police flying squad:* 1-0111; *after-hours pharmacy:* Litekem, Darling St, 461-8040 (open to 23h00); *Life Line* (equivalent of British Samaritans) 461-1111; *mountain rescue:* 1-0111; *sea rescue:* 405-3500.

THE WESTERN CAPE WINELANDS

Splendid mountain ranges, green and fertile valleys, historic towns and villages, gracious homesteads, orchards and vineyards heavy with fruit – these, in brief, are the physical elements that distinguish the Western Cape's winelands, a loosely defined region that stretches, very approximately, north-east from Cape Town to the Hex River Valley and the edge of the arid Karoo, and from Tulbagh and Ceres in the north-west to Robertson in the east.

Not that the wine industry is confined within these limits. On the contrary, the Peninsula's Constantia Valley (*see* page 234) is renowned for its superb vintages, and the newer growing areas – the Swartland, Olifants River and Piketberg, and the lands extending to and including the Little Karoo far to the east – are rapidly gaining a reputation for the quality of their table wines and, in the latter instance, for their fortified wines and brandies.

But it is the winter-rainfall areas of the southwestern Cape (a region known as the Boland), and most notably the rolling foothills around Stellenbosch, Franschhoek and Paarl and the rich alluvial soils of the Breede River Valley that consistently produce the best of the country's wines: the vineyards average between 8 and 12 tons of grapes a hectare (2.5 acres), and from the pressings come reds and whites, sherries and ports and brandies that find their way to the most discerning of tables, both in South Africa and, increasingly, abroad.

These were the first country areas to be settled by the white colonists: prompted by the need to feed an expanding Cape Town, they began infiltrating the traditional Khoisan lands of the interior during the 1660s. Stellenbosch, 41 km (25 miles) from Cape Town, was founded as an agricultural settlement in 1679, a venture that, in terms of food production, proved so successful that farmers soon began to turn their lands, their energy and surplus resources to the growing of vines.

Thereafter, river valley after river valley was occupied, the countryside turned over to pasture, to fruit, to wheat – and to grapes. By 1687 an impressive 400,000 vines had been planted

OPPOSITE: *Part of the lovely Boschendal Estate near Franschhoek. In the distance are the Groot Drakenstein Mountains.*

and were flourishing and the arrival, the next year, of a small group of French Huguenots – most of whom were skilled people, some of them well versed in the sciences of viticulture and wine-making – lent impetus to an industry that was already burgeoning.

STELLENBOSCH

The town of Stellenbosch, founded in the green and fertile valley of the Eerste River and overlooked by the forested heights of the Papegaaiberg (Parrot Mountain), grew gracefully, in keeping with the charm of its setting: the early settlers planted oak trees that were to reach splendid maturity, created open spaces, built churches and schools and thick-walled, limewashed homes with thatched roofs and timberwork of stinkwood and yellowwood, and it's all been beautifully preserved. One can see it at its best, perhaps, along Dorp Street, which has the longest row of historic buildings in the country, and around Die Braak, the village green once used for military parades and for festivals, feasting and games and still fringed by the quaintness of the past.

THE VILLAGE MUSEUM (Ryneveld Street) is a collection of historic houses dating from a number of eras, meticulously restored and furnished in period style, the gardens planted with the flowers, shrubs and trees that would have graced the original homes. The Schreuder House (1709), a smallish cottage, is believed to be the country's oldest surviving town house. Other buildings forming part of the museum include the Bletterman House (1760–1790); Grosvenor House (1800–1830), and the House of OM Bergh (1840–1870). Open daily.

DIE BRAAK (Bird Street). On and around the town square are the pretty thatched-roof Anglican Church of St Mary (1852), the Rhenish Mission, the old Burgerhuis (1797) and the VOC-Kruithuis, or Dutch East India Company powder-house (1777), now a national monument housing a small military museum.

D'OUWE WERF (Church Street) is one of the country's earliest boarding houses. Built in 1710, on the foundations of an earlier church, it's been restored and still does noble service as a lovely little hotel. If you're not staying over, do at least visit the coffee shop.

THE UNIVERSITY boasts some fine buildings, two art galleries and fine botanical gardens (on Neethling Street) noted for their displays of

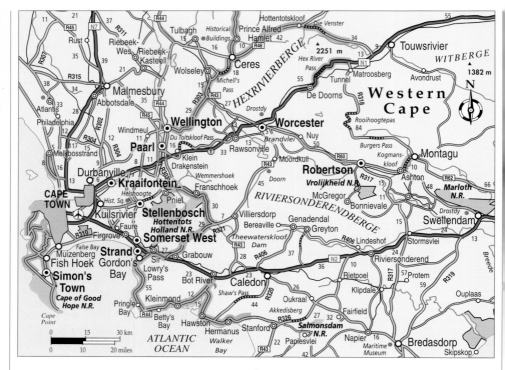

indigenous succulents, cycads, orchids, ferns, bonsai, and the strange welwitschia species that grows in the harshness of the Namib Desert.

LIBERTAS PARVA (corner of Old Strand Road and Dorp Street). An elegant, gabled mansion that incorporates both the Rembrandt van Rijn art gallery (works by leading 20th-century artists, including Pierneef, Van Wouw and Irma Stern) and, in its cellar, the Stellenryck Wine Museum (huge old vats, Cape furniture, and brassware). Both museums are open Monday to Saturday and on some public holidays.

And if it's wine you're interested in – in its history and the way it is made today – make a point, too, of visiting the:

OUDE MEESTER BRANDY MUSEUM (Old Strand Road). A wide range of relics of a fascinating past (stills, bottles and glassware) and an insight into the present. Open Monday to Saturday; Sunday afternoons.

THE BERGKELDER (on the Papegaaiberg, next to the railway station). The 'mountain cellars' have been hollowed out of the hillside; they contain some extraordinarily large and impressive vats, and they offer tours and tastings from Monday to Saturday.

THE OUDE LIBERTAS CENTRE (opposite Stellenbosch Farmers' Winery), is an enchanting venue for open-air shows – music (from classical to the sounds of Africa), drama, ballet, and opera. Performances are held in the outdoor Amphitheatre; Sunday concerts in the season (December to March) are enormously popular: bring a picnic basket and sip wine in the evening sunshine as the music washes over you. Tours of the winery by appointment.

THE LANZERAC HOTEL (Jonkershoek Road): a stately Cape Dutch mansion with excellent restaurants, a splendidly stocked wine-cellar, an art gallery (the Tinus de Jongh Memorial), a museum (early Cape furniture) and a well-patronised, unpretentious bar.

OOM SAMIE SE WINKEL (Dorp Street). For local colour, this 'algemeende handelaars' (general dealers) is an absolute must. Oom Samie was one of the town's very first all-purpose traders, and his shop's been rebuilt in period style, declared a national monument and crammed with traditional home-made preserves, bric-a-brac, curios and other goods. On the corner is De Akker, a well-known pub with a wine library and an information service.

Around Stellenbosch

Some of the most attractive of the Western Cape's vineyards, estates and homesteads are concentrated in this area, more than 20 of them along the Stellenbosch wine route (*see* page 258) and each worth visiting for its cellar tours and wine tastings; for the sustaining lunches provided by many of them, and for the beauty of the surrounding countryside. To mention, briefly, a few by name:

• **Avontuur**, on the Stellenbosch-Somerset West road. Splendid thoroughbred horses roam the beautiful farm.

• **Blaauwklippen**, 4 km (2.5 miles) along the Strand road. The charming, gabled house was built in 1789. Traditional 'Cape Malay' preserves and relishes on sale; coachman's lunch; small but intriguing museum.

• **Delaire**, at the summit of the steep Helshoogte Pass. Stunning views.

TOP LEFT: *The evocative Oom Samie se Winkel, oldest of Stellenbosch's shops.*
ABOVE: *The amphitheatre at Oude Libertas.*

• **Delheim**, situated on the high slopes of the Simonsberg and described as a 'touristic jewel and photographer's paradise'. Serves a vintner's platter during the summer months (October to April) and country soup in winter.

• **Hartenberg** (in the Devon Valley) and **Morgenhof** (in the south-western foothills of the Simonsberg); both serve vintner's lunches.

THE JEAN CRAIG POTTERY, on the Devon Valley road (off the R310 to Cape Town). Here, one stands in a central viewing area to watch the various and fascinating processes – throwing, glazing and so forth. The range of products is wide, the styles vary from the charmingly homely to the sophisticated, the quality is good. There is a shop on the premises.

CAPE DUTCH ELEGANCE

As the first wineland farms prospered, so their owners extended their sturdy but modest two- and three-roomed homes. They added wings, built cellars, stables, coach-houses, slaves' quarters, a *jonkerhuis* (a house for the eldest son), laid courtyards encircled by whitewashed walls, steepened the pitch of the roofs to allow for a gabled loft, and a distinctive architectural form began to emerge at the end of the 17th century. It was a style that drew from medieval Holland, from the France of the Huguenots and the islands of Indonesia, but which developed to become known, and admired, as Cape Dutch.

Some lovely Cape Dutch country houses grace the region. Most are gabled, a few are truly grand and they are accessible to the tourist by way of the various wine routes that have been established.

One of Stellenbosch's Cape Dutch buildings.

ABOVE: *The exquisite Franschhoek Valley, famed for its vineyards, fruit orchards and homesteads.*
OPPOSITE TOP: *The graceful Huguenot Memorial, part of Franschhoek's museum complex.*
OPPOSITE BOTTOM: *Alfresco fare at Boschendal. The estate is known for its superb Cape cuisine.*

THE FRENCH CONNECTION

Though generally of fiercely independent character, the French Huguenot (Protestant) refugees who settled in the Franschhoek area in the 1680s and 1690s were not allowed to form a separate community in the Cape hinterland but instead were mixed in with the resident Dutch and German free burghers. Within three or four decades little of significance remained of their cultural heritage: French was no longer spoken, and assimilation was all but complete. The settlers did, however, have a powerful influence on the development of the young wine industry, and on the gracious rural architecture of the period. Their national origins can still be discerned in a number of Afrikaans family names, the more common among them De Villiers, Le Roux, Du Preez, Fouché, Marais, Rousseau, Malan, Du Plessis, Theron and Du Toit; and in the names of many of the homesteads and vineyards of the Groot Drakenstein and Franschhoek region: La Provence and Haute Provence, La Bri, La Motte, Le Chêsnes, L'Ormarins and Mouton-Excelsior.

JONKERSHOEK VALLEY, not far to the east of Stellenbosch, is a scenic joy. The Eerste River rises in the area, and in one place cascades in a magnificent waterfall; to the north are the spectacular peaks known as The Twins and to the south are the imposing Stellenboschberg and Haelkop (1,490 m/4,889 ft).

Within the valley are the famed and very lovely Lanzerac and Oude Nektar estates, and the Jonkershoek State Forest, which contains the hatcheries of the Fisheries Research Station and the Assegaaibosch Nature Reserve, a 168 ha (415 acres) stretch of montane *fynbos* (heath) and sanctuary for rare proteas, small buck and some interesting bird species. The Assegaai-bosch is also noted for its wildflower garden, and there are pleasant picnic and barbecue sites and short nature trails. Larger paths and trails criss-cross the state forest, which is accessible to the public during the daylight hours of the wet season (May to September).

FRANSCHHOEK

A small centre which serves the wine and fruit farmers of the area, Franschhoek ('French corner') was founded in 1688 on land given to Huguenot refugees who had fled a Europe torn by religious strife (*see* panel, page 250).

Of note in Franschhoek itself is the large but delicately graceful Huguenot Memorial and the adjacent Huguenot Museum complex. The Franschhoek area is also something of a culinary mecca, boasting a bevy of restaurants that serve exquisite, mainly French-style dishes (*see* Advisory, page 261).

HOMESTEADS Although the Vignerons de Franschhoek is classed as a wine route, some of the wine estates belonging to it are not open to the general public (*see* page 258). Some of the cellars are, though, and others can be visited by appointment. Of special note are:

• **Bellingham** (3 km/2 miles beyond the Dwars River bridge on the Franschhoek road). The original grant for this farm dates back to 1693. The estate declined sadly during the earlier part of the 20th century but has risen, phoenix-like, during the past few decades and the cellars are now earning fame and acclaim for their excellent dry white and other wines.

A different kind of drawcard is its natural amphitheatre, which seats an audience of about 90 and in which musical and other performances are periodically staged.

• **Boschendal** (before reaching Groot Drakenstein station, on the right-hand side of the road). One of the better-known farms, the quintessence of country elegance and popular with visitors from Cape Town. The Cape Flemish-style manor house, dating from 1812 and for long the property of the De Villiers family, fell into decay in the latter part of the 19th century but has been beautifully restored and is now a museum as well as the centrepiece of a splendid wine farm. The Waenhuis now serves as a gift shop; the Taphuis as a winery and tasting room and the gardens are a delight. Boschendal's restaurant is famed for its buffet lunches (traditional Cape fare); picnic baskets are provided in summer for those who prefer to eat in the shady grounds. Open from 11h00 daily.

THE DRAKENSTEIN VALLEY, overlooked on the west by the Groot Drakenstein Mountains, is noted not only for its vineyards but also for its bountiful deciduous fruit orchards and its crops of sweet table grapes. Indeed, the area was the birthplace of South Africa's thriving export fruit industry.

SOMERSET WEST

South of Stellenbosch, 48 km (30 miles) east of Cape Town and twinned with the adjacent Strand municipality, Somerset West is an attractive and fast-growing residential centre set delightfully between the Hottentots Holland Mountains and the waters of False Bay.

VERGELEGEN Among the oldest and grandest of the historic estates, Vergelegen was the brainchild of the eccentric early Cape governor WA van der Stel. Within five years of its completion in 1701 more than half a million vines were flourishing on its broad acres, and its homestead stood as a monument to both wild extravagance and superb architectural taste.

Vergelegen's grounds are a joy, their centrepiece the exquisite Octagonal Garden. The homestead is imposing and beautifully furnished, its modern, four-level cellar a trendsetter within the wine industry. Open daily; cellar tours; teas in a garden setting.

HELDERBERG NATURE RESERVE, a lovely 400 ha (988 acres) stretch of pleasant countryside set against a backdrop of the high Helderberg peak. Principal attractions are the spectacular scenery, the area's wealth of proteas and other indigenous flora and its abundantly rich birdlife, which includes several species unique to the region (among others, the protea seedeater, Victorin's scrub warbler, and three types of redchested flufftail).

The reserve is also home to a variety of antelope, and there's a restaurant, an oak-shaded picnic spot, lily ponds, a duck pond, a herbarium, an arboretum and a small and delightful patch of natural forest (stinkwoods, yellowwoods, and rooi els). The path to the Disa Gorge and the mountain road are much favoured by discerning walkers; the cliffs a challenge to climbers. Gentle trails beckon the rambler.

SIR LOWRY'S PASS cuts through the Hottentots Holland range above Somerset West. From the heights are stunning views of the mountains, the plains below and, in the distance, Table Mountain and the Peninsula (there is a viewpoint at the top). Once over the pass, one descends to the small centres of Elgin and Grabouw, headquarters of the country's apple-growing industry.

BELOW: *Scenic grandeur is the principal feature of the Helderberg Nature Reserve.*
OPPOSITE: *The dome-shaped peaks that surmount Paarl Mountain and its nature reserve.*

THE PAARL AREA

This is a region of impressive scenic splendour. Five passes lead you over majestic mountain ranges that are often snow-capped in winter; below, the Berg River winds its way through lush countryside on its journey to the Atlantic Ocean 200 km (124 miles) away, bringing sustenance to the vineyards and orchards of what was for long known as the Pêrelvallei ('vale of pearls').

In fact, the name applies not to the general beauty of the area but derives from a dome-shaped buttress that soars high over the river – Paarl Mountain and its three attendant features, one of which, Paarl Rock, caught the eye of an early Dutch explorer, reminding him of a 'dia-mandt-ende pêrelberg' ('diamond and pearl hill') when seen at dawn, with the sunlit dew glistening on its mica-studded surface. The Rock overlooks the town of:

PAARL

A historic town, and the biggest of the Western Cape's inland centres, founded in 1720 as a farming and wagon-building settlement.

Among Paarl's claims to notability are its unusually long oak- and jacaranda-shaded Main Street, which runs a full 10 km (6 miles) from end to end; its lovely suburban gardens; its prominence in the powerful Afrikaans Language Movement; its fine buildings, and its intimate associations with the wine industry.

Paarl has its wine route (*see* page 258), and serves as the headquarters of the giant Co-operative Wine Growers' Association (KWV). The famed Nederburg wine auctions are held each year just outside town.

THE KWV is the world's largest wine co-operative: it handles some 70% of the country's wine exports. Its offices are in La Concorde, an imposing neo-classical building on Main Street. KWV's enormous wine and brandy cellar complex, in Kohler Street, is open to the public on weekdays for tours, tastings and lectures.

KWV also runs Laborie, a gracious old manor house and model wine estate nestling at the foot of Paarl Mountain. Visits by arrangement. Its adjuncts include an excellent restaurant, which is housed in a restored wine-cellar and which offers a range of delectable traditional dishes.

THE AFRIKAANS LANGUAGE MONUMENT (Taalmonument) stands on the slopes of Paarl Mountain: a splendid structure of three linked columns, a soaring spire and a fountain, each element symbolizing a debt owed by the language – to the western world, to Africa and to the Cape people of eastern origin.

EXPLORING THE WINE-WAYS

There can be few more pleasant ways of exploring the south-western Cape hinterland than to spend the day following one or other of these established routes – wine-ways inspired by the popular *Routes de Vin* of France and Germany's *Weinstrassen*. The concept was transplanted to the Cape in the early 1970s and has proved hugely successful.

For many, the routes (they are clearly sign-posted, the entrance to each farm, co-operative and estate marked by a roadside emblem) provide a good excuse to travel into the countryside for a day's or weekend's relaxation; others, more serious about wine, set out to add to their private cellar stock of favourite labels or to explore new areas, discover new tastes, perhaps picking up a bargain case-load along the way. Whatever the motives, though, those with limited time at their disposal will be able to cover only a small fraction of the ground available. There are literally hundreds of estates, farms and cooperatives, and they produce between them something over 2,000 different wines. A visit to three, maybe four and at the most five different venues along the route is probably the most one can expect to manage in a single outing.

The growers are proud of their farms, and of their wines, and the welcome they extend to visitors goes well beyond a simple quest for sales and profit. Most of the cellars offer tastings (there's no limit to the number of wines you're allowed to try, though many places charge a small fee per glass) and tours (these are at set times); some run excellent restaurants; at others you'll find a farm stall selling local specialities (produce, preserves and so on), a gift shop, perhaps a small private museum. Many of the beautiful homesteads are historic.

But whatever part of a particular route you select, it'll prove a pleasant experience indeed. You talk to people who know all the subtleties and secrets of wine-making, inspect the bottling and labelling machinery and the wooden casks tiered in the coolness of a wine- and wood-scented cellar; sample the vintages at leisure, maybe buy a bottle or two, take luncheon on the terrace, and go on to the next farm. Nothing is hurried: there is time to absorb, assess, compare, savour, enjoy.

PAARL MOUNTAIN The area's most distinctive feature – a cluster of three peaks named Britannia Rock, Gordon Rock and, as mentioned, Paarl Rock. To get there one takes Jan Philips Road from town – a circular and scenically attractive route along which there's a lovely picnic site and the Mill Stream Wild Flower Garden. The area around the mountain has been proclaimed as the:
PAARLBERG NATURE RESERVE, a pleasant 1,910 ha (4,720 acres) expanse of *fynbos* (heath) countryside dominated by the trio of peaks and graced by a variety of protea species, wild olive, aloes, bastard saffron, and wild currant; by groves of natural forest, among them (an unusual feature) a patch of woodland containing the delicate silver tree. Birds to be seen include the Cape bunting, the redwinged starling, the Cape robin, black eagle, sugarbird and sunbird. There are numerous paths and picnic/barbecue areas, and several dams in which anglers fish for black bass that are said to be the largest in the country.
LA BONHEUR CROCODILE FARM, in Suider (southern) Paarl, has over a thousand of these giant reptiles in its dams, which are traversed by raised walkways. The gift shop stocks a wide variety of hand-worked goods including, of course, crocodile-leather handbags.

Estates and wineries

There are numerous wine farms and estates in the area, many of which are on the Paarl wine route (*see* page 258). Among them are:
• **Backsberg**, on the lower slopes of the Simonsberg, has an especially pleasant tasting parlour; self-guided tours of the wine-cellars (complemented by closed-circuit TV demonstrations) and a small wine museum.
• **Fairview**, just south of Paarl Mountain, offers a variety of cheeses made from the estate's own goat's milk. At nearby Landskroon there's a splendid choice of Jersey-milk cheeses, and a vintner's platter lunch, on offer.
• **De Leuwen Jagt**, on Paarl Mountain's southwestern slopes, has beautifully restored dwellings and breathtaking views of far-off Cape Town.
• **Rhebokskloof**, just north of Paarl Mountain, has a traditional Cape restaurant; 45-minute estate tours in a four-wheel-drive vehicle.
• **Paarl Rock Brandy Cellar**, in the northern part of town. Apparently the only one of its kind in the country where you can view the entire brandy-production flow-line.

The snow-capped mountains around Ceres.

• **Nederburg**, which is perhaps the best-known of all the wine estates. Its origins and reputation for fine wines dates back to 1792; the H-shaped gabled and quite enchanting homestead, set in a wide sweep of countryside mantled by vines, has been lovingly preserved. The renowned annual Nederburg wine auction, held around mid-April, is one of the most important wine events, and social occasions, on the South African calendar: merchants, collectors, investors, private buyers and others with good (or plausible) reasons for being there come from far and wide to enjoy the sales and the carnival atmosphere. There are food and wine stalls, tastings, and a fashion parade.

THE BREEDE RIVER VALLEY

The Breede (or Breë) River Valley is the largest and probably loveliest of the south-western Cape's three wine- and fruit-producing valleys. The river rises in the high Ceres basin, a region whose mountains are often white with enough snow to attract skiers and whose main centre is the town of Ceres, named after the Roman goddess of agriculture, or fertility.

The Breede gathers momentum through the narrow and strikingly rugged Michell's Pass, plunges down between the Witsenberg and Elandskloofberg ranges and then flows south-eastwards through a lush countryside of orchards and vineyards and into the Robertson area. Of its many tributaries, the 40-km-long (25 miles) Hex River is the most notable, its valley both stunningly beautiful and hugely productive.

TULBAGH

Tulbagh began life as a tiny frontier settlement during the early 18th century, later growing into a charming country town. The 32 beautifully restored buildings (in 1969 an earthquake destroyed many buildings, and killed nine people) on Church Street are the largest single group of national monuments in South Africa.

CERES

An enchanting little town set among the mountains of the Witsenberg, the Hex River and the Skurweberg ranges.

The basin in which Ceres nestles is one of South Africa's most bountiful (and scenically most outstanding) fruit-growing areas, yielding fine crops of apples, pears, peaches and nectarines (and vast quantities of potatoes as well). Ceres boasts the southern hemisphere's largest fruit-packing enterprise. The Ceres Mountain Fynbos Reserve, to the south and west of town, was established to protect the mountain *fynbos* (heath) vegetation. A good place for walking; some fine San (Bushman) paintings can be seen.

HEX RIVER MOUNTAINS AND VALLEY

One of the world's most dramatic railway passes cuts through the heights here: a torturous route almost 1,000 m (3,281 ft) above sea level. Passengers on the Blue Train, which negotiates the mountains in daylight, enjoy breathtaking vistas. The sandstone Hex River range, whose cliffs and ravines attract mountaineers, runs southwest to north-east, rising to between 1,200 and 1,800 m (3,937 and 5,906 ft) above sea level. Highest of the pinnacles and peaks are the Matroosberg (2,251 m/7,386 ft) and Buffelshoek (2,070 m/6,792 ft). Winter snows and high average rainfall create the region's seasonal streams.

As much a delight to the eye is the valley below: fringed by grand mountains, wide and immensely fertile, its summer greens turning to lovely muted shades in the autumn and early winter, heavily irrigated and intensively cultivated, the Hex River Valley sustains nearly 200 farms that, together, produce most of the late-maturing grapes that are exported. At the entrance to the Hex River Valley is:

WORCESTER

Founded in 1818, this thriving commercial and industrial centre (and the Breede River Valley's largest town), serves as a stopover on the Cape

Town to Johannesburg route. The countryside is fertile, the farms prosperous: grapes are a major crop, grown in huge quantities.

KLEINPLASIE OPEN-AIR MUSEUM, just outside town, depicts the life and times of the early Dutch farmer. Replicas of huts and cottages, ovens, a butchery, kitchen, kiln, tobacco shed, milk room, soap kitchen and horse mill; daily demonstrations include bread-baking, wheat-milling, tobacco-rolling, candle-making, black-smithing; seasonal programmes focus on spinning, weaving, threshing, sheep-shearing, raisin-making and brandy-distilling. The cafeteria serves delicious traditional Cape food.

KAROO NATIONAL BOTANIC GARDEN, about 3 km (2 miles) off the national highway (N1). The Worcester area is along the western edge of the Little Karoo (*see* page 189); the fascinating 154 ha (381 acres) garden conserves the flora of what is called the Karoo broken veld – mainly succulents, with some trees (the International Organization for Succulents recognizes the reserve as one of the world's five authentic succulent gardens). Ten hectares (25 acres) are under cultivation, the plants grouped according to climate, region and type, and there are many special displays (succulents, carrion flowers, and bulbous species). The flowers are at their most attractive in the winter and spring. There are short walks, and a picnic area. The botanic garden is open daily, sunrise to sunset.

OPPOSITE: *The glorious autumnal colours of the Western Cape winelands.*
ABOVE: *The Montagu Spa leisure complex.*

From Worcester, the R60 highway leads you south-eastwards for about 46 km (29 miles) through the Breede River Valley, to:

ROBERTSON

A fairly substantial, pleasant town set against the high Langeberg, 160 km (100 miles) from Cape Town on the railway line between that city and Port Elizabeth far to the east.

The area is renowned for its fine wines, brandies, sherries and jerepigos (fortified, high-sugar, high-alcohol wines) and musk-flavoured muscatel grapes grown in its vineyards. There are 10 estates, five private producers and nine co-operatives in the region (*see* wine routes, page 258), one of which produces the fine Mont Blois Superior muscatel label. It's also one of the country's foremost horse-breeding areas: there are more than a dozen thoroughbred stud farms, boasting between them some 700 brood mares, within a 30 km (20 miles) radius of Robertson; the industry is sustained by lime-rich soils, superb pastorage and an excellent climate. The region hosts the annual South Cape Spring Show (sawdust track and wine garden).

THE KWV (The Co-operative Wine Growers' Association) runs South Africa's largest brandy distillery in town (it boasts about 130 stills). KWV also operates Branewynsdraai, a taphouse and excellent restaurant serving Cape food.

MONTAGU

Some 20 km (12.5 miles) east of Robertson, Montagu is set on the edge of the Little Karoo (*see* page 189) in a region of thriving fruit farms and vineyards that produce, among other things, the richly flavoured muscatel and fortified wines. The town hosts the annual Muscatel Festival.

North of Montagu is the Koo, a rugged area graced by orchards of apple, pear, apricot and peach, and by wild flowers. The Koo is a fine place for walking, and has some excellent trails.

Montagu itself is both attractive and historic. Of Long Street's houses, 14 are official national monuments (there are nine other proclaimed buildings in town). And of course there is the:
MONTAGU SPA which has drawn generations of visitors to its warm (a constant 43 °C/109 °F) and soothing waters. The spa now is served by an excellent three-star hotel, and by time-share apartments and holiday cottages.
MONTAGU MOUNTAIN RESERVE is a 1,200 ha (2,965 acres) sanctuary along the northern edge of the Langeberg range: spectacular upland

countryside on which a number of pleasant hiking trails, from about 12 km to 15 km (7.5 to 9 miles) in length, have been established. One may, though, take gentler walks. Cogmanskloof is a magnificent 6-km-long (4 miles) pass between Montagu and Ashton.

GETTING AROUND

Walks and hikes

The Western Cape's dramatic sandstone ranges and their foothills – the so-called 'Berg interface' that descends to the coastal plain in the south – combine to provide wonderful walking country. The options are virtually limitless. Among the more inviting of the shorter routes cut through the Ceres Mountain Fynbos Reserve (see page 255), the Jonkershoek Valley to the east of Stellenbosch (see page 250), the Paarlberg Nature Reserve (see page 254) and the Karoo National Botanic Garden (see page 256).

Recommended hikes which are a rather longer and harder include the Boland Trail (the Limietberg section) through the wooded uplands of the Bain's Kloof/Du Toit's Kloof/Wolseley area (about 37 km/23 miles, but there are shorter walks along particular stretches and digressions) and various routes through the spectacular Hex River Mountains (see page 256). Somewhat more gentle is the Vineyard Trail that takes you through the lush farmlands of the Stellenbosch area. Details of these and many other routes are available from the local information offices, and in a number of guidebooks which are stocked by leading bookstores.

Day drives

Again, the whole of the winelands are a delight to the eye and one doesn't need to plan too meticulously: simply wandering where the mood and moment lead will bring its rewards.

However, among the most memorable of the recommended routes is the Four Passes drive. Start from Stellenbosch (see page 247) and take the R310 over Helshoogte Pass. Turn right on the R45 for the Franschhoek Pass, Franschhoek (see page 251) and beyond, to Theewaterskloof Dam. Turn right onto the R321, travel over Viljoen's Pass, then digress right through the apple-growing centre of Grabouw; exit to join the N2 west over the precipitous Sir Lowry's Pass (see page 252) and on to Strand and Somerset West (see page 252). Return to Stellenbosch along the R44.

The wine routes

To date, nine routes have been created in South Africa, though four of them – the Constantia (see page 238), the Little Karoo (see page 189), the Swartland and the Olifants River – are not, strictly speaking, embraced by the winelands region proper. The five wine routes which fall within the parameters of this chapter are:

STELLENBOSCH The first to be established, this takes in 17 private cellars and five co-operative wineries, all located on four major roads within a 12 km (7.5 miles) radius of Stellenbosch and half-an-hour's drive from Cape Town. Some of the route's features are covered on page 247. Information: the route's offices are located in the Doornbosch buildings on Strand Road, Stellenbosch (open from Monday to Friday).

PAARL Within an hour's drive from Cape Town; smaller than the Stellenbosch route, covering just four estates and three co-operatives, some of which are discussed (see page 254). Nederburg and the KWV are in the area but are not part of the formal route. For information contact the Paarl Publicity Association, corner of Main and Auret streets, Paarl.

VIGNERONS DE FRANSCHHOEK Boschendal and Bellingham are probably the best known of the cellars on this 'route', which shouldn't really be classed as such since it's rather an exclusive association, formed to promote the fine wines of the Franschhoek Valley generally (the wines are made centrally, on a co-operative basis) and as a commemorative tribute to the early Huguenot settlers. Not all the members of the Vignerons open their cellars to the public at set hours, if at all; several offer tastings and tours by appointment only, which should be booked in advance. All their wines, however, may be sampled at the Franschhoek Vineyards Co-operative in town. Two of the estates (Bien Donné and La Provence) have stalls adjacent to the Co-operative; and Die Binnehof, a tasting shop, and Le Quartier Français, a rather lovely winehouse and restaurant (the dining room overlooks a flower and herb garden) are nearby.

WORCESTER A prolific wine-making area: about a quarter of the national grape harvest is produced in the general region (which includes Robertson, see page 259). The 22 co-operative wineries and three estates are known for their white wines, varying from dry to lusciously sweet muscatels and hanepoots. The route is rural and not too sophisticated, and visitors can enjoy country hospitality at its warmest.

For information contact Worcester Winelands Association, which maintains a presence at the Kleinplasie Open-Air Museum (*see* page 256).

ROBERTSON Also a hugely productive district; the KWV concentrate plant at Robertson is geared to process an annual 200,000 hectolitres (4.4 million gallons) of grapejuice. The Robertson Wine Trust consists of nine co-operative cellars, 10 estates and five private producers. For details regarding the routes or individual farms, contact Robertson Information.

Other speciality routes

The Cape's wine-ways are renowned, attracting thousands of visitors each year. Not so well known are a number of other thematic itineraries – fruit, cheese, antiques, historic homes, museums and, farther afield, crayfish and wool.

Hikers make their way along the Boland Trail.

THE FRUIT ROUTES Farms, co-operatives, farm stalls, packing houses and others within the region have combined to provide visitors with a comprehensive and fascinating insight into the industry in all its guises. A typical example is the Ceres Fruit Farm tours itinerary: a bus trip from Cape Town, tea and scones, lunch at a farm or hotel and visits to orchards, a fruit-drying yard and a nature reserve. Full information can be obtained from Captour or the Ceres Information Bureau (*see* Advisory, page 261).

Tours

The majority of Cape Town's tour operators offer day-long and longer trips (by coach; some by air) to and through the Cape's winelands. The packages usually include wine tastings and cellar visits, lunches, teas and sightseeing excursions. Detailed information can be obtained from Captour (*see* Advisory, page 261).

ADVISORY: THE WESTERN CAPE WINELANDS

CLIMATE

Winter-rainfall area. Hot summer periods are relieved by cool and sometimes very strong south-easterly winds; cold and wet winter spells are interspersed with warm, sunny periods. For more details, turn to the relevant sections of the previous chapter, Cape Town and the Peninsula, which covers a similar climatic area.

MAIN ATTRACTIONS

Scenic splendour ❑ Fine wines and foods ❑ Stately homesteads ❑ Sightseeing drives ❑ Walking ❑ Hiking ❑ Mountain-climbing ❑ Freshwater angling.

TRAVEL

Road. Excellent tarred roads connect the main centres with Cape Town, and with most wine route venues. Approximate distances from Cape Town: Stellenbosch 41 km/25 miles; Franschhoek 57 km/35 miles; Somerset West 48 km/30 miles; Paarl 60 km/37 miles; Ceres 130 km/81 miles; Tulbagh 153 km/95 miles; Worcester 157 km/98 miles; Robertson 160 km/99 miles; Wellington 72 km/45 miles.

Car hire: Facilities are available in Cape Town.

Coach travel: Tour operators offer a wide selection of winelands packages.

Rail. Scheduled services connect Cape Town with Stellenbosch and centres in the Western Cape and beyond.

Air. Light aircraft and helicopter tours available; for information consult Captour.

ACCOMMODATION
Select hotels and lodges

Cumberland Hotel *** Worcester. Comfort and value; 53 rooms, 2 suites; à la carte and buffet/carvery; pool; gym; tennis; squash; conference facilities. PO Box 8, Worcester 6850; tel. (0231) 7-2641, fax 7-3613.

Devon Valley Protea *** Stellenbosch area. Vineyard setting; 35 en suite rooms; à la carte and table d'hôte restaurants; 2 pools; conference facilities. PO Box 68, Stellenbosch 7599; tel. (021) 882-2012, fax 882-2610, toll-free reservations 0800 11 9000.

D'Ouwe Werf *** Stellenbosch. Historic (South Africa's oldest surviving inn); loaded with charm; 25 en suite rooms; à la carte coffee shop; small-group conference facilities available. 30 Church St, Stellenbosch 7600; tel. (021) 887-4608, fax 886-4626.

Franschhoek Mountain Manor Franschhoek area. 41 en suite rooms; table d'hôte restaurant; coffee shop; bar; pool; gym; spa; saunas; tennis; squash; bowls; horse-riding; conference facilities available. PO Box 54, Franschhoek 7690; tel. (021) 876-2071, fax 876-2077.

Goedemoed Country Inn Paarl. Bed and breakfast; family hospitality in the best Cape tradition; lovely furnishings; 9 rooms; pool. PO Box 331, Paarl 7620; tel. (021) 871-1020; fax 872-5430.

Grande Roche Hotel ***** Paarl. Luxurious; 29 suites; award-winning restaurant; wine cellar; chapel; 2 swimming pools; tennis courts; gym; sauna; conference facilities. PO Box 6038, Paarl 7620; tel. (021) 863-2727, fax 863-2220, toll-free reservations 0800 21 0257.

La Cotte Inn Franschhoek. Lovely country hotel; 10 en suite rooms; renowned à la carte restaurant; bar, wine-tasting centre; swimming pool; conference facilities available. Huguenot Rd, Franschhoek 7690; tel. (021) 876-2081.

Lanzerac Hotel **** Jonkershoek Valley, near Stellenbosch. Historic; atmospheric; 30 suites in delightful garden setting; à la carte restaurant; trattoria (serves country cuisine); bar; swimming pool; conference facilities available. PO Box 4, Stellenbosch 7599; tel. (021) 887-1132; fax 887-2310.

Le Quartier Français Franschhoek. Charming *auberge*; 14 delightful rooms overlooking garden; à la carte restaurant (lauded for its Cape Provençal cuisine and superb regional wines); alfresco lunches and teas; swimming pool. PO Box 237, Franschhoek 7690; tel. (021) 876-2151, fax 876-3105.

The Lord Charles ***** Somerset West. One of South Africa's top hotels; 196 rooms; 3 restaurants: à la carte, carvery and light meals; swimming pool; trimpark; tennis courts; 9-hole putting green; trout-fishing; conference facilities available. PO Box 5151, Helderberg 7135; tel. (024) 55-1040, fax 55-1107, toll-free reservations 0800 22 1220.

Mimosa Lodge Montagu. Edwardian charm and hospitality; 10 en suite rooms; table d'hôte restaurant; superb country cuisine. PO Box 323, Montagu 6720; tel. (0234) 4-2351, fax 4-1408.

Mountain Shadows Paarl. Tranquil; family atmosphere; 13 en suite bedrooms; breakfast (other meals available on request); swimming pool. PO Box 2501, Paarl 7620; tel. (021) 862-3192, fax 862-6796.

Roggeland Country House Noorder (northern) Paarl. The house is a national monument, set in the heart of the lovely Dal Josaphat Valley; 8 en suite bedrooms; fine country cuisine; swimming pool. PO Box 7210, Noorder Paarl 7623; tel. (021) 868-2501, fax 868-2113.

Stellenbosch Hotel Dorp St. 20 en suite rooms; à la carte restaurant; bar. PO Box 500, Stellenbosch 7599; tel. (021) 887-3644, fax 887-3673.

Self-catering and budget

The winelands offer a fair selection of guest-houses, self-contained chalets, farm-house accommodation and caravan/camping facilities. Ask Captour or the local information bureax for details.

Budget: For full information contact Bed 'n Breakfast; tel. (021) 683-3505, fax 683-5159.

Select restaurants

Good food, much of it in the traditional Cape style and often served in attractive and historic surroundings, is one of the most pleasant features of this inviting region. Some suggestions:

STELLENBOSCH AREA

Decameron, Plein St. Popular among afficionados of Italian fare; tel. (021) 883-3331.

De Volkskombuis, Old Strand Rd. Cape cuisine in historic cluster of labourers' cottages. Highly popular; tel. (021) 887-5239.

Doornbosch, Old Strand Rd. A winehouse, and one of the Cape's finest restaurants. Classical cuisine; French undertones; superb wines; tel. (021) 887-5079.

D'Ouwe Werf, Church St. Renowned country inn; serves light, home-style and delicious food in ambient setting; tel. (021) 882-4608.

Lanzerac, Lanzerac Rd. Atmospheric: the hotel is steeped in history; casual; lively; seafood a speciality; tel. (021) 885-1132.

L'Auberge Rozendal, Rozendal farm. Classical cuisine in elegant Cape Dutch setting; tel. (021) 883-8737.

Le Cameleon Bistro, Dorp St. Simple and tasty Continental food; tel. (021) 887-2776.

Le Pommier, Helshoogte Pass. Delicious Cape food in charming setting; tel. (021) 885-1269.

Lord Neethling, Neethlingshof Estate. Several rooms; full of antiques; imaginative, varied and delicious menu; tel. (021) 883-9803.

Mamma Roma, Pick 'n Pay Centre, Merriman Ave. Excellent Italian fare; cheerful, friendly atmosphere; tel. (021) 886-6064.

Café Filipe, Dorp St. Coffee shop attached to the old trading store (*see* page 246); serves light and tasty lunches; tel. (021) 887-2710.

Ralph's, Andringa St. Imaginative Continental-style menu; striking décor; tel. (021) 883-3532.

FRANSCHHOEK AREA

Boschendal, Boschendal Estate, Groot Drakenstein (*see* page 249). Gracefulness and exquisite taste are the keynotes; delicious hot and cold buffet lunches (traditional Cape fare) are served; tel. (021) 874-1252.

La Maison Chamonix. The memorable tastes of the French countryside; tel. (021) 876-2393.

Le Ballon Rouge. Superb modern French cuisine; tel. (021) 876-2651.

La Petite Ferme, Franschhoek Pass. Dramatic mountain setting; unpretentious, friendly restaurant; all-purpose menu tending to country-style food; very popular, so booking is essential. Serves lunches only; tel. (021) 876-3016.

Le Quartier Français, Huguenot Rd, Franschhoek. French-influenced Cape-style cooking; excellent. For lighter meals, visit the coffee shop next door; tel. (021) 876-2151.

SOMERSET WEST

Chez Michel, Victoria Rd. Unassuming; Continental cuisine; a big favourite with those who know food; tel. (024) 51-6069.

Drakes, Lord Charles Hotel. International menu; cordon bleu cuisine; tel. (024) 55-1040.

The Garden Terrace, Lord Charles Hotel. Enormous choice of delicious dishes (à la carte and buffet); highest standards; superb wine list; tel. (024) 55-1040.

L'Auberge de Paysan, Gallic stylishness; delightful menu; tel. (024) 42-2008.

Ou Pastorie, Colonial Dutch venue; fine French fare; tel. (024) 852-2120.

PAARL

Bosman's, Grande Roche Hotel. Among the country's finest restaurants; stylishly cosmopolitan cuisine; tel. (021) 863-2727.

TULBAGH

Paddagang Wine House, Church St. Traditional Cape-style food; in delightful setting; wine-tastings. tel. (0236) 30-0242.

WELLINGTON AREA

Blake's Rest, Onverwacht Estate. Traditional Cape setting; memorable food; tel. (021) 864-1377.

USEFUL ADDRESSES AND TELEPHONE NUMBERS

Automobile Association, tel. (021) 21-1550 (touring information and general); toll-free 0800 010101 (breakdown service); fax 419-6032.

Captour, Tourist Rendezvous Travel Centre, Adderley St, Cape Town; tel. (021) 418-5214/5; Johannesburg office: 50 Bath Ave, Rosebank; tel. (011) 442-4707.

Ceres Information Bureau, tel. (0233) 6-1287.

Franschhoek Tourism Association, tel. (021) 876-3603.

Gordon's Bay Information Office, Hendon Park, Gordon's Bay; tel. (024) 56-2321.

Montagu Information, tel. (0234) 4-1116.

Paarl Publicity Association, 216 Main St, Paarl 7646; tel. (021) 872-4842.

Satour (South African Tourism Board), Tourist Rendezvous Travel Centre, Adderley St, Cape Town; tel. (021) 21-6274, fax 419-4875.

Somerset West Information Bureau, 11 Victoria St, Somerset West 7130; tel. (024) 51-4022.

Stellenbosch Publicity Association, 36 Mark St, Stellenbosch 7600; tel. (021) 883-3584/883-9633. Wine Route Information: tel. (021) 886-4310.

Tulbagh Tourism Office Old Church Museum, 14 Church St, Tulbagh 6820; tel. (0236) 30-1020.

Wellington Information Bureau Jan van Riebeeck St, Wellington 7655; tel. (021) 873-4604.

Worcester Publicity Association 57 Kerk St, Worcester 6850; tel. (0231) 7-1408.

THE WEST COAST AND NAMAQUALAND

The Olifants is, by South African standards, a fairly large river, rising in the Great Winterhoek and Koue Bokkeveld mountains of the southern Karoo and flowing north-westwards, past the pleasant towns of Citrusdal, Clanwilliam and Vredendal before entering the Atlantic Ocean 250 km (156 miles) north of Cape Town.

Its valley is fertile, sustaining fine crops of wheat and subtropical fruits, rooibos tea, tobacco, vegetables, wine and table grapes and, most notable of all, grove upon grove of delectable Washington and Navel oranges.

To the north of the Olifants River is the region known as Namaqualand, a 48,000 km² (30,000 square miles) swathe of increasingly arid territory stretching to the lower reaches of the Orange River, beyond which is Namibia (formerly known as South West Africa) and the great dunes and drifts of the Namib desert.

Most of the coastal strip up to the Orange River is what is known as the 'sandveld', narrow for the most part, up to 50 km (30 miles) wide in places, elevated above sea level and distinguished by 'raised beaches' – sandy terraces full of seashells and wave-eroded pebbles that are the legacy of the period in far-distant prehistory when the ocean's surface was around 100 m (330 ft) higher than it is today. To the east of the sandveld is the broken country of the Hardeveld, which has an average altitude of about 900 m (2,953 ft) and which is part of South Africa's Great Escarpment (see page 10). Still farther eastward, beyond the Hardeveld, are the flattish, semi-arid and largely inhospitable wastelands of Little Bushmanland.

Altogether a dry, bleak and sparsely populated land, harsh in its moods, formidable in its great, empty spaces. But it is not without its beauty (see panel, page 265). Surface water is almost nonexistent, though the interaction of the cool Benguela ocean current and the warm desert air often produces dense mists. The region's rainfall varies between 250 mm (10 in) and a pitifully low 50 mm (2 in) a year.

OPPOSITE: The Maltese Cross, one of many strangely eroded rock features in the Cedarberg Wilderness Area, a scenically spectacular upland region that attracts hikers, climbers, campers, photographers and nature-lovers.

THE FAR NORTH

The largest town in Namaqualand proper, part of the Northern Cape province, and is at the centre of the sandveld region's spectacular springtime flower show, is:

SPRINGBOK

The place, approximately 80 km (50 miles) from the Atlantic coast, started its life when a copper mine began operating in the area in 1852. In fact the metal had featured much earlier on in the region's history: it was worked by the local Khoi centuries ago, and was much sought after by the first Dutch settlers. Governor Simon van der Stel mounted an expedition to the 'copper mountains' of Namaqualand in 1685, and the shaft his men dug can still be seen near the town. Today there are fairly large-scale workings in the area. The region is not too well geared for visitors, but it has its devotees, especially among hikers and botanists. In close proximity to the town (the entrance is 4 km (2.5 miles) beyond the airport), is the:

GOEGAP NATURE RESERVE, a 15,000 ha (37,000 acres) expanse of stark countryside, some of it flat, most of it broken by huge granite outcrops. Only part of the reserve is open to the public, but there is a game-viewing network of good gravel roads; three established walks, from 4 to 7 km (2.5 to 4.5 miles) in length, and picnic spots with barbecue facilities. Wildlife includes eland, gemsbok, springbok, klipspringer and Hartmann's mountain zebra. Open throughout the year; no accommodation.

The great, dry, harsh spaces beyond Springbok are known as:

THE RICHTERSVELD, a vast wilderness bounded in the north by the curve of the Orange River, where the terrain is hilly, rugged, and distinguished by weird, wind-sculpted rock pillars and spires and, except for the astonishingly lush greenness of irrigated land, is brown and bone dry. A spectacular feature of the northern segment is Wondergat, a deep cave which holds deep religious significance for the local Nama people. The southern section comprises scrubveld and scattered grassy plains.

Botanically, the Richtersveld is in a class of its own. A third of all known species of mesembryanthemum occur here; quiver trees and the bizarre halfmens plant are common; some of the flora has yet to be identified and classified.

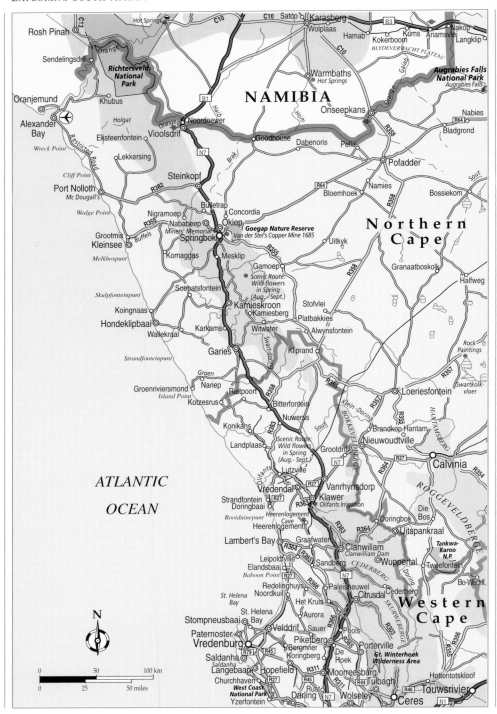

ABOVE: *The semi-arid Namaqualand region is noted for its kokerbome, or quiver trees (Aloe dichotoma), so named because early Khoikhoi made arrow-quivers from the bark of the plant.*

Those with an adventurous spirit who embark on back-packing hikes and horseback trails in this strange and lonely region really do feel like true pathfinders. You're strongly advised, though, not to venture forth into the wilderness without an experienced guide.

Some 160,000 ha (395,355 acres) have been set aside as a national park (the country's third largest). The authorities had been keen to proclaim the area for some years, but there were disputes involving the local herders (the land does, grudgingly, provide a modicum of grazing). Eventually agreement was reached to establish a 'contractual' park, safeguarding the land for the benefit of *all* – stock farmers, naturalists, tourists, animals and the precious plants.

Along the West Coast are Port Nolloth and, farther up towards the Orange, Alexander Bay. Both are fishing ports and diamond towns.

THE DIAMOND STRIP

In 1908 an ex-Kimberley labourer, Zacharius Lewala, recognized diamond chips in the sand he was shovelling at Kolmanskop, north of the Orange River and east of the small Namibian town of Lüderitz. Within a few months thousands of hectares had been pegged.

Yet, although the alluvial potential of the river estuary itself and of the coastal belt to the south had long been suspected, it wasn't until 1925 that news broke of the first big find. Prospectors converged on the desolate 80 km (50 miles) 'diamond strip' from Port Nolloth to

A WONDERLAND OF WILD FLOWERS

At first sight Namaqualand seems relentlessly harsh, intimidating in its huge emptiness, incapable of sustaining any but the simplest, least appealing forms of life. Yet the region, and especially the coastal sandveld, boasts an enormous profusion of succulents and flowering plants. After the winter rains – between August and October but most often during three weeks of September – the land is briefly and gloriously mantled by great carpets of wild flowers that stretch to the far horizons.

Namaqualand is home to about 4,000 floral species, most of which belong to the daisy and mesembryanthemum groups but also include perennial herbs, aloes, lilies and a host of other families. The small, low-growing plants are drought-resistant, their seeds lying dormant during the long dry months and then, after the life-giving rains and before the onset of the blistering desert breezes, when they sense the warming of the earth and the impending arrival of the pollinators, they burst into life, maturing in a matter of days to transform the countryside into colourful carpets of flowers.

The best flower-viewing areas vary from year to year (much depends on the local climatic conditions) but you can usually rely on spectacular displays in the Postberg Reserve next to Langebaan Lagoon, around Clanwilliam and in and around the superb Biedouw Valley to the east, Nieuwoudtville below the Cedarberg, and the town of Springbok in the distant north. Contact Flowerline on tel. (021) 418-3705 for the latest information. Coach tours – day-trips or longer – can be arranged from Cape Town; the itineraries take in other sights-to-see as well as delicious seafood meals and comfortable accommodation. Ask Captour for details.

Namaqualand's floral display.

ABOVE: *Some of the many semi-precious stones found in the Springbok area.*
ABOVE RIGHT: *Rock lobsters, known locally as crayfish, feature prominently in the West Coast fishing harvest, and on local menus.*
OPPOSITE: *A trio of Namaqualand daisies.*

the Orange to unearth hitherto unimaginable riches; some were unlucky, others made a good living, a few became wealthy overnight. Hans Merensky, a geologist, picked up 487 diamonds from a single flat rock and, in a 30-day period, collected 2,762 more near Alexander Bay.

In some areas the actual process of finding the treasure was comparatively simple – it lay everywhere, on or just beneath the ground – but it was made even simpler by a curious scientific phenomenon: the diamonds occurred in gravels containing fossils of an extinct species, the warm-water oyster *(Ostea prismatica)*. The two elements – gemstones and shellfish – have nothing in common, but were linked to some major geological upheaval that, millennia before, had changed the ocean currents, killing the oysters and sweeping the diamonds ashore. The 'oyster line' was profitably used by the prospectors as a beacon to the fabulous wealth of the ancient beach gravels.

Today, the diggings are still among the world's most lucrative. Much of the area is state-controlled and you can enter only with a permit and by prior arrangement.

PORT NOLLOTH To get to the town from Springbok, follow the N7 north and at Steinkopf turn west along the 93 km (58 miles) R382 road, through the dramatic Anenous Pass, leaving the scrubland behind to enter the sandveld.

Most of the concession divers working the offshore gravels aren't locals: they come, stay for a few months, and go away again, perhaps the richer, probably to return next year.

There is accommodation at the hotel (the Scotia Inn; fresh crayfish a speciality), a camping ground, Mamma's Italian Trattoria, and that's just about the lot, though the people are friendly and sociable and their parties lively.

ALEXANDER BAY, to the north and accessible via a tarred road from Port Nolloth, is the centre for one of the largest alluvial (sea, beach, land) diamond diggings, which can be viewed on the tours conducted each Thursday (start from the museum at 08h00). What you see is spellbinding: colossal earthmovers cutting huge slices of ground with surgical precision, the exposed gravel, screening, the sweeping of the bedrock and diamond sorting. The tour includes a seal colony and oyster farm. Accommodation is in furnished, self-catering rondavels at a farm 30 km (20 miles) distant.

THE ROAD NORTH: INLAND

The springtime glory of wild flowers is by no means confined to Namaqualand proper – the sandveld region north of the Olifants. Patchwork profusions of daisies and vygies mingle with the proteas, ericas and pincushions of the Cape Floral Kingdom's *fynbos* vegetation far to the south, gracing a region that has other, very distinctive attractions.

The main highway north from Cape Town is the N7; a wide, straight, good road that leads through the towns of Citrusdal and Clanwilliam to Springbok and then across the Namibian border and through the sandy wastelands to Windhoek, capital of Namibia. Don't be fooled by the bare simplicity of the map or by the apparent ease with which one can get to these places: the route may be a direct one but the distances are enormous. Springbok is approximately 565 km (350 miles) from Cape Town and Windhoek a further 1,000 km (621 miles).

For the first 150 km (93 miles) stretch you drive through the wheatland expanses of what is known as the Swartland, or 'black country', so named for the rich darkness of its soil. Perhaps other colours, though, would be more appropriate for in spring the fields are bright green with the splendid harvests and in summer a ripe gold. About a sixth of the national wheat crop is produced in the region, 'capital' of which is the small town of:

MALMESBURY, founded in 1743 in the valley of the Diep River and once renowned for its curative mineral springs (now in sad disuse). To the south of town is the Kalbaskraal Nature Reserve. Other features in the general (Riebeeck Valley) area are De Oude Kerk, the first church to be built in the region, now a museum housing old farming implements, utensils, and church documents; a cartwright's museum, on the farm Spes Bona (wagons, wagon-building, blacksmithing), and the house in which the great Jan Christiaan Smuts was born. This has been lovingly restored, by leading architect Gawie Fagan, and is open to the public.

MOORREESBURG AND PIKETBERG, on the N7 north of Malmesbury. The former is modestly notable for its Wheat Industry Museum, one of only three in the world; the latter for its fruit cooling and packaging complex (visitors welcome), its Edwardian-style museum, and its backcloth of imposing sandstone mountain.

Long ago the high places of the Piketberg gave sanctuary to groups of San (Bushmen), and some fine examples of their rock art can still be seen in the area. Later came the Cochoqua Khoikhoi (until recently referred to in history books as Hottentots) who, in the later 1600s, under their leader Gonnema, first traded with the white settlers and then fought them. The war lasted from 1673 to 1677, in

which year a bloodied but unbowed Gonnema struck a mutually profitable deal with the colonists, lived in relative peace thereafter, and prospered. During the hostilities the Dutch established a military outpost, or 'piquet', on the mountain slopes and it was from this that the village's name was taken.

CITRUSDAL AND CLANWILLIAM

These pleasant little towns, situated about 30 km (20 miles) apart off the N7, nestle in fertile valleys – of the Olifants (the 'Golden Valley') and the Jan Dissels respectively – and each serves as the centre of a major farming industry.

Citrusdal is set among orange groves which, collectively, comprise the third largest of South Africa's citrus-growing areas, but, because this is a frost-free winter rainfall region, it probably surpasses all in the quality of its oranges. And its estates are by far the oldest: the original orchards were planted from seedlings nurtured in Jan van Riebeeck's Cape Town garden – trees that bore their first fruits in 1661. One specimen, on the farm Hexrivier near Citrusdal, has yielded a seasonal bounty for the past 250 years and is now a proclaimed national monument.

Visitors may tour the estates. The Goede Hoop citrus co-operative operates one of the country's largest packing sheds, handling a massive 95,000 tons of oranges during the season; fresh fruit can be bought at the kiosk.

Some 50 km (30 miles) north of Citrusdal the Olifants' waters have been dammed in order to supply the needs of the irrigated farmlands of the Hantam district as well as those of:

CLANWILLIAM This is the headquarters of the country's rooibos tea industry, and is one of South Africa's ten oldest towns: farms were flourishing in the district as early as 1732.

The needle-leafed rooibos tea shrub (*Aspalathus linearis*) is a wild plant that is especially prolific on the higher slopes of the Cedarberg range that lies to the east of the Citrusdal-Clanwilliam axis (*see* page 269). The tender tips of the young shoots have been used for centuries by the black peoples, and more recently prized for their medicinal properties by the rural white communities, though systematic cultivation began only in the early 1900s. There are a number of rooibos varieties, but most aficionados consider Northier the best. The tea does not contain caffeine and it has a low tannin content, so its popularity in this

health-conscious age – both at home and abroad – is increasing by the year. Rooibos Natural Products lays on guided tours.

The area is almost as renowned for its wild flowers as for its rooibos, and is seen at its best in the springtime floral wonderland of the Biedouw Valley and the 125 ha (309 acres) Ramskop Nature Reserve, whose displays – a mix of coastal *fynbos* and Karoo succulents – are strikingly colourful between June and October. The reserve is crisscrossed by footpaths; on sale are bulbs and seeds. There's a pleasant roof-top tearoom and superb views of the Olifants River, Pakhuis Pass and the often snow-capped hills of the Cedarberg (*see* opposite page).

Worth noting, too, are the Boskloof and Kranskloof picnic and swimming spots; the Clanwilliam Dam, 18 km (11 miles) long and reckoned by water-skiers to be the country's finest venue for their sport; the Bulshoek recreational dam; and Bulshoek, which is a riverbank bathing area. San rock paintings can be seen at their best in the Agter-Pakhuis vicinity.

In a remote valley some 75 km (47 miles) from Clanwilliam, and reached via the Pakhuis Pass, is the historic Rhenish Mission village of:

WUPPERTAL, founded in 1830 and virtually unchanged since then – still a picturesque cluster of white-walled, black-thatched cottages (three terraces of them) and a winding street along which donkey-carts ply and where water flows in the furrows. The area is noted for its tobacco and rooibos tea, and for the *velskoene* – tough but comfortable walking shoes – that are made in the village. If by chance you're in the vicinity at Christmas, try to attend the carol service at the mission: it's an occasion you'll remember.

THE CEDARBERG WILDERNESS AREA

The rugged and beautiful mountain range, whose loftiest peak is the Sneeuberg (2,028 m/ 6,654 ft), takes its name from the rare and at one time almost extinct Clanwilliam cedar *(Widdringtonia cedarbergensis)*. These lovely trees suffered grievously from the axe and from uncontrolled burning during the early years of white settlement, but a few hardy specimens managed to cling to life on the upper slopes and these, now strictly protected, will hopefully prove to be the nucleus of new generations. Another, even rarer plant is the pure-white snow protea *(Protea cryophila)*, which lives precariously above the Cedarberg's snow line and occurs nowhere else in the world. For the rest, there's the rocket pincushion, the large red disa *(Disa uniflora)* and a myriad other endemic plants varying from spring annuals to fynbos and handsome indigenous forest species.

The Cedarberg is a vast controlled area of stark and strangely eroded rock formations, of waterfalls, crystal streams and clear pools, of magnificent viewsites, of caverns, overhangs, peaks and ravines. It has 254 km (158 miles) of unmarked but well defined footpaths, and it attracts hikers and backpackers, climbers, campers, photographers and nature-lovers from afar. Rock features of special interest include the 20-m-high (66 ft) pillar named the Maltese Cross; the Wolfberg Arch and the 30 m (98 ft) cleft known as the Wolfberg Cracks; the Tafelberg and its Spout. Wildlife in the area is not prolific; some 30 mammal species are present, among them klipspringer, grey rhebok, steenbok, grysbok, wild cat, caracal, bat-eared fox and baboon. Sunbirds and orangecrested sugarbirds and a number of fine raptors – black eagle, jackal buzzard, rock kestrel – can be seen.

OPPOSITE TOP: *The charming thatched cottages that distinguish the little town of Wuppertal.*
OPPOSITE BOTTOM: *Wuppertal is famed for the rough* velskoene *(walking shoes) it turns out.*
ABOVE: *The rugged Cedarberg's extraordinary Wolfberg Arch formation.*
BELOW: *San rock paintings in the Cedarberg.*

The Cedarberg is a proclaimed wilderness area and you need a permit to enter. Entry is on foot, and one can hire a guide at the Algeria forestry station. No cars or fires are allowed, for obvious reasons. You will need to arm yourself with a forestry map showing the area's paths and overnight huts. There are some 15 resident snake species: watch out for the berg adder and the puff adder. Climate: heavy winter rainfall (up to 1 000 mm/40 in a year) but it can also rain in the summer months. Snowfalls occur from May to September.

To get to the Cedarberg, turn right off the N7, 27 km (17 miles) north of Citrusdal; cross the Olifants River and drive (carefully) over the high Nieuwoudt Pass. From the summit of this pass there are fine views of the mountains; in the valley below lies the Algeria forestry station, principal starting point for a wide range of excursions into the wilderness.

Algeria has a particularly fine camping ground and picnic site, and you can, if you're feeling brave, take a refreshing dip in the close-by Rondegat River (there's an enticing, clear natural pool there). Several of the farms in the region offer pleasant and comfortable accommodation ranging from campsites to furnished chalets. For those who would prefer a touch of luxury there's also the Citrusdal Protea Hotel.

ABOVE: *Hiking in the Cedarberg Wilderness Area has become a popular pastime.*
OPPOSITE: *The West Coast is home to huge colonies of Cape gannets.*

ATLANTIC DIGRESSION

There is not much for the tourist to see beyond the Olifants River until you reach Springbok and the wild flower and diamond country of the far north (*see* page 265). Travel along the 64-km-long (40 miles) road westwards from Clanwilliam, however, and you'll arrive at:
LAMBERTS BAY, a large fishing village. This area is a bird-watcher's paradise: Bird Island – a bit of a misnomer since you can walk to it via the harbour wall – is haven to a huge colony of Cape gannets and to cormorants, penguins, seagulls and 'sterretjies' – altogether it's home to more than 150 different seabird species.

Then there's the Longvlei dam, approximately a dozen kilometres (8 miles) inland where, after good winter rains, the flamingos gather in their thousands. Farther down the coast at Elands Bay (a 48 km/30 miles drive along the gravel road; there is good beach and quite excellent surfing when the south-easter wind blows, which is often) is the West Coast's only large river estuary. In its upper reaches it is known as Verlore Vlei, or more commonly Voorvlei and here, too, great numbers of seabirds and waders congregate.

Lamberts Bay is tourist-conscious; amenities are casual but improving. People go there on family weekends (though the beach, like all the exposed West Coast venues, tends to be windswept, and the water is cold for swimming), for the birdlife and for the excellent sea-fishing. There's a museum; a caravan/camping ground; a good hotel (the Marine Protea), and an open-air, marvellously informal seafood eatery.

THE COASTAL ROUTE

An alternative way north from Cape Town is the road that takes you up the rugged western shores to the Langebaan Lagoon and Saldanha Bay.

For much of the time you're in sight of the sea, and you'll find it a pleasant enough drive. It's a scenically uncluttered and even stark but, in places, remarkably beautiful coastline of heath, sandveld, jagged cliff and wide beach. The rains don't come often, the sun can be fierce, and one is too often plagued by a high offshore winds that sweeps stinging flurries of sand into the air. But for all that the region is becoming increasingly popular among local holiday-makers, and the West Coast property and timeshare markets have been enjoying something approaching boom conditions. The journey, for the most part, will take you along the R27. You leave Cape Town at the wooden bridge at Milnerton, and bear left on the M14 to pass through:

BLOUBERGSTRAND ('blue mountain beach'). Have your camera ready: there are stunning views of Table Mountain from the shoreline

here. Incidentally, this is an increasingly sought-after residential and holiday-cottage area, and the town has a number of first-class restaurants (see page 245). If you're staying in Cape Town, an early-evening drive out followed by dinner at Ons Huisie, a restored fisherman's cottage and national monument, makes a most enjoyable outing.

THE WESTERN ISLES

To the south-west lies Dassen, one of about 40 submerged mountains off southern Africa's south and west coasts whose summits, projecting above the waters, are large enough to be termed islands, and are inhabited by huge numbers of seabirds: gulls and gannets, penguins and cormorants. They are collectively known as the Guano Islands, a name derived from their enormous surface deposits of bird-manure – a valuable source of fertilizer that has been commercially exploited for centuries (at one period they were the focus of the so-called 'guano wars' between competing interests).

Most are uninhabited, visited only by yachtsmen, conservation officials, naturalists and occasional tour parties. An exception is:
DASSEN About 223 ha (550 acres) in extent (4.5 km long by 2 km wide/2.5 miles by 1 mile) and, although it rises just 10 m (33 ft) above sea level at its highest point, boasts one or two buildings, including a lighthouse. It also supports a great many seabirds, serving as the main breeding ground of the Cape penguin (*Spheniscus demersus*), more commonly known as the jackass penguin for its harsh, braying call. Nearly 100,000 of these birds congregate in September, and again in February. Also among Dassen's residents are rock-rabbits, or dassies, which gave the island its name.

Jan van Riebeeck, who visited Dassen in the 1650s, thought very little of the place, describing it as 'not so much of an island, all sand and full of seals', but a modern scientist has termed it 'one of the naturalist's wonders of the world'.

LANGEBAAN LAGOON

Situated some 18.5 km (11 miles) to the north of Darling, 16 km long, 4.5 km at its widest and projecting southwards as an arm of Saldanha Bay, the lagoon is the focal point of a magnificent wetland wilderness area, and the burgeoning West Coast tourist industry.

The Langebaan Lagoon is an ornithological treasure-house. Its water are clear and shallow and they, and the salt marshes, the mud- and sand-banks and the rocky shores and islands of the bay are a magnet for tens of thousands of waders and other bird species. Among them are flamingos, cormorants, plovers, gulls, gannets, herons, sanderlings, knots, turnstones, and the sacred ibis – altogether, there are about 55 000 birds in residence during the summer months.

Curlew sandpipers account for two-thirds of this number. They and other migrants leave their Arctic and sub-Arctic breeding grounds for the long flight to the sunny south. They are attracted to Langebaan by the shelter it provides and the abundance of easily accessible food: molluscs, marine algae and crustaceans. There are rich fossil deposits at Langebaan – of their kind, the world's richest. The lagoon once sustained vast colonies of oysters which were killed off by changes in water temperature. Their remains lie on the lagoon bed and are commercially exploited by limeworks.

Langebaan, the islands and about 35,000 ha (86,500 acres) of the coastal zone form the West Coast National Park, which is likely to increase in size once private landowners of the area are tied into the general conservation scheme. The park encompasses the Postberg Nature Reserve, which has a modest game population, among them springbok, bontebok, kudu and gemsbok.

The terrain is, in common with much of the West Coast, virtually treeless, but the ground vegetation has its interest and, in spring, its beauty. It comprises succulents and succulent-type plants, low bushes, sedges, some coastal *fynbos* (heath) and, in their brief season, a glorious profusion of flowering annuals.

The park's headquarters and information centre is the Langebaan Lodge, which offers visitors interesting conservation displays and short guided walks to the saltmarsh and driftsand areas. The Lodge is also a very pleasant hotel, with magnificent views of Schaapen Island and the lagoon from its public rooms.

CLUB MYKONOS Just north of the lagoon mouth and outside the park's boundaries is this large hotel, timeshare and resort complex that draws its design inspiration from the Greek isles. Your accommodation is a *kalifa* (a spacious, whitewashed, colourfully trimmed and simply furnished apartment with lounge,

OPPOSITE: *The Mediterranean-style 'kalifas' of the Club Mykonos resort complex.*
ABOVE: *The fishermen of Paternoster, a small but well-known fishing village, just to the north of Saldanha Bay.*
OVERLEAF: *A fisherman's cottage stands sentinel above the rugged shores of St Helena Bay.*

kitchen, bedrooms, bathroom, shade balcony and 'braai balcony'). When you emerge, you walk along cobbled alleys and through village squares. If it weren't for the wind, and the obvious newness of everything, you could easily imagine yourself beneath an Aegean sky.

THE SALDANHA AREA

Beyond Langebaan Lagoon is the broad expanse of Saldanha Bay, one of Africa's finest natural harbours but, because the area is bone dry and drinking water scarce, little used until fairly recent times. Today, though, Saldanha is the main centre of the West Coast's fishing industry, oil storage centre, the potential site of a huge steel complex, and a deep-sea terminal for the export of iron ore, capable of accommodating the largest of bulk carrier vessels and geared to handle up to 33 million tons of ore a year.

The iron is brought from Sishen in the Northern Cape over a specially-built 861 km (535 miles) electrified railway line.

Local tourism has been slow to find its feet: Saldanha is far from Cape Town; the shores of the bay are dotted with fish-processing factories and the countryside has few immediately appealing features. But the area does have its drawcards: it's becoming popular among water-sport enthusiasts, and the town is one of the stops on the Crayfish Route. There are guided tours of the harbour and loading terminal.

North of Saldanha is St Helena Bay, 'discovered' by Vasco da Gama in November 1497 and now given over to commercial fishing: the upwelling of the cool Benguela Current here provides the nutrients that sustain vast shoals of pilchards, anchovies and mackerel.

Attractive fishing villages on this and adjacent coasts include Velddrif and Paternoster.

Velddrif is situated at the mouth of the Berg River. The estuary attracts large numbers of flamingos, spoonbills, avocets and, sometimes, the otherwise seldom-seen glossy ibis.

Paternoster is one of the more pleasant coastal hamlets, and well worth visiting for its attractiveness and for the crayfish and perlemoen taken from the waters.

ADVISORY: THE WEST COAST AND NAMAQUALAND

CLIMATE

Winter-rainfall area, but the rains are infrequent and countryside mostly dry. Hot, windy in summer; winter nights, early mornings can be very cold, days cool to warm. Best time to visit: spring (September/October).

MAIN ATTRACTIONS

Wild flowers ❏ Scenic drives ❏ Walks and trails ❏ Camping/caravanning ❏ Climbing ❏ Bird-watching ❏ Sea-fishing; crayfish diving ❏ Sailing and boating.

TRAVEL

Road. From Cape Town: Malmesbury 64 km/40 miles; Clanwilliam 240 km/149 miles; Langebaan via Malmesbury 124 km/77 miles; Saldanha Bay 149 km/93 miles; Springbok 559 km/347 miles; Port Nolloth 704 km/437 miles; Alexander Bay 784 km/487 miles; Orange River (Namibian border) 824 km/512 miles.

Main roads are excellent; minor roads can be rough. Inland route from Cape Town to Springbok and northern Namaqualand: take the N7 through Malmesbury, Citrusdal, Clanwilliam. At Steinkopf, north of Springbok, turn west on the R382 for Port Nolloth; rough coastal road from Port Nolloth to Alexander Bay. Permits needed to enter Alexander Bay; contact Alexkor, tel. (0256) 831-1330. Coastal route from Cape Town to Langebaan and Saldanha: take the R27; follow map.

Coach travel: A coach service (weekdays) operates between Cape Town and Springbok.

Air. National Airlines: weekly service between Cape Town and Springbok, serving Alexander Bay en route.

ACCOMMODATION
Select hotels

**Cedarberg Hotel ** Citrusdal. Hospitable; 26 en suite rooms; à la carte restaurant; 2 bars. PO Box 37, Citrusdal 7340; tel. (022) 921-2221, fax 921-2704.

**Hoedjiebaai Hotel ** Saldanha Bay. 16 en suite rooms; à la carte and table d'hôte restaurants; bar. PO Box 149, Saldanha Bay 7395; tel. (02281) 4-1271, fax 4-1677.

**Kokerboom Hotel ** Springbok. 34 en suite rooms; à la carte restaurant; 2 bars. PO Box 340, Springbok 8240; tel. (0251) 2-2685, fax 2-2017.

Langebaan Lodge On the lagoon. 19 en suite rooms, 2 suites; à la carte restaurant; bar; pool; conference facilities. PO Box 5, Langebaan 7357; tel. (02287) 2-2144, fax 2-2607, central reservations (021) 22-2810.

Marine Protea Hotel * Lambert's Bay. Crayfish; wild flowers; 41 rooms, 7 suites; à la carte restaurant; bar. PO Box 249, Lambert's Bay 8130; tel. (027) 432-1126, fax 432-1036, toll-free reservations 0800 11 9000.

Olifants Dam Motel Near Clanwilliam. 12 en suite rooms; à la carte restaurant. PO Box 78, Clanwilliam 8135; tel. (02682), ask for 284 or 342.

Saldanha Bay Protea Hotel * Diving school; sailing academy; 31 rooms, 2 suites; à la carte restaurant; pool; slipway. PO Box 70, Saldanha Bay 7395; tel. (02281) 4-1264, fax 4-4093, toll-free reservations 0800 11 9000.

**Samoa Hotel ** Moorreesburg. Attractive country inn; 17 en suite rooms, 1 suite; à la carte restaurant; bar; pool; conference facilities. PO Box 16, Moorreesburg 7310; tel. (0264) 3-1201, fax 3-2031.

Steenberg's Cove Hotel St Helena Bay. 12 rooms, 4 chalets; à la carte restaurant; bar. Main St, St Helena Bay 7390; tel. (02283) 6-1160.

**Strassberger's Hotel ** Clanwilliam. 23 en suite rooms; à la carte restaurant; bar; conference facilities. PO Box 4, Clanwilliam 8135; tel. (027) 482-1101, fax 482-2678.

Resort and self-catering

The region is well served by resort, guest-house and other accommodation. Contact the West Coast Publicity Association (*see* below). Some suggestions:

Club Mykonos Near lagoon. Greek-style resort; self-contained 'kalifas'; shops; restaurants; leisure facilities. For information: tel. (021) 419-4500.

Kagga Kamma ('Place of the Bushmen') Private game reserve, in Cedarberg/Karoo region east of Citrusdal (260 km/166 miles from Cape Town; take the route through Ceres). Abundant wildlife; resident San (Bushmen). Information: PO Box 7143, Paarl 7623; tel. (021) 863-8334, fax 863-8383.

Guest farms and houses: Tourist Bureau South Africa, PO Box 247, Durbanville 7550; tel./fax (021) 96-9790.

Select restaurants

The West Coast is famed for its seafood and open-air eateries known as 'skerms', including Melkbosskerm (Melkbosstrand), Die Strandloper (Langebaan), Breakwater Boma (Saldanha Bay), Die Muisbosskerm and Bosduifklip (Lambert's Bay). Bloubergstrand, near Cape Town, has fine restaurants (*see* Advisory: Cape Town and the Peninsula); Saldanha Bay Protea Hotel and Marine Protea in Lamberts Bay have superb seafood.

USEFUL ADDRESSES AND TELEPHONE NUMBERS

Automobile Association, tel. (021) 21-1550 (touring/general); toll-free 0800 010101 (breakdown service).

Captour, Tourist Rendezvous Travel Centre; Adderley St, Cape Town; tel. (021) 418-5214.

Langebaan Publicity Association, Bree St, Langebaan; tel. (02287) 2-2115.

Satour (South African Tourism Board), Tourist Rendezvous Travel Centre, Adderley St, Cape Town; tel. (021) 21-6274.

West Coast Publicity Association, tel. (02281) 4-2088, fax 4-4240.

PART THREE

VISITOR'S DIGEST

For the first-time visitor, South Africa will prove a strange and, in some respects, a confusing place, and you will need many facts at your fingertips. The information included in the following pages is designed to help you plan sensibly, and to make your trip as trouble-free as possible. Among the subjects covered are travel to and within the region, hotel and other accommodation options (these appear in more specific form in the Ad-visories at the end of the chapters), local currency and banking facilities, shopping, tipping and much else that will help you deal with the practicalities of staying in, and enjoying, the country.

A word of caution: South Africa is a region in transition, society is undergoing profound changes and these, combined with unemployment and widespread poverty, have contributed to a high crime rate. Keep your valuables is a safe place; avoid deserted areas, especially at night; bear personal security in mind at all times.

OPPOSITE: *Rugged hills grace this Klein-Karoo farm near the town of Oudtshoorn.*
ABOVE: *Fishing boats in Kalk Bay harbour.*

VISITOR'S DIGEST

ENTERING SOUTH AFRICA

ENTRY DOCUMENTS All visitors are required to have valid passports for entry into South Africa. Most foreign nationals, however, are exempt from visa requirements, including citizens of the European Community, the United States, Canada, Australia, New Zealand, Japan, Singapore, Switzerland, Lesotho, Swaziland, Botswana, Namibia and Zimbabwe.

ARRIVAL BY ROAD Travellers intending to bring their motor vehicles into the Common Customs Area (South Africa, Namibia, Lesotho, Botswana, Swaziland) must obtain a triptyque or carnet authorising temporary importation from an internationally recognized motoring organization (for example, the Automobile Association) in their country of origin.

HEALTH REQUIREMENTS Visitors coming from or passing through a yellow fever zone must have a valid International Certificate of Vaccination. The zone extends over much of tropical Africa and South America (Brazil is now regarded as a risk area). Airline passengers – those whose aircraft land for refuelling in or are otherwise in transit through a yellow fever zone – do not need a certificate provided they do not leave the aircraft.

Note: Cholera and smallpox vaccination certificates are no longer required. There are no screening procedures in force for AIDS.

If visiting the Lowveld (the region includes the Kruger National Park) or northern KwaZulu-Natal, it is advisable to begin a course of anti-malaria tablets before starting out. Tablets are available without prescription from South African pharmacies.

WHAT CLOTHING TO PACK South Africa enjoys long, hot summers; clothing is informal, although some formality (at least 'smart casual') is required after dark at theatres and art/entertainment venues and by more sophisticated hotels and restaurants. Beachwear is acceptable only on the beach. Casual clothing is customary at resorts and in game areas. For the summer months (October–April), pack lightweight clothing but include a jacket or jersey for cooler nights. Most of the country falls within the summer rainfall region, so bring an umbrella or raincoat. For winter months, pack warm clothing.

TOURIST INFORMATION

SATOUR, the South African Tourism Board maintains offices in a number of countries, among them the United Kingdom (London), the United States (New York and Los Angeles), Germany, France, Israel, Italy, Japan, the Netherlands, Switzerland, Taiwan and Zimbabwe.

Satour's headquarters are in the Menlyn Park office block, corner of Atterbury Road and Menlyn Drive, Pretoria; Private Bag X164, Pretoria 0001; tel. (012) 47-1131 and (012) 348-9521. Regional offices are located in Bloemfontein, Cape Town, Durban, East London, George, Johannesburg (city and airport), Nelspruit, Pietersburg and Port Elizabeth. Contact addresses and telephone numbers appear in the relevant Advisories in Part Two.

REGIONAL INFORMATION The major centres and tourist areas have publicity associations that provide up-to-date information on local attractions, hotels, restaurants, transport, sport, recreation, tour packages and touring routes.

AIR TRAVEL

The principal port of entry is Johannesburg International Airport, serving both Johannesburg and Pretoria. Durban and Cape Town airports also have international status. Airport passenger facilities include banks, currency exchange, post offices, duty-free and other shops, restaurants, cocktail bars, car hire, taxis and bus transport to and from the cities. Major hotels provide courtesy transport.

Domestic services: Internal destinations served by South African Airways include Bloemfontein, Cape Town, East London, George, Johannesburg, Kimberley, Port Elizabeth, Pretoria and Upington. Smaller airlines serve these cities and the smaller centres and major tourist areas. Air charter services (including helicopter hire) are widely available.

ROAD TRAVEL

This is the best way to get to know the country. The road network is extensive, comprising 200,000 km (124,000 miles) of national and provincial highways, 85 000 km (53,000 miles) of which are fully tarred. Surfaces are in good condition, though the going can be rough in the remoter rural areas.

DRIVER'S LICENCE A foreign licence is valid in South Africa provided it carries the photograph and signature of the holder and is printed in English or is accompanied by a certificate of authenticity (in English) issued by an embassy or other authority.

Alternatively, obtain an International Driving Permit before departure. The application procedure is simple and the licence is valid for 36 months.

Zimbabwe, Mozambique, Namibia, Botswana, Lesotho and Swaziland licences are valid.

PETROL Cities, towns and main highways are well served by filling stations, the remote areas less so. Many stations stay open 24 hours; others from 06h00 to 18h00, when repair services are available. Pump attendants see to your fuel and other needs; petrol, lead-free petrol and diesel are sold in litres.

MAPS AND BOOKS Excellent road maps are available from Satour and the major bookstores.

ROAD SIGNS Visiting motorists should get hold of a copy of *Pass Your Learners Easily* (available at most bookshops), which graphically illustrates South African traffic signs and the rules of the road.

THE ROUTE MARKER SYSTEM The country's main roads are identified by number rather than by name. National highways take the prefix 'N' followed by a number (the N1 is the principal south-north route from Cape Town to Johannesburg, Pretoria and beyond to the Zimbabwe border); regional highways the prefix 'R' followed by a number; metropolitan roads the prefix 'M' followed by a number and, very often, a letter indicating direction (N, S, E or W).

If the route marker has white lettering on a blue background, the road is a designated freeway: a multi-laned route which a vehicle can enter only via an on-ramp and exit via an off-ramp left of traffic flow. Other route markers have white or yellow lettering against a green background. The system sounds complicated but is in practice simple and effective. Armed with a good map – one which incorporates the route markers – the visiting motorist shouldn't find it too difficult to find his way around city, town and country.

SOME ROAD RULES Traffic keeps to the left-hand side of the road. Generally the speed limit on national highways, freeways and other major routes is 120 km/h (75 mph) – it may be lower; the roads are signposted accordingly. The general limit on rural roads is 100 km/h (62 mph); that in built-up areas 60 km/h (37 mph) unless otherwise indicated. Keep an eye open for speed-limit signs at all times. The general rule is: Keep to the left, pass on the right, even on dual and multi-laned highways.

The traffic police officer is not a member of the South African Police, but belongs to a local force trained to control the flow of traffic, render assistance at accidents, and monitor road behaviour. He or she is especially strict on motorists who exceed the speed limit (the fines are heavy) and who drive while under the influence of alcohol.

TERMINOLOGY AND LOCAL PECULIARITIES South Africa has 11 official languages; public notices and signs are most commonly expressed in both English and Afrikaans. Some of the more common words or phrases you may need, are:

ENGLISH	AFRIKAANS	XHOSA	ZULU
left	links	-khlolo	-bunxele
right	regs	-lungile(yo)	-qondile
city	stad	isixeko	indolobha
airport	lughawe	isikhululo	inkundla yezindiza
street	straat	isitalato	isitaladi
road	weg	indlela	umgwaqo
keep	hou	-gcina	-gcina
only	slegs	kuphela	kuphela
open	oop	-vulekile(yo)	-vuliwe
closed	toe	-valile(yo)	-valiweyo
beware	oppas	-lumka	-qaphela
beach	strand	unxweme	usebe lolwandle
hello	hallo	molo!	halo!
goodbye	totsiens	nisale kakuhle!	sala kahle
please	asseblief	nceda!	uxolo
thank you	dankie	enkosi!	ngiyabonga!
Where is ...?	Waar is ...?	Iphi ...?	-kuphi?

AUTOMOBILE ASSOCIATION The AA is South Africa's biggest motoring club, providing a wide range of services. These include advice on touring, caravanning, camping and places of interest; maps and brochures; preparing itineraries; insurance, car hire and accommodation reservation facilities; breakdowns and other emergencies. Trained personnel patrol major centres and the more popular tourist routes and areas. These services are offered to visitors who are able to produce the membership card of a motoring organization affiliated to the AA of SA through the AIT (*Alliance Internationale de Tourisme*) or FIA (*Fédération de l'Automobile*).

The AA's headquarters are at 66 De Korte Street, Braamfontein 2017; tel. (011) 407-1000. For AA offices in other centres, consult the relevant Advisories in Part Two, or the local telephone directory.

CAR HIRE A number of international firms, including Avis, Imperial (incorporating Hertz) and Budget, are well established in South Africa, serving all major centres, airports and some of the bigger game parks and nature reserves, including the Kruger National Park. Tariffs vary widely according to the type of vehicle, and a kilometre charge is levied. For one-way (city-to-city) rentals there are no 'drop-off' charges; delivery and pick-up services within a city are usually free of charge. Numerous local rental firms provide similar facilities. Other companies hire out caravans, campers and camp-mobiles (fully equipped with stoves, refrigerators, linen, kitchen utensils), four-wheel-drive vehicles, mini- and microbuses. For local addresses, contact Satour, or consult the Yellow Pages.

COACH TRAVEL Luxury coach services link major centres; tour operators spread the network, taking in game parks, natural wonders and scenic attractions. For details, consult a travel agent or Satour.

TRAVELLING BY RAIL

Train travel within South Africa is relatively cheap, reasonably comfortable and rather slow. Rail passenger services connect all the major centres and many of the minor ones.

Pride of the railways is the celebrated Blue Train, which travels between Pretoria, Johannesburg and Cape Town (and, on occasion, lays on special excursions to major tourist areas), offering its guests luxurious comfort, five-star cuisine and service amenities that include baths, showers, a lounge bar and a cocktail bar.

Ordinary long-distance trains have dining saloons and catering trolleys; sleeping berths in first and second class coupés (two or three passengers), and compartments (four or six passengers).

CITY TRANSPORT

Bus services in the major centres are adequate and reasonably cheap.

South African taxis do not cruise the streets in search of fares: they are found at designated ranks, at railway stations and at airports. Normally, your best course is to telephone for a cab (taxi firms are listed in the telephone directories and the Yellow Pages) or ask the hotel porter to do so for you.

Travel by taxi is expensive: if your journey is anything more than a cross-town hop, ask the driver for an estimate of the cost. Moreover, make quite sure that he can precisely locate your destination.

Less costly are the so-called 'black taxis' (locally known as Zola Budds and Mary Deckers) that ply the busier routes. These minibuses, often sociably crowded, have undesignated but customary stopping points, and provide a quick means of urban transport. Sometimes too quick: they feature prominently in the accident statistics.

Suburban train services in the Cape Peninsula and Witwatersrand metropolitan areas are extensive, fairly efficient, packed with commuters during the morning (from 07h00 to 09h00) and evening (from 16h00 to 18h00) rush hours.

MONEY MATTERS

CURRENCY The South African monetary unit is the rand (symbol: R), divided into 100 cents (symbol: c). Coins are issued in denominations of 1c, 2c, 5c, 10c, 20c, 50c, R1, R2 and R5; notes in denominations of R10, R20, R50, R100 and R200.

CURRENCY REGULATIONS There are no restrictions on the amount of foreign currency travellers may bring with them. Some countries, however, have set limits on the export of banknotes and, in these cases, visitors are advised to convert the bulk of their funds into travellers' cheques. The importation of South African currency is limited to R500 per person. Visitors can convert their foreign currency into rands at banks, bureaux de change and through such authorized exchange dealers as Thomas Cook and American Express.

BANKS The banking system is similar to and as sophisticated as those of the Western industrialized countries. Banking hours in the major centres are 09h00 to 15h30 on weekdays, 08h30 or 09h00 to 11h00 on Saturdays. There are banking facilities at the three international airports during normal hours. Special services (currency exchange, for instance) are available to passengers on incoming and outgoing international flights at other times.

TRAVELLERS' CHEQUES These may be cashed at any bank (if the currency is acceptable in South Africa), and are accepted by most hotels and shops.

CREDIT CARDS Most hotels, restaurants, shops, carriers and tour operators accept international credit cards, among which are American Express, Bank of America, Visa, Diners Club and MasterCharge.

Petrol cannot be purchased on a credit card. Some banks, however, issue a special 'petrocard'.

SERVICE CHARGES Hotels may not levy a charge for general services (though there is often a telephone service levy). Restaurants may levy a service charge but few choose to do so.

TIPPING If the service is satisfactory, it is usual to tip porters, waiters, taxi drivers, room attendants and golf caddies. Tipping petrol attendants is optional, though a window-wash and a cheerful smile do merit recognition. Generally, gratuities to waiters and taxi drivers should amount to around 10% of the cost of the service. For non-quantifiable services – porterage, for instance – it is usual to proffer a tip of between R2 and R5.

ACCOMMODATION

A voluntary grading system, covering all types of accommodation, was introduced in the early 1990s; ratings range from one to five stars.

HOTELS The best South African hotels are of international standard, but generally speaking local hoteliers still have a great deal to learn from counterparts in Europe, North America and the Pacific Rim. Among the leading hotel groups are Southern Sun/Holiday Inns, Sun International, Karos and Protea. This last group comprises establishments which have management arrangements with, but are not owned by, Protea, and thus retain their individual character. They tend to fall into the middle (two- to three-star) range; the Protea seal indicates quality.

COUNTRY GETAWAYS The major rural tourist areas, and in particular the Cape winelands and the Escarpment and Lowveld to the east of Johannesburg, are especially well endowed with secluded, restful little lodges and country guest-houses tucked away among vineyards and forested hills. Most of them are supremely comfortable, some of them highly sophisticated in terms of appointments and cuisine, all of them informal and friendly.

GAME AND NATURE RESERVES Visitors to the National Parks and the larger regional sanctuaries stay at rest camps in (usually) thatched rondavels, bungalows, chalets and cottages of varying degrees of sophistication. The bigger and better units will have their own bathrooms (or showers) and fully equipped kitchens; occupants of other units have access to communal cooking, eating and washing facilities. Some parks have shops, petrol filling stations, restaurants, swimming pools and other amenities; nearly all offer viewing drives and walking trails.

GAME LODGES Usually located in private game reserves and on game farms, these cater mainly for affluent people who like to live well while they explore the ways of the wild. Most lodges pride themselves on the degree of personal attention lavished on each guest, and on the skill of their rangers and trackers. Some of the most attractive lodges are in the areas bordering the Kruger National Park.

GAME FARMS There are many of these scattered around the northern bushveld regions. The game animals are farmed commercially, for their meat and hides, but many of the owners provide accommodation and other visitor facilities; some allow hunting on their properties.

SELF-CATERING ACCOMMODATION Options are quite varied and range from the rudimentary hiking hut through to holiday apartments and cottages to well-appointed, even luxurious, executive suites and resort chalets.

BED AND BREAKFAST The number of private homes offering this type of comfortable, convenient and comparatively cheap lodging is growing rapidly, especially in the coastal regions. Contact your travel agent, Satour or the local tourist publicity associations for details.

GENERAL INFORMATION

ELECTRICITY Generally, urban power is 220/230 volts AC at 50 cycles a second; Pretoria's system generates 250 volts; Port Elizabeth's 220/250 volts. Plugs are 5-amp, two-pin or 15-amp three-pin (round). Not all electric shavers will fit hotel and game park plug points; visitors should seek advice about adaptors from a local electrical supplier.

EMERGENCIES Emergency contact numbers for the police, ambulance and so forth are listed at the front of the telephone directory. The more important ones in the main centres appear in the relevant Advisories in Part Two. The national number for the police flying squad is 1-0111; the national ambulance number is 1-0177. Personal crisis help services include Life Line (similar to the Samaritans in Britain) and Alcoholics Anonymous. Both are listed in telephone directories.

HANDICAPPED TRAVELLERS Most hotels with two stars or more, resorts and the larger game parks and nature reserves have facilities for disabled persons (Kruger's Skukuza rest camp has several specially designed chalets). Accommodation guides, including that produced by Satour for the various touring regions, use the international access symbol to identify the facilities.

Cressida Automatics fitted with hand controls are available from Avis Rent-A-Car in the major centres. SAA and other airlines provide passenger aid units at airports. Wheelchairs and other aids for the disabled can be hired in most of the larger centres.

HOLIDAYS AND HOLY DAYS At time of writing (1996), there were 12 public holidays: New Year's Day (1 January); Human Rights Day (21 March); Good Friday (5 April); Family Day (8 April); Freedom Day (27 April); Workers' Day (1 May); Youth Day (16 June, commemorated on 17 June in 1996); National Women's Day (9 August); Heritage Day

(24 September); Day of Reconciliation (16 December); Christmas Day (25 December); Day of Goodwill (26 December). Jewish, Hindu and Islamic communities observe their traditional holy days.

The school year has four terms, which vary from province to province. The peak tourist season runs from mid-December to the first week in January.

LIQUOR AND LICENSING HOURS Bars usually open at 10h00 and close at 23h00 during the week and on Saturdays.

Nightclubs and some city bars remain open until 02h00 and later on weekdays.

The majority of liquor stores are open from 08h00 to 18h00 or 18h30; a few city outlets stay open until 20h00. Some supermarkets stock beer and wine (but not spirits); they may sell liquor only during licensing hours.

Restaurants may be fully licensed, or licensed to serve only wine and beer, or they may be unlicensed, in which case one takes along one's own beverage. Check before making a reservation.

The liquor and licensing regulations are periodically reviewed; the general trend seems to be towards a more relaxed drinking dispensation.

MEASUREMENT South Africa uses the metric system of weights and measures.

MEDICAL SERVICES South Africa does not have a 'national health' welfare scheme. Visitors are responsible for their own medical arrangements and are strongly advised to take out medical insurance prior to departure.

Public hospitals tend to be crowded and the medical and nursing staff are invariably overworked, though the standard of patient care remains remarkably high. Private hospitals generally offer a lot more comfort and individual attention, and are a great deal more expensive.

Private doctors are listed in telephone directories under 'Medical Practitioners' and, for Afrikaans-speakers, 'Mediese Praktisyns'.

Hospitalization is usually arranged through a medical practitioner, but in an emergency a visitor may telephone or go directly to the casualty department of a General Hospital or, in the smaller centres, to any hospital. Hospitals are listed under 'H' in the telephone directories.

Emergencies Ambulance and other emergency services are listed at the front of the telephone directory. The national ambulance number is 1-0177. The more important numbers in each city are given in the appropriate Advisories in Part Two.

Pharmacies Most remain open until at least 18h00 on weekdays (13h00 on Saturdays), some until much later; a few provide an all-night and limited Sunday service. Hotel reception and the hotel porter's office will have the details. Alternatively, consult the Yellow Pages.

Malaria The disease is largely under control in South Africa, though continentally it is still an extremely serious health problem (in 1986 the World Health Organization estimated that more than 750,000 Africans were dying of malaria each year).

The regions where infection is most likely to occur are eastern Mpumalanga and northern KwaZulu-Natal. The risk of contracting the disease, however, is negligible providing you take the standard precautions; tablets can be obtained from pharmacies without prescription.

Bilharzia Also known as schistosomiasis, this debilitating, waterborne tropical disease is caused by a parasitical worm that inhabits the rivers and dams of the lower-lying northern and eastern regions. When diagnosed (this can be quite difficult as the symptoms are often vague), the disease readily responds to drugs.

Precautions: be very circumspect about swimming in rivers and dams – unless there are clear assurances that they are bilharzia-free.

AIDS Although South Africa has recorded fewer cases of full-blown AIDS than many countries to the north, the disease is likely to become critical. The incidence of heterosexual AIDS, in particular, is increasing exponentially.

The risk of contracting AIDS, though, appears to be no greater here than it is in any other country, provided of course that the standard and well-publicized precautions are taken.

Drugs Drug abuse is a growing social problem in South Africa, as it is elsewhere.

Trading in and possession of illegal drugs, including marijuana (also called 'dagga' in South Africa) are criminal offences and carry severe penalties.

Marijuana is the substance most commonly abused. When smoked in conjuction with crushed Mandrax (methaqualone) pills, or 'buttons', it is known as 'white pipe', a combined use that appears to be unique to South Africa. The country has the highest incidence of Mandrax abuse in the world.

Heroin and cocaine are latecomers to the market, and fortunately remain a very small part of the South African drug scene.

Some appetite suppressants that are prescriptive elsewhere can be bought over the counter in South Africa, as can many kinds of painkillers and cough medicines containing drugs.

PHOTOGRAPHY Most international film brands and sizes are readily available from photographic shops and department stores; processing is quick (same-day; one-hour at some outlets) and relatively cheap (visitors should enquire whether process charges are included in the price of film).

Certain buildings and installations – those relating to defence (military bases, for instance) and internal security (police stations and prisons) – may not be photographed.

POSTAL SERVICE Most post offices are open from 08h00 to 16h30 on weekdays and 08h00 to 12h00 on Saturdays. Post offices in city suburbs and the smaller centres close at lunchtime (13h00 to 14h00).

An international priority mail service is available to and from Britain, the United States, Germany, France, Switzerland and a number of other countries.

SECURITY South Africa is undergoing rapid change; the transition to a fully democratic order has in many ways proved traumatic; there is a great deal of poverty, and the crime rate in some areas has been high. Take the same precautions that you would, say, in Central New York. Specifically:
• Busy streets and well-used parks, gardens and other open areas are safe enough, but don't walk alone at night in either city or suburb. Rather call a taxi.
• Avoid deserted areas, and the poorer areas, unless you are with a group.
• Don't carry large sums of cash around with you.
• Don't leave valuables in your hotel room; use a safety deposit box.

SHOPPING The full range of necessities and luxuries is available in South Africa; prices are comparable with and in many instances lower than those in other industrially advanced countries, though certain items – electrical appliances and books, for example – are a lot more expensive.

There are modern shopping complexes in and around all the major centres.

Normal shopping and business hours are from 08h30 to 17h00 Mondays to Fridays; from 08h30 to 13h00 on Saturdays. However, many of the larger supermarkets close later on weekdays and are open on Saturday afternoons, Sunday mornings and the mornings of most public holidays.

Corner cafés – suburban mini-supermarkets – are open from early morning to late evening every day of the week throughout the year. They are convenient for milk, confectionery, bread, newspapers, cigarettes and casual purchases; their prices tend to be higher than those of the larger stores.

A 14% Value Added Tax (VAT) is levied on all products and services except a few basic foodstuffs.

Some of the bigger South African retail chains are Woolworths (various departments, including a high-quality supermarket); OK Bazaars, Shoprite and Pick 'n Pay (all of these are supermarkets which stock a wide range of goods at competitive prices); Clicks (general purpose, mainly household goods); Edgars, Truworths, Foschini and Topics (wide selection of fashion clothing and accessories).

OK's Hyperama and Pick 'n Pay's Hypermarket and are extensive, no-frills, suburban shopping complexes that take bulk-buying, multi-stocking and price-paring to their extremes.

Local products of particular interest to visitors are gold, diamond and semi-precious stone jewellery; copperware; leather (including crocodile skin) and suede goods; items made from karakul wool, ostrich leather and feathers; ceramics, curios and various African handcrafts. Among the last two are intricate beadwork, wooden carvings, shields, drums, masks, game animal skins and hand-woven rugs.

South Africa's 'informal economy' has burgeoned in recent years – the product of widespread unemployment on the one hand and more relaxed trading regulations on the other – and bustling street markets (and craft fairs) now enliven most of the larger centres and provide excellent opportunities for bargain hunters.

TELEPHONES The South African telephone system is fully automatic and one can dial direct to most centres in South and southern Africa as well as to most parts of the world. All the dialling codes are listed near the front of the telephone directory. Both local and long-distance calls are metered.

Calls from hotels often carry a heavy surcharge and visitors are advised to double-check the charges that appear on their bills.

Telex and facsimile transmission (fax) facilities are widely available in South Africa.

TIME Throughout the year, South African Standard Time is two hours ahead of Greenwich Mean Time, one hour ahead of Central European Winter Time, and seven hours ahead of the USA's Eastern Standard Winter Time.

VENOMOUS CREATURES The ordinary visitor to South Africa faces very little risk from snakes, spiders or scorpions in the main tourist areas. Those taking part in safaris and walking trails, however, should obviously be rather more wary, and follow the advice of the group leader.